Early in his career, **George Bernard Shaw** (1856–1950) wrote for newspapers and magazines as a critic of art, literature, music, and drama. From 1893 to 1939, the most active period of his career, Shaw wrote forty-seven plays. By 1915, his international fame was firmly established and productions of *Candida, Man and Superman, Arms and the Man*, and *The Devil's Disciple* appeared in many countries around the world. He went on to write such dramas as *Heartbreak House, Back to Methuselah, Androcles and the Lion*, and *St. Joan*. In 1925, the playwright was awarded the Nobel Prize.

Eric Bentley is an eminent playwright, translator, and drama critic whose numerous books include *The Playwright as Thinker: A Study of Drama in Modern Times, Bernard Shaw 1856–1950, In Search of Theater*, and the widely acclaimed *The Life of the Drama*.

Norman Lloyd is perhaps most well known for his role as the wise and avuncular Dr. Auschlander on the popular television drama *St. Elsewhere*, but he has appeared in many other television series as well as feature films such as Hitchcock's *Saboteur, The Age of Innocence* and *Dead Poets Society*. He began his career as an apprentice at Eva LeGallienne's Civic Repertory Theatre and later joined with Orson Welles and John Houseman in the formation of the Mercury Theatre. An acclaimed director and producer, he has been a frequent guest lecturer at colleges and universities and has served on the teaching staff of the American Film Institute. He is the author of *Stages: Of Life in Theatre, Film and Television*.

Plays By

GEORGE BERNARD SHAW

MRS. WARREN'S PROFESSION

ARMS AND THE MAN

CANDIDA

MAN AND SUPERMAN

With an Introduction by
Eric Bentley
and a New Afterword by
Norman Lloyd

C

SIGNET CLASSICS

SIGNET CLASSICS
Published by New American Library, a division of
Penguin Group (USA) Inc., 375 Hudson Street,
New York, New York 10014, USA
Penguin Group (Canada), 90 Eglinton Avenue East, Suite 700, Toronto,
Ontario M4P 2Y3, Canada (a division of Pearson Penguin Canada Inc.)
Penguin Books Ltd., 80 Strand, London WC2R 0RL, England
Penguin Ireland, 25 St. Stephen's Green, Dublin 2,
Ireland (a division of Penguin Books Ltd.)
Penguin Group (Australia), 250 Camberwell Road, Camberwell, Victoria 3124,
Australia (a division of Pearson Australia Group Pty. Ltd.)
Penguin Books India Pvt. Ltd., 11 Community Centre, Panchsheel Park,
New Delhi - 110 017, India
Penguin Group (NZ), 67 Apollo Drive, Rosedale, North Shore 0632,
New Zealand (a division of Pearson New Zealand Ltd.)
Penguin Books (South Africa) (Pty.) Ltd., 24 Sturdee Avenue,
Rosebank, Johannesburg 2196, South Africa

Penguin Books Ltd., Registered Offices:
80 Strand, London WC2R 0RL, England

Published by Signet Classics, an imprint of New American Library,
a division of Penguin Group (USA) Inc.

First Signet Classics Printing, August 1960
First Signet Classics Printing (Lloyd Afterword), August 2004
10 9 8 7 6 5

Introduction copyright © New American Library, a division of Penguin Group
(USA) Inc., 1960
Afterword copyright © Norman Lloyd, 2004
All rights reserved

Acknowledgment is made to the Public Trustee and the Society of Authors
(London).

 REGISTERED TRADEMARK—MARCA REGISTRADA

Printed in the United States of America

CONTENTS

INTRODUCTION:
THE MAKING OF A DRAMATIST
(1892–1903)
vii

MRS. WARREN'S PROFESSION
1

ARMS AND THE MAN
99

CANDIDA
169

MAN AND SUPERMAN
239

AFTERWORD:
G.B.S.: AN ACTOR'S APPRECIATION
481

SELECTED BIBLIOGRAPHY
487

INTRODUCTION:
THE MAKING OF A DRAMATIST
(1892–1903)

It was clear from the start that Bernard Shaw was a man of ideas. Later it turned out that he was a fabulous entertainer. But few have granted that the two Shaws were one. The old tendency was to grant that he was a publicist, a critic, an essayist, even a philosopher, but to add: "not, of course, a dramatist." The later tendency was to concede that he was a great showman but to discount his thoughtful side. As Egon Friedell said, you could suck the theatrical sugar from the pill of propaganda, and put the pill itself back on the plate.

Neither in the old days, then, nor in the later ones was Shaw considered a dramatist, for even the later generations have only thought him a master of the theatrical occasion, a man with a theatrical line of talk and a theatrical bag of tricks, a highly histrionic jokester—a comedian, certainly, but hardly a writer of serious comedy. The fact is that the shock of that long career in the theater has still not been absorbed. Shaw has not yet been seen in perspective.

In these circumstances, it is interesting to go back and look at what happened in the eighteen nineties. In 1891, Bernard Shaw had still not written a play, though he was thirty-five years old. A dozen years later, though he could describe himself as "an unperformed playwright in London," he had written *Widowers' Houses* (1892), *The Philanderer* (1893), *Mrs. Warren's Profession* (1893–94), *Arms and the Man* (1894), *Candida* (1894–95), *The Man of Destiny* (1895), *You Never Can Tell* (1895–96), *The Devil's Disciple* (1896–97), *Caesar and Cleopatra* (1898), *Captain Brassbound's Conversion* (1899), *The Admirable Bashville* (1901), and *Man and Superman* (1901–03).

Let us take for granted that these plays are full of ideas and jokes, and ask if they do not also meet the demands of dramatic criticism as such. The drama, everyone agrees, presents character in action. Human actions become "an action" in the drama when they are arranged effectively—when, that is, they are given what we can recognize as a proper and praiseworthy structure. Of character dramatic critics have required many different things. One of them is emotional substance.

Let us ask, then, how Shaw, when he set about playwriting, tackled the problem of structure; and let us ask if he gave his characters' existence the requisite emotional substance.

Structure

How did Shaw put a play together? To think of questions about Shaw is to think also of the answers he invariably provided to them. In this case, he said: "I avoid plots like the plague. . . . My procedure is to imagine characters and let them rip. . . ." The quotation is from his *Table-talk* but (again, as usual) he said the same thing on many other occasions. One always has to ask not what he means (which may be clear) but what he is getting at. All Shaw's critical prose is polemical, as he freely admitted, and his writing on the theater is devoted to the destruction of some kinds of drama and their replacement by some others (or one other). Here the enemy is the kind of play which had been dominant throughout the latter half of the nineteenth century—"the well-made play," as perfected by Eugène Scribe. In this dramaturgy, the Aristotelian doctrine of the primacy of plot had been driven to an improper extreme. The plot was now not primus inter pares, but all that mattered. It lost its originally organic relation to character and theme. So it became anathema to the apostles of the New Drama at the century's close. As late as 1946, when Allardyce Nicoll declared that Shaw was himself influenced by the well-made play, the old playwright went into print to deny it.

If the well-made play is defined as having no serious content, if it is defined by the relation (or lack of relation) of its plot to character and theme, then obviously Shaw did not write well-made plays. Yet, Professor Nicoll had a point, and a strong one, which was that, for all the disclaimers, Shaw's plays did have plots and, furthermore, that these plots tended to be old acquaintances for those who knew their well-made play. Actually, the playwright had no need to be scandalized, for no dramatist had been more influenced by the well-made play than his own idol of those days, Henrik Ibsen. The Norwegian had begun his theatrical career by directing a large number of these plays; he made an exact imitation of them in his own *Lady Inger of Östråt;* and he had continued to the end to use many of their characteristic devices. Hence, it would have been quite possible for a writer in 1890 to denounce Scribe and Sardou and simultaneously to steal their bag of tricks—from Ibsen. It is doubtful, though, if Bernard Shaw needed to deceive himself in this way. It seems more likely that he took the main situation in *Arms and the Man* from one of Scribe's most successful plays, *Bataille de Dames.*

A situation is not, of course, a plot, and the plot of *Arms and the Man* is not simply lifted from Scribe, even though parts of it may have been. Plagiarism is not the point. The point is that even when Shaw's story diverges from Scribe, it remains Scribean. The play *Arms and the Man* is hung, as it were, on the cunningly told tale of the lost coat with the photograph in its pocket. The reader need only go through the text and mark the hints, incidents, accidents, and contretemps of this tale and he will be finding the layout, the plan—yes, the plot—of this play. Or at any rate, the plot of what could have been a first draft of the play. Shaw, one gathers, did not write such first drafts but, supposing he had, what would be the difference between the first draft and the final one? In the answer of this question lies the secret of the Shavian dramaturgy.

A corollary of the view that "plot is all" is this proposition: the cause of any incident is another incident. It is known that Scribe used to chart out a configuration of incidents and then write his play. This is to go far beyond Aristotle. It is to set no store at all by human initiative and assign to events themselves a kind of fatality: they are a network in which mankind is caught. Granted that the conception might in certain hands have its awesomeness; in Scribe's hands it had only triviality, because he manipulated the events till the issue was a pleasant one. It is curious how often that manipulation had to be arbitrary and drastic. Do events, when given their head, rush downward to disaster? To guarantee a happy ending, the well-making playwrights often needed their emergency weapon: sheer accident. Hence the Shavian complaint that well-made plays were badly made, after all.

Hence also Bernard Shaw's first drama, which is an adaptation of an adaptation of a well-made play. The subject is one that Scribe and the younger Dumas brought to the nineteenth-century theater: marrying, or refusing to marry, money. The immediate source is an unfinished play of William Archer's, *Rhinegold*. Archer's source is *La Ceinture Dorée*, by Emile Augier. When a young man discovers that his young lady's inherited money was acquired by her father in an immoral way, what does he do? William Archer's answer was: he pitches it into the Rhine. One presumes that Archer's action would have been set on a convenient balcony beside that river. Augier's hero is not so privileged. To preserve his honor, he would simply have to forgo the pleasure of marrying the lady, if the author did not provide him and the play with a convenient accident (or money *ex machina*). The whole French economy has to meet with a crisis (war breaks out) so that our heroine's father may be reduced to poverty; it is now honorable for our hero to propose to our heroine. In the well-made play, one incident leads to another with a logic that is inescapable—except when the author decides to escape it. Perhaps Shaw's objection was less to the inescapability than to the egregious, last-minute escapes.

His first play, *Widowers' Houses,* may not be great art but it is a great reversal of custom. Shaw's key decision was to refuse to accept Augier's ending, to refuse to have àccident (masquerading as fate or otherwise) intervene. Such a refusal leads a man—leads a born playwright, at least—back and back into the earlier stages of a story and he ends up writing an utterly different play—an utterly different *kind* of play.

Not one but two conceptions of Augier's were being rejected: not just the solution-by-sheer-accident (which condemns a play to meaninglessness) but also the autonomy-of-incidents—something, by the way, which was no part of Augier's conscious philosophy but was imposed on him by the Scribean design. Dramatists are committed to the doctrine of free will. They can say they don't believe in it, but they have to write their plays as if they did. (In this they resemble human beings in general, for your most ardent determinist acts on the assumption that determinism is false.) People in plays have got to be able to make decisions, and these decisions have got to be both real and influential: they have to affect events. I see no reason to object to Aristotle's declaration that plot is the soul

of the drama, but Aristotle would have objected to
Scribe's attempt to cut the soul off from the body—
that is, from character.

What *does* a young man do when he finds that his
bride's dowry comes from a tainted source? There are
two ways for a writer to arrive at an answer. He can
say: "I can think of several answers—on the basis of
several different possibilities of 'theater.' Answer A
will give you Big Scene X; Answer B will give you
Ending Y; and so on." Or he can say: "I cannot give
you any answer at all until the terms of the proposition are defined, including the term 'tainted.' Above
all, I need to know who these people are: what bride?
what young man?" The first way to arrive at an answer would commonly be thought the playwright's
way: the reasoning is "craftsmanlike" and "of the theater," and would earn a man commendation on
Broadway in 1960. The second way is only the human
way. That makes it the way of the real dramatist and
so of Bernard Shaw.

It could be said that we have this perfectly function-
ing machine of the well-made play and that a Bernard
Shaw is throwing a monkey wrench into it—the monkey wrench of character. That is how it must seem
from the Scribean viewpoint. From the viewpoint of
dramatic art, however, one would say that this particular engine had been revolving all too fast and use-
lessly; only when a Shaw slips in the clutch can the
gear engage and the vehicle prove itself a vehicle by
moving.

"My procedure is to imagine characters and let
them rip. . . ." The pertinence of this remark may by
now be clearer: if the young man has been "imagined," the dramatist can find the decision he would
make as to the young lady's money. But at this point,
we realize that Shaw's words leave out of account the
fact that the situation confronting the young man had
been established in advance of the imagining of his
character. It had been established by Augier and Archer and by Shaw's own decision to use their work.

Hence, Shaw's own interpretation is both helpful and misleading—or, perhaps, is helpful only if those who are helped do a lot of work on their own.

Shaw put *Widowers' Houses* together—how? He took from certain predecessors not only a situation but a story, and not only a story but that clever, orderly, and theatrical arrangement of a story which we call a plot. Then he changed the plot—or as he would have said, let the characters change it for him. Now, had he retained Augier's characters, they could only have caused him to break off the action one scene earlier than Augier did: instead of the happy ending created by a national emergency, we would get the unhappy ending which the emergency reversed.

Characters in a well-made play are "conventional"—that is, they behave, not according to laws of psychology but according to the expectations of an audience in a theater. A type of drama in which the plot is given a free hand cannot afford any less passive or more obtrusive *personae*. Conversely, if a playwright abandons the plot-determined play, he will have to be more inventive as to character. To assume the initiative, his characters will have to be capable of it. So Shaw's first contribution to the drama was: more active characters. They were more active, first of all, in the most obvious fashion: they were violent. More important, they made decisions which affected the course of events, and they made them on the basis of their own nature, not of the spectator's. And so these characters were surprising. For a number of years, they were too surprising to be acceptable. Like all surprising art, Shaw's dramaturgy was damned as nonart. The critics' formula was: Not a Play.

Augier's hero could not consider being the husband of a woman with a tainted dowry. Shaw creates a hero who has the effrontery to ask the heroine to throw up her dowry for his sake. But the Shavian joke—the Shavian reversal—is already what it would characteristically be in the future: a double one. To this demanding hero he adds an even more demanding heroine: she simply refuses to be poor to preserve her innocence. That is the nub of the first Shaw comedy. Then Shaw works his way out of the apparent deadlock, not by having the heroine weaken (that is, "improve"), but by having the hero renew his strength (that is, "deteriorate"). This the latter does by way of recovering from a shock. The shock comes from without and might be called an accident (like Augier's outbreak of war), except that it belongs to the logic of the situation. It turns out that the source of the hero's own unearned income is the same as that of his girl's father. End of Act Two. In the third and last act, our hero comes around and gets the girl by accepting the nature of capitalism. Socialist propaganda? Precisely. Shaw boasted of it. But he boasted with equal reason that he was writing comedy in the most traditional sense.

"Take what would be done by Scribe, Sardou, Dumas *fils*, or Augier and do the opposite." Is that the Shavian formula? It is certain that Shavian comedy is parodistic in a way, or to an extent, that Plautus, Jonson, and Molière were not. These others, one would judge, took a convention they respected and brought it to the realization of its best possibilities. Shaw took conventions in which he saw no possibilities—except insofar as he would expose their bankruptcy. The injunction "Do the opposite" was not whimsical. Shaw decided to "do the opposite" of Scribe in much the way Marx decided to do the opposite of Hegel—not to stand everything on its head (Hegel, he held, had done this) but to set everything back on its feet again. That was revolutionary thinking, and Shaw's art, for all the polite and charming trappings, was revolutionary art. The usual relations were reversed.

Such reversals as we see in the ending of *Widowers' Houses* are relatively simple. Shaw's weakest plays are those in which he has done little more than turn the ending around: the price you pay for the brilliant ending of *The Devil's Disciple* is that of a rather dull, and decidedly conventional, first act. His best plays are those in which the principle of reversal has pervaded the whole. Such a play is *Arms and the Man*.

The idea of taking two couples and causing them to exchange partners is hardly novel and, as I have said, the little tale of the coat and the portrait is Scribean in pattern. But Shaw can justifiably plead that this is no well-made play because the artifices of the plot are not what ultimately achieve the result. Here is one of the decisive turns in the action:

> BLUNTSCHLI. When you get into that noble attitude and speak in that thrilling voice, I admire you; but I find it impossible to believe a single word you say.
>
> RAINA. Captain Bluntschli!
>
> BLUNTSCHLI. Yes?
>
> RAINA. Do you mean what you said just now? Do you *know* what you said just now?
>
> BLUNTSCHLI. I do.
>
> RAINA. I! I!!! How did you find me out?

With this last query, Raina passes over forever from Sergius's world to Bluntschli's: as a result of nothing in the Scribean arrangement of incidents, but of words, words, words. It is here that, to many, the Shavian drama seems vulnerable. In drama, actions are supposed to speak louder than words. Writers on the subject invariably know their etymology— "drama" derives from a Greek verb meaning "to do"—and use it as a cudgel. Their error is a vulgar one: action need not be external. It can often be carried by words alone. Shaw used to remark that his plays were all words just as Raphael's paintings were all paint.

There is a degree of legerdemain in that remark, for Scribe, too, put down his plays in words. What was confusing to Shaw's readers and spectators half a century ago was that after indicating unmistakably that he was playing Scribe's game, Shaw proceeded to break the rules. The fact that Bluntschli conquers by words gains its peculiar force from a context in which the opposite was to be expected. To look over *Arms and the Man* with an eye to technique would be to conclude that what we have here is Scribe most subtly interwoven with Shaw. Yet this formulation is inadequate, for who did the interweaving? There was a Scribe in Shaw, and there was a counter-Scribe in Shaw; what makes his works dramatic is the interaction of the two.

The passion and preoccupation of Scribe was the idea of climax: to the Big Scene at the end—or, rather, a little before the end—all his arts are dedicated. In Bernard Shaw there was almost as great a predilection for anticlimax. It is the Shavian "effect" par excellence; no other playwright has come near finding so many possibilities in it. The bit I have quoted from Bluntschli and Raina is an apt example. *Arms and the Man* contains a corresponding scene between Sergius and Louka. Where, in a well-made play, Bluntschli and Louka would have to soar to the heights of Raina and Sergius, in the Shaw play Raina and Sergius drop with a bump to the level of Bluntschli and Louka. Such is resolution by anticlimax. It is dramaturgically effective, and it enforces the author's theme. But this is not all of Shaw: it is only the counter-Scribe.

The dual anticlimaxes do not round off *Arms and the Man*. What does? Not the disenchantment of Raina and Sergius but the discovery that Bluntschli the realist is actually an enchanted soul whom nothing will disenchant. He has destroyed their romanticism but is himself "incurably romantic." This is another point that is made in "mere words"—"mere words stuck on at the end," if you wish—and yet stuck on very well, for they are firmly attached to that little tale of the coat and the photograph which gives the work its continuity and shape:

BLUNTSCHLI.—Yes: that's the coat I mean. . . . Do you suppose I am the sort of fellow a young girl falls in love with? Why, look at our ages! I'm thirty-four:

I don't suppose the young lady is much over seven-teen. All that adventure which was life or death to me, was only a schoolgirl's game to her . . . would a woman who took the affair seriously have sent me this and written on it: "Raina, to her chocolate cream soldier—a souvenir"?

PETKOFF. That's what I was looking for. How the deuce did it get there?

BLUNTSCHLI. I have put everything right, I hope, gracious young lady!

RAINA. I quite agree with your account of yourself. You are a romantic idiot. Next time I hope you will know the difference between a schoolgirl of seventeen and a woman of twenty-three.

In this scene, plot and theme reach completion together, and the play of thesis and antithesis ends in synthesis.

The supreme triumph of Shaw's dramaturgical dialectics is to be found in *Man and Superman,* and, for all the blarney in the preface about the medieval *Everyman* and the eighteenth-century *Don Giovanni,* the method is the conversion of old materials into nineteenth-century terms, both thematic and technical. Shaw's claim to be returning to a pristine Don Juan is valid to the extent that the theme had originally been less of psychological than of philosophical, indeed theological, interest. It is also true that Don Juan had run away from his women. However, he had run away from them only after possessing them. In Shaw's play, he runs away to prevent *them* from possessing *him.* It is a comic parody of the old motif, embodying Shaw's standard new motif: the courting of the man by the woman. And where the old dramatists and librettists had used the old, "open" type of plot (or nonplot), Shaw substitutes an utterly Scribean "closed" structure.

This very "modern" and "twentieth-century" play is made up of narrative materials familiar to every Victorian theatergoer. We have a hero who spends the entire evening hotly pursued by his foes; a clandestine

marriage celebrated in defiance of a hostile father; a
lovelorn hero who sacrifices himself so that the girl
will go to his rival; a villain whose function is to constitute for a while the barrier to denouement and happy
ending. The subplot about the Malone family rests
upon two separate uses of the "secret skillfully withheld," then skillfully released. Traditional farcical coincidence binds together Straker and Mendoza. The
play bears every sign of careful workmanship—all of
it School of Scribe.

But as with *Arms and the Man,* as soon as we examine particulars, we find, interwoven with the Scribean
elements, those typically Shavian verbal exchanges
which constitute further action. Violet's marriage
could have been made a secret of in any Scribe play,
and Scribe could have been relied on to choose an
effective moment for the release of the secret. In
Shaw, what creates both the fun and the point of the
news release is not the organization of the incidents
but their relation to theme:

> TANNER. . . . I know, and the whole world really
> knows, though it dare not say so, that you were right
> to follow your instinct; that vitality and bravery are
> the greatest qualities a woman can have, and mother-
> hood her solemn initiation into womanhood; and that
> the fact of your not being legally married matters not
> one scrap either to your own worth or to our real
> regard for you.
>
> VIOLET. Oh! You think me a wicked woman, like
> the rest. . . . I won't bear such a horrible insult as to
> be complimented by Jack on being one of the wretches
> of whom he approves. I have kept my marriage a se-
> cret for my husband's sake.

An incident which Tanner wishes to use to illustrate his
"modern" philosophy thus comes to illustrate a contrasting
thesis: that Violet lives by a nonmodern philosophy.

Simple? Yes, but closely linked to a point that is
unsimple enough to have generally been missed: Tan-

ner is a windbag. Indeed, the mere fact of the woman
courting the man would probably not yield comedy at
all were it not for a further and more dynamic reversal: the woman, who makes no great claims for herself,
has all the shrewdness, the real *Lebensweisheit,* while
the man, who knows everything and can discourse like
Bernard Shaw, is—a fool. Tanner is, in fact, like Molière's Alceste, the traditional fool of comedy in highly
sophisticated intellectual disguise. Ann Whitefield,
into whose trap Tanner falls, is the knave—in skirts.

While Don Juan Tenorio is Superman—or is on
the road to him—John Tanner, M.I.R.C., is merely
Man, and as such belongs to The World As It Is. Of
dramaturgical interest is that the kind of plot Shaw
evidently considers capable of giving an image of The
World As It Is should be the kind that is generally
considered (by himself, for instance) artificial, unreal,
arbitrary, inane. Shaw the critic championed the new
Naturalism, and among French dramatists especially
favored Brieux, who produced dully literal theatrical
documentaries. Yet, when Shaw wrote an essay entitled "A Dramatic Realist to His Critics," the example of "realism" he gave from his own work was
Arms and the Man—on the grounds that the characters respond naturally even if the situations aren't
natural. We are entitled, then, to insist on his choice
of "unnatural" situations. He must intuitively have
understood something which, as a critic, he failed to
grasp: that plot does not merely reproduce external
reality. The violence and intrigue in Shakespeare,
which Shaw the critic declared extraneous, provides
the objective correlative of Shakespeare's feelings
about life, and the "idiocies" of the plot of *Man and
Superman* provide an objective correlative for Shaw's
sense of modern life. The very fact that Shaw despised Scribe helps to explain the particular use he
made of him.

The Don Juan episode in Act Three is neither a
well-made play nor a portion of a well-made play. It
stands apart as something appropriately more austere

and august. It is not a traditional work of any kind, not even a Platonic dialogue, the relation between Socrates and his interlocutors being quite different. It is not even a debate, for two of the speakers, the Commander and Ana, hardly present arguments at all: they simply represent a point of view. Do even the Devil and Don Juan *discuss* anything? A devil is scarcely a being one can convert to a Cause, and if the Don is busy convincing anyone it is himself. Certainly it is the philosophy of Bernard Shaw that he is given to speak, but is persuasion exercised—even on the audience? Rather, the contributions of the four presences come together as a vision of life—and an intimation of superlife.

Man—and Superman. The comedy of John Tanner—and the vision of Don Juan Tenorio. Shaw—and counter-Shaw. Thesis and antithesis are, to be sure, of separate interest, and yet, as usual, the great Shavian achievement is to have related one to the other. Tanner seems a wise man and proves a fool. Don Juan passes for a philanderer but proves an explorer and a missionary of the truth. In our trivial, tawdry, clever, Scribean world, intellect is futile and ever at the mercy of instinct. Take away the episode in hell, and Shaw has written an anti-intellectual comedy. The episode assigns to intellect the highest role. No longer, therefore, is Ann the center and source of things—only a possible mother for Superman. Here Don Juan dominates. Here (or rather, in heaven) intellect is at home, and the Don is cured of that occupational disease of Shavian heroes—homelessness. He "comes to a good end"—only it is not an end, it is an episode, and from these celestial-infernal heights we must descend to earth with the shock of Shavian anticlimax, to earth and to Tanner, from Superman back to Man. One section of the play gets an electric charge from the other.

Of Shaw's "playmaking" one must conclude that he knew how to put together a Scribean plot; that he knew how to subordinate such a plot to his own purposes; and that, in *Man and Superman*, he knew how to take the resultant Shavian comedy and combine it dynamically with a disquisition on (and by) Don Juan.

Emotional Substance

If Shaw's plays are, or begin by being, a parody of the more conventional drama of his time, that parody is by no means confined to the form. We have already seen that the themes, too, tend to get turned around: these compositions not only do the opposite, as it were, but say the opposite.

What of the emotions? Whatever the ultimate purpose of drama, its immediate impact is a strongly emotional one, and one cannot conceive of a story having an emotional effect upon an audience unless it is an emotional story and has a certain emotional structure. I may be forgiven for stating so rudimentary a principle because the Shavian drama presents us with a paradox: it has flooded a thousand theaters with emotion and yet has often been held to be emotionless.

Of course, this common opinion is absurd, bolstered though it can be with remarks of Shaw's own about being a mere "work machine" and the like. What we confront here is originality. Shaw may not have been an original thinker; he tried, rather, to make a synthesis of what certain others had thought. But he was an original person. What fitted him so well for the role of the enemy of convention was that his natural responses were not those of other people but all his own. His emotional constitution was a peculiar one, and that peculiarity is reflected in his plays.

Sex is, without doubt, the crucial issue. Comedy remains fertility worship, however sublimated, and it is fair enough to ask what Bernard Shaw made of the old sexual rigmarole—courtship and the barriers thereto. It is even fair to use any facts about Shaw himself that are a matter of public record.

On the other hand, one is not honor-bound to side

with "modern" opinion against "Victorian" as to
what is good and bad. The very "modern" Dr. Kinsey
implied that human vitality could be measured in sta-
tistics on orgasms. Our subject Bernard Shaw will not
pass into any Kinseyite paradise. Though he lived to
be ninety-four, he seems to have experienced sexual
intercourse only between the ages of twenty-nine and
forty-three. "I lived a continent virgin . . . until I was
29. . . . During the fourteen years before my marriage
at 43 there was always some lady in the case. . . . As
man and wife we found a new relation in which sex
had no part. It ended the old gallantries, flirtations,
and philanderings for both of us." This quotation is
from a letter to Frank Harris, who, as a Kinseyite
before Kinsey, wrote: "Compare his [Shaw's] private
life with Shakespeare's. While Mary Fitton was banished from London Shakespeare could write nothing
but tragedies. That went on for five years. When the
Queen died and Shakespeare's Dark Lady returned,
he wrote *Antony and Cleopatra,* his greatest love
story. As nothing like that happened in Shaw's life
we can only get a textbooky, sexless type of play."
A remarkable blend of ignorance, invention, and arbitrary assumption! For, actually, Shaw concealed
from Harris most of his private life; nothing whatever
is known about Shakespeare's feelings for any
woman; and no critic or psychologist of repute has
ever argued that a man's writing has to be "textbooky" and "sexless" unless he is carrying on an
adulterous romance; a more familiar argument would
be that precisely the abstinent man's imagination
might well be crammed with sex. But there is no
settling the question a priori.

   William Archer declared that Shaw's plays reeked
with sex. It is a more suggestive declaration than
Harris's. It reminds us that Shaw was able to re-
create the sexual charm of both men and women to
a degree unequaled by any English dramatist except
Shakespeare. To be sure, he doesn't need bedroom
scenes to do this. Morell only has to talk and we

understand "Prossy's complaint." Undershaft only
has to talk and we understand why he is a problem
to his daughter. To say nothing of the long line of
sirens from Candida to Orinthia! Few of the "sexy"
ladies of Restoration comedy, by contrast, have any
sex appeal at all. One thing Archer is sure to have
had in mind is that the women in Shaw pursue a
sexual purpose in a way absolutely unknown to Victorian literature. Of all the reversals in Shavian
drama, this is inevitably the most famous: the reversal
in the roles of the sexes. Shaw once committed himself to the view that all superior women are masculine and all superior men are feminine. In his
comedies, most often, the woman is active, the man
passive. Perhaps by 1960 the theme has been restated
ad nauseam; to Archer it was startling—as was
Shaw's determination to rub the sore places of the
sexual morality of his time. *Mrs. Warren's Profession*
was for many years too "raw" a play for production
in London, and it created a memorable scandal when
it was produced in New Haven and New York in
1905. Like most of the major modern dramatists and
novelists, Shaw mentioned the unmentionable. He
even claimed to have "put the physical act of sexual
intercourse on the stage" (in *Overruled*). Archer evidently felt that Shaw could not give the subject of
sex a rest: he may not always have been at the center
of it but he was forever touching its fringes.

Here Frank Harris would have interjected: "He was
always *avoiding* the center of it." And the interjection
is called for. The impression that a man is unemotional
in general and sexless in particular does not come
from nowhere. Nor are the kinds of sex I have been
noting what the average spectator is looking for if he
demands a "sexy" show. *Overruled* does not really
"put the physical act of sexual intercourse on the
stage," and, even if it did, it would do so comically—
depriving the act of precisely that element which people miss in Shaw, which is not sex in general but the
torridity of sexual romance. At that, if this element

were simply absent, Shaw might very well have got away with the omission. But it is explicitly rejected. It is not that a Shavian couple cannot consider intercourse but that they are likely to consider it and decide not to. If the characteristic act of the French drama of the period was the plunge into bed, that of the Shavian drama is the precipitate retreat from the bedroom door.

Harris would be right in reminding us that such was Bernard Shaw's emotional constitution. What other writer has ever created all the normal expectations in a scene between a king and his mistress (*The Apple Cart*), only to reveal later that their relationship is purely platonic? *Captain Brassbound's Conversion* shows the Shavian pattern to perfection. Is there sexual feeling in the play? There is. The process by which Brassbound and Lady Cicely are brought closer and closer is positively titillating. After which, what happens? They are parted. The play has a superb final curtain. "How glorious!" says Lady Cicely, "how glorious!" Then with one of those quick changes of tone that mark the Shavian dialogue: "And what an escape!" Is this unemotional? No. But the emotion is not erotic—rather, it is relief at a release from the erotic. Such is the emotional content of this particular Shavian anticlimax.

As far as conscious intention goes, all Shaw's plays might bear the title he gave to three of them—Plays for Puritans—for that intention is to show romance transcended by a higher-than-erotic purpose. It is a classic intention—an application, really, of the traditional conflict of love and honor, with honor winning hands down, as it did in Corneille and even in one masterpiece of Racine's, *Bérénice*. We are concerned here not with philosophic intention but psychological substance. Where the philosopher insists that Shaw does not cross the threshold of the bedroom, the psychologist asks: why does he hover at the bedroom door?

We know from the correspondence with Mrs. Pat Campbell that Shaw liked to play with fire. Even the correspondence with Ellen Terry entailed a playfulness not quite devoid of "danger." The boy Shaw had been witness to an odd household arrangement whereby his mother's music teacher contrived to be (it would seem) almost but not quite her lover. A slightly older Shaw has recently been portrayed as the intruder into a friend's marriage, like his own Eugene Marchbanks: this is speculation. Let us look at the play *Candida*, which is a fact.

It has a notable Big Scene at the end, which is characterized by an equally notable improbability. A comfortable, sensible parson's wife doesn't let herself get jockeyed into "choosing" between her husband and an almost total stranger. People—such people at least—don't do such things. A respectable woman's choice was made before the banns were read.

Perhaps Candida is not really respectable? That is the line of interpretation taken by Beatrice Webb, who declared her a prostitute. Will the play, taken as a play, bear this interpretation out? A dramatist's license to have the truth turn out different from the impression given to the audience is very limited, for it is to a large extent by giving impressions that he creates characters. Shaw has given the impression that Candida is *not* a prostitute.

Against this it can be urged that Shaw himself took Beatrice Webb's side and attacked Candida—in remarks he made about her in letters to James Huneker, Richard Burton, and others. True, but was that legitimate? He himself admitted that he had no more right to say what his plays meant than any other critic. One might add that he may have had less, for when an author intervenes to correct our impressions of his work, he is often intervening to change or misinterpret that work.

Outside the play, Shaw is against Candida. Inside it, he is both for and against her, but he is for her effectually, and against her ineffectually, because the direct impression is favorable, while it is only by throwing logic back into the story when it is over that you can reach an unfavorable judgment. This means, I should think, that though Shaw's intellect is against Candida, his emotions are for her.

What is it that this play has always projected in the theater, and can always be counted on to project again? The charm of Candida. This is a reality so immediate and all-pervasive that it is hard for any other element in the play to make headway against it. Leading actresses know this, and hearing their director speak of Candida's essential badness, can afford to smile a Candida smile, strong in the knowledge that there is nothing a director can do about this badness, once that smile has been displayed on stage as well as off.

I would say that it is a confused play but that the confusion goes unnoticed because of Candida's charm and may even be the cause of a degree of emotional tension unusual in a Shaw play. Candida is made out of a Shavian ambivalence: he would like to reject this kind of woman, but actually he dotes on her. One quickly senses that he *is* Marchbanks. One also finds he protests (too much) that he is *not* Marchbanks. "I had in mind De Quincey's account of his adolescence in his Confessions," he wrote. "I certainly never thought of myself as a model." From the empty pretence of being De Quincey, no doubt, comes the prodigious unreality of many of the lines. As a character, Marchbanks must be reckoned a failure. Shaw was hiding. What better image to hide behind than that of the kind of writer he himself was not—a romantic poet? Especially if De Quincey would do the job for him?

It didn't work, of course, except as pure histrionics. (Marchbanks, though a poorly drawn character, is always an effective stage role, and still seems to correspond to the actors' idea of a poet.) But if no one in the play can reject Candida, there is a noteworthy niche in it for the man whom she will reject. This niche Marchbanks can fill nobly, and has his dramatic moment as he marches into it: his final exit is a magnificent piece of action. Possibly everything before that (in this role) is just an improvisation. Shaw could not make us believe in the poet's poetry, but he does make us believe in his pain and his nobility, for at these points he could identify himself with Eugene completely without having to "think of himself as a model."

Dramatists usually speak of their characters individually, and that could be regarded as strange, because the drama, all through the centuries, has done much less with separate persons than with relationships. The traditional characters are, if you will, simplified to the point of crudity. What is not crude, as treated by the old dramatists, is the interaction of these characters: the dynamics of human relations are fully rendered. If what you do not get is the detailed psychological biography, what you do get is the essence of such relations as parent and child, boy and girl, man and wife.

Now, modern playwrights, happily, have not departed from the classic patterns as much as they are supposed to have, and what rings true, emotionally, in *Candida* corresponds to Shaw's ability to find and re-create some of these elemental relationships. An inner obstacle, one would judge, hampered him when he tried to "do" the Marchbanks-Candida relationship, but the Morell-Candida relation is both clear and challenging. It is, as Shaw himself said, the relationship of Nora and Torvald Helmer turned around: in Shaw's play the man is the doll. But where Ibsen tells the story of a doll who finally comes to life, Shaw tells the story of a seemingly living person who turns out to have been a doll all along. (In other words, the relation of Shaw to Ibsen, instead of being as direct as it might seem, is an inverse one, exactly like the relation of Shaw to other nineteenth-century drama.) Into Morell Shaw can put that part of himself (a child) which finds Candida irresistible, just as into Candida he can put that part of Woman which he finds irresistible—the mother in her. One would have to be as naïve a psychologist as Frank Harris to consider the mother-and-child relation less emotional than that of lovers.

Or less dramatic. Relationships become dramatic not in the degree of their eroticism but to the extent that they contain conflict. Pure love would not be a dramatic subject at all. Love becomes dramatic when it is impure—when the loving element is submerged in a struggle for power. The axis about which *Candida* revolves is that of strength and weakness, not love and hate. And if one knows Shaw's views on the topic of the "weaker sex" in general, the conclusion of *Candida* follows naturally: instead of the little woman reaching up toward the arms of the strong man, we have the strong woman reaching down to pick up her child. It is remarkable how far Shaw's thought is from the standard "advanced thinking" of his generation, with its prattle of equality and comradeship. He is closer to Nietzsche.

Of the ending of *A Doll's House* it has been said: perhaps Nora has walked out in a mere tantrum and will be back in the morning. How much more savage is the ending of *Candida*! Only Strindberg could have written a sequel to it. The cruelty of the heroine— merely implicit in the present play—would have to come to the surface in any continuation of the story. Candida has chosen to let her husband discover his shame: she, as well as he, will have to take the consequences. Let the stage manager hold razors and strait jackets in readiness!

One reason why Shaw got so little credit for his treatment of the emotions is that the emotions he treats are not the ones people expect. The very fact that his favorite device is anticlimax should tell us that what he most insistently feels is "letdown." It may be retorted that on the contrary, Bernard Shaw was the most buoyant and vivacious of men. That is also true. The axis "strength-weakness" is not more important to Shaw's content than the axis "elation-depression" is to his form. The dialogue ripples gaily along; then comes the sudden letdown. The circus has familiarized us with the pattern: it is the light of heart who take the pratfall. Even as the fool pops up in Shavian comedy in the highly intellectualized shape of a Jack Tanner, so the pratfall is transmuted into an anticlimax that has a positively climactic force. It has been customary to take these anticlimaxes as expressions of an idea—the idea of disenchantment. It is *the* idea of modern literature, and it is inseparable from an emotion far commoner and far more influential than romantic excitement. There seems to be no name for this emotion—and that, too, is significant. Let us call it desolation.

You cannot be disenchanted without having been enchanted. One is sometimes tempted to believe that our human desolation might have been avoided if only we had not started out so undesolate. It is not the fact that we don't have things that worries us, but that we have lost them—or rather, been deprived of them. Desolation is the feeling of having been driven from paradise.

A friend of Bernard Shaw's said that when he saw *The Wild Duck,* the bottom dropped out of the universe. One difference between Ibsen and Shaw is that the former produced this effect on the audience, whereas the latter produced it on the characters in a play. Just as a character in a melodrama loses a fortune, so a character in a Shaw play loses a universe. The experience may be given a playful treatment, as with Raina and Sergius. In the case of Morell, the treatment is only partly playful. It gets more serious as the play *Candida* proceeds. Morell finally loses his image of his wife and of himself. The curtain has to be rung down to save us from the Strindberg play that would have to follow.

What of *Mrs. Warren's Profession*? The starting point was a treatment by Maupassant of the theme of a girl finding out that her mother is a courtesan. In an early version of the tale, Maupassant had the girl kill herself. In the later and better-known text (*Yvette*), he saves her life to engineer for himself an ironic-poignant ending: she becomes a kept woman like her mother before her. Curtain! That is the kind of inversion of a suicidal ending which Shaw did *not* go in for. Or not any more. If Shaw had shown a "surrender to the system" (in comical fashion) in the ending of *Widowers' Houses,* he was now intent on showing a rejection of the system. In the first instance, Vivie Warren's revolt represents Shaw's rational rejection of capitalism, but the play culminates in a scene that has no necessary connection with economics—a scene of family crisis, a scene in which a daughter rejects her mother. Which, after all, is archetypal Shaw: instead of the emotions of lover and mistress, he renders the emotions of parents and children, and particularly the emotion of the child rejecting the parent. *Major Barbara* is perhaps the grandest example of this archetype. The great last act of *Pygmalion* is the same thing in disguise, for Henry Higgins is the progenitor of the new Eliza, and that is why she must break free of him. Shaw's Joan has a father, too—in heaven—and she comes at times almost to the point of breaking with Him. That she does not quite do so is the upshot of a play which, while it shows Joan's isolation from men, ends with a stretching of arms toward the heavenly Father. Vivie Warren is already a Saint Joan in that the experience Shaw gives her is that of being desolated. It is the experience he felt most deeply—presumably because it was the experience he had most deeply experienced. In any event, the two long scenes between Vivie and Mrs. Warren are emotional playwriting such as England had not seen for a couple of centuries.

The background, however, is blurred. A Scribean climax is arranged to provide *élan* for the announcement that Vivie's romance is incestuous:

CROFTS . . . Allow me, Mister Frank, to introduce you to your half-sister, the eldest daughter of the Reverend Samuel Gardner. Miss Vivie: your half-brother. Good morning.

FRANK [. . . *raising the rifle*]. You'll testify before the coroner that it's an accident, Viv. [*He takes aim at the retreating figure of Crofts. Vivie seizes the muzzle and pulls it round against her breast.*]

VIVIE. Fire now. You may.

Direct climax (as against anticlimax) was not really in Shaw's line, and in failing to parody Scribe here, Shaw has himself tumbled into the ridiculous. Perhaps the following act was bound to be an anticlimax in a way not intended—a mere disappointment. Yet, it is hard to believe that the particular disappointments it brings are simply the result of a technical ineptitude. Rather, they involve hesitations about the subject. After so strongly creating the impression of incest, Shaw shuffles the notion off in the next act in a surprisingly ambiguous way. It would be easy enough, from a technical viewpoint, to make clear that no incest had been committed. Why did Shaw leave the situation doubtful? So that Vivie could dismiss the issue as irrelevant? In that case, what is relevant? Why is she giving Frank up? One can think of possible reasons, but what reason is one *supposed* to think of?

Unclarity in the work of so careful a craftsman, a writer, moreover, who has more than once been accused of excessive clarity, surely bears witness to inner uncertainty and conflict. To think of *Mrs. Warren's Profession* in this personal way is to realize what powerful aggressions it embodies. Shaw combined the themes of prostitution and incest in order to make quite a rational point: our mad society draws back in horror from incest, which is certainly not a pressing menace and perhaps not even a bad thing, while it encourages prostitution, which is a virulent social pestilence. But both themes have a resonance far beyond the bounds of intellect. It is as if they proved more than Shaw had bargained for. The incest theme is sounded—all too boldly. Then the young dramatist has no idea what to do with it. He takes it back. Only, it is too late. So he half takes it back. After all, what is troubling Vivie does go beyond the rationally established causes. Deep water! And Shaw flounders in it. Which has some interest for the student of the emotions. Even where Shaw's plays are faulty, they are not unemotional. On the contrary, it is because of a certain emotional involvement in the material, not because of incapacity for such involvement, that Shaw was not able to resolve certain problems and truly finish certain plays. *Candida* and *Mrs. Warren's Profession* could be cited in evidence. There is material in both which was not successfully "worked through."

Is there similar material in Shaw's collected plays which *was* worked through? To my mind, a good answer would be: yes, *Pygmalion.* This play might well have proved just as ambiguous as the others, for it might have seemed that Eliza must love Higgins, and therefore that her leaving him is but an overrational afterthought of the author's, like his afterthoughts on Candida. Some people, including the author of *My Fair Lady,* think that is just what the Shavian ending is. I, on the other hand, feel—and it is feeling that is in question—that Eliza's rebellion grows organically out of what preceded. She is Higgins's creation: she cannot *be* at all unless she become independent of her creator. If she has "sex appeal," that makes the break more difficult but not less necessary. A girl's father quite normally has sex appeal for her. That is not to justify incest. Here Shaw does cope with incest, and in the best way—by avoiding it.

The ending of *Pygmalion* is the classic Shavian situation: someone is clamorously refusing to enter the bedroom. The friends of Frank Harris are thereby disgusted. That is their right. But there is a point to be made about Shaw's rendering of emotion. Refusal is emotional. There is more turbulence in conflict between Eliza and Higgins as conceived by Shaw than in romance between them as in *My Fair Lady.*

Man and Superman, on the other hand, might seem to be without emotional substance. The attempt made at a straightforward emotional climax is certainly rather unsuccessful:

> TANNER. I love you. The Life Force enchants me: I have the whole world in my arms when I clasp you. But I am fighting for my freedom: for my honor, for my self, one and indivisible.
>
> ANN. Your happiness will be worth them all.
>
> TANNER. You would sell freedom and honor and self for happiness?
>
> ANN. It will not be all happiness for me. Perhaps death.
>
> TANNER [*groaning*]. Oh, that clutch holds and hurts. What have you grasped in me? Is there a father's heart as well as a mother's?

If there is capital here, it is the kind that yields no dramatic return, and indeed a criticism of this false climax would lead us to complain of the introduction of the "Life Force" in the first place. There seems no such organic relation between Tanner and Ann as there is between Vivie and her mother, Eliza and Higgins, Candida and Morell. The pair are sometimes compared to Benedick and Beatrice. The comparison is not apt. Shakespeare shows the erotically "dangerous" element in the hostility of his couple. But Tanner and Ann draw no sparks from each other. A cynic might say: here there can be no love since there is no hate. There is really no relationship at all, except that she insists on having him and he cannot evade her successfully because the author won't let him. In this case, we have either to conclude that Frank Harris's kind of criticism applies—or that this is "drama of ideas" and we must not ask it to be otherwise.

Emotional substance? The farce of Tanner and Ann, taken in isolation, has very little, but oddly enough, the episode in hell has a good deal, and this spreads itself over the work as a whole. Even here, though, there is a discrepancy between intention and achievement. The final effect of the Don Juan scene is not that we find the positive message inspiring. We find it at best important, at worst gallant—a brave effort to make sense of things that cannot be made sense of. It is all rather like a speech made in wartime, saying that our side is bound to win because we are right. Perhaps. Perhaps. But the words that burn with irrefutability are all words expressing not aspiration toward a better future, but recognition of a bad present. Don Juan himself is at his best when denouncing people. The speech that steals the show ("And is Man any the less destroying himself . . .") is made by the Devil. Which is because it is not only a very reasonable speech but a very emotional one, a speech that springs from that very desolation which Shaw's best people experience.

This note of personal poignancy is not heard very often after *Saint Joan* (1923). So much the worse, perhaps, for the later plays. They have considerable merit, yet they often lack urgency even when the author makes Urgent Statements in them. And it is interesting that they lack not only dynamic and turbulent personal relationships but also close structure. There had been a connection between the emotional and the dramaturgic construction of the earlier plays; and when one went, so did the other.

I am not proposing a complete theory of the Shavian drama. Nor am I asking my reader to assume that all is dominated by the emotional conflicts of its author, much less that it ought to be. For that matter, I have had to remark that unresolved conflict sometimes resulted in unresolved art. What I am affirming is, first, that some Shaw plays communicate personal feeling of great intensity and, second, that even some Shaw plays which are less overtly emotional do embody powerful feelings, though not of the kind that is usually expected.

—ERIC BENTLEY

Mrs. Warren's Profession

*The harlot's cry from street to street
Shall weave old England's winding sheet.*

—William Blake

THE AUTHOR'S APOLOGY

Mrs. Warren's Profession has been performed at last, after a delay of only eight years; and I have once more shared with Ibsen the triumphant amusement of startling all but the strongest-headed of the London theatre critics clean out of the practice of their profession. No author who has ever known the exultation of sending the press into an hysterical tumult of protest, of moral panic, of involuntary and frantic confession of sin, of a horror of conscience in which the power of distinguishing between the work of art on the stage and the real life of the spectator is confused and overwhelmed, will ever care for the stereotyped compliments which every successful farce or melodrama elicits from the newspapers. Give me that critic who rushed from my play to declare furiously that Sir George Crofts ought to be kicked. What a triumph for the actor, thus to reduce a jaded London journalist to the condition of the simple sailor in the Wapping gallery, who shouts execrations at Iago and warnings to Othello not to believe him! But dearer still than such simplicity is that sense of the sudden earthquake shock to the foundations of morality which sends a pallid crowd of critics into the street shrieking that the pillars of society are cracking and the ruin of the state at hand. Even the Ibsen champions of ten years ago remonstrate with me just as the veterans of those brave days remonstrated with them. Mr. Grein, the hardy iconoclast who first launched my plays on the stage alongside *Ghosts* and *The Wild Duck,* exclaims that I have shattered his ideals. Actually his ideals! What would Dr. Relling say? And Mr. William Archer himself disowns me because I "cannot touch pitch without wallowing in it." Truly my play must be more needed than I knew; and yet I thought I knew how little the others know.

Do not suppose, however, that the consternation of the press reflects any consternation among the general public. Anybody can upset the theatre critics, in a turn of the wrist, by substituting for the romantic commonplaces of the stage the moral commonplaces of the pulpit, the platform, or the library. Play *Mrs. Warren's Profession* to an audience of clerical members of the Christian Social Union and of women well experienced in Rescue, Temperance, and Girls' Club work,* and no moral panic will arise: every man and woman present will know that as long as poverty makes virtue hideous and the spare pocket-money of rich bachelordom makes vice dazzling, their daily hand-to-hand fight against prostitution with prayer and persuasion, shelters and scanty alms, will be a losing one. There was a time when they were able to urge that though "the white-lead factory where Anne Jane was poisoned" may be a far more terrible place than Mrs. Warren's house, yet hell is still more dreadful. Nowadays they no longer believe in hell; and the girls among whom they are working know that they do not believe in it, and would laugh at them if they did. So well have the rescuers learnt that Mrs. Warren's defence of herself and indictment of society is the thing that most needs saying, that those who know me personally reproach me, not for writing this play, but for wasting my energies on "pleasant plays" for the amusement of frivolous people, when I can build up such excellent stage sermons on their own work. *Mrs. Warren's Profession* is the one play of mine which I could submit to a censorship without doubt of the result; only, it must not be the censorship of the minor theatre critic, nor of an innocent court official like the King's Reader of Plays, much less of people who consciously profit by Mrs. War-

---

* Many a specialist of the stalls will shudder at his own dreary conception of such an audience: but I can assure him that he would hardly know where he was on such an occasion, so much more vital would the atmosphere be, and so much jollier and better looking the people.

ren's profession, or who personally make use of it, or who hold the widely whispered view that it is an indispensable safety-valve for the protection of domestic virtue, or, above all, who are smitten with a sentimental affection for our fallen sister, and would "take her up tenderly, lift her with care, fashioned so slenderly, young, and *so* fair." Nor am I prepared to accept the verdict of the medical gentlemen who would compulsorily examine and register Mrs. Warren, whilst leaving Mrs. Warren's patrons, especially her military patrons, free to destroy her health and anybody else's without fear of reprisals. But I should be quite content to have my play judged by, say, a joint committee of the Central Vigilance Society and the Salvation Army. And the sterner moralists the members of the committee were, the better.

Some of the journalists I have shocked reason so unripely that they will gather nothing from this but a confused notion that I am accusing the National Vigilance Association and the Salvation Army of complicity in my own scandalous immorality. It will seem to them that people who would stand this play would stand anything. They are quite mistaken. Such an audience as I have described would be revolted by many of our fashionable plays. They would leave the theatre convinced that the Plymouth Brother who still regards the playhouse as one of the gates of hell is perhaps the safest adviser on the subject of which he knows so little. If I do not draw the same conclusion, it is not because I am one of those who claim that art is exempt from moral obligations, and not that the writing or performance of a play is a moral act, to be treated on exactly the same footing as theft or murder if it produces equally mischievous consequences. I am convinced that fine art is the subtlest, the most seductive, the most effective instrument of moral propagandism in the world, excepting only the example of personal conduct; and I waive even this exception in favor of the art of the stage, because it works by exhibiting examples of personal conduct made intelligible and moving to crowds of unobservant unreflecting people to whom real life means nothing. I have pointed out again and again that the influence of the theatre in England is growing so great that whilst private conduct, religion, law, science, politics, and morals are becoming more and more theatrical, the theatre itself remains impervious to common sense, religion, science, politics, and morals. That is why I fight the theatre, not with pamphlets and sermons and treatises, but with plays; and so effective do I find the dramatic method that I have no doubt I shall at last persuade even London to take its conscience and its brains with it when it goes to the theatre, instead of leaving them at home with its prayer book as it does at present. Consequently, I am the last man to deny that if the net effect of performing *Mrs. Warren's Profession* were an increase in the number of persons entering that profession, its performance should be dealt with accordingly.

Now let us consider how such recruiting can be encouraged by the theatre. Nothing is easier. Let the King's Reader of Plays, backed by the press, make an unwritten but perfectly well understood regulation that members of Mrs. Warren's profession shall be tolerated on the stage only when they are beautiful, exquisitely dressed, and sumptuously lodged and fed; also that they shall, at the end of the play, die of consumption to the sympathetic tears of the whole audience, or step into the next room to commit suicide, or at least be turned out by their protectors and passed on to be "redeemed" by old and faithful lovers who have adored them in spite of all their levities. Naturally the poorer girls in the gallery will believe in the beauty, in the exquisite dresses, and the luxurious living, and will see that there is no real necessity for the consumption, the suicide, or the ejectment: mere pious forms, all of them, to save the Censor's face. Even if these purely official catastrophes carried any conviction, the majority of English girls remain so poor, so dependent, so well aware that the drudgeries of such honest work as is within their reach are likely enough to lead them eventually to lung disease, premature death, and domestic desertion or brutality, that they would still see reason to prefer the primrose path to the strait path of virtue, since both, vice at worst and virtue at best, lead to the same end in poverty and overwork. It is true that the Board School mistress will tell you that only girls of a certain kind will reason in this way. But alas! that certain kind turns out on inquiry to be simply the pretty, dainty kind: that is, the only kind that gets the chance of acting on such reasoning. Read the first report of the Commission on the Housing of the Working Classes [Bluebook C 4402, 1889]; read the Report on Home Industries (sacred word, Home!) issued by the Women's Industrial Council [Home Industries of Women in London, 1897]; and ask yourself whether, if the lot in life therein described were your lot in life, you would prefer the lot of Cleopatra, of Theodora, of the Lady of the Camellias, of Mrs. Tanqueray, of Zaza, or Iris. If you can go deep enough into things to be able to say no, how many ignorant half-starved girls will believe you are speaking sincerely? To them the lot of Iris is heavenly in comparison with their own. Yet our King, like his predecessors, says to the dramatist "Thus, and thus only, shall you present Mrs. Warren's profession on the stage, or you shall starve. Witness Shaw, who told the untempting truth about it, and whom We, by the Grace of God, accordingly disallow and suppress, and do what in Us lies to silence." Fortunately, Shaw cannot be silenced. "The harlot's cry from street to street" is louder than the voices of all the kings. I am not dependent on the theatre, and cannot be starved into making my play a standing advertisement of the attractive side of Mrs. Warren's business.

Here I must guard myself against a misunderstanding. It is not the fault of their authors that the long string of wantons' tragedies, from *Antony and Cleopatra* to *Iris,* are snares to poor girls, and are objected to on that account by many earnest men and women who consider *Mrs. Warren's Profession* an excellent sermon. Mr. Pinero is in no way bound to suppress the fact that his Iris is a person to be envied by millions of better women. If he made his play false to life by inventing fictitious disadvantages for her, he would be acting as unscrupulously as any tract writer. If society chooses to provide for its Irises better than for its working women, it must not expect honest playwrights to manufacture spurious evidence to save its credit. The mischief lies in the deliberate suppression of the other side of the case: the refusal to allow Mrs. Warren to expose the drudgery and repulsiveness of plying for hire among coarse, tedious drunkards; the determination not to let the Parisian girl in Brieux's *Les Avariés* come on the stage and drive into people's minds what her diseases mean for her and for themselves. All that, says the King's Reader in effect, is horrifying, loathsome. Precisely: what does he expect it to be? would he have us represent it as beautiful and gratifying? The answer to this question, I fear, must be a blunt Yes; for it seems impossible to root out of an Englishman's mind the notion that vice is delightful, and that abstention from it is privation. At all events, as long as the tempting side of it is kept towards the public, and softened by plenty of sentiment and sympathy, it is welcomed by our Censor, whereas the slightest attempt to place it in the light of the policeman's lantern or the Salvation Army shelter is checkmated at once as not merely disgusting, but, if you please, unnecessary.

Everybody will, I hope, admit that this state of things is intolerable; that the subject of Mrs. Warren's profession must be either tapu altogether, or else exhibited with the warning side as freely displayed as the tempting side. But many persons will vote for a complete tapu, and an impartial clean sweep from the boards of Mrs. Warren and Gretchen and the rest: in short, for banishing the sexual instincts from the stage altogether. Those who think this impossible can hardly have considered the number and importance of the subjects which are actually banished from the stage. Many plays, among them *Lear, Hamlet, Macbeth, Coriolanus, Julius Caesar,* have no sex complications: the thread of their action can be followed by children who could not understand a single scene of *Mrs. Warren's Profession* or *Iris.* None of our plays rouse the sympathy of the audience by an exhibition of the pains of maternity, as Chinese plays constantly do. Each nation has its particular set of tapus in addition to the common human stock; and though each of these tapus limits the scope of the dramatist, it does not make drama impossible. If Redford were to refuse to license plays with female characters in them, he would only be doing to the stage what our tribal customs already do to the pulpit and the bar. I have myself written a rather entertaining play with only one woman in it, and she quite heartwhole; and I could just as easily write a play without a woman in it at all. I will even go as far as to promise Redford my support if he will introduce this limitation for part of the year, say during Lent, so as to make a chosen season for that dullest of stock dramatic subjects, adultery, and force our managers and authors to find out what all great dramatists find out spontaneously: to wit, that people who sacrifice every other consideration to love are as hopelessly unheroic on the stage as lunatics or dipsomaniacs. Hector is the world's hero; not Paris nor Antony.

But though I do not question the possibility of a drama in which love should be as effectively ignored as cholera is at present, there is not the slightest chance of that way out of the difficulty being taken by Redford. If he attempted it there would be a revolt in which he would be swept away, in spite of my single-handed efforts to defend him. A complete tapu is politically impossible. A complete toleration is equally impossible to Redford, because his occupation would be gone if there were no tapu to enforce. He is therefore compelled to maintain the present compromise of a partial tapu, applied, to the best of his judgment, with a careful respect to persons and to public opinion. And a very sensible English solution of the difficulty, too, most readers will say. I should not dispute it if dramatic poets really were what English public opinion generally assumes them to be during their lifetime: that is, a licentiously irregular group to be kept in order in a rough and ready way by a magistrate who will stand no nonsense from them. But I cannot admit that the class represented by Aeschylus, Sophocles, Aristophanes, Euripides, Shakespeare, Goethe, Ibsen, and Tolstoy, not to mention our own contemporary playwrights, is as much in place in Mr. Redford's office as a pickpocket is in Bow Street. Further, it is not true that the Censorship, though it certainly suppresses Ibsen and Tolstoy, and would suppress Shakespeare but for the absurd rule that a play once licensed is always licensed (so that Wycherly is permitted and Shelley prohibited), also suppresses unscrupulous playwrights. I challenge Mr. Redford to mention any extremity of sexual misconduct which any manager in his senses would risk presenting on the London stage that has not been presented under his license and that of his predecessor. The compromise, in fact, works out in practice in favor of loose plays as against earnest ones.

To carry conviction on this point, I will take the extreme course of narrating the plots of two plays witnessed within the last ten years by myself at London West End theatres, one licensed by the late Queen Victoria's Reader of Plays, the other by the present Reader to the King. Both plots conform to the strictest rules of the period when *La Dame aux Camellias* was still a forbidden play, and when *The Second Mrs. Tanqueray* would have been tolerated only on condition that she carefully explained to the audience that when she met Captain Ardale she sinned "but in intention."

Play number one. A prince is compelled by his parents to marry the daughter of a neighboring king, but loves another maiden. The scene represents a hall in the king's palace at night. The wedding has taken place that day; and the closed door of the nuptial chamber is in view of the audience. Inside, the princess awaits her bridegroom. A duenna is in attendance. The bridegroom enters. His sole desire is to escape from a marriage which is hateful to him. An idea strikes him. He will assault the duenna, and get ignominiously expelled from the palace by his indignant father-in-law. To his horror, when he proceeds to carry out this stratagem, the duenna, far from raising an alarm, is flattered, delighted, and compliant. The assaulter becomes the assaulted. He flings her angrily to the ground, where she remains placidly. He flies. The father enters; dismisses the duenna; and listens at the keyhole of his daughter's nuptial chamber, uttering various pleasantries, and declaring, with a shiver, that a sound of kissing, which he supposes to proceed from within, makes him feel young again.

In deprecation of the scandalized astonishment with which such a story as this will be read, I can only say that it was not presented on the stage until its propriety had been certified.

Story number two. A German officer finds himself in an inn with a French lady who has wounded his national vanity. He resolves to humble her by committing a rape upon her. He announces his purpose. She remonstrates, implores, flies to the doors and finds them locked, calls for help and finds none at hand, runs screaming from side to side, and, after a harrowing scene, is overpowered and faints. Nothing further being possible on the stage without actual felony, the officer then relents and leaves her. When she recovers, she believes that he has carried out his threat; and during the rest of the play she is represented as vainly vowing vengeance upon him, whilst she is really falling in love with him under the influence of his imaginary crime against her. Finally she consents to marry him; and the curtain falls on their happiness.

This story was certified by the present King's Reader, acting for the Lord Chamberlain, as void in its general tendency of "anything immoral or otherwise improper for the stage." But let nobody conclude therefore that Mr. Redford is a monster, whose policy it is to deprave the theatre. As a matter of fact, both the above stories are strictly in order from the official point of view. The incidents of sex which they contain, though carried in both to the extreme point at which another step would be dealt with, not by the King's Reader, but by the police, do not involve adultery, nor any allusion to Mrs. Warren's profession, nor to the fact that the children of any polyandrous group will, when they grow up, inevitably be confronted, as those of Mrs. Warren's group are in my play, with the insoluble problem of their own possible consanguinity. In short, by depending wholly on the coarse humors and the physical fascination of sex, they comply with all the formulable requirements of the Censorship, whereas plays in which these humors and fascinations are discarded, and the social problems created by sex seriously faced and dealt with, inevitably ignore the official formula and are suppressed. If the old rule against the exhibition of illicit sex relations on the stage were revived, and the subject absolutely barred, the only result would be that *Antony and Cleopatra*, *Othello* (because of the Bianca episode), *Troilus and Cressida*, *Henry IV*, *Measure for Measure*, *Timon of Athens*, *La Dame aux Camellias*, *The Profligate*, *The Second*

Mrs. Tanqueray, The Notorious Mrs. Ebbsmith, The Gay Lord Quex, Mrs. Dane's Defence, and *Iris* would be swept from the stage, and placed under the same ban as Tolstoy's *Dominion of Darkness* and *Mrs. Warren's Profession,* whilst such plays as the two described above would have a monopoly of the theatre as far as sexual interest is concerned.

What is more, the repulsiveness of the worst of the certified plays would protect Censorship against effective exposure and criticism. Not long ago an American Review of high standing asked me for an article on the Censorship of the English Stage. I replied that such an article would involve passages too disagreeable for publication in a magazine for general family reading. The editor persisted nevertheless; but not until he had declared his readiness to face this, and had pledged himself to insert the article unaltered (the particularity of the pledge extending even to a specification of the exact number of words in the article) did I consent to the proposal. What was the result? The editor, confronted with the two stories given above, threw his pledge to the winds, and, instead of returning the article, printed it with the illustrative examples omitted, and nothing left but the argument from political principle against the Censorship. In doing this he fired my broadside after withdrawing the cannon balls; for neither the Censor nor any other Englishman, except perhaps Mr. Leslie Stephen and a few other veterans of the dwindling old guard of Benthamism, cares a dump about political principle. The ordinary Briton thinks that if every other Briton is not under some form of tutelage, the more childish the better, he will abuse his freedom viciously. As far as its principle is concerned, the Censorship is the most popular institution in England; and the playwright who criticizes it is slighted as a blackguard agitating for impunity. Consequently nothing can really shake the confidence of the public in the Lord Chamberlain's department except a remorseless and unbowdlerized narration of the licentious fictions which slip through its net, and are hallmarked by it with the approval of the throne. But as such stories cannot be made public without great difficulty, owing to the obligation an editor is under not to deal unexpectedly with matters that are not *virginibus puerisque*, the chances are heavily in favor of the Censor escaping all remonstrance. With the exception of such comments as I was able to make in my own critical articles in the *World* and the *Saturday Review* when the pieces I have described were first produced, and a few ignorant protests by churchmen against much better plays which they confessed they had not seen nor read, nothing has been said in the press that could seriously disturb the easy-going notion that the stage would be much worse than it admittedly is but for the vigilance of the King's Reader. The truth is, that no manager would dare produce on his own responsibility the pieces he can now get royal certificates for at two guineas per piece.

I hasten to add that I believe these evils to be inherent in the nature of all censorship, and not merely a consequence of the form the institution takes in London. No doubt there is a staggering absurdity in appointing an ordinary clerk to see that the leaders of European literature do not corrupt the morals of the nation, and to restrain Sir Henry Irving, as a rogue and a vagabond, from presuming to impersonate Samson or David on the stage, though any other sort of artist may daub these scriptural figures on a signboard or carve them on a tombstone without hindrance. If the General Medical Council, the Royal College of Physicians, the Royal Academy of Arts, the Incorporated Law Society, and Convocation were abolished, and their functions handed over to Mr. Redford, the Concert of Europe would presumably declare England mad and treat her accordingly. Yet, though neither medicine nor painting nor law nor the Church moulds the character of the nation as potently as the theatre does, nothing can come on the stage unless its dimensions admit of its first passing through Mr. Redford's mind! Pray do not think that I question Mr. Redford's honesty. I am quite sure that he sincerely thinks me a blackguard, and my play a grossly improper one, because, like Tolstoy's *Dominion of Darkness,* it produces, as they are both meant to produce, a very strong and very painful impression of evil. I do not doubt for a moment that the rapine play which I have described, and which he licensed, was quite incapable in manuscript of producing any particular effect on his mind at all, and that when he was once satisfied that the ill-conducted hero was a German and not an English officer, he passed the play without studying its moral tendencies. Even if he had undertaken that study, there is no more reason to suppose that he is a competent moralist than there is to suppose that I am a competent mathematician. But truly it does not matter whether he is a moralist or not. Let nobody dream for a moment that what is wrong with the Censorship is the shortcoming of the gentleman who happens at any moment to be acting as Censor. Replace him tomorrow by an Academy of Letters and an Academy of Dramatic Poetry, and the new filter will still exclude original and epoch-making work, whilst passing conventional, old-fashioned, and vulgar work without question. The conclave which compiles the Index of the Roman Catholic Church is the most august, ancient, learned, famous, and authoritative censorship in Europe. Is it more enlightened, more liberal, more tolerant than the comparatively infinitesimal office of the Lord Chamberlain? On the contrary, it has reduced itself to a degree of absurdity which makes a Catholic university a contradiction in terms. All censorships exist to prevent anyone from challenging current conceptions and existing institutions. All progress is initiated by challenging current conceptions, and executed by supplanting existing institutions. Consequently the first condition of progress is the removal of censorships. There is the whole case against censorships in a nutshell.

It will be asked whether theatrical managers are to be allowed to produce what they like, without regard to the public interest. But that is not the alternative. The managers of our London music halls are not subject to any censorship. They produce their entertainments on their own responsibility, and have no two-guinea certificates to plead if their houses are conducted viciously. They know that if they lose their character, the County Council will simply refuse to renew their license at the end of the year; and nothing in the history of popular art is more amazing than the improvement in music halls that this simple arrangement has produced within a few years. Place the theatres on the same footing, and we shall promptly have a similar revolution: a whole class of frankly blackguardly plays, in which unscrupulous low comedians attract crowds to gaze at bevies of girls who have nothing to exhibit but their prettiness, will vanish like the obscene songs which were supposed to enliven the squalid dulness, incredible to the younger generation, of the music halls fifteen years ago. On the other hand, plays which treat sex questions as problems for thought instead of as aphrodisiacs will be freely performed. Gentlemen of Mr. Redford's way of thinking will have plenty of opportunity of protesting against them in Council; but the result will be that Mr. Redford will find his natural level; Ibsen and Tolstoy theirs; so no harm will be done.

This question of the Censorship reminds me that I have to apologize to those who went to the recent performance of *Mrs. Warren's Profession* expecting to find it what I have just called an aphrodisiac. That was not my fault: it was Mr. Redford's. After the specimens I have given of the tolerance of his department, it was natural enough for thoughtless people to infer that a play which overstepped his indulgence must be a very exciting play indeed. Accordingly, I find one critic so explicit as to the nature of his disappointment as to say candidly that "such airy talk as there is upon the matter is utterly unworthy of acceptance as being a representation of what people with blood in them think or do on such occasions." Thus am I crushed between the upper millstone of Mr. Redford, who thinks me a libertine, and the nether popular critic, who thinks me a prude. Critics of all grades and ages, middle-aged fathers of families no less than ardent young enthusiasts, are equally indignant with me. They revile me as lacking in passion, in feeling, in manhood. Some of them even sum the matter up by denying me any dramatic power: a melancholy betrayal of what dramatic power has come to mean on our stage under the Censorship! Can I be expected to refrain from laughing at the spectacle of a number of respectable gentlemen lamenting because a playwright lures them to the theatre by a promise to excite their senses in a very special and sensational manner, and then, having successfully trapped them in exceptional numbers, proceeds to ignore their senses and ruthlessly improve their minds? But I protest again that the lure was not mine. The play had been in print for four years; and I have spared no pains to make known that my plays are built to induce, not voluptuous reverie but intellectual interest, not romantic rhapsody but humane concern. Accordingly, I do not find those critics who are gifted with intellectual appetite and political conscience complaining of want of dramatic power. Rather do they protest, not altogether unjustly, against a few relapses into staginess and caricature which betray the young playwright and the old playgoer in this early work of mine. As to the voluptuaries, I can assure them that the playwright, whether he be myself or another, will always disappoint them. The drama can do little to delight the senses: all the apparent instances to the contrary are instances of the personal fascination of the performers. The drama of pure feeling is no longer in the hands of the playwright: it has been conquered by the musician, after whose enchantments all the verbal arts seem cold and tame. *Romeo and Juliet* with the loveliest Juliet is dry, tedious, and rhetorical in comparison with Wagner's *Tristan,* even though Isolde be both fourteen stone and forty, as she often is in Germany. Indeed, it needed no Wagner to convince the public of this. The voluptuous sentimentality of Gounod's *Faust* and Bizet's *Carmen* has captured the common playgoer; and there is, flatly, no future now for any drama without music except the drama of thought. The attempt to produce a genus of opera without music—and this absurdity is what our fashionable theatres have been driving at for a long time past without knowing it—is far less hopeful than my own determination to accept problem as the normal material of the drama.

That this determination will throw me into a long conflict with our theatre critics, and with the few playgoers who go to the theatre as often as the critics, I well know; but I am too well equipped for the strife to be deterred by it, or to bear malice towards the losing side. In trying to produce the sensuous effects of opera, the fashionable drama has become so flaccid in its sentimentality, and the intellect of its frequenters so atrophied by disuse, that the reintroduction of problem, with its remorseless logic and iron framework of fact, inevitably produces at first an overwhelming impression of coldness and inhuman rationalism. But this will soon pass away. When the intellectual muscle and moral nerve of the critics has been developed in the struggle with modern problem plays, the pettish luxuriousness of the clever ones, and the sulky sense of disadvantaged weakness in the sentimental ones, will clear away; and it will be seen that only in the problem play is there any real drama, because drama is no mere setting up of the camera to nature: it is the presentation in parable of the conflict between Man's will and his environment: in a word, of problem. The vapidness of such drama as the pseudo-operatic plays contain lies in the fact that in them animal passion, sentimentally diluted, is shown in conflict, not with real circumstances, but with a set of conventions and assumptions half of which do not exist off the stage, whilst the other half can either be evaded by a pretence of compliance or defied with complete impunity by any reasonably strong-minded person. Nobody can feel that such conventions are really compulsory; and consequently nobody can believe in the stage pathos that accepts them as an inexorable fate, or in the reality of the figures who indulge in such pathos. Sitting at such plays we do not believe: we make believe. And the habit of make believe becomes at last so rooted, that criticism of the theatre insensibly ceases to be criticism at all, and becomes more and more a chronicle of the fashionable enterprises of the only realities left on the stage: that is, the performers in their own persons. In this phase the playwright who attempts to revive genuine drama produces the disagreeable impression of the pedant who attempts to start a serious discussion at a fashionable at-home. Later on, when he has driven the tea services out and made the people who had come to use the theatre as a drawing-room understand that it is they and not the dramatists who are the intruders, he has to face the accusation that his plays ignore human feeling, an illusion produced by that very resistance of fact and law to human feeling which creates drama. It is the *deus ex machina* who, by suspending that resistance, makes the fall of the curtain an immediate necessity, since drama ends exactly where resistance ends. Yet the introduction of this resistance produces so strong an impression of heartlessness nowadays that a distinguished critic has summed up the impression made on him by *Mrs. Warren's Profession,* by declaring that "the difference between the spirit of Tolstoy and the spirit of Mr. Shaw is the difference between the spirit of Christ and the spirit of Euclid." But the epigram would be as good if Tolstoy's name were put in place of mine and D'Annunzio's in place of Tolstoy's. At the same time I accept the enormous compliment to my reasoning powers with sincere complacency; and I promise my flatterer that when he is sufficiently accustomed to and therefore undazzled by problem on the stage to be able to attend to the familiar factor of humanity in it as well as to the unfamiliar one of a real environment, he will both see and feel that *Mrs. Warren's Profession* is no mere theorem, but a play of instincts and temperaments in conflict with each other and with a flinty social problem that never yields an inch to mere sentiment.

I go further than this. I declare that the real secret of the cynicism and inhumanity of which shallower critics accuse me is the unexpectedness with which my characters behave like human beings, instead of conforming to the romantic logic of the stage. The axioms and postulates of that dreary mimanthropometry are so well known that it is almost impossible for its slaves to write tolerable last acts to their plays, so conventionally do their conclusions follow from their premises. Because I have thrown this logic ruthlessly overboard, I am accused of ignoring, not state logic, but, of all things, human feeling. People with completely theatrified imaginations tell me that no girl would treat her mother as Vivie Warren does, meaning that no stage heroine would in a popular sentimental play. They say this just as they might say that no two straight lines would inclose a space. They do not see how completely inverted their vision has become even when I throw its preposterousness in their faces, as I repeatedly do in this very play. Praed, the sentimental artist (fool that I was not to make him a playwright instead of an architect!), burlesques them by expecting all through the piece that the feelings of the others will be logically deducible from their family relationships and from his "conventionally unconventional" social code. The sarcasm is lost on the critics: they, saturated with the same logic, only think him the sole sensible person on the stage. Thus it comes about that the more completely the dramatist is emancipated from the illusion that men and women are primarily reasonable beings, and the more powerfully he insists on the ruthless indifference of their great dramatic antagonist, the external world, to their whims and emotions, the surer he is to be denounced as blind to the very distinction on which his whole work is built. Far from ignoring idiosyncrasy, will, passion, impulse, whim, as factors in human action, I have placed them so nakedly on the stage that the elderly citizen, accustomed to see them clothed with the veil of manufactured logic about duty, and to disguise even his own impulses from himself in this way, finds the picture as unnatural as Carlyle's suggested painting of parliament sitting without its clothes.

I now come to those critics who, intellectually baffled by the problem in *Mrs. Warren's Profession,* have made a virtue of running away from it. I will illustrate their method by a quotation from Dickens, taken from the fifth chapter of *Our Mutual Friend:*

"Hem!" began Wegg. "This, Mr. Boffin and Lady, is the first chapter of the first wollume of the Decline and Fall off——" here he looked hard at the book, and stopped.

"What's the matter, Wegg?"

"Why it comes into my mind, do you know, sir," said Wegg with an air of insinuating frankness (having first again looked hard at the book), "that you made a little mistake this morning which I had meant to set you right in; only something put it out of my head. I think you said Rooshan Empire, sir?"

"It is Rooshan; ain't it Wegg?"

"No, sir. Roman. Roman."

"What's the difference, Wegg?"

"The difference, sir?" Mr. Wegg was faltering and

in danger of breaking down, when a bright thought flashed upon him. "The difference, sir? There you place me in a difficulty, Mr. Boffin. Suffice it to observe that the difference is best postponed to some other occasion when Mrs. Boffin does not honor us with her company. In Mrs. Boffin's presence, sir, we had better drop it."

Mr. Wegg thus came out of his disadvantage with quite a chivalrous air, and not only that, but by dint of repeating with a manly delicacy, "In Mrs. Boffin's presence, sir, we had better drop it!" turned the disadvantage on Boffin, who felt that he had committed himself in a very painful manner.

I am willing to let Mr. Wegg drop it on these terms, provided that I am allowed to mention here that *Mrs. Warren's Profession* is a play for women; that it was written for women; that it has been performed and produced mainly through the determination of women that it should be performed and produced; that the enthusiasm of women made its first performance excitingly successful; and that not one of these women had any inducement to support it except their belief in the timeliness and the power of the lesson the play teaches. Those who were "surprised to see ladies present" were men; and when they proceeded to explain that the journals they represented could not possibly demoralize the public by describing such a play, their editors cruelly devoted the space saved by their delicacy to an elaborate and respectful account of the progress of a young lord's attempt to break the bank at Monte Carlo. A few days sooner Mrs. Warren would have been crowded out of their papers by an exceptionally abominable police case. I do not suggest that the police case should have been suppressed; but neither do I believe that regard for public morality had anything to do with their failure to grapple with the performance of the Stage Society. And, after all, there was no need to fall back on Silas Wegg's subterfuge. Several critics saved the faces of their papers easily enough by the simple expedient of saying all they had to say in the tone of a shocked governess lecturing a naughty child. To them, I might plead, in Mrs. Warren's words, "Well, it's only good manners to be ashamed, dearie;" but it surprises me, recollecting as I do Fanny Brough's delivery of that line, that gentlemen who shivered like violets in a zephyr as it swept through them, should so completely miss the full width of its application as to go home and straightway make a public exhibition of mock modesty.

My old Independent Theatre manager, Mr. Grein, besides that reproach to me for shattering his ideals, complains that Mrs. Warren is not wicked enough, and names several romancers who would have clothed her black soul with all the terrors of tragedy. I have no doubt they would; but that is just what I did not want to do. Nothing would please our sanctimonious British public more than to throw the whole guilt of Mrs. Warren's profession on Mrs. Warren herself. Now, the whole aim of my play is to throw that guilt on the British public itself. You may remember that when you produced my first play, *Widowers' Houses,* exactly the same misunderstanding arose. When the virtuous young gentleman rose up in wrath against the slum landlord, the slum landlord very effectually shewed him that slums are the product, not of individual Harpagons, but of the indifference of virtuous young gentlemen to the condition of the city they live in, provided they live at the west end of it on money earned by somebody else's labor. The notion that prostitution is created by the wickedness of Mrs. Warren is as silly as the notion—prevalent, nevertheless, to some extent in Temperance circles—that drunkenness is created by the wickedness of the publican. Mrs. Warren is not a whit a worse woman than the reputable daughter who cannot endure her. Her indifference to the ultimate social consequences of her means of making money, and her discovery of that means by the ordinary method of taking the line of least resistance to getting it, are too common in English society to call for any special remark. Her vitality, her thrift, her energy, her outspokenness, her wise care of her daughter, and the managing capacity which has enabled her and her sister to climb from the fried fish shop down by the mint to the establishments of which she boasts, are all high English social virtues. Her defence of herself is so overwhelming that it provokes the *St. James's Gazette* to declare that "the tendency of the play is wholly evil" because "it contains one of the boldest and most specious defences of an unmoral life for poor women that has ever been penned." Happily the *St. James's Gazette* here speaks in its haste. Mrs. Warren's defence of herself is not only bold and specious, but valid and unanswerable. But it is no defence at all of the vice which she organizes. It is no defence of an immoral life to say that the alternative offered by society collectively to poor women is a miserable life, starved, overworked, fetid, ailing, ugly. Though it is quite natural and *right* for Mrs. Warren to choose what is, according to her lights, the least immoral alternative, it is none the less infamous of society to offer such alternatives. For the alternatives offered are not morality and immorality, but two sorts of immorality. The man who cannot see that starvation, overwork, dirt, and disease are as immoral as prostitution—that they are the vices and crimes of a nation, and not merely its misfortunes—is (to put it as politely as possible) a hopelessly Private Person.

The notion that Mrs. Warren must be a fiend is only an example of the violence and passion which the slightest reference to sex rouses in undisciplined minds, and which makes it seem natural to our lawgivers to punish silly and negligible indecencies with a ferocity unknown in dealing with, for example, ruinous financial swindling. Had my play been entitled *Mr. Warren's Profession,* and Mr. Warren been a bookmaker, nobody would have expected me to make him a villain as well. Yet gambling is a vice, and bookmaking an institution, for which there is absolutely nothing to be said. The moral and economic evil done by trying to get other people's money without working for it (and this is the essence of gambling) is not only enormous but uncompensated. There are no two sides to the question of gambling, no circumstances which force us to tolerate it lest its suppression lead to worse things, no consensus of opinion among responsible classes, such as magistrates and military commanders, that it is a necessity, no Athenian records of gambling made splendid by the talents of its professors, no contention that instead of violating morals it only violates a legal institution which is in many respects oppressive and unnatural, no possible plea that the instinct on which it is founded is a vital one. Prostitution can confuse the issue with all these excuses: gambling has none of them. Consequently, if Mrs. Warren must needs be a demon, a bookmaker must be a cacodemon. Well, does anybody who knows the sporting world really believe that bookmakers are worse than their neighbors? On the contrary, they have to be a good deal better; for in that world nearly everybody whose social rank does not exclude such an occupation would be a bookmaker if he could; but the strength of character required for handling large sums of money and for strict settlements and unflinching payment of losses is so rare that successful bookmakers are rare too. It may seem that at least public spirit cannot be one of a bookmaker's virtues; but I can testify from personal experience that excellent public work is done with money subscribed by bookmakers. It is true that there are abysses in bookmaking: for example, welshing. Mr. Grein hints that there are abysses in Mrs. Warren's profession also. So there are in every profession: the error lies in supposing that every member of them sounds these depths. I sit on a public body which prosecutes Mrs. Warren zealously; and I can assure Mr. Grein that she is often leniently dealt with because she has conducted her business "respectably" and held herself above its vilest branches. The degrees in infamy are as numerous and as scrupulously observed as the degrees in the peerage. The moralist's notion that there are depths at which the moral atmosphere ceases is as delusive as the rich man's notion that there are no social jealousies or snobberies among the very poor. No: had I drawn Mrs. Warren as a fiend in human form, the very people who now rebuke me for flattering her would probably be the first to deride me for deducing character logically from occupation instead of observing it accurately in society.

One critic is so enslaved by this sort of logic that he calls my portraiture of the Rev. Samuel Gardner an attack on religion. According to this view Subaltern Iago is an attack on the army, Sir John Falstaff an attack on knighthood, and King Claudius an attack on royalty.

Here again the clamor for naturalness and human feeling, raised by so many critics when they are confronted by the real thing on the stage, is really a clamor for the most mechanical and superficial sort of logic. The dramatic reason for making the clergyman what Mrs. Warren calls "an old stick-in-the-mud," whose son, in spite of much capacity and charm, is a cynically worthless member of society, is to set up a mordant contrast between him and the woman of infamous profession, with her well-brought-up, straightforward, hardworking daughter. The critics who have missed the contrast have doubtless observed often enough that many clergymen are in the church through no genuine calling, but simply because, in circles which can command preferment, it is the refuge of "the fool of the family"; and that clergymen's sons are often conspicuous reactionists against the restraints imposed on them in childhood by their father's profession. These critics must know, too, from history if not from experience, that women as unscrupulous as Mrs. Warren have distinguished themselves as administrators and rulers, both commercially and politically. But both observation and knowledge are left behind when journalists go to the theatre. Once in their stalls, they assume that it is "natural" for clergymen to be saintly, for soldiers to be heroic, for lawyers to be hard-hearted, for sailors to be simple and generous, for doctors to perform miracles with little bottles, and for Mrs. Warren to be a beast and a demon. All this is not only not natural, but not dramatic. A man's profession only enters into the drama of his life when it comes into conflict with his nature. The result of this conflict is tragic in Mrs. Warren's case, and comic in the clergyman's case (at least we are savage enough to laugh at it); but in both cases it is illogical, and in both cases natural. I repeat, the critics who accuse me of sacrificing nature to logic are so sophisticated by their profession that to them logic is nature, and nature absurdity.

Many friendly critics are too little skilled in social questions and moral discussions to be able to conceive that respectable gentlemen like themselves, who would instantly call the police to remove Mrs. Warren if she ventured to canvass them personally, could possibly be in any way responsible for her proceedings. They remonstrate sincerely, asking me what good such painful exposures can possibly do. They might as well ask what good Lord Shaftesbury did by devoting his life to the exposure of evils (by no means yet remedied) compared to which the worst things brought into view or even into surmise in this play are trifles. The good of mentioning them is that you make people so extremely uncomfortable about them that they finally stop blaming "human nature" for them, and begin to support measures for their reform. Can anything be more absurd than the copy of *The Echo* which contains a notice of the performance of my play? It is edited by a gentleman who, having devoted his life to work of the Shaftesbury type, exposes social evils and clamors for their reform in every column except one; and that one is occupied by the declaration of the paper's kindly theatre critic, that the performance left him "wondering what useful purpose the play was intended to serve." The balance has to be redressed by the more fashionable papers, which usually combine capable art criticism with West-End solecism on politics and sociology. It is very noteworthy, however, on comparing the press explosion produced by *Mrs. Warren's Profession* in 1902 with that produced by *Widowers' Houses* about ten years earlier, that whereas in 1892 the facts were frantically denied and the persons of the drama flouted as monsters of wickedness, in 1902 the facts are admitted, and the characters recognized, though it is suggested that this is exactly why no gentleman should mention them in public. Only one writer has ventured to imply this time that the poverty mentioned by Mrs. Warren has since been quietly relieved, and need not have been dragged back to the footlights. I compliment him on his splendid mendacity, in which he is unsupported, save by a little plea in a theatrical paper which is innocent enough to think that ten guineas a year with board and lodging is an impossibly low wage for a barmaid. It goes on to cite Mr. Charles Booth as having testified that there are many laborers' wives who are happy and contented on eighteen shillings a week. But I can go further than that myself. I have seen an Oxford agricultural laborer's wife looking cheerful on eight shillings a week;

but that does not console me for the fact that agriculture
in England is a ruined industry. If poverty does not matter as long as it is contented, then crime does not matter
as long as it is unscrupulous. The truth is that it is only
then that it does matter most desperately. Many persons
are more comfortable when they are dirty than when
they are clean; but that does not recommend dirt as a
national policy.

Here I must for the present break off my arduous
work of educating the press. We shall resume our studies
later on; but just now I am tired of playing the preceptor;
and the eager thirst of my pupils for improvement does
not console me for the slowness of their progress. Besides I must reserve space to gratify my own vanity and
do justice to the six artists who acted my play, by placing
on record the hitherto unchronicled success of the first
representation. It is not often that an author, after a
couple of hours of those rare alternations of excitement
and intensely attentive silence which only occur in the
theatre when actors and audience are reacting on one
another to the utmost, is able to step on the stage and
apply the strong word genius to the representation with
the certainty of eliciting an instant and overwhelming
assent from the audience. That was my good fortune on
the afternoon of Sunday, the fifth of January last. I was
certainly extremely fortunate in my interpreters in the
enterprise, and that not alone in respect of their artistic
talent; for had it not been for their superhuman patience,
their imperturbable good humor and good fellowship,
there could have been no performance. The terror of the
Censor's power gave us trouble enough to break up any
ordinary commercial enterprise. Managers promised and
even engaged their theatres to us after the most explicit
warnings that the play was unlicensed, and at the last
moment suddenly realized that Mr. Redford had their
livelihoods in the hollow of his hand, and backed out.
Over and over again the date and place were fixed and
the tickets printed, only to be canceled, until at last the
desperate and overworked manager of the Stage Society
could only laugh, as criminals broken on the wheel used
to laugh at the second stroke. We rehearsed under great

difficulties. Christmas pieces and plays for the new year
were being prepared in all directions; and my six actor
colleagues were busy people, with engagements in these
pieces in addition to their current professional work
every night. On several raw winter days stages for re-
hearsal were unattainable even by the most distinguished
applicants; and we shared corridors and saloons with
them whilst the stage was given over to children in training for Boxing night. At last we had to rehearse at an
hour at which no actor or actress has been out of bed
within the memory of man; and we sardonically congrat-
ulated one another every morning on our rosy matutinal
looks and the improvement wrought by early rising in
our healths and characters. And all this, please observe,
for a society without treasury or commercial prestige,
for a play which was being denounced in advance as
unmentionable, for an author without influence at the
fashionable theatres! I victoriously challenge the West
End managers to get as much done for interested motives, if they can.

Three causes made the production the most notable
that has fallen to my lot. First, the veto of the Censor,
which put the supporters of the play on their mettle.
Second, the chivalry of the Stage Society, which, in spite
of my urgent advice to the contrary, and my demonstration of the difficulties, dangers, and expenses the enterprise would cost, put my discouragements to shame and
resolved to give battle at all costs to the attempt of the
Censorship to suppress the play. Third, the artistic spirit
of the actors, who made the play their own and carried
it through triumphantly in spite of a series of disappointments and annoyances much more trying to the dramatic
temperament than mere difficulties.

The acting, too, required courage and character as
well as skill and intelligence. The veto of the Censor
introduced a quite novel element of moral responsibility
into the undertaking. And the characters were very unusual in the English stage. The young heroine is, like
her mother, an Englishwoman to the backbone, and not,
like the heroines of our fashionable drama, a prima
donna of Italian origin. Consequently she was sure to be
denounced as unnatural and undramatic by the critics.

The most vicious man in the play is not in the least a
stage villain: indeed, he regards his own moral character
with the sincere complacency of a hero of melodrama.
The amiable devotee of romance and beauty is shown
at an age which brings out the futilization which these
worships are apt to produce if they are made the staple
of life instead of the sauce. The attitude of the clever
young people to their elders is faithfully presented as
one of pitiless ridicule and unsympathetic criticism, and
forms a spectacle incredible to those who, when young,
were not cleverer than their nearest elders, and painful
to those sentimental parents who shrink from the cruelty
of youth, which pardons nothing because it knows nothing. In short, the characters and their relations are of a
kind that the routineer critic has not learned to place; so
that their misunderstanding was a foregone conclusion.
Nevertheless, there was no hesitation behind the curtain.
When it went up at last, a stage much too small for the
company was revealed to an auditorium much too small
for the audience. But the players, though it was impossible for them to forget their own discomfort, at once
made the spectators forget theirs. It certainly was a
model audience, responsible from the first line to the
last; and it got no less than it deserved in return.

  I grieve to have to add that the second performance,
given for the edification of the London press and of
those members of the Stage Society who cannot attend
the Sunday performances, was a less inspiriting one than
the first. A solid phalanx of theatre-weary journalists in
an afternoon humor, most of them committed to irrecon-
cilable disparagement of problem plays, and all of them
bound by etiquette to be as undemonstrative as possible,
is not exactly the sort of audience that rises at the performers and cures them of the inevitable reaction after
an excitingly successful first night. The artist nature is a
sensitive and therefore a vindictive one; and masterful
players have a way with recalcitrant audiences of rubbing a play into them instead of delighting them with it.
I should describe the second performance of *Mrs. Warren's Profession,* especially as to its earlier stages, as decidedly a rubbed-in one. The rubbing was no doubt
salutary; but it must have hurt some of the thinner skins.

The charm of the lighter passages fled; and the strong scenes, though they again carried everything before them, yet discharged that duty in a grim fashion, doing execution on the enemy rather than moving them to repentance and confession. Still, to those who had not seen the first performance, the effect was sufficiently impressive; and they had the advantage of a fresh development in Mrs. Warren, who, artistically jealous, as I took it, of the overwhelming effect of the end of the second act on the previous day, threw herself into the fourth act in quite a new way, and achieved the apparently impossible feat of surpassing herself. The compliments paid to Miss Fanny Brough by the critics, eulogistic as they are, are the compliments of men three-fourths duped as Partridge was duped by Garrick. By much of her acting they were so completely taken in that they did not recognize it as acting at all. Indeed, none of the six players quite escaped this consequence of their own thoroughness. There was a distinct tendency among the less experienced critics to complain of their sentiments and behavior. Naturally, the author does not share that grievance.

Piccard's Cottage, January, 1902.

ACT ONE

*S*ummer afternoon in a cottage garden on the eastern
slope of a hill a little south of Haslemere in Surrey.
Looking up the hill, the cottage is seen in the left hand
corner of the garden, with its thatched roof and porch,
and a large latticed window to the left of the porch. Farther back a little wing is built out, making an angle with
the right side wall. From the end of this wing a paling
curves across and forward, completely shutting in the garden, except for a gate on the right. The common rises
uphill beyond the paling to the sky line. Some folded
canvas garden chairs are leaning against the side bench
in the porch. A lady's bicycle is propped against the wall,
under the window. A little to the right of the porch a
hammock is slung from two posts. A big canvas umbrella,
stuck in the ground, keeps the sun off the hammock, in
which a young lady lies reading and making notes, her
head towards the cottage and her feet towards the gate.
In front of the hammock, and within reach of her hand,
is a common kitchen chair, with a pile of serious-looking
books and a supply of writing paper upon it.

A gentleman walking on the common comes into sight
from behind the cottage. He is hardly past middle age, with
something of the artist about him, unconventionally but
carefully dressed, and clean-shaven except for a moustache,
with an eager, susceptible face and very amiable and considerate manners. He has silky black hair, with waves of grey
and white in it. His eyebrows are white, his moustache
black. He seems not certain of his way. He looks over the
paling; takes stock of the place; and sees the young lady.

*   *   *

THE GENTLEMAN [*taking off his hat*]. I beg your pardon. Can you direct me to Hindhead View—Mrs. Alison's?

THE YOUNG LADY [*glancing up from her book*]. This is Mrs. Alison's. [*She resumes her work.*]

THE GENTLEMAN. Indeed! Perhaps—may I ask are you Miss Vivie Warren?

THE YOUNG LADY [*sharply, as she turns on her elbow to get a good look at him*]. Yes.

THE GENTLEMAN [*daunted and conciliatory*]. I'm afraid I appear intrusive. My name is Praed. [*Vivie at once throws her books upon the chair, and gets out of the hammock.*] Oh, pray don't let me disturb you.

VIVIE [*striding to the gate and opening it for him*]. Come in, Mr. Praed. [*He comes in.*] Glad to see you. [*She proffers her hand and takes his with a resolute and hearty grip. She is an attractive specimen of the sensible, able, highly-educated young middle-class Englishwoman. Age 22. Prompt, strong, confident, self-possessed. Plain, businesslike dress, but not dowdy. She wears a chatelaine at her belt, with a fountain pen and a paper knife among its pendants.*]

PRAED. Very kind of you indeed, Miss Warren. [*She shuts the gate with a vigorous slam: he passes in to the middle of the garden, exercising his fingers, which are slightly numbed by her greeting.*] Has your mother arrived?

VIVIE [*quickly, evidently scenting aggression*]. Is she coming?

PRAED [*surprised*]. Didn't you expect us?

VIVIE. No.

PRAED. Now, goodness me, I hope I've not mistaken the day. That would be just like me, you know. Your mother arranged that she was to come down from London and that I was to come over from Horsham to be introduced to you.

VIVIE [*not at all pleased*]. Did she? H'm! My mother has rather a trick of taking me by surprise—to see how I behave myself when she's away, I suppose. I fancy I shall take my mother very much by surprise one of these days, if she makes arrangements that concern me without consulting me beforehand. She hasn't come.

PRAED [*embarrassed*]. I'm really very sorry.

VIVIE [*throwing off her displeasure*]. It's not your fault, Mr. Praed, is it? And I'm very glad you've come, believe me. You are the only one of my mother's friends I have asked her to bring to see me.

PRAED [*relieved and delighted*]. Oh, now this is really very good of you, Miss Warren!

VIVIE. Will you come indoors; or would you rather sit out here whilst we talk?

PRAED. It will be nicer out here, don't you think?

VIVIE. Then I'll go and get you a chair. [*She goes to the porch for a garden chair.*]

PRAED [*following her*]. Oh, pray, pray! Allow me. [*He lays hands on the chair.*]

VIVIE [*letting him take it*]. Take care of your fingers: they're rather dodgy things, those chairs. [*She goes across to the chair with the books on it; pitches them into the hammock; and brings the chair forward with one swing.*]

PRAED [*who has just unfolded his chair*]. Oh, now do let me take that hard chair! I like hard chairs.

VIVIE. So do I. [*She sits down.*] Sit down, Mr. Praed. [*This invitation is given with genial peremptoriness, his anxiety to please her clearly striking her as a sign of weakness of character on his part.*]

PRAED. By the way, though, hadn't we better go to the station to meet your mother?

VIVIE [*coolly*]. Why? She knows the way. [*Praed hesitates, and then sits down in the garden chair, rather disconcerted.*] Do you know, you are just like what I expected. I hope you are disposed to be friends with me?

PRAED [*again beaming*]. Thank you, my dear Miss Warren; thank you. Dear me! I'm so glad your mother hasn't spoilt you!

VIVIE. How?

PRAED. Well, in making you too conventional. You know, my dear Miss Warren, I am a born anarchist. I hate authority. It spoils the relations between parent and child—even between mother and daughter. Now I was always afraid that your mother would strain her authority to make you very conventional. It's such a relief to find that she hasn't.

VIVIE. Oh! have I been behaving unconventionally?

PRAED. Oh, no: oh, dear no. At least not conventionally unconventionally, you understand. [*She nods. He goes on, with a cordial outburst.*] But it was so charming of you to say that you were disposed to be friends with me! You modern young ladies are splendid—perfectly splendid!

VIVIE [*dubiously*]. Eh? [*watching him with dawning disappointment as to the quality of his brains and character.*]

PRAED. When I was your age, young men and women were afraid of each other: there was no good fellowship—nothing real—only gallantry copied out of novels, and as vulgar and affected as it could be. Maidenly reserve!—gentlemanly chivalry!—always saying no when you meant yes!—simple purgatory for shy and sincere souls!

VIVIE. Yes, I imagine there must have been a frightful waste of time—especially women's time.

PRAED. Oh, waste of life, waste of everything. But things are improving. Do you know, I have been in a positive state of excitement about meeting you ever since your magnificent achievements at Cambridge—a thing unheard of in my day. It was perfectly splendid, your tieing with the third wrangler. Just the right place, you know. The first wrangler is always a dreamy, morbid fellow, in whom the thing is pushed to the length of a disease.

VIVIE. It doesn't pay. I wouldn't do it again for the same money.

PRAED [*aghast*]. The same money!

VIVIE. I did it for £50. Perhaps you don't know how it was. Mrs. Latham, my tutor at Newnham, told my mother that I could distinguish myself in the mathematical tripos if I went for it in earnest. The papers were full just then of Phillipa Summers beating the senior wrangler—you remember about it; and nothing would please my mother but that I should do the same thing. I said flatly that it was not worth my while to face the grind since I was not going in for teaching; but I offered to try for fourth wrangler or thereabouts for £50. She closed with me at that, after a little grumbling; and I was better than my bargain. But I wouldn't do it again for that. £200 would have been nearer the mark.

PRAED [*much damped*]. Lord bless me! That's a very practical way of looking at it.

VIVIE. Did you expect to find me an unpractical person?

PRAED. No, no. But surely it's practical to consider not only the work these honors cost, but also the culture they bring.

VIVIE. Culture! My dear Mr. Praed: do you know what the mathematical tripos means? It means grind, grind, grind, for six to eight hours a day at mathematics, and nothing but mathematics. I'm supposed to know something about science; but I know nothing except the mathematics it involves. I can make calculations for engineers, electricians, insurance companies, and so on; but I know next to nothing about engineering or electricity or insurance. I don't even know arithmetic well. Outside mathematics, lawn tennis, eating, sleeping, cycling, and walking, I'm a more ignorant barbarian than any woman could possibly be who hadn't gone in for the tripos.

PRAED [*revolted*]. What a monstrous, wicked, rascally system! I knew it! I felt at once that it meant destroying all that makes womanhood beautiful.

VIVIE. I don't object to it on that score in the least. I shall turn it to very good account, I assure you.

PRAED. Pooh! In what way?

VIVIE. I shall set up in chambers in the city and work at actuarial calculations and conveyancing. Under cover of that I shall do some law, with one eye on the Stock Exchange all the time. I've come down here by myself to read law—not for a holiday, as my mother imagines. I hate holidays.

PRAED. You make my blood run cold. Are you to have no romance, no beauty in your life?

VIVIE. I don't care for either, I assure you.

PRAED. You can't mean that.

VIVIE. Oh yes I do. I like working and getting paid for it. When I'm tired of working, I like a comfortable chair, a cigar, a little whisky, and a novel with a good detective story in it.

PRAED [*in a frenzy of repudiation*]. I don't believe

not stereotype

it. I am an artist; and I can't believe it: I refuse to believe it. [*Enthusiastically.*] Ah, my dear Miss Warren, you haven't discovered yet, I see, what a wonderful world art can open up to you.

VIVIE. Yes, I have. Last May I spent six weeks in London with Honoria Fraser. Mamma thought we were doing a round of sight-seeing together; but I was really at Honoria's chambers in Chancery Lane every day, working away at actuarial calculations for her, and helping her as well as a greenhorn could. In the evenings we smoked and talked, and never dreamt of going out except for exercise. And I never enjoyed myself more in my life. I cleared all my expenses and got initiated into the business without a fee into the bargain.

PRAED. But bless my heart and soul, Miss Warren, do you call that trying art?

VIVIE. Wait a bit. That wasn't the beginning. I went up to town on an invitation from some artistic people in Fitzjohn's Avenue: one of the girls was a Newnham chum. They took me to the National Gallery, to the Opera, and to a concert where the band played all the evening—Beethoven and Wagner and so on. I wouldn't go through that experience again for anything you could offer me. I held out for civility's sake until the third day; and then I said, plump out, that I couldn't stand any more of it, and went off to Chancery Lane. Now you know the sort of perfectly splendid modern young lady I am. How do you think I shall get on with my mother?

PRAED [*startled*]. Well, I hope—er—

VIVIE. It's not so much what you hope as what you believe, that I want to know.

PRAED. Well, frankly, I am afraid your mother will be a little disappointed. Not from any shortcoming on your part—I don't mean that. But you are so different from her ideal.

VIVIE. What is her ideal like?

PRAED. Well, you must have observed, Miss Warren, that people who are dissatisfied with their own bringing up generally think that the world would be all right if everybody were to be brought up quite differently. Now your mother's life has been—er—I suppose you know—

VIVIE. I know nothing. [*Praed is appalled. His con-*

sternation grows as she continues.] That's exactly my difficulty. You forget, Mr. Praed, that I hardly know my mother. Since I was a child I have lived in England, at school or college, or with people paid to take charge of me. I have been boarded out all my life; and my mother has lived in Brussels or Vienna and never let me go to her. I only see her when she visits England for a few days. I don't complain; it's been very pleasant; for people have been very good to me; and there has always been plenty of money to make things smooth. But don't imagine I know anything about my mother. I know far less than you do.

PRAED [*very ill at ease*]. In that case—[*He stops, quite at a loss. Then, with a forced attempt at gaiety.*] But what nonsense we are talking! Of course you and your mother will get on capitally. [*He rises, and looks abroad at the view.*] What a charming little place you have here!

VIVIE [*unmoved*]. If you think you are doing anything but confirming my worst suspicions by changing the subject like that, you must take me for a much greater fool than I hope I am.

PRAED. Your worst suspicions! Oh, pray don't say that. Now don't.

VIVIE. Why won't my mother's life bear being talked about?

PRAED. Pray think, Miss Vivie. It is natural that I should have a certain delicacy in talking to my old friend's daughter about her behind her back. You will have plenty of opportunity of talking to her about it when she comes. [*Anxiously.*] I wonder what is keeping her.

VIVIE. No: She won't talk about it either. [*Rising.*] However, I won't press you. Only mind this, Mr. Praed. I strongly suspect there will be a battle royal when my mother hears of my Chancery Lane project.

PRAED [*ruefully*]. I'm afraid there will.

VIVIE. I shall win the battle, because I want nothing but my fare to London to start there to-morrow earning my own living by devilling for Honoria. Besides, I have no mysteries to keep up; and it seems she has. I shall use that advantage over her if necessary.

PRAED [*greatly shocked*]. Oh, no. No, pray. You'd not do such a thing.

VIVIE. Then tell me why not.

PRAED. I really cannot. I appeal to your good feeling. [*She smiles at his sentimentality.*] Besides, you may be too bold. Your mother is not to be trifled with when she's angry.

VIVIE. You can't frighten me, Mr. Praed. In that month at Chancery Lane I had opportunities of taking the measure of one or two women very like my mother who came to consult Honoria. You may back me to win. But if I hit harder in my ignorance than I need, remember that it is you who refuse to enlighten me. Now let us drop the subject. [*She takes her chair and replaces it near the hammock with the same vigorous swing as before.*]

PRAED [*taking a desperate resolution*]. One word, Miss Warren. I had better tell you. It's very difficult; but—

[*Mrs. Warren and Sir George Crofts arrive at the gate. Mrs. Warren is a woman between 40 and 50, good-looking, showily dressed in a brilliant hat and a gay blouse fitting tightly over her bust and flanked by fashionable sleeves. Rather spoiled and domineering, but, on the whole, a genial and fairly presentable old blackguard of a woman.*

Crofts is a tall, powerfully-built man of about 50, fashionably dressed in the style of a young man. Nasal voice, reedier than might be expected from his strong frame. Clean-shaven, bull-dog jaws, large flat ears, and thick neck, gentlemanly combination of the most brutal types of city man, sporting man, and man about town.]

VIVIE. Here they are. [*Coming to them as they enter the garden.*] How do, mater. Mr. Praed's been here this half hour, waiting for you.

MRS. WARREN. Well, if you've been waiting, Praddy, it's your own fault: I thought you'd have had the gumption to know I was coming by the 3:10 train. Vivie, put your hat on, dear: you'll get sunburnt. Oh, forgot to introduce you. Sir George Crofts, my little Vivie.

[*Crofts advances to Vivie with his most courtly manner. She nods, but makes no motion to shake hands.*]

CROFTS. May I shake hands with a young lady whom I have known by reputation very long as the daughter of one of my oldest friends?

VIVIE [*who has been looking him up and down sharply*]. If you like. [*She takes his tenderly proffered hand and gives it a squeeze that makes him open his eyes; then turns away and says to her mother*] Will you come in, or shall I get a couple more chairs? [*She goes into the porch for the chairs.*]

MRS. WARREN. Well, George, what do you think of her?

CROFTS [*ruefully*]. She has a powerful fist. Did you shake hands with her, Praed?

PRAED. Yes: it will pass off presently.

CROFTS. I hope so. [*Vivie reappears with two more chairs. He hurries to her assistance.*] Allow me.

MRS. WARREN [*patronizingly*]. Let Sir George help you with the chairs, dear.

VIVIE [*almost pitching two into his arms*]. Here you are. [*She dusts her hands and turns to Mrs. Warren.*] You'd like some tea, wouldn't you?

MRS. WARREN [*sitting in Praed's chair and fanning herself*]. I'm dying for a drop to drink.

VIVIE. I'll see about it. [*She goes into the cottage. Sir George has by this time managed to unfold a chair and plant it beside Mrs. Warren, on her left. He throws the other on the grass and sits down, looking dejected and rather foolish, with the handle of his stick in his mouth. Praed, still very uneasy, fidgets about the garden on their right.*]

MRS. WARREN [*to Praed, looking at Crofts*]. Just look at him, Praddy: he looks cheerful, don't he? He's been worrying my life out these three years to have that little girl of mine shewn to him; and now that I've done it, he's quite out of countenance. [*Briskly.*] Come! sit up, George; and take your stick out of your mouth. [*Crofts sulkily obeys.*]

PRAED. I think, you know—if you don't mind my saying so—that we had better get out of the habit of thinking of her as a little girl. You see she has really distinguished herself; and I'm not sure, from what I have seen of her, that she is not older than any of us.

MRS. WARREN [*greatly amused*]. Only listen to him, George! Older than any of us! Well, she has been stuffing you nicely with her importance.

PRAED. But young people are particularly sensitive about being treated in that way.

MRS. WARREN. Yes; and young people have to get all that nonsense taken out of them, and a good deal more besides. Don't you interfere, Praddy. I know how to treat my own child as well as you do. [*Praed, with a grave shake of his head, walks up the garden with his hands behind his back. Mrs. Warren pretends to laugh, but looks after him with perceptible concern. Then she whispers to Crofts.*] What's the matter with him? What does he take it like that for?

CROFTS [*morosely*]. You're afraid of Praed.

MRS. WARREN. What! Me! Afraid of dear old Praddy! Why, a fly wouldn't be afraid of him.

CROFTS. You're afraid of him.

MRS. WARREN [*angry*]. I'll trouble you to mind your own business, and not try any of your sulks on me. I'm not afraid of you, anyhow. If you can't make yourself agreeable, you'd better go home. [*She gets up, and, turning her back on him, finds herself face to face with Praed.*] Come, Praddy, I know it was only your tender-heartedness. You're afraid I'll bully her.

PRAED. My dear Kitty: you think I'm offended. Don't imagine that: pray don't. But you know I often notice things that escape you; and though you never take my advice, you sometimes admit afterwards that you ought to have taken it.

MRS. WARREN. Well, what do you notice now?

PRAED. Only that Vivie is a grown woman. Pray, Kitty, treat her with every respect.

MRS. WARREN [*with genuine amazement*]. Respect! Treat my own daughter with respect! What next, pray!

VIVIE [*appearing at the cottage door and calling to Mrs. Warren*]. Mother: will you come up to my room and take your bonnet off before tea?

MRS. WARREN. Yes, dearie. [*She laughs indulgently at Praed and pats him on the cheek as she passes him on her way to the porch. She follows Vivie into the cottage.*]

CROFTS [*furtively*]. I say, Praed.

PRAED. Yes.

CROFTS. I want to ask you a rather particular question.

PRAED. Certainly. [*He takes Mrs. Warren's chair and sits close to Crofts.*]

CROFTS. That's right: they might hear us from the window. Look here: did Kitty ever tell you who that girl's father is?

PRAED. Never.

CROFTS. Have you any suspicion of who it might be?

PRAED. None.

CROFTS [*not believing him*]. I know, of course, that you perhaps might feel bound not to tell if she had said anything to you. But it's very awkward to be uncertain about it now that we shall be meeting the girl every day. We don't exactly know how we ought to feel towards her.

PRAED. What difference can that make? We take her on her own merits. What does it matter who her father was?

CROFTS [*suspiciously*]. Then you know who he was?

PRAED [*with a touch of temper*]. I said no just now. Did you not hear me?

CROFTS. Look here, Praed. I ask you as a particular favor. If you do know [*movement of protest from Praed*]—I only say, if you know, you might at least set my mind at rest about her. The fact is I feel attracted towards her. Oh, don't be alarmed: it's quite an innocent feeling. That's what puzzles me about it. Why, for all I know, *I* might be her father.

PRAED. You! Impossible! Oh, no, nonsense!

CROFTS [*catching him up cunningly*]. You know for certain that I'm not?

PRAED. I know nothing about it, I tell you, any more than you. But really, Crofts—oh, no, it's out of the question. There's not the least resemblance.

CROFTS. As to that, there's no resemblance between her and her mother that I can see. I suppose she's not *your* daughter, is she?

PRAED [*He meets the question with an indignant stare; then recovers himself with an effort and answers gently and gravely*]. Now listen to me, my dear Crofts. I have nothing to do with that side of Mrs. Warren's life, and never had. She has never spoken to me about it; and of course I have never spoken to her about it. Your delicacy will tell you that a handsome woman needs some friends who are not—well, not on that footing with her. The effect of her own beauty would become a torment to her if she could not escape from it occasionally. You are probably on much more confidential terms with Kitty than I am. Surely you can ask her the question yourself.

CROFTS [*rising impatiently*]. I have asked her often enough. But she's so determined to keep the child all to herself that she would deny that it ever had a father if she could. No: there's nothing to be got out of her— nothing that one can believe, anyhow. I'm thoroughly uncomfortable about it, Praed.

PRAED [*rising also*]. Well, as you are, at all events, old enough to be her father, I don't mind agreeing that we both regard Miss Vivie in a parental way, as a young girl whom we are bound to protect and help. All the more, as the real father, whoever he was, was probably a blackguard. What do you say?

CROFTS [*aggressively*]. I'm no older than you, if you come to that.

PRAED. Yes, you are, my dear fellow: you were born old. I was born a boy: I've never been able to feel the assurance of a grown-up man in my life.

MRS. WARREN [*calling from within the cottage*]. Praddee! George! Tea-ea-ea-ea!

CROFTS [*hastily*]. She's calling us. [*He hurries in. Praed shakes his head bodingly, and is following slowly when he is hailed by a young gentleman who has just appeared on the common, and is making for the gate. He is a pleasant, pretty, smartly dressed, and entirely good-for-nothing young fellow, not long turned 20, with a charming voice and agreeably disrespectful manner. He carries a very light sporting magazine rifle.*]

THE YOUNG GENTLEMAN. Hallo! Praed!

PRAED. Why, Frank Gardner! [*Frank comes in and shakes hands cordially.*] What on earth are you doing here?

FRANK. Staying with my father.

PRAED. The Roman father?

FRANK. He's rector here. I'm living with my people this autumn for the sake of economy. Things came to a crisis in July: the Roman father had to pay my debts. He's stony broke in consequence; and so am I. What are you up to in these parts? Do you know the people here?

PRAED. Yes: I'm spending the day with a Miss Warren.

FRANK [*enthusiastically*]. What! Do you know Vivie? Isn't she a jolly girl! I'm teaching her to shoot—you see [*shewing the rifle.*]! I'm so glad she knows you: you're just the sort of fellow she ought to know. [*He smiles, and raises the charming voice almost to a singing tone as he exclaims*] It's ever so jolly to find you here, Praed. Ain't it, now?

PRAED. I'm an old friend of her mother's. Mrs. Warren brought me over to make her daughter's acquaintance.

FRANK. The mother! Is she here?

PRAED. Yes—inside at tea.

MRS. WARREN [*calling from within*]. Prad-dee-ee-ee-eee! The tea-cake'll be cold.

PRAED [*calling*]. Yes, Mrs. Warren. In a moment. I've just met a friend here.

MRS. WARREN. A what?

PRAED [*louder*]. A friend.

MRS. WARREN. Bring him up.

PRAED. All right. [*To Frank.*] Will you accept the invitation?

FRANK [*incredulous, but immensely amused*]. Is that Vivie's mother?

PRAED. Yes.

FRANK. By Jove! What a lark! Do you think she'll like me?

PRAED. I've no doubt you'll make yourself popular, as usual. Come in and try [*moving towards the house*].

FRANK. Stop a bit. [*Seriously.*] I want to take you into my confidence.

PRAED. Pray don't. It's only some fresh folly, like the barmaid at Redhill.

FRANK. It's ever so much more serious than that. You say you've only just met Vivie for the first time?

PRAED. Yes.

FRANK [*rhapsodically*]. Then you can have no idea what a girl she is. Such character! Such sense! And her cleverness! Oh, my eye, Praed, but I can tell you she is clever! And the most loving little heart that—

CROFTS [*putting his head out of the window*]. I say, Praed: what are you about? Do come along. [*He disappears.*]

FRANK. Hallo! Sort of chap that would take a prize at a dog show, ain't he? Who's he?

PRAED. Sir George Crofts, an old friend of Mrs. Warren's. I think we had better come in.

[*On their way to the porch they are interrupted by a call from the gate. Turning, they see an elderly clergyman looking over it.*]

THE CLERGYMAN [*calling*]. Frank!

FRANK. Hallo! [*To Praed.*] The Roman father. [*To the clergyman.*] Yes, gov'nor: all right: presently. [*To Praed.*] Look here, Praed: you'd better go in to tea. I'll join you directly.

PRAED. Very good. [*He raises his hat to the clergyman, who acknowledges the salute distantly. Praed goes into the cottage. The clergyman remains stiffly outside the gate, with his hands on the top of it. The Rev. Samuel Gardner, a beneficed clergyman of the Established Church, is over 50. He is a pretentious, booming, noisy person, hopelessly asserting himself as a father and a clergyman without being able to command respect in either capacity.*]

REV. S. Well, sir. Who are your friends here, if I may ask?

FRANK. Oh, it's all right, gov'nor! Come in.

REV. S. No, sir; not until I know whose garden I am entering.

FRANK. It's all right. It's Miss Warren's.

REV. S. I have not seen her at church since she came.

FRANK. Of course not: she's a third wrangler—ever so intellectual!—took a higher degree than you did; so why should she go to hear you preach?

REV. S. Don't be disrespectful, sir.

FRANK. Oh, it don't matter: nobody hears us. Come in. [*He opens the gate, unceremoniously pulling his father with it into the garden.*] I want to introduce you to her. She and I get on rattling well together: she's charming. Do you remember the advice you gave me last July, gov'nor?

REV. S. [*severely*]. Yes. I advised you to conquer your idleness and flippancy, and to work your way into an honorable profession and live on it and not upon me.

FRANK. No: that's what you thought of afterwards. What you actually said was that since I had neither brains nor money, I'd better turn my good looks to account by marrying somebody with both. Well, look here. Miss Warren has brains: you can't deny that.

REV. S. Brains are not everything.

FRANK. No, of course not: there's the money—

REV. S. [*interrupting him austerely*]. I was not thinking of money, sir. I was speaking of higher things—social position, for instance.

FRANK. I don't care a rap about that.

REV. S. But I do, sir.

FRANK. Well, nobody wants you to marry her. Anyhow, she has what amounts to a high Cambridge degree; and she seems to have as much money as she wants.

REV. S. [*sinking into a feeble vein of humor*]. I greatly doubt whether she has as much money as you will want.

FRANK. Oh, come: I haven't been so very extravagant. I live ever so quietly; I don't drink; I don't bet much; and I never go regularly on the razzle-dazzle as you did when you were my age.

REV. S. [*booming hollowly*]. Silence, sir.

FRANK. Well, you told me yourself, when I was making ever such an ass of myself about the barmaid at Redhill, that you once offered a woman £50 for the letters you wrote to her when—

REV. S. [*terrified*]. Sh-sh-sh, Frank, for Heaven's sake! [*He looks round apprehensively. Seeing no one within earshot he plucks up courage to boom again, but more subduedly.*] You are taking an ungentlemanly advantage of what I confided to you for your own good, to save you from an error you would have repented all your life long. Take warning by your father's follies, sir; and don't make them an excuse for your own.

FRANK. Did you ever hear the story of the Duke of Wellington and his letters?

REV. S. No, sir; and I don't want to hear it.

FRANK. The old Iron Duke didn't throw away £50—not he. He just wrote: "My dear Jenny: Publish and be damned! Yours affectionately, Wellington." That's what you should have done.

REV. S. [*piteously*]. Frank, my boy: when I wrote those letters I put myself into that woman's power. When I told you about her I put myself, to some extent, I am sorry to say, in your power. She refused my money with these words, which I shall never forget: "Knowledge is power," she said; "and I never sell power." That's more than twenty years ago; and she has never made use of her power or caused me a moment's uneasiness. You are behaving worse to me than she did, Frank.

FRANK. Oh, yes, I dare say! Did you ever preach at her the way you preach at me every day?

REV. S. [*wounded almost to tears*]. I leave you, sir. You are incorrigible. [*He turns towards the gate.*]

FRANK [*utterly unmoved*]. Tell them I shan't be home to tea, will you, gov'nor, like a good fellow? [*He goes towards the cottage door and is met by Vivie coming out, followed by Praed, Crofts, and Mrs. Warren.*]

VIVIE [*to Frank*]. Is that your father, Frank? I do so want to meet him.

FRANK. Certainly. [*Calling after his father.*] Gov'nor. [*The Rev. S. turns at the gate, fumbling nervously at his hat. Praed comes down the garden on the opposite side, beaming in anticipation of civilities. Crofts prowls about near the hammock, poking it with his stick to make it swing. Mrs. Warren halts on the threshold, staring hard at the clergyman.*] Let me introduce—my father: Miss Warren.

VIVIE [*going to the clergyman and shaking his hand*]. Very glad to see you here, Mr. Gardner. Let me introduce everybody. Mr. Gardner—Mr. Frank Gardner—Mr. Praed—Sir George Crofts, and— [*As the men are raising their hats to one another, Vivie is interrupted by an exclamation from her mother, who swoops down on the Reverend Samuel*].

MRS. WARREN. Why, it's Sam Gardner, gone into the church! Don't you know us, Sam? This is George Crofts, as large as life and twice as natural. Don't you remember me?

REV. S. [*very red*]. I really—er—

MRS. WARREN. Of course you do. Why, I have a whole album of your letters still: I came across them only the other day.

REV. S. [*miserably confused*]. Miss Vavasour, I believe.

MRS. WARREN [*correcting him quickly in a loud whisper*]. Tch! Nonsense—Mrs. Warren: don't you see my daughter there?

ACT TWO

Inside the cottage after nightfall. Looking eastward from within instead of westward from without, the latticed window, with its curtains drawn, is now seen in the middle of the front wall of the cottage, with the porch door to the left of it. In the left-hand side wall is the door leading to the wing. Farther back against the same wall is a dresser with a candle and matches on it, and Frank's rifle standing beside them, with the barrel resting in the plate-rack. In the centre a table stands with a lighted lamp on it. Vivie's books and writing materials are on a table to the right of the window, against the wall. The fireplace is on the right, with a settle: there is no fire. Two of the chairs are set right and left of the table.

The cottage door opens, shewing a fine starlit night without; and Mrs. Warren, her shoulders wrapped in a shawl borrowed from Vivie, enters, followed by Frank. She has had enough of walking, and gives a gasp of relief as she unpins her hat; takes it off; sticks the pin through the crown; and puts it on the table.

MRS. WARREN. O Lord! I don't know which is the worst of the country, the walking or the sitting at home with nothing to do: I could do a whisky and soda now very well, if only they had such a thing in this place.

FRANK [*helping her to take off her shawl, and giving her shoulders the most delicate possible little caress with his fingers as he does so*]. Perhaps Vivie's got some.

MRS. WARREN [*glancing back at him for an instant from the corner of her eye as she detects the pressure*]. Nonsense! What would a young girl like her be doing with such things! Never mind: it don't matter. [*She throws herself wearily into a chair at the table.*] I wonder how she passes her time here! I'd a good deal rather be in Vienna.

FRANK. Let me take you there. [*He folds the shawl neatly; hangs it on the back of the other chair; and sits down opposite Mrs. Warren.*]

MRS. WARREN. Get out! I'm beginning to think you're a chip off the old block.

FRANK. Like the gov'nor, eh?

MRS. WARREN. Never you mind. What do you know about such things? You're only a boy.

FRANK. Do come to Vienna with me? It'd be ever such larks.

MRS. WARREN. No, thank you. Vienna is no place for you—at least not until you're a little older. [*She nods at him to emphasize this piece of advice. He makes a mock-piteous face, belied by his laughing eyes. She looks at him; then rises and goes to him.*] Now, look here, little boy [*taking his face in her hands and turning it up to her*]: I know you through and through by your likeness to your father, better than you know yourself. Don't you go taking any silly ideas into your head about me. Do you hear?

FRANK [*gallantly wooing her with his voice*]. Can't help it, my dear Mrs. Warren: it runs in the family. [*She pretends to box his ears; then looks at the pretty, laughing, upturned face for a moment, tempted. At last she kisses him and immediately turns away, out of patience with herself.*]

MRS. WARREN. There! I shouldn't have done that. I am wicked. Never you mind, my dear: it's only a motherly kiss. Go and make love to Vivie.

FRANK. So I have.

MRS. WARREN [*turning on him with a sharp note of alarm in her voice*]. What!

FRANK. Vivie and I are ever such chums.

MRS. WARREN. What do you mean? Now, see here: I won't have any young scamp tampering with my little girl. Do you hear? I won't have it.

FRANK [quite unabashed]. My dear Mrs. Warren: don't you be alarmed. My intentions are honorable— ever so honorable; and your little girl is jolly well able to take care of herself. She don't need looking after half so much as her mother. She ain't so handsome, you know.

MRS. WARREN [taken aback by his assurance]. Well, you have got a nice, healthy two inches thick of cheek all over you. I don't know where you got it—not from your father, anyhow. [Voices and footsteps in the porch]. Sh! I hear the others coming in. [She sits down hastily.] Remember: you've got your warning. [The Rev. Samuel comes in, followed by Crofts.] Well, what became of you two? And where's Praddy and Vivie?

CROFTS [putting his hat on the settle and his stick in the chimney corner]. They went up the hill. We went to the village. I wanted a drink. [He sits down on the settle, putting his legs up along the seat.]

MRS. WARREN. Well, she oughtn't to go off like that without telling me. [To Frank.] Get your father a chair, Frank: where are your manners? [Frank springs up and gracefully offers his father his chair; then takes another from the wall and sits down at the table, in the middle, with his father on his right and Mrs. Warren on his left.] George: where are you going to stay to-night? You can't stay here. And what's Praddy going to do?

CROFTS. Gardner'll put me up.

MRS. WARREN. Oh, no doubt you've taken care of yourself! But what about Praddy?

CROFTS. Don't know. I suppose he can sleep at the inn.

MRS. WARREN. Haven't you room for him, Sam?

REV. S. Well, er—you see, as rector here, I am not free to do as I like exactly. Er—what is Mr. Praed's social position?

MRS. WARREN. Oh, he's all right: he's an architect. What an old-stick-in-the-mud you are, Sam!

FRANK. Yes, it's all right, gov'nor. He built that

place down in Monmouthshire for the Duke of Beaufort—Tintern Abbey they call it. You must have heard of it. [*He winks with lightning smartness at Mrs. Warren, and regards his father blandly.*]

REV. S. Oh, in that case, of course we shall only be too happy. I suppose he knows the Duke of Beaufort personally.

FRANK. Oh, ever so intimately! We can stick him in Georgina's old room.

MRS. WARREN. Well, that's settled. Now, if those two would only come in and let us have supper. They've no right to stay out after dark like this.

CROFTS [*aggressively*]. What harm are they doing you?

MRS. WARREN. Well, harm or not, I don't like it.

FRANK. Better not wait for them, Mrs. Warren. Praed will stay out as long as possible. He has never known before what it is to stray over the heath on a summer night with my Vivie.

CROFTS [*sitting up in some consternation*]. I say, you know. Come!

REV. S. [*startled out of his professional manner into real force and sincerity*]. Frank, once for all, it's out of the question. Mrs. Warren will tell you that it's not to be thought of.

CROFTS. Of course not.

FRANK [*with enchanting placidity*]. Is that so, Mrs. Warren?

MRS. WARREN [*reflectively*]. Well, Sam, I don't know. If the girl wants to get married, no good can come of keeping her unmarried.

REV. S. [*astounded*]. But married to him!—your daughter to my son! Only think: it's impossible.

CROFTS. Of course it's impossible. Don't be a fool, Kitty.

MRS. WARREN [*nettled*]. Why not? Isn't my daughter good enough for your son?

REV. S. But surely, my dear Mrs. Warren, you know the reason—

MRS. WARREN [*defiantly*]. I know no reasons. If you know any, you can tell them to the lad, or to the girl, or to your congregation, if you like.

REV. S. [*helplessly*]. You know very well that I couldn't tell anyone the reasons. But my boy will believe me when I tell him there are reasons.

FRANK. Quite right, Dad: he will. But has your boy's conduct ever been influenced by your reasons?

CROFTS. You can't marry her; and that's all about it. [*He gets up and stands on the hearth, with his back to the fireplace, frowning determinedly.*]

MRS. WARREN [*turning on him sharply*]. What have you got to do with it, pray?

FRANK [*with his prettiest lyrical cadence*]. Precisely what I was going to ask, myself, in my own graceful fashion.

CROFTS [*to Mrs. Warren*]. I suppose you don't want to marry the girl to a man younger than herself and without either a profession or twopence to keep her on. Ask Sam, if you don't believe me. [*To the Rev. S.*] How much more money are you going to give him?

REV. S. Not another penny. He has had his patrimony; and he spent the last of it in July. [*Mrs. Warren's face falls.*]

CROFTS [*watching her*]. There! I told you. [*He resumes his place on the settle and puts up his legs on the seat again, as if the matter were finally disposed of.*]

FRANK [*plaintively*]. This is ever so mercenary. Do you suppose Miss Warren's going to marry for money? If we love one another—

MRS. WARREN. Thank you. Your love's a pretty cheap commodity, my lad. If you have no means of keeping a wife, that settles it: you can't have Vivie.

FRANK [*much amused*]. What do you say, gov'nor, eh?

REV. S. I agree with Mrs. Warren.

FRANK. And good old Crofts has already expressed his opinion.

CROFTS [*turning angrily on his elbow*]. Look here: I want none of your cheek.

FRANK [*pointedly*]. I'm ever so sorry to surprise you, Crofts; but you allowed yourself the liberty of speaking to me like a father a moment ago. One father is enough, thank you.

CROFTS [*contemptuously*]. Yah! [*He turns away again.*]

FRANK [*rising*]. Mrs. Warren: I cannot give my Vivie up even for your sake.

MRS. WARREN [*muttering*]. Young scamp!

FRANK [*continuing*]. And as you no doubt intend to hold out other prospects to her, I shall lose no time in placing my case before her. [*They stare at him; and he begins to declaim gracefully*]

> He either fears his fate too much,
>   Or his deserts are small,
> That dares not put it to the touch
>   To gain or lose it all.

[*The cottage door opens whilst he is reciting; and Vivie and Praed come in. He breaks off. Praed puts his hat on the dresser. There is an immediate improvement in the company's behaviour. Crofts takes down his legs from the settle and pulls himself together as Praed joins him at the fireplace. Mrs. Warren loses her ease of manner, and takes refuge in querulousness.*]

MRS. WARREN. Wherever have you been, Vivie?

VIVIE [*taking off her hat and throwing it carelessly on the table*]. On the hill.

MRS. WARREN. Well, you shouldn't go off like that without letting me know. How could I tell what had become of you—and night coming on, too!

VIVIE [*going to the door of the inner room and opening it, ignoring her mother*]. Now, about supper? We shall be rather crowded in here, I'm afraid.

MRS. WARREN. Did you hear what I said, Vivie?

VIVIE [*quietly*]. Yes, mother. [*Reverting to the supper difficulty.*] How many are we? [*Counting.*] One, two, three, four, five, six. Well, two will have to wait until the rest are done: Mrs. Alison has only plates and knives for four.

PRAED. Oh, it doesn't matter about me. I—

VIVIE. You have had a long walk and are hungry, Mr. Praed: you shall have your supper at once. I can

wait myself. I want one person to wait with me. Frank:
are you hungry?

FRANK. Not the least in the world—completely off
my peck, in fact.

MRS. WARREN [*to Crofts*]. Neither are you, George.
You can wait.

CROFTS. Oh, hang it, I've eaten nothing since tea-
time. Can't Sam do it?

FRANK. Would you starve my poor father?

REV. S. [*testily*]. Allow me to speak for myself, sir. I
am perfectly willing to wait.

VIVIE [*decisively*]. There's no need. Only two are
wanted. [*She opens the door of the inner room.*] Will you
take my mother in, Mr. Gardner. [*The Rev. S. takes Mrs.
Warren; and they pass into the next room. Praed and
Crofts follow. All except Praed clearly disapprove of the
arrangement, but do not know how to resist it. Vivie
stands at the door looking in at them.*] Can you squeeze
past to that corner, Mr. Praed: it's rather a tight fit. Take
care of your coat against the white-wash—that's right.
Now, are you all comfortable?

PRAED [*within*]. Quite, thank you.

MRS. WARREN [*within*]. Leave the door open, dearie.
[*Frank looks at Vivie; then steals to the cottage door and
softly sets it wide open.*] Oh, Lor', what a draught! You'd
better shut it, dear. [*Vivie shuts it promptly. Frank noise-
lessly shuts the cottage door.*]

FRANK [*exulting*]. Aha! Got rid of 'em. Well, Vivvums: what do you think of my governor!

VIVIE [*preoccupied and serious*]. I've hardly spoken
to him. He doesn't strike me as being a particularly
able person.

FRANK. Well, you know, the old man is not altogether such a fool as he looks. You see, he's rector here;
and in trying to live up to it he makes a much bigger
ass of himself than he really is. No, the gov'nor ain't so
bad, poor old chap; and I don't dislike him as much as
you might expect. He means well. How do you think
you'll get on with him?

VIVIE [*rather grimly*]. I don't think my future life
will be much concerned with him, or with any of that

old circle of my mother's, except perhaps Praed. What do you think of my mother?

FRANK. Really and truly?

VIVIE. Yes, really and truly.

FRANK. Well, she's ever so jolly. But she's rather a caution, isn't she? And Crofts! Oh, my eye, Crofts!

VIVIE. What a lot, Frank!

FRANK. What a crew!

VIVIE [*with intense contempt for them*]. If I thought that *I* was like that—that I was going to be a waster, shifting along from one meal to another with no purpose, and no character, and no grit in me, I'd open an artery and bleed to death without one moment's hesitation.

FRANK. Oh, no, you wouldn't. Why should they take any grind when they can afford not to? I wish I had their luck. No: what I object to is their form. It isn't the thing: it's slovenly, ever so slovenly.

VIVIE. Do you think your form will be any better when you're as old as Crofts, if you don't work?

FRANK. Of course I do—ever so much better. Vivvums mustn't lecture: her little boy's incorrigible. [*He attempts to take her face caressingly in his hands.*]

VIVIE [*striking his hands down sharply*]. Off with you: Vivvums is not in a humor for petting her little boy this evening.

FRANK. How unkind!

VIVIE [*stamping at him*]. Be serious. I'm serious.

FRANK. Good. Let us talk learnedly. Miss Warren: do you know that all the most advanced thinkers are agreed that half the diseases of modern civilization are due to starvation of the affections in the young. Now, I—

VIVIE [*cutting him short*]. You are getting tiresome. [*She opens the inner door.*] Have you room for Frank there? He's complaining of starvation.

MRS. WARREN [*within*]. Of course there is [*clatter of knives and glasses as she moves the things on the table*]. Here: there's room now beside me. Come along, Mr. Frank.

FRANK [*aside to Vivie, as he goes*]. Her little boy will be ever so even with his Vivvums for this. [*He goes into the other room.*]

MRS. WARREN [*within*]. Here, Vivie: come on, you too, child. You must be famished. [*She enters, followed by Crofts, who holds the door open for Vivie with marked deference. She goes out without looking at him; and he shuts the door after her.*] Why, George, you can't be done: you've eaten nothing.

CROFTS. Oh, all I wanted was a drink. [*He thrusts his hands in his pockets and begins prowling about the room, restless and sulky.*]

MRS. WARREN. Well, I like enough to eat. But a little of that cold beef and cheese and lettuce goes a long way. [*With a sigh of only half repletion she sits down lazily at the table.*]

CROFTS. What do you go encouraging that young pup for?

MRS. WARREN [*on the alert at once*]. Now see here, George: what are you up to about that girl? I've been watching your way of looking at her. Remember: I know you and what your looks mean.

CROFTS. There's no harm in looking at her, is there?

MRS. WARREN. I'd put you out and pack you back to London pretty soon if I saw any of your nonsense. My girl's little finger is more to me than your whole body and soul. [*Crofts receives this with a sneering grin. Mrs. Warren, flushing a little at her failure to impose on him in the character of a theatrically devoted mother, adds in a lower key.*] Make your mind easy: the young pup has no more chance than you have.

CROFTS. Mayn't a man take an interest in a girl?

MRS. WARREN. Not a man like you.

CROFTS. How old is she?

MRS. WARREN. Never you mind how old she is.

CROFTS. Why do you make such a secret of it?

MRS. WARREN. Because I choose.

CROFTS. Well, I'm not fifty yet; and my property is as good as it ever was—

MRS. WARREN [*interrupting him*]. Yes; because you're as stingy as you're vicious.

CROFTS [*continuing*]. And a baronet isn't to be picked up every day. No other man in my position would put up with you for a mother-in-law. Why shouldn't she marry me?

MRS. WARREN. You!

CROFTS. We three could live together quite comfortably. I'd die before her and leave her a bouncing widow with plenty of money. Why not? It's been growing in my mind all the time I've been walking with that fool inside there.

MRS. WARREN [*revolted*]. Yes; it's the sort of thing that would grow in your mind. [*He halts in his prowling; and the two look at one another, she steadfastly, with a sort of awe behind her contemptuous disgust: he stealthily, with a carnal gleam in his eye and a loose grin, tempting her.*]

CROFTS [*suddenly becoming anxious and urgent as he sees no sign of sympathy in her*]. Look here, Kitty: you're a sensible woman: you needn't put on any moral airs. I'll ask no more questions; and you need answer none. I'll settle the whole property on her; and if you want a cheque for yourself on the wedding day, you can name any figure you like—in reason.

MRS. WARREN. Faugh! So it's come to that with you, George, like all the other worn out old creatures.

CROFTS [*savagely*]. Damn you! [*She rises and turns fiercely on him; but the door of the inner room is opened just then; and the voices of the others are heard returning. Crofts, unable to recover his presence of mind, hurries out of the cottage. The clergyman comes back.*]

REV. S. [*looking round*]. Where is Sir George?

MRS. WARREN. Gone out to have a pipe. [*She goes to the fireplace, turning her back on him to compose herself. The clergyman goes to the table for his hat. Meanwhile Vivie comes in, followed by Frank, who collapses into the nearest chair with an air of extreme exhaustion. Mrs. Warren looks round at Vivie and says, with her affectation of maternal patronage even more forced than usual.*] Well, dearie: have you had a good supper?

VIVIE. You know what Mrs. Alison's suppers are. [*She turns to Frank and pets him.*] Poor Frank! was all the beef gone? did it get nothing but bread and cheese and ginger beer? [*Seriously, as if she had done quite enough trifling for one evening.*] Her butter is really awful. I must get some down from the stores.

FRANK. Do, in Heaven's name!

[*Vivie goes to the writing-table and makes a memorandum to order the butter. Praed comes in from the inner room, putting up his handkerchief, which he has been using as a napkin.*]

REV. S. Frank, my boy: it is time for us to be thinking of home. Your mother does not know yet that we have visitors.

PRAED. I'm afraid we're giving trouble.

FRANK. Not the least in the world, Praed: my mother will be delighted to see you. She's a genuinely intellectual, artistic woman; and she sees nobody here from one year's end to another except the gov'nor; so you can imagine how jolly dull it pans out for her. [*To the Rev. S.*] You're not intellectual or artistic, are you, pater? So take Praed home at once; and I'll stay here and entertain Mrs. Warren. You'll pick up Crofts in the garden. He'll be excellent company for the bull-pup.

PRAED [*taking his hat from the dresser, and coming close to Frank*]. Come with us, Frank. Mrs. Warren has not seen Miss Vivie for a long time; and we have prevented them from having a moment together yet.

FRANK [*quite softened, and looking at Praed with romantic admiration*]. Of course: I forgot. Ever so thanks for reminding me. Perfect gentleman, Praddy. Always were—my ideal through life. [*He rises to go, but pauses a moment between the two older men, and puts his hand on Praed's shoulder.*] Ah, if you had only been my father instead of this unworthy old man! [*He puts his other hand on his father's shoulder.*]

REV. S. [*blustering*]. Silence, sir, silence: you are profane.

MRS. WARREN [*laughing heartily*]. You should keep him in better order, Sam. Good-night. Here: take George his hat and stick with my compliments.

REV. S. [*taking them*]. Good-night. [*They shake hands. As he passes Vivie he shakes hands with her also and bids her good-night. Then, in booming command, to Frank.*] Come along, sir, at once. [*He goes out. Meanwhile Frank has taken his cap from the dresser and his rifle from the rack. Praed shakes hands with Mrs. Warren and Vivie and goes out, Mrs. Warren accompanying him idly to the door, and looking out after him as he goes across the garden. Frank silently begs a kiss from Vivie; but she, dismissing him with a stern glance, takes a couple of books and some paper from the writing-table, and sits down with them at the middle table, so as to have the benefit of the lamp.*]

FRANK [*at the door, taking Mrs. Warren's hand*]. Good-night, dear Mrs. Warren. [*He squeezes her hand. She snatches it away, her lips tightening, and looks more than half disposed to box his ears. He laughs mischievously and runs off, clapping-to the door behind him.*]

MRS. WARREN [*coming back to her place at the table, opposite Vivie, resigning herself to an evening of boredom now that the men are gone*]. Did you ever in your life hear anyone rattle on so? Isn't he a tease? [*She sits down.*] Now that I think of it, dearie, don't you go encouraging him. I'm sure he's a regular good-for-nothing.

VIVIE. Yes: I'm afraid poor Frank is a thorough good-for-nothing. I shall have to get rid of him; but I shall feel sorry for him, though he's not worth it, poor lad. That man Crofts does not seem to me to be good for much either, is he?

MRS. WARREN [*galled by Vivie's cool tone*]. What do you know of men, child, to talk that way about them? You'll have to make up your mind to see a good deal of Sir George Crofts, as he's a friend of mine.

VIVIE [*quite unmoved*]. Why? Do you expect that we shall be much together—you and I, I mean?

MRS. WARREN [*staring at her*]. Of course—until you're married. You're not going back to college again.

VIVIE. Do you think my way of life would suit you? I doubt it.

MRS. WARREN. Your way of life! What do you mean?

VIVIE [*cutting a page of her book with the paper knife on her chatelaine*]. Has it really never occurred to you, mother, that I have a way of life like other people?

MRS. WARREN. What nonsense is this you're trying to talk? Do you want to shew your independence, now that you're a great little person at school? Don't be a fool, child.

VIVIE [*indulgently*]. That's all you have to say on the subject, is it, mother?

MRS. WARREN [*puzzled, then angry*]. Don't you keep on asking me questions like that. [*Violently.*] Hold your tongue. [*Vivie works on, losing no time, and saying nothing.*] You and your way of life, indeed! What next? [*She looks at Vivie again. No reply.*] Your way of life will be what I please, so it will. [*Another pause.*] I've been noticing these airs in you ever since you got that tripos or whatever you call it. If you think I'm going to put up with them you're mistaken; and the sooner you find it out, the better. [*Muttering.*] All I have to say on the subject, indeed! [*Again raising her voice angrily.*] Do you know who you're speaking to, Miss?

VIVIE [*looking across at her without raising her head from her book*]. No. Who are you? What are you?

MRS. WARREN [*rising breathless*]. You young imp!

VIVIE. Everybody knows my reputation, my social standing, and the profession I intend to pursue. I know nothing about you. What is that way of life which you invite me to share with you and Sir George Crofts, pray?

MRS. WARREN. Take care. I shall do something I'll be sorry for after, and you, too.

VIVIE [*putting aside her books with cool decision*]. Well, let us drop the subject until you are better able to face it. [*Looking critically at her mother.*] You want some good walks and a little lawn tennis to set you up. You are shockingly out of condition: you were not able to manage twenty yards uphill to-day without stopping to pant; and your wrists are mere rolls of fat. Look at mine. [*She holds out her wrists.*]

MRS. WARREN [*after looking at her helplessly, begins to whimper*]. Vivie—

VIVIE [*springing up sharply*]. Now pray don't begin to cry. Anything but that. I really cannot stand whimpering. I will go out of the room if you do.

MRS. WARREN [*piteously*]. Oh, my darling, how can you be so hard on me? Have I no rights over you as your mother?

VIVIE. Are you my mother?

MRS. WARREN [*appalled*]. Am I your mother! Oh, Vivie!

VIVIE. Then where are our relatives—my father— our family friends? You claim the rights of a mother:

the right to call me fool and child; to speak to me as no woman in authority over me at college dare speak to me; to dictate my way of life; and to force on me the acquaintance of a brute whom anyone can see to be the most vicious sort of London man about town. Before I give myself the trouble to resist such claims, I may as well find out whether they have any real existence.

MRS. WARREN [*distracted, throwing herself on her knees*]. Oh, no, no. Stop, stop. I am your mother: I swear it. Oh, you can't mean to turn on me—my own child: it's not natural. You believe me, don't you? Say you believe me.

VIVIE. Who was my father?

MRS. WARREN. You don't know what you're asking. I can't tell you.

VIVIE [*determinedly*]. Oh, yes, you can, if you like. I have a right to know; and you know very well that I have that right. You can refuse to tell me, if you please; but if you do, you will see the last of me to-morrow morning.

MRS. WARREN. Oh, it's too horrible to hear you talk like that. You wouldn't—you couldn't leave me.

VIVIE [*ruthlessly*]. Yes, without a moment's hesitation, if you trifle with me about this. [*Shivering with disgust.*] How can I feel sure that I may not have the contaminated blood of that brutal waster in my veins?

MRS. WARREN. No, no. On my oath it's not he, nor any of the rest that you have ever met. I'm certain of that, at least. [*Vivie's eyes fasten sternly on her mother as the significance of this flashes on her.*]

VIVIE [*slowly*]. You are certain of that, at least. Ah! You mean that that is all you are certain of. [*Thoughtfully.*] I see. [*Mrs. Warren buries her face in her hands.*] Don't do that, mother: you know you don't feel it a bit. [*Mrs. Warren takes down her hands and looks up deplorably at Vivie, who takes out her watch and says*] Well, that is enough for to-night. At what hour would you like breakfast? Is half-past eight too early for you?

MRS. WARREN [*wildly*]. My God, what sort of woman are you?

VIVIE [*coolly*]. The sort the world is mostly made of, I should hope. Otherwise I don't understand how it gets its business done. Come [*taking her mother by the wrist, and pulling her up pretty resolutely*]: pull yourself together. That's right.

MRS. WARREN [*querulously*]. You're very rough with me, Vivie.

VIVIE. Nonsense. What about bed? It's past ten.

MRS. WARREN [*passionately*]. What's the use of my going to bed? Do you think I could sleep?

VIVIE. Why not? I shall.

MRS. WARREN. You! you've no heart. [*She suddenly breaks out vehemently in her natural tongue—the dialect of a woman of the people—with all her affectations of maternal authority and conventional manners gone, and an overwhelming inspiration of true conviction and scorn in her.*] Oh, I won't bear it: I won't put up with the injustice of it. What right have you to set yourself up above me like this? You boast of what you are to me—to me, who gave you the chance of being what you are. What chance had I? Shame on you for a bad daughter and a stuck-up prude!

VIVIE [*cool and determined, but no longer confident; for her replies, which have sounded convincingly sensible and strong to her so far, now begin to ring rather woodenly and even priggishly against the new tone of her mother*]. Don't think for a moment I set myself above you in any way. You attacked me with the conventional authority of a mother: I defended myself with the conventional superiority of a respectable woman. Frankly, I am not going to stand any of your nonsense; and when you drop it I shall not expect you to stand any of mine. I shall always respect your right to your own opinions and your own way of life.

MRS. WARREN. My own opinions and my own way of life! Listen to her talking! Do you think I was brought up like you—able to pick and choose my own way of life? Do you think I did what I did because I liked it, or thought it right, or wouldn't rather have gone to college and been a lady if I'd had the chance?

VIVIE. Everybody has some choice, mother. The poorest girl alive may not be able to choose between being Queen of England or Principal of Newnham; but she can choose between ragpicking and flowerselling, ac-

cording to her taste. People are always blaming their
circumstances for what they are. I don't believe in circumstances. The people who get on in this world are the
people who get up and look for the circumstances they
want, and, if they can't find them, make them.

MRS. WARREN. Oh, it's easy to talk, very easy, isn't
it? Here!—would you like to know what my circumstances were?

VIVIE. Yes: you had better tell me. Won't you sit
down?

MRS. WARREN. Oh, I'll sit down: don't you be afraid.
[*She plants her chair farther forward with brazen energy,
and sits down. Vivie is impressed in spite of herself.*]
D'you know what your gran'mother was?

VIVIE. No.

MRS. WARREN. No, you don't. I do. She called herself
a widow and had a fried-fish shop down by the Mint,
and kept herself and four daughters out of it. Two of us
were sisters: that was me and Liz; and we were both
good-looking and well made. I suppose our father was
a well-fed man: mother pretended he was a gentleman;
but I don't know. The other two were only half sisters—
undersized, ugly, starved looking, hard working, honest
poor creatures: Liz and I would have half-murdered
them if mother hadn't half-murdered us to keep our
hands off them. They were the respectable ones. Well,
what did they get by their respectability? I'll tell you.
One of them worked in a whitelead factory twelve hours
a day for nine shillings a week until she died of lead
poisoning. She only expected to get her hands a little
paralyzed; but she died. The other was always held up
to us as a model because she married a Government
laborer in the Deptford victualling yard, and kept his
room and the three children neat and tidy on eighteen
shillings a week—until he took to drink. That was worth
being respectable for, wasn't it?

VIVIE [*now thoughtfully attentive*]. Did you and your
sister think so?

MRS. WARREN. Liz didn't, I can tell you: she had
more spirit. We both went to a church school—that was
part of the ladylike airs we gave ourselves to be superior
to the children that knew nothing and went nowhere—

and we stayed there until Liz went out one night and never came back. I know the schoolmistress thought I'd soon follow her example; for the clergyman was always warning me that Lizzie'd end by jumping off Waterloo Bridge. Poor fool: that was all he knew about it! But I was more afraid of the whitelead factory than I was of the river; and so would you have been in my place. That clergyman got me a situation as scullery maid in a temperance restaurant where they sent out for anything you liked. Then I was waitress; and then I went to the bar at Waterloo station—fourteen hours a day serving drinks and washing glasses for four shillings a week and my board. That was considered a great promotion for me. Well, one cold, wretched night, when I was so tired I could hardly keep myself awake, who should come up for a half of Scotch but Lizzie, in a long fur cloak, elegant and comfortable, with a lot of sovereigns in her purse.

VIVIE [*grimly*]. My aunt Lizzie!

MRS. WARREN. Yes: and a very good aunt to have, too. She's living down at Winchester now, close to the cathedral, one of the most respectable ladies there—chaperones girls at the county ball, if you please. No river for Liz, thank you! You remind me of Liz a little: she was a first-rate business woman—saved money from the beginning—never let herself look too like what she was—never lost her head or threw away a chance. When she saw I'd grown up good-looking she said to me across the bar: "What are you doing there, you little fool? wearing out your health and your appearance for other people's profit!" Liz was saving money then to take a house for herself in Brussels: and she thought we two could save faster than one. So she lent me some money and gave me a start; and I saved steadily and first paid her back, and then went into business with her as her partner. Why shouldn't I have done it? The house in Brussels was real high class—a much better place for a woman to be in than the factory where Anne Jane got poisoned. None of our girls were ever treated as I was treated in the scullery of that temperance place, or at the Waterloo bar, or at home. Would you have had me stay in them and become a worn out old drudge before I was forty?

VIVIE [*intensely interested by this time*]. No; but why did you choose that business? Saving money and good management will succeed in any business.

MRS. WARREN. Yes, saving money. But where can a woman get the money to save in any other business? Could you save out of four shillings a week and keep yourself dressed as well? Not you. Of course, if you're a plain woman and can't earn anything more; or if you have a turn for music, or the stage, or newspaper-writing: that's different. But neither Liz nor I had any turn for such things: all we had was our appearance and our turn for pleasing men. Do you think we were such fools as to let other people trade in our good looks by employing us as shopgirls, or barmaids, or waitresses, when we could trade in them ourselves and get all the profits instead of starvation wages? Not likely.

VIVIE. You were certainly quite justified—from the business point of view.

MRS. WARREN. Yes; or any other point of view. What is any respectable girl brought up to do but to catch some rich man's fancy and get the benefit of his money by marrying him?—as if a marriage ceremony could make any difference in the right or wrong of the thing! Oh, the hypocrisy of the world makes me sick! Liz and I had to work and save and calculate just like other people; elseways we should be as poor as any good-for-nothing, drunken waster of a woman that thinks her luck will last for ever. [*With great energy.*] I despise such people: they've no character; and if there's a thing I hate in a woman, it's want of character.

VIVIE. Come, now, mother: frankly! Isn't it part of what you call character in a woman that she should greatly dislike such a way of making money?

MRS. WARREN. Why, of course. Everybody dislikes having to work and make money; but they have to do it all the same. I'm sure I've often pitied a poor girl, tired out and in low spirits, having to try to please some man that she doesn't care two straws for—some half-drunken fool that thinks he's making himself agreeable when he's teasing and worrying and disgusting a woman so that hardly any money could pay her for putting up with it. But she has to bear with disagreeables and take the rough with the smooth, just like a nurse in a hospital or anyone else. It's not work that any woman would do for pleasure, goodness knows; though to hear the pious people talk you would suppose it was a bed of roses.

VIVIE. Still you consider it worth while. It pays.

MRS. WARREN. Of course it's worth while to a poor girl, if she can resist temptation and is good-looking and well conducted and sensible. It's far better than any other employment open to her. I always thought that oughtn't to be. It can't be right, Vivie, that there shouldn't be better opportunities for women. I stick to that: it's wrong. But it's so, right or wrong; and a girl must make the best of it. But, of course, it's not worth while for a lady. If you took to it you'd be a fool; but I should have been a fool if I'd taken to anything else.

VIVIE [*more and more deeply moved*]. Mother: suppose we were both as poor as you were in those wretched old days, are you quite sure that you wouldn't advise me to try the Waterloo bar, or marry a labourer, or even go into the factory?

MRS. WARREN [*indignantly*]. Of course not. What sort of mother do you take me for! How could you keep your self-respect in such starvation and slavery? And what's a woman worth? what's life worth? without self-respect! Why am I independent and able to give my daughter a first-rate education, when other women that had just as good opportunities are in the gutter? Because I always knew how to respect myself and control myself. Why is Liz looked up to in a cathedral town? The same reason. Where would we be now if we'd minded the clergyman's foolishness? Scrubbing floors for one and sixpence a day and nothing to look forward to but the workhouse infirmary. Don't you be led astray by people who don't know the world, my girl. The only way for a woman to provide for herself decently is for her to be good to some man that can afford to be good to her. If she's in his own station of life, let her make him marry her; but if she's far beneath him she can't expect it— why should she? It wouldn't be for her own happiness. Ask any lady in London society that has daughters; and she'll tell you the same, except that I tell you straight and she'll tell you crooked. That's all the difference.

VIVIE [*fascinated, gazing at her*]. My dear mother: you are a wonderful woman—you are stronger than all England. And are you really and truly not one wee bit doubtful—or—or—ashamed?

MRS. WARREN. Well, of course, dearie, it's only good manners to be ashamed of it, it's expected from a woman. Women have to pretend to feel a great deal that they don't feel. Liz used to be angry with me for plumping out the truth about it. She used to say that when every woman could learn enough from what was going on in the world before her eyes, there was no need to talk about it to her. But then Liz was such a perfect lady! She had the true instinct of it; while I was always a bit of a vulgarian. I used to be so pleased when you sent me your photographs to see that you were growing up like Liz: you've just her ladylike, determined way. But I can't stand saying one thing when everyone knows I mean another. What's the use in such hypocrisy? If people arrange the world that way for women, there's no good pretending that it's arranged the other way. I never was a bit ashamed really. I consider that I had a right to be proud that we managed everything so respectably, and never had a word against us, and that the girls were so well taken care of. Some of them did very well: one of them married an ambassador. But of course now I daren't talk about such things: whatever would they think of us! [*She yawns.*] Oh, dear! I do believe I'm getting sleepy after all. [*She stretches herself lazily, thoroughly relieved by her explosion, and placidly ready for her night's rest.*]

VIVIE. I believe it is I who will not be able to sleep now. [*She goes to the dresser and lights the candle. Then she extinguishes the lamp, darkening the room a good deal.*] Better let in some fresh air before locking up. [*She opens the cottage door, and finds that it is broad moonlight.*] What a beautiful night! Look! [*She draws aside the curtains of the window. The landscape is seen bathed in the radiance of the harvest moon rising over Blackdown.*]

MRS. WARREN [*with a perfunctory glance at the scene*]. Yes, dear: but take care you don't catch your death of cold from the night air.

VIVIE [*contemptuously*]. Nonsense.

MRS. WARREN [*querulously*]. Oh, yes: everything I say is nonsense, according to you.

VIVIE [*turning to her quickly*]. No: really that is not so, mother. You have got completely the better of me to-night, though I intended it to be the other way. Let us be good friends now.

MRS. WARREN [*shaking her head a little ruefully*]. So it has been the other way. But I suppose I must give in to it. I always got the worst of it from Liz; and now I suppose it'll be the same with you.

VIVIE. Well, never mind. Come; good-night, dear old mother. [*She takes her mother in her arms.*]

MRS. WARREN [*fondly*]. I brought you up well, didn't I, dearie?

VIVIE. You did.

MRS. WARREN. And you'll be good to your poor old mother for it, won't you?

VIVIE. I will, dear. [*Kissing her.*] Good-night.

MRS. WARREN [*with unction*]. Blessings on my own dearie darling—a mother's blessing! [*She embraces her daughter protectingly, instinctively looking upward as if to call down a blessing.*]

ACT THREE

In the Rectory garden next morning, with the sun shining and the birds in full song. The garden wall has a five-barred wooden gate, wide enough to admit a carriage, in the middle. Beside the gate hangs a bell on a coiled spring, communicating with a pull outside. The carriage drive comes down the middle of the garden and then swerves to its left, where it ends in a little gravelled circus opposite the rectory porch. Beyond the gate is seen the dusty high road, parallel with the wall, bounded on the farther side by a strip of turf and an unfenced pine wood. On the lawn, between the house and the drive, is a clipped yew tree, with a garden bench in its shade. On the opposite side the garden is shut in by a box hedge; and there

*is a sundial on the turf, with an iron chair near it. A little
path leads off through the box hedge, behind the sundial.*

*Frank, seated on the chair near the sundial, on which
he has placed the morning papers, is reading the* Standard. *His father comes from the house, red-eyed and shiv-
ery, and meets Frank's eyes with misgiving.*

FRANK [*looking at his watch*]. Half-past eleven. Nice
hour for a rector to come down to breakfast!

REV. S. Don't mock, Frank: don't mock. I'm a little—
er— [*Shivering.*]————

FRANK. Off colour?

REV. S. [*repudiating the expression*]. No, sir: unwell
this morning. Where's your mother?

FRANK. Don't be alarmed: she's not here. Gone to
town by the 11:13 with Bessie. She left several messages
for you. Do you feel equal to receiving them now, or
shall I wait till you've breakfasted?

REV. S. I have breakfasted, sir. I am surprised at
your mother going to town when we have people staying
with us. They'll think it very strange.

FRANK. Possibly she has considered that. At all
events, if Crofts is going to stay here, and you are going
to sit up every night with him until four, recalling the
incidents of your fiery youth, it is clearly my mother's
duty, as a prudent housekeeper, to go up to the stores
and order a barrel of whisky and a few hundred siphons.

REV. S. I did not observe that Sir George drank
excessively.

FRANK. You were not in a condition to, gov'nor.

REV. S. Do you mean to say that I—

FRANK [*calmly*]. I never saw a beneficed clergyman
less sober. The anecdotes you told about your past career were so awful that I really don't think Praed would
have passed the night under your roof if it hadn't been
for the way my mother and he took to one another.

REV. S. Nonsense, sir. I am Sir George Crofts' host.
I must talk to him about something; and he has only
one subject. Where is Mr. Praed now?

FRANK. He is driving my mother and Bessie to the
station.

REV. S. Is Crofts up yet?

FRANK. Oh, long ago. He hasn't turned a hair: he's in much better practice than you—has kept it up ever since, probably. He's taken himself off somewhere to smoke. [*Frank resumes his paper. The Rev. S. turns disconsolately towards the gate; then comes back irresolutely.*]

REV. S. Er—Frank.

FRANK. Yes.

REV. S. Do you think the Warrens will expect to be asked here after yesterday afternoon?

FRANK. They've been asked already. Crofts informed us at breakfast that you told him to bring Mrs. Warren and Vivie over here to-day, and to invite them to make this house their home. It was after that communication that my mother found she must go to town by the 11:13 train.

REV. S. [*with despairing vehemence*]. I never gave any such invitation. I never thought of such a thing.

FRANK [*compassionately*]. How do you know, gov'nor, what you said and thought last night? Hallo! here's Praed back again.

PRAED [*coming in through the gate*]. Good morning.

REV. S. Good morning. I must apologize for not having met you at breakfast. I have a touch of—of—

FRANK. Clergyman's sore throat, Praed. Fortunately not chronic.

PRAED [*changing the subject*]. Well, I must say your house is in a charming spot here. Really most charming.

REV. S. Yes: it is indeed. Frank will take you for a walk, Mr. Praed, if you like. I'll ask you to excuse me: I must take the opportunity to write my sermon while Mrs. Gardner is away and you are all amusing yourselves. You won't mind, will you?

PRAED. Certainly not. Don't stand on the slightest ceremony with me.

REV. S. Thank you. I'll—er—er— [*He stammers his way to the porch and vanishes into the house*].

PRAED [*sitting down on the turf near Frank, and hugging his ankles*]. Curious thing it must be writing a sermon every week.

FRANK. Ever so curious, if he did it. He buys 'em. He's gone for some soda water.

PRAED. My dear boy: I wish you would be more

respectful to your father. You know you can be so nice
when you like.

FRANK. My dear Praddy: you forget that I have to
live with the governor. When two people live together—it don't matter whether they're father and son,
husband and wife, brother and sister—they can't keep
up the polite humbug which comes so easy for ten minutes on an afternoon call. Now the governor, who
unites to many admirable domestic qualities the irreso-
luteness of a sheep and the pompousness and aggressiveness of a jackass—

PRAED. No, pray, pray, my dear Frank, remember!
He is your father.

FRANK. I give him due credit for that. But just imagine his telling Crofts to bring the Warrens over here! He
must have been ever so drunk. You know, my dear
Praddy, my mother wouldn't stand Mrs. Warren for a
moment. Vivie mustn't come here until she's gone back
to town.

PRAED. But your mother doesn't know anything
about Mrs. Warren, does she?

FRANK. I don't know. Her journey to town looks as
if she did. Not that my mother would mind in the ordinary way: she has stuck like a brick to lots of women
who had got into trouble. But they were all nice women.
That's what makes the real difference. Mrs. Warren, no
doubt, has her merits; but she's ever so rowdy; and my
mother simply wouldn't put up with her. So—hallo!
[*This exclamation is provoked by the reappearance of the
clergyman, who comes out of the house in haste and
dismay.*]

REV. S. Frank: Mrs. Warren and her daughter are
coming across the heath with Crofts: I saw them from
the study windows. What am I to say about your
mother?

FRANK [*jumping up energetically*]. Stick on your hat
and go out and say how delighted you are to see them;
and that Frank's in the garden; and that mother and
Bessie have been called to the bedside of a sick relative,
and were ever so sorry they couldn't stop; and that you
hope Mrs. Warren slept well; and—and—say any blessed
thing except the truth, and leave the rest to Providence.

REV. S. But how are we to get rid of them afterwards?

FRANK. There's no time to think of that now. Here! [*He bounds into the porch and returns immediately with a clerical felt hat, which he claps on his father's head.*] Now: off with you. Praed and I'll wait here, to give the thing an unpremeditated air. [*The clergyman, dazed, but obedient, hurries off through the gate. Praed gets up from the turf, and dusts himself.*]

FRANK. We must get that old lady back to town somehow, Praed. Come! honestly, dear Praddy, do you like seeing them together—Vivie and the old lady?

PRAED. Oh, why not?

FRANK [*his teeth on edge*]. Don't it make your flesh creep ever so little?—that wicked old devil, up to every villainy under the sun, I'll swear, and Vivie—ugh!

PRAED. Hush, pray. They're coming. [*The clergyman and Crofts are seen coming along the road, followed by Mrs. Warren and Vivie walking affectionately together.*]

FRANK. Look: she actually has her arm round the old woman's waist. It's her right arm: she began it. She's gone sentimental, by God! Ugh! ugh! Now do you feel the creeps? [*The clergyman opens the gate; and Mrs. Warren and Vivie pass him and stand in the middle of the garden looking at the house. Frank, in an ecstasy of dissimulation, turns gaily to Mrs. Warren, exclaiming*] Ever so delighted to see you, Mrs. Warren. This quiet old rectory garden becomes you perfectly.

MRS. WARREN. Well, I never! Did you hear that, George? He says I look well in a quiet old rectory garden.

REV. S. [*still holding the gate for Crofts, who loafs through it, heavily bored*]. You look well everywhere, Mrs. Warren.

FRANK. Bravo, gov'nor! Now look here: let's have an awful jolly time of it before lunch. First let's see the church. Everyone has to do that. It's a regular old thirteenth century church, you know: the gov'nor's ever so fond of it, because he got up a restoration fund and had it completely rebuilt six years ago. Praed will be able to show its points.

REV. S. [*mooning hospitably at them*]. I shall be

pleased, I'm sure, if Sir George and Mrs. Warren really care about it.

MRS. WARREN. Oh, come along and get it over. It'll do George good: I'll lay he doesn't trouble church much.

CROFTS [*turning back towards the gate*]. I've no objection.

REV. S. Not that way. We go through the fields, if you don't mind. Round here. [*He leads the way by the little path through the box hedge.*]

CROFTS. Oh, all right. [*He goes with the parson. Praed follows with Mrs. Warren. Vivie does not stir, but watches them until they have gone, with all the lines of purpose in her face marking it strongly.*]

FRANK. Ain't you coming.

VIVIE. No. I want to give you a warning, Frank. You were making fun of my mother just now when you said that about the rectory garden. That is barred in future. Please treat my mother with as much respect as you treat your own.

FRANK. My dear Viv: she wouldn't appreciate it. She's not like my mother: the same treatment wouldn't do for both cases. But what on earth has happened to you? Last night we were perfectly agreed as to your mother and her set. This morning I find you attitudinizing sentimentally with your arm round your parent's waist.

VIVIE [*flushing*]. Attitudinizing!

FRANK. That was how it struck me. First time I ever saw you do a second-rate thing.

VIVIE [*controlling herself*]. Yes, Frank: there has been a change; but I don't think it a change for the worse. Yesterday I was a little prig.

FRANK. And to-day?

VIVIE [*wincing; then looking at him steadily*]. To-day I know my mother better than you do.

FRANK. Heaven forbid!

VIVIE. What do you mean?

FRANK. Viv; there's a freemasonry among thoroughly immoral people that you know nothing of. You've too much character. That's the bond between your mother and me: that's why I know her better than you'll ever know her.

VIVIE. You are wrong: you know nothing about her. If you knew the circumstances against which my mother had to struggle—

FRANK [*adroitly finishing the sentence for her*]. I should know why she is what she is, shouldn't I? What difference would that make? Circumstances or no circumstances, Viv, you won't be able to stand your mother.

VIVIE [*very angry*]. Why not?

FRANK. Because she's an old wretch, Viv. If you ever put your arm round her waist in my presence again, I'll shoot myself there and then as a protest against an exhibition which revolts me.

VIVIE. Must I choose between dropping your acquaintance and dropping my mother's?

FRANK [*gracefully*]. That would put the old lady at ever such a disadvantage. No, Viv: your infatuated little boy will have to stick to you in any case. But he's all the more anxious that you shouldn't make mistakes. It's no use, Viv: your mother's impossible. She may be a good sort; but she's a bad lot, a very bad lot.

VIVIE [*hotly*]. Frank—! [*He stands his ground. She turns away and sits down on the bench under the yew tree, struggling to recover her self-command. Then she says*] Is she to be deserted by all the world because she's what you call a bad lot? Has she no right to live?

FRANK. No fear of that, Viv: she won't ever be deserted. [*He sits on the bench beside her.*]

VIVIE. But I am to desert her, I suppose.

FRANK [*babyishly, lulling her and making love to her with his voice*]. Mustn't go live with her. Little family group of mother and daughter wouldn't be a success. Spoil our little group.

VIVIE [*falling under the spell*]. What little group?

FRANK. The babes in the wood: Vivie and little Frank. [*He slips his arm round her waist and nestles against her like a weary child.*] Let's go and get covered up with leaves.

VIVIE [*rhythmically, rocking him like a nurse*]. Fast asleep, hand in hand, under the trees.

FRANK. The wise little girl with her silly little boy.

VIVIE. The dear little boy with his dowdy little girl.

FRANK. Ever so peaceful, and relieved from the imbecility of the little boy's father and the questionableness of the little girl's—

VIVIE [*smothering the word against her breast*]. Sh-sh-sh-sh! little girl wants to forget all about her mother. [*They are silent for some moments, rocking one another. Then Vivie wakes up with a shock, exclaiming*] What a pair of fools we are! Come: sit up. Gracious! your hair. [*She smooths it.*] I wonder do all grown up people play in that childish way when nobody is looking. I never did it when I was a child.

FRANK. Neither did I. You are my first playmate. [*He catches her hand to kiss it, but checks himself to look round first. Very unexpectedly he sees Crofts emerging from the box hedge.*] Oh, damn!

VIVIE. Why damn, dear?

FRANK [*whispering*]. Sh! Here's this brute Crofts. [*He sits farther away from her with an unconcerned air.*]

VIVIE. Don't be rude to him, Frank. I particularly wish to be polite to him. It will please my mother. [*Frank makes a wry face.*]

CROFTS. Could I have a few words with you, Miss Vivie?

VIVIE. Certainly.

CROFTS [*to Frank*]. You'll excuse me, Gardner. They're waiting for you in the church, if you don't mind.

FRANK [*rising*]. Anything to oblige you, Crofts—except church. If you want anything, Vivie, ring the gate bell, and a domestic will appear. [*He goes into the house with unruffled suavity.*]

CROFTS [*watching him with a crafty air as he disappears, and speaking to Vivie with an assumption of being on privileged terms with her*]. Pleasant young fellow that, Miss Vivie. Pity he has no money, isn't it?

VIVIE. Do you think so?

CROFTS. Well, what's he to do? No profession, no property. What's he good for?

VIVIE. I realize his disadvantages, Sir George.

CROFTS [*a little taken aback at being so precisely interpreted*]. Oh, it's not that. But while we're in this world we're in it; and money's money. [*Vivie does not answer.*] Nice day, isn't it?

VIVIE [*with scarcely veiled contempt for this effort at conversation*]. Very.

CROFTS [*with brutal good humor, as if he liked her pluck*]. Well, that's not what I came to say. [*Affecting frankness.*] Now listen, Miss Vivie. I'm quite aware that I'm not a young lady's man.

VIVIE. Indeed, Sir George?

CROFTS. No; and to tell you the honest truth, I don't want to be either. But when I say a thing I mean it; when I feel sentiment I feel it in earnest; and what I value I pay hard money for. That's the sort of man I am.

VIVIE. It does you great credit, I'm sure.

CROFTS. Oh, I don't mean to praise myself. I have my faults, Heaven knows: no man is more sensible of that than I am. I know I'm not perfect: that's one of the advantages of being a middle-aged man; for I'm not a young man, and I know it. But my code is a simple one, and, I think, a good one. Honor between man and man; fidelity between man and woman; and no cant about this religion, or that religion, but an honest belief that things are making for good on the whole.

VIVIE [*with biting irony*]. "A power, not ourselves, that makes for righteousness," eh?

CROFTS [*taking her seriously*]. Oh, certainly, not ourselves, of course. You understand what I mean. [*He sits down beside her, as one who has found a kindred spirit.*] Well, now as to practical matters. You may have an idea that I've flung my money about; but I haven't: I'm richer to-day than when I first came into the property. I've used my knowledge of the world to invest my money in ways that other men have overlooked; and whatever else I may be, I'm a safe man from the money point of view.

VIVIE. It's very kind of you to tell me all this.

CROFTS. Oh, well, come, Miss Vivie: you needn't pretend you don't see what I'm driving at. I want to settle down with a Lady Crofts. I suppose you think me very blunt, eh?

VIVIE. Not at all: I am much obliged to you for being so definite and business-like. I quite appreciate the offer: the money, the position, Lady Crofts, and so on. But I think I will say no, if you don't mind. I'd rather not.

[*She rises, and strolls across to the sundial to get out of his immediate neighborhood.*]

CROFTS [*not at all discouraged, and taking advantage of the additional room left him on the seat to spread himself comfortably, as if a few preliminary refusals were part of the inevitable routine of courtship*]. I'm in no hurry. It was only just to let you know in case young Gardner should try to trap you. Leave the question open.

VIVIE [*sharply*]. My no is final. I won't go back from it. [*She looks authoritatively at him. He grins; leans forward with his elbows on his knees to prod with his stick at some unfortunate insect in the grass; and looks cunningly at her. She turns away impatiently.*]

CROFTS. I'm a good deal older than you—twenty-five years—quarter of a century. I shan't live for ever; and I'll take care that you shall be well off when I'm gone.

VIVIE. I am proof against even that inducement, Sir George. Don't you think you'd better take your answer? There is not the slightest chance of my altering it.

CROFTS [*rising, after a final slash at a daisy, and beginning to walk to and fro*]. Well, no matter. I could tell you some things that would change your mind fast enough; but I won't, because I'd rather win you by honest affection. I was a good friend to your mother: ask her whether I wasn't. She'd never have made the money that paid for your education if it hadn't been for my advice and help, not to mention the money I advanced her. There are not many men would have stood by her as I have. I put not less than £40,000 into it, from first to last.

VIVIE [*staring at him*]. Do you mean to say you were my mother's business partner?

CROFTS. Yes. Now just think of all the trouble and the explanations it would save if we were to keep the whole thing in the family, so to speak. Ask your mother whether she'd like to have to explain all her affairs to a perfect stranger.

VIVIE. I see no difficulty, since I understand that the business is wound up, and the money invested.

CROFTS [*stopping short, amazed*]. Wound up! Wind

up a business that's paying 35 per cent in the worst years! Not likely. Who told you that?

VIVIE [*her colour quite gone*]. Do you mean that it is still—? [*She stops abruptly, and puts her hand on the sundial to support herself. Then she gets quickly to the iron chair and sits down.*] What business are you talking about?

CROFTS. Well, the fact is, it's not what would be considered exactly a high-class business in my set—the county set, you know—our set it will be if you think better of my offer. Not that there's any mystery about it: don't think that. Of course you know by your mother's being in it that it's perfectly straight and honest. I've known her for many years; and I can say of her that she'd cut off her hands sooner than touch anything that was not what it ought to be. I'll tell you all about it if you like. I don't know whether you've found in travelling how hard it is to find a really comfortable private hotel.

VIVIE [*sickened, averting her face*]. Yes: go on.

CROFTS. Well, that's all it is. Your mother has a genius for managing such things. We've got two in Brussels, one in Berlin, one in Vienna, and two in Buda-Pesth. Of course there are others besides ourselves in it; but we hold most of the capital; and your mother's indispensable as managing director. You've noticed, I daresay, that she travels a good deal. But you see you can't mention such things in society. Once let out the word hotel and everybody says you keep a public-house. You wouldn't like people to say that of your mother, would you? That's why we're so reserved about it. By the bye, you'll keep it to yourself, won't you? Since it's been a secret so long, it had better remain so.

VIVIE. And this is the business you invite me to join you in?

CROFTS. Oh, no. My wife shan't be troubled with business. You'll not be in it more than you've always been.

VIVIE. *I* always been! What do you mean?

CROFTS. Only that you've always lived on it. It paid for your education and the dress you have on your back. Don't turn up your nose at business, Miss Vivie: where would your Newnhams and Girtons be without it?

VIVIE [*rising, almost beside herself*]. Take care. I know what this business is.

CROFTS [*starting, with a suppressed oath*]. Who told you?

VIVIE. Your partner—my mother.

CROFTS [*black with rage*]. The old— [*Vivie looks quickly at him. He swallows the epithet and stands swearing and raging foully to himself. But he knows that his cue is to be sympathetic. He takes refuge in generous indignation.*] She ought to have had more consideration for you. I'd never have told you.

VIVIE. I think you would probably have told me when we were married: it would have been a convenient weapon to break me in with.

CROFTS [*quite sincerely*]. I never intended that. On my word as a gentleman I didn't.

[*Vivie wonders at him. Her sense of the irony of his protest cools and braces her. She replies with contemptuous self-possession*].

VIVIE. It does not matter. I suppose you understand that when we leave here to-day our acquaintance ceases.

CROFTS. Why? Is it for helping your mother?

VIVIE. My mother was a very poor woman who had no reasonable choice but to do as she did. You were a rich gentleman; and you did the same for the sake of 35 per cent. You are a pretty common sort of scoundrel, I think. That is my opinion of you.

CROFTS [*after a stare—not at all displeased, and much more at his ease on these frank terms than on their former ceremonious ones*]. Ha, ha, ha, ha! Go it, little missie, go it: it doesn't hurt me and it amuses you. Why the devil shouldn't I invest my money that way? I take the interest on my capital like other people: I hope you don't think I dirty my own hands with the work. Come: you wouldn't refuse the acquaintance of my mother's cousin, the Duke of Belgravia, because some of the rents he gets are earned in queer ways. You wouldn't cut the Archbishop of Canterbury, I suppose, because the Ecclesiastical Commissioners have a few publicans and sinners among their tenants? Do you remember your Crofts scholarship at Newnham? Well, that was founded by my brother the M.P. He gets his 22 per cent out of a factory

with 600 girls in it, and not one of them getting wages
enough to live on. How d'ye suppose most of them manage? Ask your mother. And do you expect me to turn
my back on 35 per cent when all the rest are pocketing
what they can, like sensible men? No such fool! If you're
going to pick and choose your acquaintances on moral
principles, you'd better clear out of this country, unless
you want to cut yourself out of all decent society.

VIVIE [*conscience stricken*]. You might go on to
point out that I myself never asked where the money I
spent came from. I believe I am just as bad as you.

CROFTS [*greatly reassured*]. Of course you are; and
a very good thing, too! What harm does it do after all?
[*Rallying her jocularly.*] So you don't think me such a
scoundrel now you come to think it over. Eh?

VIVIE. I have shared profits with you; and I admitted
you just now to the familiarity of knowing what I think
of you.

CROFTS [*with serious friendliness*]. To be sure you
did. You won't find me a bad sort: I don't go in for
being superfine intellectually; but I've plenty of honest
human feeling; and the old Crofts breed comes out in a
sort of instinctive hatred of anything low, in which I'm
sure you'll sympathize with me. Believe me, Miss Vivie,
the world isn't such a bad place as the croakers make
out. So long as you don't fly openly in the face of society,
society doesn't ask any inconvenient questions; and it
makes precious short work of the cads who do. There
are no secrets better kept than the secrets that everybody guesses. In the society I can introduce you to, no
lady or gentleman would so far forget themselves as to
discuss my business affairs or your mother's. No man
can offer you a safer position.

VIVIE [*studying him curiously*]. I suppose you really
think you're getting on famously with me.

CROFTS. Well, I hope I may flatter myself that you
think better of me than you did at first.

VIVIE [*quietly*]. I hardly find you worth thinking
about at all now. [*She rises and turns towards the gate,
pausing on her way to contemplate him and say almost
gently, but with intense conviction.*] When I think of the
society that tolerates you, and the laws that protect

you—when I think of how helpless nine out of ten young girls would be in the hands of you and my mother—the unmentionable woman and her capitalist bully—

CROFTS [*livid*]. Damn you!

VIVIE. You need not. I feel among the damned already.

[*She raises the latch of the gate to open it and go out. He follows her and puts his hand heavily on the top bar to prevent its opening.*]

CROFTS [*panting with fury*]. Do you think I'll put up with this from you, you young devil, you?

VIVIE [*unmoved*]. Be quiet. Some one will answer the bell. [*Without flinching a step she strikes the bell with the back of her hand. It clangs harshly; and he starts back involuntarily. Almost immediately Frank appears at the porch with his rifle.*]

FRANK [*with cheerful politeness*]. Will you have the rifle, Viv; or shall I operate?

VIVIE. Frank: have you been listening?

FRANK. Only for the bell, I assure you; so that you shouldn't have to wait. I think I showed great insight into your character, Crofts.

CROFTS. For two pins I'd take that gun from you and break it across your head.

FRANK [*stalking him cautiously*]. Pray don't. I'm ever so careless in handling firearms. Sure to be a fatal accident, with a reprimand from the coroner's jury for my negligence.

VIVIE. Put the rifle away, Frank: it's quite unnecessary.

FRANK. Quite right, Viv. Much more sportsmanlike to catch him in a trap. [*Crofts, understanding the insult, makes a threatening movement.*] Crofts: there are fifteen cartridges in the magazine here; and I am a dead shot at the present distance at an object of your size.

CROFTS. Oh, you needn't be afraid. I'm not going to touch you.

FRANK. Ever so magnanimous of you under the circumstances! Thank you.

CROFTS. I'll just tell you this before I go. It may interest you, since you're so fond of one another. Allow me, Mister Frank, to introduce you to your half-sister, the eldest daughter of the Reverend Samuel Gardner.

Miss Vivie: your half-brother. Good morning. [*He goes out through the gate and along the road.*]

FRANK [*after a pause of stupefaction, raising the rifle*]. You'll testify before the coroner that it's an accident, Viv. [*He takes aim at the retreating figure of Crofts. Vivie seizes the muzzle and pulls it round against her breast.*]

VIVIE. Fire now. You may.

FRANK [*dropping his end of the rifle hastily*]. Stop! take care. [*She lets it go. It falls on the turf.*] Oh, you've given your little boy such a turn. Suppose it had gone off—ugh! [*He sinks on the garden seat, overcome.*]

VIVIE. Suppose it had: do you think it would not have been a relief to have some sharp physical pain tearing through me?

FRANK [*coaxingly*]. Take it ever so easy, dear Viv. Remember: even if the rifle scared that fellow into telling the truth for the first time in his life, that only makes us the babes in the wood in earnest. [*He holds out his arms to her.*] Come and be covered up with leaves again.

VIVIE [*with a cry of disgust*]. Ah, not that, not that. You make all my flesh creep.

FRANK. Why, what's the matter?

VIVIE. Good-bye. [*She makes for the gate.*]

FRANK [*jumping up*]. Hallo! Stop! Viv! Viv! [*She turns in the gateway.*] Where are you going to? Where shall we find you?

VIVIE. At Honoria Fraser's chambers, 67 Chancery Lane, for the rest of my life. [*She goes off quickly in the opposite direction to that taken by Crofts.*]

FRANK. But I say—wait—dash it! [*He runs after her*].

ACT FOUR

Honoria Fraser's chambers in Chancery Lane. An office at the top of New Stone Buildings, with a plate-glass window, distempered walls, electric light, and a patent stove. Saturday afternoon. The chimneys of Lincoln's Inn and the western sky beyond are seen through the window. There is a double writing table in the middle of the room, with a cigar box, ash pans, and a portable electric reading lamp almost snowed up in heaps of papers and books. This table has knee holes and chairs right and left and is very untidy. The clerk's desk, closed and tidy, with its high stool, is against the wall, near a door communicating with the inner rooms. In the opposite wall is the door leading to the public corridor. Its upper panel is of opaque glass, lettered in black on the outside, "Fraser and Warren." A baize screen hides the corner between this door and the window.

Frank, in a fashionable light-colored coaching suit, with his stick, gloves, and white hat in his hands, is pacing up and down the office. Somebody tries the door with a key.

FRANK [*calling*]. Come in. It's not locked.

[*Vivie comes in, in her hat and jacket. She stops and stares at him.*]

VIVIE [*sternly*]. What are you doing here?

FRANK. Waiting to see you. I've been here for hours. Is this the way you attend to your business? [*He puts his hat and stick on the table, and perches himself with a vault on the clerk's stool, looking at her with every appearance of being in a specially restless, teasing, flippant mood.*]

VIVIE. I've been away exactly twenty minutes for a cup of tea. [*She takes off her hat and jacket and hangs them up behind the screen.*] How did you get in?

FRANK. The staff had not left when I arrived. He's gone to play football on Primrose Hill. Why don't you employ a woman, and give your sex a chance?

VIVIE. What have you come for?

FRANK [*springing off the stool and coming close to her*]. Viv: let's go and enjoy the Saturday half-holiday somewhere, like the staff. What do you say to Richmond, and then a music hall, and a jolly supper?

VIVIE. Can't afford it. I shall put in another six hours' work before I go to bed.

FRANK. Can't afford it, can't we? Aha! Look here. [*He takes out a handful of sovereigns and makes them chink.*] Gold, Viv, gold!

VIVIE. Where did you get it?

FRANK. Gambling, Viv, gambling. Poker.

VIVIE. Pah! It's meaner than stealing it. No: I'm not coming. [*She sits down to work at the table, with her back to the glass door, and begins turning over the papers.*]

FRANK [*remonstrating piteously*]. But, my dear Viv, I want to talk to you ever so seriously.

VIVIE. Very well: sit down in Honoria's chair and talk here. I like ten minutes' chat after tea. [*He murmurs.*] No use groaning: I'm inexorable. [*He takes the opposite seat disconsolately.*] Pass that cigar box, will you?

FRANK [*pushing the cigar box across*]. Nasty womanly habit. Nice men don't do it any longer.

VIVIE. Yes: they object to the smell in the office; and we've had to take to cigarets. See! [*She opens the box and takes out a cigaret, which she lights. She offers him one; but he shakes his head with a wry face. She settles herself comfortably in her chair, smoking.*] Go ahead.

FRANK. Well, I want to know what you've done— what arrangements you've made.

VIVIE. Everything was settled twenty minutes after I arrived here. Honoria has found the business too much for her this year; and she was on the point of sending for me and proposing a partnership when I walked in and told her I hadn't a farthing in the world. So I installed myself and packed her off for a fortnight's holiday. What happened at Haslemere when I left?

FRANK. Nothing at all. I said you'd gone to town on particular business.

VIVIE. Well?

FRANK. Well, either they were too flabbergasted to say anything, or else Crofts had prepared your mother. Anyhow, she didn't say anything; and Crofts didn't say anything; and Praddy only stared. After tea they got up and went; and I've not seen them since.

VIVIE [*nodding placidly with one eye on a wreath of smoke*]. That's all right.

FRANK [*looking round disparagingly.*] Do you intend to stick in this confounded place?

VIVIE [*blowing the wreath decisively away and sitting straight up*]. Yes. These two days have given me back all my strength and self-possession. I will never take a holiday again as long as I live.

FRANK [*with a very wry face*]. Mps! You look quite happy—and as hard as nails.

VIVIE [*grimly*]. Well for me that I am!

FRANK [*rising*]. Look here, Viv: we must have an explanation. We parted the other day under a complete misunderstanding.

VIVIE [*putting away the cigaret*]. Well: clear it up.

FRANK. You remember what Crofts said?

VIVIE. Yes.

FRANK. That revelation was supposed to bring about a complete change in the nature of our feeling for one another. It placed us on the footing of brother and sister.

VIVIE. Yes.

FRANK. Have you ever had a brother?

VIVIE. No.

FRANK. Then you don't know what being brother and sister feels like? Now I have lots of sisters: Jessie and Georgina and the rest. The fraternal feeling is quite familiar to me; and I assure you my feeling for you is not the least in the world like it. The girls will go their way; I will go mine; and we shan't care if we never see one another again. That's brother and sister. But as to you, I can't be easy if I have to pass a week without seeing you. That's not brother and sister. It's exactly what I felt an hour before Crofts made his revelation. In short, dear Viv, it's love's young dream.

VIVIE [*bitingly*]. The same feeling, Frank, that brought your father to my mother's feet. Is that it?

FRANK [*revolted*]. I very strongly object, Viv, to have my feelings compared to any which the Reverend Samuel is capable of harboring; and I object still more to a comparison of you to your mother. Besides, I don't believe the story. I have taxed my father with it, and obtained from him what I consider tantamount to a denial.

VIVIE. What did he say?

FRANK. He said he was sure there must be some mistake.

VIVIE. Do you believe him?

FRANK. I am prepared to take his word as against Crofts'.

VIVIE. Does it make any difference? I mean in your

imagination or conscience; for of course it makes no real difference.

FRANK [*shaking his head*]. None whatever to me.

VIVIE. Nor to me.

FRANK [*staring*]. But this is ever so surprising! I thought our whole relations were altered in your imagination and conscience, as you put it, the moment those words were out of that brute's muzzle.

VIVIE. No: it was not that. I didn't believe him. I only wish I could.

FRANK. Eh?

VIVIE. I think brother and sister would be a very suitable relation for us.

FRANK. You really mean that?

VIVIE. Yes. It's the only relation I care for, even if we could afford any other. I mean that.

FRANK [*raising his eyebrows like one on whom a new light has dawned, and speaking with quite an effusion of chivalrous sentiment*]. My dear Viv: why didn't you say so before? I am ever so sorry for persecuting you. I understand, of course.

VIVIE [*puzzled*]. Understand what?

FRANK. Oh, I'm not a fool in the ordinary sense— only in the Scriptural sense of doing all the things the wise man declared to be folly, after trying them himself on the most extensive scale. I see I am no longer Vivvums' little boy. Don't be alarmed: I shall never call you Vivvums again—at least unless you get tired of your new little boy, whoever he may be.

VIVIE. My new little boy!

FRANK [*with conviction*]. Must be a new little boy. Always happens that way. No other way, in fact.

VIVIE. None that you know of, fortunately for you. [*Someone knocks at the door.*]

FRANK. My curse upon yon caller, whoe'er he be!

VIVIE. It's Praed. He's going to Italy and wants to say good-bye. I asked him to call this afternoon. Go and let him in.

FRANK. We can continue our conversation after his departure for Italy. I'll stay him out. [*He goes to the door and opens it.*] How are you, Praddy? Delighted to see you. Come in. [*Praed, dressed for travelling, comes in, in high spirits, excited by the beginning of his journey.*]

PRAED. How do you do, Miss Warren. [*She presses his hand cordially, though a certain sentimentality in his high spirits jars on her.*] I start in an hour from Holborn Viaduct. I wish I could persuade you to try Italy.

VIVIE. What for?

PRAED. Why, to saturate yourself with beauty and romance, of course. [*Vivie, with a shudder, turns her chair to the table, as if the work waiting for her there were a consolation and support to her. Praed sits opposite to her. Frank places a chair just behind Vivie, and drops lazily and carelessly into it, talking at her over his shoulder.*]

FRANK. No use, Praddy. Viv is a little Philistine. She is indifferent to my romance, and insensible to my beauty.

VIVIE. Mr. Praed: once for all, there is no beauty and no romance in life for me. Life is what it is; and I am prepared to take it as it is.

PRAED [*enthusiastically*]. You will not say that if you come to Verona and on to Venice. You will cry with delight at living in such a beautiful world.

FRANK. This is most eloquent, Praddy. Keep it up.

PRAED. Oh, I assure you *I* have cried—I shall cry again, I hope—at fifty! At your age, Miss Warren, you would not need to go so far as Verona. Your spirits would absolutely fly up at the mere sight of Ostend. You would be charmed with the gaiety, the vivacity, the happy air of Brussels. [*Vivie recoils.*] What's the matter?

FRANK. Hallo, Viv!

VIVIE [*to Praed with deep reproach*]. Can you find no better example of your beauty and romance than Brussels to talk to me about?

PRAED [*puzzled*]. Of course it's very different from Verona. I don't suggest for a moment that—

VIVIE [*bitterly*]. Probably the beauty and romance come to much the same in both places.

PRAED [*completely sobered and much concerned*]. My dear Miss Warren: I— [*looking enquiringly at Frank*] Is anything the matter?

FRANK. She thinks your enthusiasm frivolous, Praddy. She's had ever such a serious call.

VIVIE [*sharply*]. Hold your tongue, Frank. Don't be silly.

FRANK [*calmly*]. Do you call this good manners, Praed?

PRAED [*anxious and considerate*]. Shall I take him away, Miss Warren? I feel sure we have disturbed you at your work. [*He is about to rise.*]

VIVIE. Sit down: I'm not ready to go back to work yet. You both think I have an attack of nerves. Not a bit of it. But there are two subjects I want dropped, if you don't mind. One of them [*to Frank*] is love's young dream in any shape or form: the other [*to Praed*] is the romance and beauty of life, especially as exemplified by the gaiety of Brussels. You are welcome to any illusions you may have left on these subjects: I have none. If we three are to remain friends, I must be treated as a woman of business, permanently single [*to Frank*] and permanently unromantic [*to Praed*].

FRANK. I also shall remain permanently single until you change your mind. Praddy: change the subject. Be eloquent about something else.

PRAED [*diffidently*]. I'm afraid there's nothing else in the world that I can talk about. The Gospel of Art is the only one I can preach. I know Miss Warren is a great devotee of the Gospel of Getting On; but we can't discuss that without hurting your feelings, Frank, since you are determined not to get on.

FRANK. Oh, don't mind my feelings. Give me some improving advice by all means; it does me ever so much good. Have another try to make a successful man of me, Viv. Come: let's have it all: energy, thrift, foresight, self-respect, character. Don't you hate people who have no character, Viv?

VIVIE [*wincing*]. Oh, stop: stop: let us have no more of that horrible cant. Mr. Praed: if there are really only those two gospels in the world, we had better all kill ourselves; for the same taint is in both, through and through.

FRANK [*looking critically at her*]. There is a touch of poetry about you to-day, Viv, which has hitherto been lacking.

PRAED [*remonstrating*]. My dear Frank: aren't you a little unsympathetic?

VIVIE [*merciless to herself*]. No: it's good for me. It keeps me from being sentimental.

FRANK [*bantering her*]. Checks your strong natural propensity that way, don't it?

VIVIE [*almost hysterically*]. Oh, yes: go on: don't spare me. I was sentimental for a moment in my life—beautifully sentimental—by moonlight; and now—

FRANK [*quickly*]. I say, Viv: take care. Don't give yourself away.

VIVIE. Oh, do you think Mr. Praed does not know all about my mother? [*Turning on Praed.*] You had better have told me that morning, Mr. Praed. You are very old-fashioned in your delicacies, after all.

PRAED. Surely it is you who are a little old-fashioned in your prejudices, Miss Warren. I feel bound to tell you, speaking as an artist, and believing that the most intimate human relationships are far beyond and above the scope of the law, that though I know that your mother is an unmarried woman, I do not respect her the less on that account. I respect her more.

FRANK [*airily*]. Hear, hear!

VIVIE [*staring at him*]. Is that all you know?

PRAED. Certainly that is all.

VIVIE. Then you neither of you know anything. Your guesses are innocence itself compared to the truth.

PRAED [*startled and indignant, preserving his politeness with an effort*]. I hope not. [*More emphatically.*] I hope not, Miss Warren. [*Frank's face shows that he does not share Praed's incredulity. Vivie utters an exclamation of impatience. Praed's chivalry droops before their conviction. He adds, slowly*] If there is anything worse—that is, anything else—are you sure you are right to tell us, Miss Warren?

VIVIE. I am sure that if I had the courage I should spend the rest of my life in telling it to everybody—in stamping and branding it into them until they felt their share in its shame and horror as I feel mine. There is nothing I despise more than the wicked convention that protects these things by forbidding a woman to mention them. And yet I can't tell you. The two infamous words that describe what my mother is are ringing in my ears and struggling on my tongue; but I can't utter them: my instinct is too strong for me. [*She buries her face in her hands. The two men, astonished, stare at one another and then at her. She raises her head again desperately and takes a sheet of paper and a pen.*] Here: let me draft you a prospectus.

FRANK. Oh, she's mad. Do you hear, Viv, mad. Come: pull yourself together.

VIVIE. You shall see. [*She writes.*] "Paid up capital: not less than £40,000 standing in the name of Sir George Crofts, Baronet, the chief shareholder." What comes next?—I forget. Oh, yes: "Premises at Brussels, Berlin, Vienna and Buda-Pesth. Managing director: Mrs. Warren;" and now don't let us forget her qualifications: the two words. There! [*She pushes the paper to them.*] Oh, no: don't read it: don't! [*She snatches it back and tears it to pieces; then seizes her head in her hands and hides her face on the table. Frank, who has watched the writing carefully over her shoulder, and opened his eyes very widely at it, takes a card from his pocket; scribbles a couple of words; and silently hands it to Praed, who looks at it with amazement. Frank then remorsefully stoops over Vivie.*]

FRANK [*whispering tenderly*]. Viv, dear: that's all right. I read what you wrote: so did Praddy. We understand. And we remain, as this leaves us at present, yours ever so devotedly. [*Vivie slowly raises her head.*]

PRAED. We do, indeed, Miss Warren. I declare you are the most splendidly courageous woman I ever met. [*This sentimental compliment braces Vivie. She throws it away from her with an impatient shake, and forces herself to stand up, though not without some support from the table.*]

FRANK. Don't stir, Viv, if you don't want to. Take it easy.

VIVIE. Thank you. You can always depend on me for two things, not to cry and not to faint. [*She moves a few steps towards the door of the inner rooms, and stops close to Praed to say*] I shall need much more courage than that when I tell my mother that we have come to the parting of the ways. Now I must go into the next room for a moment to make myself neat again, if you don't mind.

PRAED. Shall we go away?

VIVIE. No: I'll be back presently. Only for a moment. [*She goes into the other room, Praed opening the door for her.*]

PRAED. What an amazing revelation! I'm extremely disappointed in Crofts: I am indeed.

FRANK. I'm not in the least. I feel he's perfectly accounted for at last. But what a facer for me, Praddy! I can't marry her now.

PRAED [*sternly*]. Frank! [*The two look at one another, Frank unruffled, Praed deeply indignant.*] Let me tell you, Gardner, that if you desert her now you will behave very despicably.

FRANK. Good old Praddy! Ever chivalrous! But you mistake: it's not the moral aspect of the case: it's the money aspect. I really can't bring myself to touch the old woman's money now.

PRAED. And was that what you were going to marry on?

FRANK. What else? *I* haven't any money, nor the smallest turn for making it. If I married Viv now she would have to support me; and I should cost her more than I am worth.

PRAED. But surely a clever, bright fellow like you can make something by your own brains.

FRANK. Oh, yes, a little. [*He takes out his money again.*] I made all that yesterday—in an hour and a half. But I made it in a highly speculative business. No, dear Praddy: even if Jessie and Georgina marry millionaires and the governor dies after cutting them off with a shilling, I shall have only four hundred a year. And he won't die until he's three score and ten: he hasn't originality enough. I shall be on short allowance for the next twenty years. No short allowance for Viv, if I can help it. I withdraw gracefully and leave the field to the gilded youth of England. So that's settled. I shan't worry her about it: I'll just send her a little note after we're gone. She'll understand.

PRAED [*grasping his hand*]. Good fellow, Frank! I heartily beg your pardon. But must you never see her again?

FRANK. Never see her again! Hang it all, be reasonable. I shall come along as often as possible, and be her brother. I cannot understand the absurd consequences you romantic people expect from the most ordinary transactions. [*A knock at the door.*] I wonder who this is. Would you mind opening the door? If it's a client it will look more respectable than if I appeared.

PRAED. Certainly. [*He goes to the door and opens it. Frank sits down in Vivie's chair to scribble a note.*] My dear Kitty: come in, come in.

[*Mrs. Warren comes in, looking apprehensively round for Vivie. She has done her best to make herself matronly and dignified. The brilliant hat is replaced by a sober bonnet, and the gay blouse covered by a costly black silk mantle. She is pitiably anxious and ill at ease—evidently panic-stricken.*]

MRS. WARREN [*to Frank*]. What! You're here, are you?

FRANK [*turning in his chair from his writing, but not rising*]. Here, and charmed to see you. You come like a breath of spring.

MRS. WARREN. Oh, get out with your nonsense. [*In a low voice.*] Where's Vivie?

[*Frank points expressively to the door of the inner room, but says nothing.*]

MRS. WARREN [*sitting down suddenly and almost beginning to cry*]. Praddy: won't she see me, don't you think?

PRAED. My dear Kitty: don't distress yourself. Why should she not?

MRS. WARREN. Oh, you never can see why not: you're too amiable. Mr. Frank: did she say anything to you?

FRANK [*folding his note*]. She must see you, if [*very expressively*] you wait until she comes in.

MRS. WARREN [*frightened*]. Why shouldn't I wait?

[*Frank looks quizzically at her; puts his note carefully on the ink-bottle, so that Vivie cannot fail to find it when next she dips her pen; then rises and devotes his attention entirely to her.*]

FRANK. My dear Mrs. Warren: suppose you were a sparrow—ever so tiny and pretty a sparrow hopping in the roadway—and you saw a steam roller coming in your direction, would you wait for it?

MRS. WARREN. Oh, don't bother me with your sparrows. What did she run away from Haslemere like that for?

FRANK. I'm afraid she'll tell you if you wait until she comes back.

MRS. WARREN. Do you want me to go away?

FRANK. No. I always want you to stay. But I advise you to go away.

MRS. WARREN. What! And never see her again!

FRANK. Precisely.

MRS. WARREN [*crying again*]. Praddy: don't let him be cruel to me. [*She hastily checks her tears and wipes her eyes.*] She'll be so angry if she sees I've been crying.

FRANK [*with a touch of real compassion in his airy tenderness*]. You know that Praddy is the soul of kindness, Mrs. Warren. Praddy: what do you say? Go or stay?

PRAED [*to Mrs. Warren*]. I really should be very sorry to cause you unnecessary pain; but I think perhaps you had better not wait. The fact is— [*Vivie is heard at the inner door.*]

FRANK. Sh! Too late. She's coming.

MRS. WARREN. Don't tell her I was crying. [*Vivie comes in. She stops gravely on seeing Mrs. Warren, who greets her with hysterical cheerfulness.*] Well, dearie. So here you are at last.

VIVIE. I am glad you have come: I want to speak to you. You said you were going, Frank, I think.

FRANK. Yes. Will you come with me, Mrs. Warren? What do you say to a trip to Richmond, and the theatre in the evening? There is safety in Richmond. No steam roller there.

VIVIE. Nonsense, Frank. My mother will stay here.

MRS. WARREN [*scared*]. I don't know: perhaps I'd better go. We're disturbing you at your work.

VIVIE [*with quiet decision*]. Mr. Praed: please take Frank away. Sit down, mother. [*Mrs. Warren obeys helplessly.*]

PRAED. Come, Frank. Good-bye, Miss Vivie.

VIVIE [*shaking hands*]. Good-bye. A pleasant trip.

PRAED. Thank you: thank you. I hope so.

FRANK [to Mrs. Warren]. Good-bye: you'd ever so much better have taken my advice. [He shakes hands with her. Then airily to Vivie] Bye-bye, Viv.

VIVIE. Good-bye. [He goes out gaily without shaking hands with her. Praed follows. Vivie, composed and extremely grave, sits down in Honoria's chair, and waits for her mother to speak. Mrs. Warren, dreading a pause, loses no time in beginning.]

MRS. WARREN. Well, Vivie, what did you go away like that for without saying a word to me? How could you do such a thing! And what have you done to poor George? I wanted him to come with me; but he shuffled out of it. I could see that he was quite afraid of you. Only fancy: he wanted me not to come. As if [trembling] I should be afraid of you, dearie. [Vivie's gravity deepens.] But of course I told him it was all settled and comfortable between us, and that we were on the best of terms. [She breaks down.] Vivie: what's the meaning of this? [She produces a paper from an envelope; comes to the table; and hands it across.] I got it from the bank this morning.

VIVIE. It is my month's allowance. They sent it to me as usual the other day. I simply sent it back to be placed to your credit, and asked them to send you the lodgment receipt. In future I shall support myself.

MRS. WARREN [not daring to understand]. Wasn't it enough? Why didn't you tell me? [With a cunning gleam in her eye.] I'll double it: I was intending to double it. Only let me know how much you want.

VIVIE. You know very well that that has nothing to do with it. From this time I go my own way in my own business and among my own friends. And you will go yours. [She rises.] Good-bye.

MRS. WARREN [appalled]. Good-bye?

VIVIE. Yes: good-bye. Come: don't let us make a useless scene: you understand perfectly well. Sir George Crofts has told me the whole business.

MRS. WARREN [angrily]. Silly old— [She swallows an epithet, and turns white at the narrowness of her escape from uttering it.] He ought to have his tongue cut out.

But I explained it all to you; and you said you didn't mind.

VIVIE [*steadfastly*]. Excuse me: I do mind. You explained how it came about. That does not alter it.

[*Mrs. Warren, silenced for a moment, looks forlornly at Vivie, who waits like a statue, secretly hoping that the combat is over. But the cunning expression comes back into Mrs. Warren's face; and she bends across the table, sly and urgent, half whispering.*]

MRS. WARREN. Vivie: do you know how rich I am?

VIVIE. I have no doubt you are very rich.

MRS. WARREN. But you don't know all that that means: you're too young. It means a new dress every day; it means theatres and balls every night; it means having the pick of all the gentlemen in Europe at your feet; it means a lovely house and plenty of servants; it means the choicest of eating and drinking; it means everything you like, everything you want, everything you can think of. And what are you here? A mere drudge, toiling and moiling early and late for your bare living and two cheap dresses a year. Think it over. [*Soothingly.*] You're shocked, I know. I can enter into your feelings; and I think they do you credit; but trust me, nobody will blame you: you may take my word for that. I know what young girls are; and I know you'll think better of it when you've turned it over in your mind.

VIVIE. So that's how it's done, is it? You must have said all that to many a woman, mother, to have it so pat.

MRS. WARREN [*passionately*]. What harm am I asking you to do? [*Vivie turns away contemptuously. Mrs. Warren follows her desperately.*] Vivie: listen to me: you don't understand: you've been taught wrong on purpose: you don't know what the world is really like.

VIVIE [*arrested*]. Taught wrong on purpose! What do you mean?

MRS. WARREN. I mean that you're throwing away all your chances for nothing. You think that people are what they pretend to be—that the way you were taught at school and college to think right and proper is the way things really are. But it's not: it's all only a pretence, to keep the cowardly, slavish, common run of people

quiet. Do you want to find that out, like other women,
at forty, when you've thrown yourself away and lost your
chances; or won't you take it in good time now from
your own mother, that loves you and swears to you that
it's truth—gospel truth? [*Urgently.*] Vivie: the big people,
the clever people, the managing people, all know it.
They do as I do, and think what I think. I know plenty
of them. I know them to speak to, to introduce you to,
to make friends of for you. I don't mean anything wrong:
that's what you don't understand: your head is full of
ignorant ideas about me. What do the people that taught
you know about life or about people like me? When did
they ever meet me, or speak to me, or let anyone tell
them about me?—the fools! Would they ever have done
anything for you if you hadn't paid them? Haven't I told
you that I want you to be respectable? Haven't I brought
you up to be respectable? And how can you keep it up
without my money and my influence and Lizzie's
friends? Can't you see that you're cutting your own
throat as well as breaking my heart in turning your back
on me?

VIVIE. I recognise the Crofts philosophy of life,
mother. I heard it all from him that day at the Gardners'.

MRS. WARREN. You think I want to force that played-
out old sot on you! I don't, Vivie: on my oath I don't.

VIVIE. It would not matter if you did: you would not
succeed. [*Mrs. Warren winces, deeply hurt by the implied
indifference towards her affectionate intention. Vivie, neither understanding this nor concerning herself about it,
goes on calmly*] Mother: you don't at all know the sort
of person I am. I don't object to Crofts more than to
any other coarsely built man of his class. To tell you the
truth, I rather admire him for being strong-minded
enough to enjoy himself in his own way and make plenty
of money instead of living the usual shooting, hunting,
dining-out, tailoring, loafing life of his set merely because all the rest do it. And I'm perfectly aware that if
I'd been in the same circumstances as my aunt Liz, I'd
have done exactly what she did. I don't think I'm more
prejudiced or straitlaced than you: I think I'm less. I'm
certain I'm less sentimental. I know very well that fashionable morality is all a pretence: and that if I took your

money and devoted the rest of my life to spending it
fashionably, I might be as worthless and vicious as the
silliest woman could possibly want to be without having
a word said to me about it. But I don't want to be worthless. I shouldn't enjoy trotting about the park to adver-
tise my dressmaker and carriage builder, or being bored
at the opera to show off a shop windowful of diamonds.

MRS. WARREN [*bewildered*]. But—

VIVIE. Wait a moment: I've not done. Tell me why
you continue your business now that you are independent of it. Your sister, you told me, has left all that
behind her. Why don't you do the same?

MRS. WARREN. Oh, it's all very easy for Liz: she likes
good society, and has the air of being a lady. Imagine
me in a cathedral town! Why, the very rooks in the trees
would find me out even if I could stand the dulness of
it. I must have work and excitement, or I should go
melancholy mad. And what else is there for me to do?
The life suits me: I'm fit for it and not for anything else.
If I didn't do it somebody else would; so I don't do any
real harm by it. And then it brings in money; and I like
making money. No: it's no use: I can't give it up—not
for anybody. But what need you know about it? I'll
never mention it. I'll keep Crofts away. I'll not trouble
you much: you see I have to be constantly running about
from one place to another. You'll be quit of me altogether when I die.

VIVIE. No: I am my mother's daughter. I am like
you: I must have work, and must make more money
than I spend. But my work is not your work, and my
way not your way. We must part. It will not make much
difference to us: instead of meeting one another for perhaps a few months in twenty years, we shall never meet:
that's all.

MRS. WARREN [*her voice stifled in tears*]. Vivie: I
meant to have been more with you: I did indeed.

VIVIE. It's no use, mother: I am not to be changed
by a few cheap tears and entreaties any more than you
are, I dare say.

MRS. WARREN [*wildly*]. Oh, you call a mother's
tears cheap.

VIVIE. They cost you nothing; and you ask me to

give you the peace and quietness of my whole life in exchange for them. What use would my company be to you if you could get it? What have we two in common that could make either of us happy together?

MRS. WARREN [*lapsing recklessly into her dialect*]. We're mother and daughter. I want my daughter. I've a right to you. Who is to care for me when I'm old? Plenty of girls have taken to me like daughters and cried at leaving me; but I let them all go because I had you to look forward to. I kept myself lonely for you. You've no right to turn on me now and refuse to do your duty as a daughter.

VIVIE [*jarred and antagonized by the echo of the slums in her mother's voice*]. My duty as a daughter! I thought we should come to that presently. Now once for all, mother, you want a daughter and Frank wants a wife. I don't want a mother; and I don't want a husband. I have spared neither Frank nor myself in sending him about his business. Do you think I will spare you?

MRS. WARREN [*violently*]. Oh, I know the sort you are—no mercy for yourself or anyone else. *I* know. My experience has done that for me anyhow: I can tell the pious, canting, hard, selfish woman when I meet her. Well, keep yourself to yourself: *I* don't want you. But listen to this. Do you know what I would do with you if you were a baby again—aye, as sure as there's a Heaven above us?

VIVIE. Strangle me, perhaps.

MRS. WARREN. No: I'd bring you up to be a real daughter to me, and not what you are now, with your pride and your prejudices and the college education you stole from me—yes, stole: deny it if you can: what was it but stealing? I'd bring you up in my own house, so I would.

VIVIE [*quietly*]. In one of your own houses.

MRS. WARREN [*screaming*]. Listen to her! listen to how she spits on her mother's grey hairs! Oh, may you live to have your own daughter tear and trample on you as you have trampled on me. And you will: you will. No woman ever had luck with a mother's curse on her.

VIVIE. I wish you wouldn't rant, mother. It only hardens me. Come: I suppose I am the only young woman you ever had in your power that you did good to. Don't spoil it all now.

MRS. WARREN. Yes. Heaven forgive me, it's true; and you are the only one that ever turned on me. Oh, the injustice of it, the injustice, the injustice! I always wanted to be a good woman. I tried honest work; and I was slave-driven until I cursed the day I ever heard of honest work. I was a good mother; and because I made my daughter a good woman she turns me out as if I was a leper. Oh, if I only had my life to live over again! I'd talk to that lying clergyman in the school. From this time forth, so help me Heaven in my last hour, I'll do wrong and nothing but wrong. And I'll prosper on it.

VIVIE. Yes: it's better to choose your line and go through with it. If I had been you, mother, I might have done as you did; but I should not have lived one life and believed in another. You are a conventional woman at heart. That is why I am bidding you good-bye now. I am right, am I not?

MRS. WARREN [taken aback]. Right to throw away all my money!

VIVIE. No: right to get rid of you? I should be a fool not to? Isn't that so?

MRS. WARREN [sulkily]. Oh, well, yes, if you come to that, I suppose you are. But Lord help the world if everybody took to doing the right thing! And now I'd better go than stay where I'm not wanted. [She turns to the door.]

VIVIE [kindly]. Won't you shake hands?

MRS. WARREN [after looking at her fiercely for a moment with a savage impulse to strike her]. No, thank you. Good-bye.

VIVIE [matter-of-factly]. Good-bye. [Mrs. Warren goes out, slamming the door behind her. The strain on Vivie's face relaxes; her grave expression breaks up into one of joyous content; her breath goes out in a half sob, half laugh of intense relief. She goes buoyantly to her place at the writing table; pushes the electric lamp out of the way; pulls over a great sheaf of papers; and is in the act of dipping her pen in the ink when she finds Frank's note. She opens it unconcernedly and reads it quickly, giving a little laugh at some quaint turn of expression in *it.*] And good-bye, Frank. [*She tears the note up and tosses the pieces into the wastepaper basket without a second thought. Then she goes at her work with a plunge, and soon becomes absorbed in her figures.*]

Arms and
the Man

ACT ONE

Night. A lady's bedchamber in Bulgaria, in a small town near the Dragoman Pass. It is late in November in the year 1885, and through an open window with a little balcony on the left can be seen a peak of the Balkans, wonderfully white and beautiful in the starlit snow. The interior of the room is not like anything to be seen in the east of Europe. It is half rich Bulgarian, half cheap Viennese. The counterpane and hangings of the bed, the window curtains, the little carpet, and all the ornamental textile fabrics in the room are oriental and gorgeous: the paper on the walls is occidental and paltry. Above the head of the bed, which stands against a little wall cutting off the right hand corner of the room diagonally, is a painted wooden shrine, blue and gold, with an ivory image of Christ, and a light hanging before it in a pierced metal ball suspended by three chains. On the left, further forward, is an ottoman. The washstand, against the wall on the left, consists of an enamelled iron basin with a pail beneath it in a painted metal frame, and a single towel on the rail at the side. A chair near it is Austrian bent wood, with cane seat. The dressing table, between the bed and the window, is an ordinary pine table, covered with a cloth of many colors, but with an expensive toilet mirror on it. The door is on the right; and there is a chest of drawers between the door and the bed. This chest of drawers is also covered by a variegated native cloth, and on it there is a pile of paper backed novels, a box of chocolate creams, and a miniature easel, on which is a large photograph of an extremely handsome officer, whose lofty bearing and magnetic glance can be felt even from the portrait. The room is lighted by a candle on the chest of drawers, and another on the dressing table, with a box of matches beside it.

The window is hinged doorwise and stands wide open, folding back to.the left. Outside a pair of wooden shutters, opening outwards, also stand open. On the balcony, a young lady, intensely conscious of the romantic beauty of the night, and of the fact that her own youth and beauty is a part of it, is on the balcony, gazing at the snowy Balkans. She is covered by a long mantle of furs, worth, on a moderate estimate, about three times the furniture of her room.

Her reverie is interrupted by her mother, Catherine Petkoff, a woman over forty, imperiously energetic, with magnificent black hair and eyes, who might be a very splendid specimen of the wife of a mountain farmer, but is determined to be a Viennese lady, and to that end wears a fashionable tea gown on all occasions.

CATHERINE [*entering hastily, full of good news*]. Raina— [*she pronounces it Rah-eena, with the stress on the ee*] Raina— [*she goes to the bed, expecting to find Raina there.*] Why, where— [*Raina looks into the room.*] Heavens! child, are you out in the night air instead of in your bed? You'll catch your death. Louka told me you were asleep.

RAINA [*coming in*]. I sent her away. I wanted to be alone. The stars are so beautiful! What is the matter?

CATHERINE. Such news. There has been a battle!

RAINA [*her eyes dilating*]. Ah! [*She throws the cloak on the ottoman, and comes eagerly to Catherine in her nightgown, a pretty garment, but evidently the only one she has on.*]

CATHERINE. A great battle at Slivnitza! A victory! And it was won by Sergius.

RAINA [*with a cry of delight*]. Ah! [*Rapturously.*] Oh, mother! [*Then, with sudden anxiety*] Is father safe?

CATHERINE. Of course: he sent me the news. Sergius is the hero of the hour, the idol of the regiment.

RAINA. Tell me, tell me. How was it! [*Ecstatically.*] Oh, mother, mother, mother! [*Raina pulls her mother down on the ottoman; and they kiss one another frantically.*]

CATHERINE [*with surging enthusiasm*]. You can't guess how splendid it is. A cavalry charge—think of that! He defied our Russian commanders—acted without orders—led a charge on his own responsibility—headed it himself—was the first man to sweep through their guns. Can't you see it, Raina; our gallant splendid Bulgarians with their swords and eyes flashing, thundering down like an avalanche and scattering the wretched Servian dandies like chaff. And you—you kept Sergius waiting a year before you would be betrothed to him. Oh, if you have a drop of Bulgarian blood in your veins, you will worship him when he comes back.

RAINA. What will he care for my poor little worship after the acclamations of a whole army of heroes? But no matter: I am so happy—so proud! [*She rises and walks about excitedly.*] It proves that all our ideas were real after all.

CATHERINE [*indignantly*]. Our ideas real! What do you mean?

RAINA. Our ideas of what Sergius would do—our patriotism—our heroic ideals. Oh, what faithless little creatures girls are!— I sometimes used to doubt whether they were anything but dreams. When I buckled on Sergius's sword he looked so noble: it was treason to think of disillusion or humiliation or failure. And yet—and yet— [*Quickly.*] Promise me you'll never tell him.

CATHERINE. Don't ask me for promises until I know what I am promising.

RAINA. Well, it came into my head just as he was holding me in his arms and looking into my eyes, that perhaps we only had our heroic ideas because we are so fond of reading Byron and Pushkin, and because we were so delighted with the opera that season at Bucharest. Real life is so seldom like that—indeed never, as far as I knew it then. [*Remorsefully.*] Only think, mother, I doubted him: I wondered whether all his heroic qualities and his soldiership might not prove mere imagination when he went into a real battle. I had an uneasy fear that he might cut a poor figure there beside all those clever Russian officers.

CATHERINE. A poor figure! Shame on you! The Servians have Austrian officers who are just as clever as
our Russians; but we have beaten them in every battle
for all that.

RAINA [*laughing and sitting down again*]. Yes, I was
only a prosaic little coward. Oh, to think that it was all
true—that Sergius is just as splendid and noble as he
looks—that the world is really a glorious world for
women who can see its glory and men who can act its
romance! What happiness! what unspeakable fulfilment!
Ah! [*She throws herself on her knees beside her mother
and flings her arms passionately round her. They are interrupted by the entry of Louka, a handsome, proud girl
in a pretty Bulgarian peasant's dress with double apron,
so defiant that her servility to Raina is almost insolent.
She is afraid of Catherine, but even with her goes as far
as she dares. She is just now excited like the others; but
she has no sympathy for Raina's raptures and looks contemptuously at the ecstasies of the two before she addresses them.*]

LOUKA. If you please, madam, all the windows are
to be closed and the shutters made fast. They say there
may be shooting in the streets. [*Raina and Catherine rise
together, alarmed.*] The Servians are being chased right
back through the pass; and they say they may run into
the town. Our cavalry will be after them; and our people
will be ready for them you may be sure, now that they
are running away. [*She goes out on the balcony and pulls
the outside shutters to; then steps back into the room.*]

RAINA. I wish our people were not so cruel. What
glory is there in killing wretched fugitives?

CATHERINE [*businesslike, her housekeeping instincts
aroused*]. I must see that everything is made safe downstairs.

RAINA [*to Louka*]. Leave the shutters so that I can
just close them if I hear any noise.

CATHERINE [*authoritatively, turning on her way to
the door*]. Oh, no, dear, you must keep them fastened.
You would be sure to drop off to sleep and leave them
open. Make them fast, Louka.

LOUKA. Yes, madam. [*She fastens them.*]

RAINA. Don't be anxious about me. The moment I

hear a shot, I shall blow out the candles and roll myself up in bed with my ears well covered.

CATHERINE. Quite the wisest thing you can do, my love. Good-night.

RAINA. Good-night. [*They kiss one another, and Raina's emotion comes back for a moment.*] Wish me joy of the happiest night of my life—if only there are no fugitives.

CATHERINE. Go to bed, dear, and don't think of them. [*She goes out.*]

LOUKA [*secretly, to Raina*]. If you would like the shutters open, just give them a push like this. [*She pushes them: they open: she pulls them to again.*] One of them ought to be bolted at the bottom; but the bolt's gone.

RAINA [*with dignity, reproving her*]. Thanks, Louka; but we must do what we are told. [*Louka makes a grimace.*] Good-night.

LOUKA [*carelessly*]. Good-night. [*She goes out, swaggering.*]

[*Raina, left alone, goes to the chest of drawers, and adores the portrait there with feelings that are beyond all expression. She does not kiss it or press it to her breast, or shew it any mark of bodily affection; but she takes it in her hands and elevates it like a priestess.*]

RAINA [*looking up at the picture with worship*]. Oh, I shall never be unworthy of you any more, my hero—never, never, never. [*She replaces it reverently, and selects a novel from the little pile of books. She turns over the leaves dreamily; finds her page; turns the book inside out at it; and then, with a happy sigh, gets into bed and prepares to read herself to sleep. But before abandoning herself to fiction, she raises her eyes once more, thinking of the blessed reality and murmurs*] My hero! my hero! [*A distant shot breaks the quiet of the night outside. She starts, listening; and two more shots, much nearer, follow, startling her so that she scrambles out of bed, and hastily blows out the candle on the chest of drawers. Then, putting her fingers in her ears, she runs to the dressing-table and blows out the light there, and hurries back to bed. The room is now in darkness: nothing is visible but the glimmer of the light in the pierced ball before the image, and the starlight seen through the slits at the top of the*

*shutters. The firing breaks out again: there is a startling
fusillade quite close at hand. Whilst it is still echoing, the
shutters disappear, pulled open from without, and for an
instant the rectangle of snowy starlight flashes out with
the figure of a man in black upon it. The shutters close
immediately and the room is dark again. But the silence
is now broken by the sound of panting. Then there is a
scrape; and the flame of a match is seen in the middle of
the room.*]

RAINA [*crouching on the bed*]. Who's there? [*The
match is out instantly.*] Who's there? Who is that?

A MAN'S VOICE [*in the darkness, subduedly, but
threateningly*]. Sh—sh! Don't call out or you'll be shot.
Be good; and no harm will happen to you. [*She is heard
leaving her bed, and making for the door.*] Take care,
there's no use in trying to run away. Remember, if you
raise your voice my pistol will go off. [*Commandingly.*]
Strike a light and let me see you. Do you hear? [*Another
moment of silence and darkness. Then she is heard retreating to the dressing table. She lights a candle, and the
mystery is at an end. A man of about 35, in a deplorable
plight, bespattered with mud and blood and snow, his belt
and the strap of his revolver case keeping together the
torn ruins of the blue coat of a Servian artillery officer.
As far as the candlelight and his unwashed, unkempt condition make it possible to judge, he is a man of middling
stature and undistinguished appearance, with strong neck
and shoulders, a roundish, obstinate looking head covered with short crisp bronze curls, clear quick blue eyes
and good brows and mouth, a hopelessly prosaic nose
like that of a strong-minded baby, trim soldierlike carriage and energetic manner, and with all his wits about
him in spite of his desperate predicament—even with a
sense of humor of it, without, however, the least intention
of trifling with it or throwing away a chance. He reckons
up what he can guess about Raina—her age, her social
position, her character, the extent to which she is frightened—at a glance, and continues, more politely but still
most determinedly*] Excuse my disturbing you; but you
recognise my uniform—Servian. If I'm caught I shall be
killed. [*Determinedly.*] Do you understand that?

RAINA. Yes.

MAN. Well, I don't intend to get killed if I can help it. [*Still more determinedly.*] Do you understand that? [*He locks the door with a snap.*]

RAINA [*disdainfully*]. I suppose not. [*She draws herself up superbly, and looks him straight in the face, saying with emphasis*] Some soldiers, I know, are afraid of death.

MAN [*with grim goodhumor*]. All of them, dear lady, all of them, believe me. It is our duty to live as long as we can, and kill as many of the enemy as we can. Now if you raise an alarm—

RAINA [*cutting him short*]. You will shoot me. How do you know that I am afraid to die?

MAN [*cunningly*]. Ah; but suppose I don't shoot you, what will happen then? Why, a lot of your cavalry—the greatest blackguards in your army—will burst into this pretty room of yours and slaughter me here like a pig; for I'll fight like a demon: they shan't get me into the street to amuse themselves with: I know what they are. Are you prepared to receive that sort of company in your present undress? [*Raina, suddenly conscious of her nightgown, instinctively shrinks and gathers it more closely about her. He watches her, and adds, pitilessly*] It's rather scanty, eh? [*She turns to the ottoman. He raises his pistol instantly, and cries*] Stop! [*She stops.*] Where are you going?

RAINA [*with dignified patience*]. Only to get my cloak.

MAN [*darting to the ottoman and snatching the cloak*]. A good idea. No: I'll keep the cloak: and you will take care that nobody comes in and sees you without it. This is a better weapon than the pistol. [*He throws the pistol down on the ottoman.*]

RAINA [*revolted*]. It is not the weapon of a gentleman!

MAN. It's good enough for a man with only you to stand between him and death. [*As they look at one another for a moment, Raina hardly able to believe that even a Servian officer can be so cynically and selfishly unchivalrous, they are startled by a sharp fusillade in the street. The chill of imminent death hushes the man's voice as he adds*] Do you hear? If you are going to bring those scoundrels in on me you shall receive them as you are. [*Raina meets his eye with unflinching scorn. Suddenly he starts, listening. There is a step outside. Someone tries the door, and then knocks hurriedly and urgently at it. Raina looks at the man, breathless. He throws up his head with the gesture of a man who sees that it is all over with him, and, dropping the manner which he has been assuming to intimidate her, flings the cloak to her, exclaiming, sincerely and kindly*] No use: I'm done for. Quick! wrap yourself up: they're coming!

RAINA [*catching the cloak eagerly*]. Oh, thank you. [*She wraps herself up with great relief. He draws his sabre and turns to the door, waiting.*]

LOUKA [*outside, knocking*]. My lady, my lady! Get up, quick, and open the door.

RAINA [*anxiously*]. What will you do?

MAN [*grimly*]. Never mind. Keep out of the way. It will not last long.

RAINA [*impulsively*]. I'll help you. Hide yourself, oh, hide yourself, quick, behind the curtain. [*She seizes him by a torn strip of his sleeve, and pulls him towards the window.*]

MAN [*yielding to her*]. There is just half a chance, if you keep your head. Remember: nine soldiers out of ten are born fools. [*He hides behind the curtain, looking out for a moment to say, finally*] If they find me, I promise you a fight—a devil of a fight! [*He disappears. Raina takes off the cloak and throws it across the foot of the bed. Then with a sleepy, disturbed air, she opens the door. Louka enters excitedly.*]

LOUKA. A man has been seen climbing up the water-pipe to your balcony—a Servian. The soldiers want to search for him; and they are so wild and drunk and furious. My lady says you are to dress at once.

RAINA [*as if annoyed at being disturbed*]. They shall not search here. Why have they been let in?

CATHERINE [*coming in hastily*]. Raina, darling, are you safe? Have you seen anyone or heard anything?

RAINA. I heard the shooting. Surely the soldiers will not dare come in here?

CATHERINE. I have found a Russian officer, thank

Heaven: he knows Sergius. [*Speaking through the door to someone outside.*] Sir, will you come in now! My daughter is ready.

[*A young Russian officer, in Bulgarian uniform, enters, sword in hand.*]

THE OFFICER [*with soft, feline politeness and stiff military carriage*]. Good evening, gracious lady; I am sorry to intrude, but there is a fugitive hiding on the balcony. Will you and the gracious lady your mother please to withdraw whilst we search?

RAINA [*petulantly*]. Nonsense, sir, you can see that there is no one on the balcony. [*She throws the shutters wide open and stands with her back to the curtain where the man is hidden, pointing to the moonlit balcony. A couple of shots are fired right under the window, and a bullet shatters the glass opposite Raina, who winks and gasps, but stands her ground, whilst Catherine screams, and the officer rushes to the balcony.*]

THE OFFICER [*on the balcony, shouting savagely down to the street*]. Cease firing there, you fools: do you hear? Cease firing, damn you. [*He glares down for a moment; then turns to Raina, trying to resume his polite manner.*] Could anyone have got in without your knowledge? Were you asleep?

RAINA. No, I have not been to bed.

THE OFFICER [*impatiently, coming back into the room*]. Your neighbours have their heads so full of runaway Servians that they see them everywhere. [*Politely.*] Gracious lady, a thousand pardons. Good-night. [*Military bow, which Raina returns coldly. Another to Catherine, who follows him out. Raina closes the shutters. She turns and sees Louka, who has been watching the scene curiously.*]

RAINA. Don't leave my mother, Louka, whilst the soldiers are here. [*Louka glances at Raina, at the ottoman, at the curtain; then purses her lips secretively, laughs to herself, and goes out. Raina follows her to the door, shuts it behind her with a slam, and locks it violently. The man immediately steps out from behind the curtain, sheathing his sabre, and dismissing the danger from his mind in a businesslike way.*]

MAN. A narrow shave; but a miss is as good as a

mile. Dear young lady, your servant until death. I wish for your sake I had joined the Bulgarian army instead of the Servian. I am not a native Servian.

RAINA [*haughtily*]. No, you are one of the Austrians who set the Servians on to rob us of our national liberty, and who officer their army for them. We hate them!

MAN. Austrian! not I. Don't hate me, dear young lady. I am only a Swiss, fighting merely as a professional soldier. I joined Servia because it was nearest to me. Be generous: you've beaten us hollow.

RAINA. Have I not been generous?

MAN. Noble!—heroic! But I'm not saved yet. This particular rush will soon pass through; but the pursuit will go on all night by fits and starts. I must take my chance to get off during a quiet interval. You don't mind my waiting just a minute or two, do you?

RAINA. Oh, no: I am sorry you will have to go into danger again. [*Motioning towards ottoman.*] Won't you sit—[*She breaks off with an irrepressible cry of alarm as she catches sight of the pistol. The man, all nerves, shies like a frightened horse.*]

MAN [*irritably*]. Don't frighten me like that. What is it?

RAINA. Your pistol! It was staring that officer in the face all the time. What an escape!

MAN [*vexed at being unnecessarily terrified*]. Oh, is that all?

RAINA [*staring at him rather superciliously, conceiving a poorer and poorer opinion of him, and feeling proportionately more and more at her ease with him*]. I am sorry I frightened you. [*She takes up the pistol and hands it to him.*] Pray take it to protect yourself against me.

MAN [*grinning wearily at the sarcasm as he takes the pistol*]. No use, dear young lady: there's nothing in it. It's not loaded. [*He makes a grimace at it, and drops it disparagingly into his revolver case.*]

RAINA. Load it by all means.

MAN. I've no ammunition. What use are cartridges in battle? I always carry chocolate instead; and I finished the last cake of that yesterday.

RAINA [*outraged in her most cherished ideals of man-*

hood]. Chocolate! Do you stuff your pockets with sweets—like a schoolboy—even in the field?

MAN. Yes. Isn't it contemptible?

[*Raina stares at him, unable to utter her feelings. Then she sails away scornfully to the chest of drawers, and returns with the box of confectionery in her hand.*]

RAINA. Allow me. I am sorry I have eaten them all except these. [*She offers him the box.*]

MAN [*ravenously*]. You're an angel! [*He gobbles the comfits.*] Creams! Delicious! [*He looks anxiously to see whether there are any more. There are none. He accepts the inevitable with pathetic goodhumor, and says, with grateful emotion*] Bless you, dear lady. You can always tell an old soldier by the inside of his holsters and cartridge boxes. The young ones carry pistols and cartridges; the old ones, grub. Thank you. [*He hands back the box. She snatches it contemptuously from him and throws it away. This impatient action is so sudden that he shies again.*] Ugh! Don't do things so suddenly, gracious lady. Don't revenge yourself because I frightened you just now.

RAINA [*superbly*]. Frighten me! Do you know, sir, that though I am only a woman, I think I am at heart as brave as you.

MAN. I should think so. You haven't been under fire for three days as I have. I can stand two days without shewing it much; but no man can stand three days: I'm as nervous as a mouse. [*He sits down on the ottoman, and takes his head in his hands.*] Would you like to see me cry?

RAINA [*quickly*]. No.

MAN. If you would, all you have to do is to scold me just as if I were a little boy and you my nurse. If I were in camp now they'd play all sorts of tricks on me.

RAINA [*a little moved*]. I'm sorry. I won't scold you. [*Touched by the sympathy in her tone, he raises his head and looks gratefully at her: she immediately draws back and says stiffly*] You must excuse me: our soldiers are not like that. [*She moves away from the ottoman*].

MAN. Oh, yes, they are. There are only two sorts of soldiers: old ones and young ones. I've served fourteen years: half of your fellows never smelt powder before. Why, how is it that you've just beaten us? Sheer ignorance of the art of war, nothing else. [*Indignantly.*] I never saw anything so unprofessional.

RAINA [*ironically*]. Oh, was it unprofessional to beat you?

MAN. Well, come, is it professional to throw a regiment of cavalry on a battery of machine guns, with the dead certainty that if the guns go off not a horse or man will ever get within fifty yards of the fire? I couldn't believe my eyes when I saw it.

RAINA [*eagerly turning to him, as all her enthusiasm and her dream of glory rush back on her*]. Did you see the great cavalry charge? Oh, tell me about it. Describe it to me.

MAN. You never saw a cavalry charge, did you?

RAINA. How could I?

MAN. Ah, perhaps not—of course. Well, it's a funny sight. It's like slinging a handful of peas against a window pane: first one comes; then two or three close behind him; and then all the rest in a lump.

RAINA [*her eyes dilating as she raises her clasped hands ecstatically*]. Yes, first One!—the bravest of the brave!

MAN [*prosaically*]. Hm! you should see the poor devil pulling at his horse.

RAINA. Why should he pull at his horse?

MAN [*impatient of so stupid a question*]. It's running away with him, of course: do you suppose the fellow wants to get there before the others and be killed? Then they all come. You can tell the young ones by their wildness and their slashing. The old ones come bunched up under the number one guard: they know that they are mere projectiles, and that it's no use trying to fight. The wounds are mostly broken knees, from the horses cannoning together.

RAINA. Ugh! But I don't believe the first man is a coward. I believe he is a hero!

MAN [*goodhumoredly*]. That's what you'd have said if you'd seen the first man in the charge to-day.

RAINA [*breathless*]. Ah, I knew it! Tell me—tell me about him.

MAN. He did it like an operatic tenor—a regular handsome fellow, with flashing eyes and lovely moustache, shouting a war-cry and charging like Don Quixote at the windmills. We nearly burst with laughter at him; but when the sergeant ran up as white as a sheet, and told us they'd sent us the wrong cartridges, and that we couldn't fire a shot for the next ten minutes, we laughed at the other side of our mouths. I never felt so sick in my life, though I've been in one or two very tight places. And I hadn't even a revolver cartridge—nothing but chocolate. We'd no bayonets—nothing. Of course, they just cut us to bits. And there was Don Quixote flourishing like a drum major, thinking he'd done the cleverest thing ever known, whereas he ought to be courtmartialled for it. Of all the fools ever let loose on a field of battle, that man must be the very maddest. He and his regiment simply committed suicide—only the pistol missed fire, that's all.

RAINA [*deeply wounded, but steadfastly loyal to her ideals*]. Indeed! Would you know him again if you saw him?

MAN. Shall I ever forget him. [*She again goes to the chest of drawers. He watches her with a vague hope that she may have something else for him to eat. She takes the portrait from its stand and brings it to him.*]

RAINA. That is a photograph of the gentleman—the patriot and hero—to whom I am betrothed.

MAN [*looking at it*]. I'm really very sorry. [*Looking at her.*] Was it fair to lead me on? [*He looks at the portrait again.*] Yes: that's him: not a doubt of it. [*He stifles a laugh.*]

RAINA [*quickly*]. Why do you laugh?

MAN [*shamefacedly, but still greatly tickled*]. I didn't laugh, I assure you. At least I didn't mean to. But when I think of him charging the windmills and thinking he was doing the finest thing— [*chokes with suppressed laughter*].

RAINA [*sternly*]. Give me back the portrait, sir.

MAN [*with sincere remorse*]. Of course. Certainly. I'm really very sorry. [*She deliberately kisses it, and looks him straight in the face, before returning to the chest of drawers to replace it. He follows her, apologizing.*] Perhaps I'm quite wrong, you know: no doubt I am. Most likely he had got wind of the cartridge business somehow, and knew it was a safe job.

RAINA. That is to say, he was a pretender and a coward! You did not dare say that before.

MAN [*with a comic gesture of despair*]. It's no use, dear lady: I can't make you see it from the professional point of view. [*As he turns away to get back to the ottoman, the firing begins again in the distance.*]

RAINA [*sternly, as she sees him listening to the shots*]. So much the better for you.

MAN [*turning*]. How?

RAINA. You are my enemy; and you are at my mercy. What would I do if I were a professional soldier?

MAN. Ah, true, dear young lady: you're always right. I know how good you have been to me: to my last hour I shall remember those three chocolate creams. It was unsoldierly; but it was angelic.

RAINA [*coldly*]. Thank you. And now I will do a soldierly thing. You cannot stay here after what you have just said about my future husband; but I will go out on the balcony and see whether it is safe for you to climb down into the street. [*She turns to the window.*]

MAN [*changing countenance*]. Down that waterpipe! Stop! Wait! I can't! I daren't! The very thought of it makes me giddy. I came up it fast enough with death behind me. But to face it now in cold blood!— [*He sinks on the ottoman.*] It's no use: I give up: I'm beaten. Give the alarm. [*He drops his head in his hands in the deepest dejection.*]

RAINA [*disarmed by pity*]. Come, don't be disheartened. [*She stoops over him almost maternally: he shakes his head.*] Oh, you are a very poor soldier—a chocolate cream soldier. Come, cheer up: it takes less courage to climb down than to face capture—remember that.

MAN [*dreamily, lulled by her voice*]. No, capture only means death; and death is sleep—oh, sleep, sleep, sleep, undisturbed sleep! Climbing down the pipe means doing something—exerting myself—thinking! Death ten times over first.

RAINA [*softly and wonderingly, catching the rhythm of his weariness*]. Are you so sleepy as that?

MAN. I've not had two hours undisturbed sleep since the war began. I'm on the staff: you don't know what that means. I haven't closed my eyes for thirty-six hours.

RAINA [*desperately*]. But what am I to do with you?

MAN [*staggering up*]. Of course I must do something. [*He shakes himself; pulls himself together; and speaks with rallied vigour and courage.*] You see, sleep or no sleep, hunger or no hunger, tired or not tired, you can always do a thing when you know it must be done. Well, that pipe must be got down—[*He hits himself on the chest, and adds*]—Do you hear that, you chocolate cream soldier? [*He turns to the window.*]

RAINA [*anxiously*]. But if you fall?

MAN. I shall sleep as if the stones were a feather bed. Good-bye. [*He makes boldly for the window, and his hand is on the shutter when there is a terrible burst of firing in the street beneath.*]

RAINA [*rushing to him*]. Stop! [*She catches him by the shoulder, and turns him quite round.*] They'll kill you.

MAN [*coolly, but attentively*]. Never mind: this sort of thing is all in my day's work. I'm bound to take my chance. [*Decisively.*] Now do what I tell you. Put out the candles, so that they shan't see the light when I open the shutters. And keep away from the window, whatever you do. If they see me, they're sure to have a shot at me.

RAINA [*clinging to him*]. They're sure to see you: it's bright moonlight. I'll save you—oh, how can you be so indifferent? You want me to save you, don't you?

MAN. I really don't want to be troublesome. [*She shakes him in her impatience.*] I am not indifferent, dear young lady, I assure you. But how is it to be done?

RAINA. Come away from the window—please. [*She coaxes him back to the middle of the room. He submits humbly. She releases him, and addresses him patronizingly.*] Now listen. You must trust to our hospitality. You do not yet know in whose house you are. I am a Petkoff.

MAN. What's that?

RAINA [*rather indignantly*]. I mean that I belong to the family of the Petkoffs, the richest and best known in our country.

MAN. Oh, yes, of course. I beg your pardon. The Petkoffs, to be sure. How stupid of me!

RAINA. You know you never heard of them until this minute. How can you stoop to pretend?

MAN. Forgive me: I'm too tired to think; and the change of subject was too much for me. Don't scold me.

RAINA. I forgot. It might make you cry. [*He nods, quite seriously. She pouts and then resumes her patronizing tone.*] I must tell you that my father holds the highest command of any Bulgarian in our army. He is [*proudly*] a Major.

MAN [*pretending to be deeply impressed*]. A Major! Bless me! Think of that!

RAINA. You shewed great ignorance in thinking that it was necessary to climb up to the balcony, because ours is the only private house that has two rows of windows. There is a flight of stairs inside to get up and down by.

MAN. Stairs! How grand! You live in great luxury indeed, dear young lady.

RAINA. Do you know what a library is?

MAN. A library? A roomful of books.

RAINA. Yes, we have one, the only one in Bulgaria.

MAN. Actually a real library! I should like to see that.

RAINA [*affectedly*]. I tell you these things to shew you that you are not in the house of ignorant country folk who would kill you the moment they saw your Servian uniform, but among civilized people. We go to Bucharest every year for the opera season; and I have spent a whole month in Vienna.

MAN. I saw that, dear young lady. I saw at once that you knew the world.

RAINA. Have you ever seen the opera of Ernani?

MAN. Is that the one with the devil in it in red velvet, and a soldier's chorus?

RAINA [*contemptuously*]. No!

MAN [*stifling a heavy sigh of weariness*]. Then I don't know it.

RAINA. I thought you might have remembered the great scene where Ernani, flying from his foes just as you are tonight, takes refuge in the castle of his bitterest enemy, an old Castilian noble. The noble refuses to give him up. His guest is sacred to him.

MAN [*quickly waking up a little*]. Have your people got that notion?

RAINA [*with dignity*]. My mother and I can understand that notion, as you call it. And if instead of threatening me with your pistol as you did, you had simply thrown yourself as a fugitive on our hospitality, you would have been as safe as in your father's house.

MAN. Quite sure?

RAINA [*turning her back on him in disgust*]. Oh, it is useless to try and make you understand.

MAN. Don't be angry: you see how awkward it would be for me if there was any mistake. My father is a very hospitable man: he keeps six hotels; but I couldn't trust him as far as that. What about your father?

RAINA. He is away at Slivnitza fighting for his country. I answer for your safety. There is my hand in pledge of it. Will that reassure you? [*She offers him her hand.*]

MAN [*looking dubiously at his own hand*]. Better not touch my hand, dear young lady. I must have a wash first.

RAINA [*touched*]. That is very nice of you. I see that you are a gentleman.

MAN [*puzzled*]. Eh?

RAINA. You must not think I am surprised. Bulgarians of really good standing—people in our position—wash their hands nearly every day. But I appreciate your delicacy. You may take my hand. [*She offers it again.*]

MAN [*kissing it with his hands behind his back*]. Thanks, gracious young lady: I feel safe at last. And now would you mind breaking the news to your mother? I had better not stay here secretly longer than is necessary.

RAINA. If you will be so good as to keep perfectly still whilst I am away.

MAN. Certainly. [*He sits down on the ottoman.*] [*Raina goes to the bed and wraps herself in the fur cloak. His eyes close. She goes to the door, but on turning for a last look at him, sees that he is dropping off to sleep.*]

RAINA [*at the door*]. You are not going asleep, are you? [*He murmurs inarticulately: she runs to him and shakes him.*] Do you hear? Wake up: you are falling asleep.

MAN. Eh? Falling aslee—? Oh, no, not the least in the world: I was only thinking. It's all right: I'm wide awake.

RAINA [*severely*]. Will you please stand up while I am away. [*He rises reluctantly.*] All the time, mind.

MAN [*standing unsteadily*]. Certainly—certainly: you may depend on me.

[*Raina looks doubtfully at him. He smiles foolishly. She goes reluctantly, turning again at the door, and almost catching him in the act of yawning. She goes out.*]

MAN [*drowsily*]. Sleep, sleep, sleep, sleep, slee— [*The words trail off into a murmur. He wakes again with a shock on the point of falling.*] Where am I? That's what I want to know: where am I? Must keep awake. Nothing keeps me awake except danger—remember that— [*intently*] danger, danger, danger, dan— Where's danger? Must find it. [*He starts off vaguely around the room in search of it.*] What am I looking for? Sleep—danger—don't know. [*He stumbles against the bed.*] Ah, yes: now I know. All right now. I'm to go to bed, but not to sleep—be sure not to sleep—because of danger. Not to lie down, either, only sit down. [*He sits on the bed. A blissful expression comes into his face.*] Ah! [*With a happy sigh he sinks back at full length; lifts his boots into the bed with a final effort; and falls fast asleep instantly.*]

[*Catherine comes in, followed by Raina.*]

RAINA [*looking at the ottoman*]. He's gone! I left him here.

CATHERINE. Here! Then he must have climbed down from the—

RAINA [*seeing him*]. Oh! [*She points.*]

CATHERINE [*scandalized*]. Well! [*She strides to the left side of the bed, Raina following and standing opposite her on the right.*] He's fast asleep. The brute!

RAINA [*anxiously*]. Sh!

CATHERINE [*shaking him*]. Sir! [*Shaking him again, harder.*] Sir!! [*Vehemently shaking very hard.*] Sir!!!

RAINA [*catching her arm*]. Don't, mamma: the poor dear is worn out. Let him sleep.

CATHERINE [*letting him go and turning amazed to Raina*]. The poor dear! Raina!!! [*She looks sternly at her daughter. The man sleeps profoundly.*]

ACT TWO

The sixth of March, 1886. In the garden of Major Pet-koff's house. It is a fine spring morning; and the garden looks fresh and pretty. Beyond the paling the tops of a couple of minarets can be seen, shewing that there is a valley there, with the little town in it. A few miles further the Balkan mountains rise and shut in the view. Within the garden the side of the house is seen on the right, with a garden door reached by a little flight of steps. On the left the stable yard, with its gateway, encroaches on the garden. There are fruit bushes along the paling and house, covered with washing hung out to dry. A path runs by the house, and rises by two steps at the corner where it turns out of the sight along the front. In the middle a small table, with two bent wood chairs at it, is laid for breakfast with Turkish coffee pot, cups, rolls, etc.; but the cups have been used and the bread broken. There is a wooden garden seat against the wall on the left.

Louka, smoking a cigaret, is standing between the table and the house, turning her back with angry disdain on a manservant who is lecturing her. He is a middle-aged man of cool temperament and low but clear and keen intelligence, with the complacency of the servant who values himself on his rank in servility, and the imperturbability of the accurate calculator who has no illusions. He wears a white Bulgarian costume jacket with decorated border, sash, wide knickerbockers, and decorated gaiters. His head is shaved up to the crown, giving him a high Japanese forehead. His name is Nicola.

NICOLA. Be warned in time, Louka: mend your manners. I know the mistress. She is so grand that she never dreams that any servant could dare to be disrespectful to her; but if she once suspects that you are defying her, out you go.

LOUKA. I do defy her. I will defy her. What do I care for her?

NICOLA. If you quarrel with the family, I never can marry you. It's the same as if you quarrelled with me!

LOUKA. You take her part against me, do you?

NICOLA [*sedately*]. I shall always be dependent on the good will of the family. When I leave their service and start a shop in Sofea, their custom will be half my capital: their bad word would ruin me.

LOUKA. You have no spirit. I should like to see them dare say a word against me!

NICOLA [*pityingly*]. I should have expected more sense from you, Louka. But you're young, you're young!

LOUKA. Yes; and you like me the better for it, don't you? But I know some family secrets they wouldn't care to have told, young as I am. Let them quarrel with me if they dare!

NICOLA [*with compassionate superiority*]. Do you know what they would do if they heard you talk like that?

LOUKA. What could they do?

NICOLA. Discharge you for untruthfulness. Who would believe any stories you told after that? Who would give you another situation? Who in this house would dare be seen speaking to you ever again? How long would your father be left on his little farm? [*She impatiently throws away the end of her cigaret, and stamps on it.*] Child, you don't know the power such high people have over the like of you and me when we try to rise out of our poverty against them. [*He goes close to her and lowers his voice.*] Look at me, ten years in their service. Do you think I know no secrets? I know things about the mistress that she wouldn't have the master know for a thousand levas. I know things about him that she wouldn't let him hear the last of for six months if I blabbed them to her. I know things about Raina that would break off her match with Sergius if—

LOUKA [*turning on him quickly*]. How do you know? I never told you!

NICOLA [*opening his eyes cunningly*]. So that's your little secret, is it? I thought it might be something like that. Well, you take my advice, and be respectful; and make the mistress feel that no matter what you know or don't know, they can depend on you to hold your tongue and serve the family faithfully. That's what they like; and that's how you'll make most out of them.

LOUKA [*with searching scorn*]. You have the soul of a servant, Nicola.

NICOLA [*complacently*]. Yes: that's the secret of success in service.

[*A loud knocking with a whip handle on a wooden door, outside on the left, is heard.*]

MALE VOICE OUTSIDE. Hollo! Hollo there! Nicola!

LOUKA. Master! back from the war!

NICOLA [*quickly*]. My word for it, Louka, the war's over. Off with you and get some fresh coffee. [*He runs out into the stable yard.*]

LOUKA [*as she puts the coffee pot and the cups upon the tray, and carries it into the house*]. You'll never put the soul of a servant into me.

[*Major Petkoff comes from the stable yard, followed by Nicola. He is a cheerful, excitable, insignificant, unpolished man of about 50, naturally unambitious except as to his income and his importance in local society, but just now greatly pleased with the military rank which the war has thrust on him as a man of consequence in his town. The fever of plucky patriotism which the Servian attack roused in all the Bulgarians has pulled him through the war; but he is obviously glad to be home again.*]

PETKOFF [*pointing to the table with his whip*]. Breakfast out here, eh?

NICOLA. Yes, sir. The mistress and Miss Raina have just gone in.

PETKOFF [*sitting down and taking a roll*]. Go in and say I've come; and get me some fresh coffee.

NICOLA. It's coming, sir. [*He goes to the house door. Louka, with fresh coffee, a clean cup, and a brandy bottle on her tray meets him.*] Have you told the mistress?

LOUKA. Yes: she's coming.

[*Nicola goes into the house. Louka brings the coffee to the table.*]

PETKOFF. Well, the Servians haven't run away with you, have they?

LOUKA. No, sir.

PETKOFF. That's right. Have you brought me some cognac?

LOUKA [*putting the bottle on the table*]. Here, sir.

PETKOFF. That's right. [*He pours some into his coffee.*]

[*Catherine who has at this early hour made only a very*

perfunctory toilet, and wears a Bulgarian apron over a once brilliant, but now half worn out red dressing gown, and a colored handkerchief tied over her thick black hair, with Turkish slippers on her bare feet, comes from the house, looking astonishingly handsome and stately under all the circumstances. Louka goes into the house.]

CATHERINE. My dear Paul, what a surprise for us. [*She stoops over the back of his chair to kiss him.*] Have they brought you fresh coffee?

PETKOFF. Yes, Louka's been looking after me. The war's over. The treaty was signed three days ago at Bucharest; and the decree for our army to demobilize was issued yesterday.

CATHERINE [*springing erect, with flashing eyes*]. The war over! Paul: have you let the Austrians force you to make peace?

PETKOFF [*submissively*]. My dear: they didn't consult me. What could *I* do? [*She sits down and turns away from him.*] But of course we saw to it that the treaty was an honorable one. It declares peace—

CATHERINE [*outraged*]. Peace!

PETKOFF [*appeasing her*]. —but not friendly relations: remember that. They wanted to put that in; but I insisted on its being struck out. What more could I do?

CATHERINE. You could have annexed Servia and made Prince Alexander Emperor of the Balkans. That's what I would have done.

PETKOFF. I don't doubt it in the least, my dear. But I should have had to subdue the whole Austrian Empire first; and that would have kept me too long away from you. I missed you greatly.

CATHERINE [*relenting*]. Ah! [*Stretches her hand affectionately across the table to squeeze his.*]

PETKOFF. And how have you been, my dear?

CATHERINE. Oh, my usual sore throats, that's all.

PETKOFF [*with conviction*]. That comes from washing your neck every day. I've often told you so.

CATHERINE. Nonsense, Paul!

PETKOFF [*over his coffee and cigaret*]. I don't believe in going too far with these modern customs. All this washing can't be good for the health: it's not natural. There was an Englishman at Phillipopolis who used to

wet himself all over with cold water every morning when
he got up. Disgusting! It all comes from the English:
their climate makes them so dirty that they have to be
perpetually washing themselves. Look at my father: he
never had a bath in his life; and he lived to be ninety-
eight, the healthiest man in Bulgaria. I don't mind a
good wash once a week to keep up my position; but
once a day is carrying the thing to a ridiculous extreme.

CATHERINE. You are a barbarian at heart still, Paul.
I hope you behaved yourself before all those Russian
officers.

PETKOFF. I did my best. I took care to let them know
that we had a library.

CATHERINE. Ah; but you didn't tell them that we
have an electric bell in it? I have had one put up.

PETKOFF. What's an electric bell?

CATHERINE. You touch a button; something tinkles
in the kitchen; and then Nicola comes up.

PETKOFF. Why not shout for him?

CATHERINE. Civilized people never shout for their
servants. I've learnt that while you were away.

PETKOFF. Well, I'll tell you something I've learnt,
too. Civilized people don't hang out their washing to dry
where visitors can see it; so you'd better have all that
[indicating the clothes on the bushes] put somewhere else.

CATHERINE. Oh, that's absurd, Paul: I don't believe
really refined people notice such things.

[Someone is heard knocking at the stable gates.]

PETKOFF. There's Sergius. [Shouting.] Hollo, Nicola!

CATHERINE. Oh, don't shout, Paul: it really isn't
nice.

PETKOFF. Bosh! [He shouts louder than before.]
Nicola!

NICOLA [appearing at the house door]. Yes, sir.

PETKOFF. If that is Major Saranoff, bring him round
this way. [He pronounces the name with the stress on the
second syllable—Sarah noff.]

NICOLA. Yes, sir. [He goes into the stable yard.]

PETKOFF. You must talk to him, my dear, until
Raina takes him off our hands. He bores my life out
about our not promoting him—over my head, mind you.

CATHERINE. He certainly ought to be promoted when

he marries Raina. Besides, the country should insist on
having at least one native general.

PETKOFF. Yes, so that he could throw away whole
brigades instead of regiments. It's no use, my dear: he
has not the slightest chance of promotion until we are
quite sure that the peace will be a lasting one.

NICOLA [*at the gate, announcing*]. Major Sergius Saranoff! [*He goes into the house and returns presently with
a third chair, which he places at the table. He then
withdraws.*]

[*Major Sergius Saranoff, the original of the portrait in
Raina's room, is a tall, romantically handsome man, with
the physical hardihood, the high spirit, and the susceptible
imagination of an untamed mountaineer chieftain. But his
remarkable personal distinction is of a characteristically
civilized type. The ridges of his eyebrows, curving with a
ram's-horn twist round the marked projections at the
outer corners, his jealously observant eye, his nose, thin,
keen, and apprehensive in spite of the pugnacious high
bridge and large nostril, his assertive chin, would not be
out of place in a Paris salon. In short, the clever, imaginative barbarian has an acute critical faculty which has been
thrown into intense activity by the arrival of western civilization in the Balkans; and the result is precisely what
the advent of nineteenth century thought first produced in
England: to-wit, Byronism. By his brooding on the perpetual failure, not only of others, but of himself, to live
up to his imaginative ideals, his consequent cynical scorn
for humanity, the jejune credulity as to the absolute valid-
ity of his ideals and the unworthiness of the world in
disregarding them, his wincings and mockeries under the
sting of the petty disillusions which every hour spent
among men brings to his infallibly quick observation, he
has acquired the half tragic, half ironic air, the mysterious
moodiness, the suggestion of a strange and terrible history
that has left him nothing but undying remorse, by which
Childe Harold fascinated the grandmothers of his English
contemporaries. Altogether it is clear that here or nowhere
is Raina's ideal hero. Catherine is hardly less enthusiastic,
and much less reserved in shewing her enthusiasm. As he
enters from the stable gate, she rises effusively to greet*

*him. Petkoff is distinctly less disposed to make a fuss
about him.*]

PETKOFF. Here already, Sergius. Glad to see you!

CATHERINE. My dear Sergius! [*She holds out both
her hands.*]

SERGIUS [*kissing them with scrupulous gallantry*]. My
dear mother, if I may call you so.

PETKOFF [*drily*]. Mother-in-law, Sergius; mother-in-
law! Sit down, and have some coffee.

SERGIUS. Thank you, none for me. [*He gets away
from the table with a certain distaste for Petkoff's enjoyment of it, and posts himself with conscious grace against
the rail of the steps leading to the house.*]

CATHERINE. You look superb—splendid. The campaign has improved you. Everybody here is mad about
you. We were all wild with enthusiasm about that magnificent cavalry charge.

SERGIUS [*with grave irony*]. Madam: it was the cradle
and the grave of my military reputation.

CATHERINE. How so?

SERGIUS. I won the battle the wrong way when our
worthy Russian generals were losing it the right way.
That upset their plans, and wounded their self-esteem.
Two of their colonels got their regiments driven back on
the correct principles of scientific warfare. Two major-
generals got killed strictly according to military etiquette.
Those two colonels are now major-generals; and I am
still a simple major.

CATHERINE. You shall not remain so, Sergius. The
women are on your side; and they will see that justice
is done you.

SERGIUS. It is too late. I have only waited for the
peace to send in my resignation.

PETKOFF [*dropping his cup in his amazement*].
Your resignation!

CATHERINE. Oh, you must withdraw it!

SERGIUS [*with resolute, measured emphasis, folding
his arms*]. I never withdraw!

PETKOFF [*vexed*]. Now who could have supposed you
were going to do such a thing?

SERGIUS [*with fire*]. Everyone that knew me. But

enough of myself and my affairs. How is Raina; and where is Raina?

RAINA [*suddenly coming round the corner of the house and standing at the top of the steps in the path*]. Raina is here. [*She makes a charming picture as they all turn to look at her. She wears an underdress of pale green silk, draped with an overdress of thin ecru canvas embroidered with gold. On her head she wears a pretty Phrygian cap of gold tinsel. Sergius, with an exclamation of pleasure, goes impulsively to meet her. She stretches out her hand: he drops chivalrously on one knee and kisses it.*]

PETKOFF [*aside to Catherine, beaming with parental pride*]. Pretty, isn't it? She always appears at the right moment.

CATHERINE [*impatiently*]. Yes: she listens for it. It is an abominable habit.

[*Sergius leads Raina forward with splendid gallantry, as if she were a queen. When they come to the table, she turns to him with a bend of the head; he bows; and thus they separate, he coming to his place, and she going behind her father's chair.*]

RAINA [*stooping and kissing her father*]. Dear father! Welcome home!

PETKOFF [*patting her cheek*]. My little pet girl. [*He kisses her; she goes to the chair left by Nicola for Sergius, and sits down.*]

CATHERINE. And so you're no longer a soldier, Sergius.

SERGIUS. I am no longer a soldier. Soldiering, my dear madam, is the coward's art of attacking mercilessly when you are strong, and keeping out of harm's way when you are weak. That is the whole secret of successful fighting. Get your enemy at a disadvantage; and never, on any account, fight him on equal terms. Eh, Major!

PETKOFF. They wouldn't let us make a fair stand-up fight of it. However, I suppose soldiering has to be a trade like any other trade.

SERGIUS. Precisely. But I have no ambition to succeed as a tradesman; so I have taken the advice of that bagman of a captain that settled the exchange of prisoners with us at Peerot, and given it up.

PETKOFF. What, that Swiss fellow? Sergius: I've often thought of that exchange since. He over-reached us about those horses.

SERGIUS. Of course he over-reached us. His father was a hotel and livery stable keeper; and he owed his first step to his knowledge of horse-dealing. [*With mock enthusiasm.*] Ah, he was a soldier—every inch a soldier! If only I had bought the horses for my regiment instead of foolishly leading it into danger, I should have been a field-marshal now!

CATHERINE. A Swiss? What was he doing in the Servian army?

PETKOFF. A volunteer of course—keen on picking up his profession. [*Chuckling.*] We shouldn't have been able to begin fighting if these foreigners hadn't shewn us how to do it: we knew nothing about it; and neither did the Servians. Egad, there'd have been no war without them.

RAINA. Are there many Swiss officers in the Servian Army?

PETKOFF. No—all Austrians, just as our officers were all Russians. This was the only Swiss I came across. I'll never trust a Swiss again. He cheated us—humbugged us into giving him fifty able bodied men for two hundred confounded worn out chargers. They weren't even eatable!

SERGIUS. We were two children in the hands of that consummate soldier, Major: simply two innocent little children.

RAINA. What was he like?

CATHERINE. Oh, Raina, what a silly question!

SERGIUS. He was like a commercial traveller in uniform. Bourgeois to his boots.

PETKOFF [*grinning*]. Sergius: tell Catherine that queer story his friend told us about him—how he escaped after Slivnitza. You remember?—about his being hid by two women.

SERGIUS [*with bitter irony*]. Oh, yes, quite a romance. He was serving in the very battery I so unprofessionally charged. Being a thorough soldier, he ran away like the rest of them, with our cavalry at his heels. To escape their attentions, he had the good taste to take refuge in the chamber of some patriotic young Bulgarian lady. The young lady was enchanted by his persuasive commercial traveller's manners. She very modestly entertained him for an hour or so and then called in her mother lest her conduct should appear unmaidenly. The old lady was equally fascinated; and the fugitive was sent on his way in the morning, disguised in an old coat belonging to the master of the house, who was away at the war.

RAINA [*rising with marked stateliness*]. Your life in the camp has made you coarse, Sergius. I did not think you would have repeated such a story before me. [*She turns away coldly.*]

CATHERINE [*also rising*]. She is right, Sergius. If such women exist, we should be spared the knowledge of them.

PETKOFF. Pooh! nonsense! what does it matter?

SERGIUS [*ashamed*]. No, Petkoff: I was wrong. [*To Raina, with earnest humility.*] I beg your pardon. I have behaved abominably. Forgive me, Raina. [*She bows reservedly.*] And you, too, madam. [*Catherine bows graciously and sits down. He proceeds solemnly, again addressing Raina.*] The glimpses I have had of the seamy side of life during the last few months have made me cynical; but I should not have brought my cynicism here—least of all into your presence, Raina. I— [*Here, turning to the others, he is evidently about to begin a long speech when the Major interrupts him.*]

PETKOFF. Stuff and nonsense, Sergius. That's quite enough fuss about nothing: a soldier's daughter should be able to stand up without flinching to a little strong conversation. [*He rises.*] Come: it's time for us to get to business. We have to make up our minds how those three regiments are to get back to Phillipopolis:—there's no forage for them on the Sophia route. [*He goes towards the house.*] Come along. [*Sergius is about to follow him when Catherine rises and intervenes.*]

CATHERINE. Oh, Paul, can't you spare Sergius for a few moments? Raina has hardly seen him yet. Perhaps I can help you to settle about the regiments.

SERGIUS [*protesting*]. My dear madam, impossible: you—

CATHERINE [*stopping him playfully*]. You stay here, my dear Sergius: there's no hurry. I have a word or two to say to Paul. [*Sergius instantly bows and steps back.*] Now, dear [*taking Petkoff's arm*], come and see the electric bell.

PETKOFF. Oh, very well, very well. [*They go into the house together affectionately. Sergius, left alone with Raina, looks anxiously at her, fearing that she may be still offended. She smiles, and stretches out her arms to him.*]

SERGIUS [*hastening to her, but refraining from touching her without express permission*]. Am I forgiven?

RAINA [*placing her hands on his shoulder as she looks up at him with admiration and worship*]. My hero! My king.

SERGIUS. My queen! [*He kisses her on the forehead with holy awe.*]

RAINA. How I have envied you, Sergius! You have been out in the world, on the field of battle, able to prove yourself there worthy of any woman in the world; whilst I have had to sit at home inactive—dreaming—useless—doing nothing that could give me the right to call myself worthy of any man.

SERGIUS. Dearest, all my deeds have been yours. You inspired me. I have gone through the war like a knight in a tournament with his lady looking on at him!

RAINA. And you have never been absent from my thoughts for a moment. [*Very solemnly.*] Sergius: I think we two have found the higher love. When I think of you, I feel that I could never do a base deed, or think an ignoble thought.

SERGIUS. My lady, and my saint! [*Clasping her reverently.*]

RAINA [*returning his embrace*]. My lord and my g—

SERGIUS. Sh—sh! Let me be the worshipper, dear. You little know how unworthy even the best man is of a girl's pure passion!

RAINA. I trust you. I love you. You will never disappoint me, Sergius. [*Louka is heard singing within the house. They quickly release each other.*] Hush! I can't pretend to talk indifferently before her: my heart is too full. [*Louka comes from the house with her tray. She goes*

*to the table, and begins to clear it, with her back turned
to them.*] I will go and get my hat; and then we can go
out until lunch time. Wouldn't you like that?

SERGIUS. Be quick. If you are away five minutes, it
will seem five hours. [*Raina runs to the top of the steps
and turns there to exchange a look with him and wave
him a kiss with both hands. He looks after her with emotion for a moment, then turns slowly away, his face radi-
ant with the exultation of the scene which has just passed.
The movement shifts his field of vision, into the corner
of which there now comes the tail of Louka's double
apron. His eye gleams at once. He takes a stealthy look
at her, and begins to twirl his moustache nervously, with
his left hand akimbo on his hip. Finally, striking the
ground with his heels in something of a cavalry swagger,
he strolls over to the left of the table, opposite her, and
says*] Louka: do you know what the higher love is?

LOUKA [*astonished*]. No, sir.

SERGIUS. Very fatiguing thing to keep up for any
length of time, Louka. One feels the need of some relief
after it.

LOUKA [*innocently*]. Perhaps you would like some
coffee, sir? [*She stretches her hand across the table for
the coffee pot.*]

SERGIUS [*taking her hand*]. Thank you, Louka.

LOUKA [*pretending to pull*]. Oh, sir, you know I
didn't mean that. I'm surprised at you!

SERGIUS [*coming clear of the table and drawing her
with him*]. I am surprised at myself, Louka. What would
Sergius, the hero of Slivnitza, say if he saw me now?
What would Sergius, the apostle of the higher love, say
if he saw me now? What would the half dozen Sergiuses
who keep popping in and out of this handsome figure
of mine say if they caught us here? [*Letting go her hand
and slipping his arm dexterously round her waist.*] Do
you consider my figure handsome, Louka?

LOUKA. Let me go, sir. I shall be disgraced. [*She
struggles: he holds her inexorably.*] Oh, will you let go?

SERGIUS [*looking straight into her eyes*]. No.

LOUKA. Then stand back where we can't be seen.
Have you no common sense?

SERGIUS. Ah, that's reasonable. [*He takes her into*

the stable-yard gateway, where they are hidden from the house.]

LOUKA [*complaining*]. I may have been seen from the windows: Miss Raina is sure to be spying about after you.

SERGIUS [*stung—letting her go*]. Take care, Louka. I may be worthless enough to betray the higher love; but do not you insult it.

LOUKA [*demurely*]. Not for the world, sir, I'm sure. May I go on with my work please, now?

SERGIUS [*again putting his arm round her*]. You are a provoking little witch, Louka. If you were in love with me, would you spy out of windows on me?

LOUKA. Well, you see, sir, since you say you are half a dozen different gentlemen all at once, I should have a great deal to look after.

SERGIUS [*charmed*]. Witty as well as pretty. [*He tries to kiss her.*]

LOUKA [*avoiding him*]. No, I don't want your kisses. Gentlefolk are all alike—you making love to me behind Miss Raina's back, and she doing the same behind yours.

SERGIUS [*recoiling a step*]. Louka!

LOUKA. It shews how little you really care!

SERGIUS [*dropping his familiarity and speaking with freezing politeness*]. If our conversation is to continue, Louka, you will please remember that a gentleman does not discuss the conduct of the lady he is engaged to with her maid.

LOUKA. It's so hard to know what a gentleman considers right. I thought from your trying to kiss me that you had given up being so particular.

SERGIUS [*turning from her and striking his forehead as he comes back into the garden from the gateway*]. Devil! devil!

LOUKA. Ha! ha! I expect one of the six of you is very like me, sir, though I am only Miss Raina's maid. [*She goes back to her work at the table, taking no further notice of him.*]

SERGIUS [*speaking to himself*]. Which of the six is the real man?—that's the question that torments me. One of them is a hero, another a buffoon, another a humbug, another perhaps a bit of a blackguard. [*He pauses and looks furtively at Louka, as he adds with deep bitterness*] And one, at least, is a coward—jealous, like all cowards. [*He goes to the table.*] Louka.

LOUKA. Yes?

SERGIUS. Who is my rival?

LOUKA. You shall never get that out of me, for love or money.

SERGIUS. Why?

LOUKA. Never mind why. Besides, you would tell that I told you; and I should lose my place.

SERGIUS [*holding out his right hand in affirmation*]. No; on the honor of a— [*He checks himself, and his hand drops nerveless as he concludes, sardonically*] —of a man capable of behaving as I have been behaving for the last five minutes. Who is he?

LOUKA. I don't know. I never saw him. I only heard his voice through the door of her room.

SERGIUS. Damnation! How dare you?

LOUKA [*retreating*]. Oh, I mean no harm: you've no right to take up my words like that. The mistress knows all about it. And I tell you that if that gentleman ever comes here again, Miss Raina will marry him, whether he likes it or not. I know the difference between the sort of manner you and she put on before one another and the real manner. [*Sergius shivers as if she had stabbed him. Then, setting his face like iron, he strides grimly to her, and grips her above the elbows with both hands.*]

SERGIUS. Now listen you to me!

LOUKA [*wincing*]. Not so tight: you're hurting me!

SERGIUS. That doesn't matter. You have stained my honor by making me a party to your eavesdropping. And you have betrayed your mistress—

LOUKA [*writhing*]. Please—

SERGIUS. That shews that you are an abominable little clod of common clay, with the soul of a servant. [*He lets her go as if she were an unclean thing, and turns away, dusting his hands of her, to the bench by the wall, where he sits down with averted head, meditating gloomily.*]

LOUKA [*whimpering angrily with her hands up her sleeves, feeling her bruised arms*]. You know how to hurt with your tongue as well as with your hands. But I don't care, now I've found out that whatever clay I'm made of, you're made of the same. As for her, she's a liar; and her fine airs are a cheat; and I'm worth six of her. [*She shakes the pain off hardily; tosses her head; and sets to work to put the things on the tray. He looks doubtfully at her once or twice. She finishes packing the tray, and laps the cloth over the edges, so as to carry all out together. As she stoops to lift it, he rises.*]

SERGIUS. Louka! [*She stops and looks defiantly at him with the tray in her hands.*] A gentleman has no right to hurt a woman under any circumstances. [*With profound humility, uncovering his head.*] I beg your pardon.

LOUKA. That sort of apology may satisfy a lady. Of what use is it to a servant?

SERGIUS [*thus rudely crossed in his chivalry, throws it off with a bitter laugh and says slightingly*]. Oh, you wish to be paid for the hurt? [*He puts on his shako, and takes some money from his pocket.*]

LOUKA [*her eyes filling with tears in spite of herself*]. No, I want my hurt made well.

SERGIUS [*sobered by her tone*]. How? [*She rolls up her left sleeve; clasps her arm with the thumb and fingers of her right hand; and looks down at the bruise. Then she raises her head and looks straight at him. Finally, with a superb gesture she presents her arm to be kissed. Amazed, he looks at her; at the arm; at her again; hesitates; and then, with shuddering intensity, exclaims*] Never! [*and gets away as far as possible from her.*]

[*Her arm drops. Without a word, and with unaffected dignity, she takes her tray, and is approaching the house when Raina returns wearing a hat and jacket in the height of the Vienna fashion of the previous year, 1885. Louka makes way proudly for her, and then goes into the house.*]

RAINA. I'm ready! What's the matter? [*Gaily.*] Have you been flirting with Louka?

SERGIUS [*hastily*]. No, no. How can you think such a thing?

RAINA [*ashamed of herself*]. Forgive me, dear: it was only a jest. I am so happy to-day.

[*He goes quickly to her, and kisses her hand remorsefully. Catherine comes out and calls to them from the top of the steps.*]

CATHERINE [*coming down to them*]. I am sorry to disturb you, children; but Paul is distracted over those three regiments. He does not know how to get them to Phillipopolis; and he objects to every suggestion of mine. You must go and help him, Sergius. He is in the library.

RAINA [*disappointed*]. But we are just going out for a walk.

SERGIUS. I shall not be long. Wait for me just five minutes. [*He runs up the steps to the door.*]

RAINA [*following him to the foot of the steps and looking up at him with timid coquetry*]. I shall go round and wait in full view of the library windows. Be sure you draw father's attention to me. If you are a moment longer than five minutes, I shall go in and fetch you, regiments or no regiments.

SERGIUS [*laughing*]. Very well. [*He goes in. Raina watches him until he is out of her sight. Then, with a perceptible relaxation of manner, she begins to pace up and down about the garden in a brown study.*]

CATHERINE. Imagine their meeting that Swiss and hearing the whole story! The very first thing your father asked for was the old coat we sent him off in. A nice mess you have got us into!

RAINA [*gazing thoughtfully at the gravel as she walks*]. The little beast!

CATHERINE. Little beast! What little beast?

RAINA. To go and tell! Oh, if I had him here, I'd stuff him with chocolate creams till he couldn't ever speak again!

CATHERINE. Don't talk nonsense. Tell me the truth, Raina. How long was he in your room before you came to me?

RAINA [*whisking round and recommencing her march in the opposite direction*]. Oh, I forget.

CATHERINE. You cannot forget! Did he really climb up after the soldiers were gone, or was he there when that officer searched the room?

RAINA. No. Yes, I think he must have been there then.

CATHERINE. You think! Oh, Raina, Raina! Will anything ever make you straightforward? If Sergius finds out, it is all over between you.

RAINA [*with cool impertinence*]. Oh, I know Sergius is your pet. I sometimes wish you could marry him instead of me. You would just suit him. You would pet him, and spoil him, and mother him to perfection.

CATHERINE [*opening her eyes very widely indeed*]. Well, upon my word!

RAINA [*capriciously—half to herself*]. I always feel a longing to do or say something dreadful to him—to shock his propriety—to scandalize the five senses out of him! [*To Catherine perversely.*] I don't care whether he finds out about the chocolate cream soldier or not. I half hope he may. [*She again turns flippantly away and strolls up the path to the corner of the house.*]

CATHERINE. And what should I be able to say to your father, pray?

RAINA [*over her shoulder, from the top of the two steps*]. Oh, poor father! As if he could help himself! [*She turns the corner and passes out of sight.*]

CATHERINE [*looking after her, her fingers itching*]. Oh, if you were only ten years younger! [*Louka comes from the house with a salver, which she carries hanging down by her side.*] Well?

LOUKA. There's a gentleman just called, madam—a Servian officer—

CATHERINE [*flaming*]. A Servian! How dare he—[*Checking herself bitterly.*] Oh, I forgot. We are at peace now. I suppose we shall have them calling every day to pay their compliments. Well, if he is an officer why don't you tell your master? He is in the library with Major Saranoff. Why do you come to me?

LOUKA. But he asks for you, madam. And I don't think he knows who you are: he said the lady of the house. He gave me this little ticket for you. [*She takes a card out of her bosom; puts it on the salver and offers it to Catherine.*]

CATHERINE [*reading*]. "Captain Bluntschli!" That's a German name.

LOUKA. Swiss, madam, I think.

CATHERINE [*with a bound that makes Louka jump back*]. Swiss! What is he like?

LOUKA [*timidly*]. He has a big carpet bag, madam.

CATHERINE. Oh, Heavens, he's come to return the coat! Send him away—say we're not at home—ask him to leave his address and I'll write to him— Oh, stop: that will never do. Wait! [*She throws herself into a chair to think it out. Louka waits.*] The master and Major Saranoff are busy in the library, aren't they?

LOUKA. Yes, madam.

CATHERINE [*decisively*]. Bring the gentleman out here at once. [*Imperatively.*] And be very polite to him. Don't delay. Here [*impatiently snatching the salver from her*]: leave that here; and go straight back to him.

LOUKA. Yes, madam. [*Going.*]

CATHERINE. Louka!

LOUKA [*stopping*]. Yes, madam.

CATHERINE. Is the library door shut?

LOUKA. I think so, madam.

CATHERINE. If not, shut it as you pass through.

LOUKA. Yes, madam. [*Going.*]

CATHERINE. Stop! [*Louka stops.*] He will have to go out that way [*indicating the gate of the stable yard.*] Tell Nicola to bring his bag here after him. Don't forget.

LOUKA [*surprised*]. His bag?

CATHERINE. Yes, here, as soon as possible. [*Vehemently.*] Be quick! [*Louka runs into the house. Catherine snatches her apron off and throws it behind a bush. She then takes up the salver and uses it as a mirror, with the result that the handkerchief tied round her head follows the apron. A touch to her hair and a shake to her dressing gown makes her presentable.*] Oh, how—how—how can a man be such a fool! Such a moment to select! [*Louka appears at the door of the house, announcing "Captain Bluntschli;" and standing aside at the top of the steps to let him pass before she goes in again. He is the man of the adventure in Raina's room. He is now clean, well brushed, smartly uniformed, and out of trouble, but still unmistakably the same man. The moment Louka's back is turned, Catherine swoops on him with hurried, urgent, coaxing appeal.*] Captain Bluntschli, I am very glad to see you; but you must leave this house at once. [*He raises his eyebrows.*] My husband has just returned, with my future son-in-law; and they know nothing. If they did, the consequences would be terrible. You are a foreigner: you do not feel our national animosities as we do. We still hate the Servians: the only effect of the peace on my husband is to make him feel like a lion baulked of his prey. If he discovered our secret, he would never forgive me; and my daughter's life would hardly be safe. Will you, like the chivalrous gentleman and soldier you are, leave at once before he finds you here?

BLUNTSCHLI [*disappointed, but philosophical*]. At once, gracious lady. I only came to thank you and return the coat you lent me. If you will allow me to take it out of my bag and leave it with your servant as I pass out, I need detain you no further. [*He turns to go into the house.*]

CATHERINE [*catching him by the sleeve*]. Oh, you must not think of going back that way. [*Coaxing him across to the stable gates.*] This is the shortest way out. Many thanks. So glad to have been of service to you. Good-bye.

BLUNTSCHLI. But my bag?

CATHERINE. It will be sent on. You will leave me your address.

BLUNTSCHLI. True. Allow me. [*He takes out his card-case, and stops to write his address, keeping Catherine in an agony of impatience. As he hands her the card, Petkoff, hatless, rushes from the house in a fluster of hospitality, followed by Sergius.*]

PETKOFF [*as he hurries down the steps*]. My dear Captain Bluntschli—

CATHERINE. Oh Heavens! [*She sinks on the seat against the wall.*]

PETKOFF [*too preoccupied to notice her as he shakes Bluntschli's hand heartily*]. Those stupid people of mine thought I was out here, instead of in the—haw!—library. [*He cannot mention the library without betraying how proud he is of it.*] I saw you through the window. I was wondering why you didn't come in. Saranoff is with me: you remember him, don't you?

SERGIUS [*saluting humorously, and then offering his hand with great charm of manner*]. Welcome, our friend the enemy!

PETKOFF. No longer the enemy, happily. [*Rather anxiously.*] I hope you've come as a friend, and not on business.

CATHERINE. Oh, quite as a friend, Paul. I was just asking Captain Bluntschli to stay to lunch; but he declares he must go at once.

SERGIUS [*sardonically*]. Impossible, Bluntschli. We want you here badly. We have to send on three cavalry regiments to Phillipopolis; and we don't in the least know how to do it.

BLUNTSCHLI [*suddenly attentive and businesslike*]. Phillipopolis! The forage is the trouble, eh?

PETKOFF [*eagerly*]. Yes, that's it. [*To Sergius.*] He sees the whole thing at once.

BLUNTSCHLI. I think I can shew you how to manage that.

SERGIUS. Invaluable man! Come along! [*Towering over Bluntschli, he puts his hand on his shoulder and takes him to the steps, Petkoff following. As Bluntschli puts his foot on the first step, Raina comes out of the house.*]

RAINA [*completely losing her presence of mind*]. Oh, the chocolate cream soldier!

[*Bluntschli stands rigid. Sergius, amazed, looks at Raina, then at Petkoff, who looks back at him and then at his wife.*]

CATHERINE [*with commanding presence of mind*]. My dear Raina, don't you see that we have a guest here—Captain Bluntschli, one of our new Servian friends?

[*Raina bows; Bluntschli bows.*]

RAINA. How silly of me! [*She comes down into the centre of the group, between Bluntschli and Petkoff.*] I made a beautiful ornament this morning for the ice pudding; and that stupid Nicola has just put down a pile of plates on it and spoiled it. [*To Bluntschli, winningly.*] I hope you didn't think that you were the chocolate cream soldier, Captain Bluntschli.

BLUNTSCHLI [*laughing*]. I assure you I did. [*Stealing a whimsical glance at her.*] Your explanation was a relief.

PETKOFF [*suspiciously, to Raina*]. And since when, pray, have you taken to cooking?

CATHERINE. Oh, whilst you were away. It is her latest fancy.

PETKOFF [*testily*]. And has Nicola taken to drinking? He used to be careful enough. First he shews Captain Bluntschli out here when he knew quite well I was in the—hum!—library; and then he goes downstairs and breaks Raina's chocolate soldier. He must— [*At this moment Nicola appears at the top of the steps R., with a carpet bag. He descends; places it respectfully before Bluntschli; and waits for further orders. General amazement. Nicola, unconscious of the effect he is producing, looks perfectly satisfied with himself. When Petkoff recovers his power of speech, he breaks out at him with*] Are you mad, Nicola?

NICOLA [*taken aback*]. Sir?

PETKOFF. What have you brought that for?

NICOLA. My lady's orders, sir. Louka told me that—

CATHERINE [*interrupting him*]. My orders! Why should I order you to bring Captain Bluntschli's luggage out here? What are you thinking of, Nicola?

NICOLA [*after a moment's bewilderment, picking up the bag as he addresses Bluntschli with the very perfection of servile discretion*]. I beg your pardon, sir, I am sure. [*To Catherine.*] My fault, madam! I hope you'll overlook it! [*He bows, and is going to the steps with the bag, when Petkoff addresses him angrily.*]

PETKOFF. You'd better go and slam that bag, too, down on Miss Raina's ice pudding! [*This is too much for Nicola. The bag drops from his hands on Petkoff's corns, eliciting a roar of anguish from him.*] Begone, you butter-fingered donkey.

NICOLA [*snatching up the bag, and escaping into the house*]. Yes, sir.

CATHERINE. Oh, never mind, Paul, don't be angry!

PETKOFF [*muttering*]. Scoundrel. He's got out of hand while I was away. I'll teach him. [*Recollecting his guest.*] Oh, well, never mind. Come, Bluntschli, let's have no more nonsense about you having to go away. You know very well you're not going back to Switzerland yet. Until you do go back you'll stay with us.

RAINA. Oh, do, Captain Bluntschli.

PETKOFF [*to Catherine*]. Now, Catherine, it's of you that he's afraid. Press him and he'll stay.

CATHERINE. Of course I shall be only too delighted if [*appealingly*] Captain Bluntschli really wishes to stay. He knows my wishes.

BLUNTSCHLI [*in his driest military manner*]. I am at madame's orders.

SERGIUS [*cordially*]. That settles it!

PETKOFF [*heartily*]. Of course!

RAINA. You see, you must stay!

BLUNTSCHLI [*smiling*]. Well, if I must, I must!

[*Gesture of despair from Catherine.*]

ACT THREE

In the library after lunch. It is not much of a library, its literary equipment consisting of a single fixed shelf stocked with old paper covered novels, broken backed, coffee stained, torn and thumbed, and a couple of little hanging shelves with a few gift books on them, the rest of the wall space being occupied by trophies of war and the chase. But it is a most comfortable sitting-room. A row of three large windows in the front of the house shew a mountain panorama, which is just now seen in one of its softest aspects in the mellowing afternoon light. In the left hand corner, a square earthenware stove, a perfect tower of colored pottery, rises nearly to the ceiling and guarantees plenty of warmth. The ottoman in the middle is a circular bank of decorated cushions, and the window seats are well upholstered divans. Little Turkish tables, one of them with an elaborate hookah on it, and a screen to match them, complete the handsome effect of the furnishing. There is one object, however, which is hopelessly out of keeping with its surroundings. This is a small kitchen table, much the worse for wear, fitted as a writing table with an old canister full of pens, an eggcup filled with ink, and a deplorable scrap of severely used pink blotting paper.

At the side of this table, which stands on the right, Bluntschli is hard at work, with a couple of maps before him, writing orders. At the head of it sits Sergius, who is also supposed to be at work, but who is actually gnawing the feather of a pen, and contemplating Bluntschli's quick, sure, businesslike progress with a mixture of envious irritation at his own incapacity, and awestruck wonder at an ability which seems to him almost miraculous, though its prosaic character forbids him to esteem it. The major is comfortably established on the ottoman, with a newspaper in his hand and the tube of the hookah within his reach. Catherine sits at the stove, with her back to them, embroidering. Raina, reclining on the divan under the left hand window, is gazing in a daydream out at the Balkan landscape, with a neglected novel in her lap.

The door is on the left. The button of the electric bell is between the door and the fireplace.

PETKOFF [*looking up from his paper to watch how they are getting on at the table*]. Are you sure I can't help you in any way, Bluntschli?

BLUNTSCHLI [*without interrupting his writing or looking up*]. Quite sure, thank you. Saranoff and I will manage it.

SERGIUS [*grimly*]. Yes: we'll manage it. He finds out what to do; draws up the orders; and I sign 'em. Division of labour, Major. [*Bluntschli passes him a paper.*] Another one? Thank you. [*He plants the papers squarely before him; sets his chair carefully parallel to them; and signs with the air of a man resolutely performing a difficult and dangerous feat.*] This hand is more accustomed to the sword than to the pen.

PETKOFF. It's very good of you, Bluntschli, it is indeed, to let yourself be put upon in this way. Now are you quite sure I can do nothing?

CATHERINE [*in a low, warning tone*]. You can stop interrupting, Paul.

PETKOFF [*starting and looking round at her*]. Eh? Oh! Quite right, my love, quite right. [*He takes his newspaper up, but lets it drop again.*] Ah, you haven't been campaigning, Catherine: you don't know how pleasant it is for us to sit here, after a good lunch, with nothing to do but enjoy ourselves. There's only one thing I want to make me thoroughly comfortable.

CATHERINE. What is that?

PETKOFF. My old coat. I'm not at home in this one: I feel as if I were on parade.

CATHERINE. My dear Paul, how absurd you are about that old coat! It must be hanging in the blue closet where you left it.

PETKOFF. My dear Catherine, I tell you I've looked there. Am I to believe my own eyes or not? [*Catherine quietly rises and presses the button of the electric bell by the fireplace*]. What are you shewing off that bell for? [*She looks at him majestically, and silently resumes her chair and her needlework.*] My dear: if you think the obstinacy of your sex can make a coat out of two old dressing gowns of Raina's, your waterproof, and my mackintosh, you're mistaken. That's exactly what the blue closet contains at present. [*Nicola presents himself.*]

CATHERINE [*unmoved by Petkoff's sally*]. Nicola: go to the blue closet and bring your master's old coat here—the braided one he usually wears in the house.

NICOLA. Yes, madam. [*Nicola goes out.*]

PETKOFF. Catherine.

CATHERINE. Yes, Paul?

PETKOFF. I bet you any piece of jewellery you like to order from Sophia against a week's housekeeping money, that the coat isn't there.

CATHERINE. Done, Paul.

PETKOFF [*excited by the prospect of a gamble*]. Come: here's an opportunity for some sport. Who'll bet on it? Bluntschli: I'll give you six to one.

BLUNTSCHLI [*imperturbably*]. It would be robbing you, Major. Madame is sure to be right. [*Without looking up, he passes another batch of papers to Sergius.*]

SERGIUS [*also excited*]. Bravo, Switzerland! Major: I bet my best charger against an Arab mare for Raina that Nicola finds the coat in the blue closet.

PETKOFF [*eagerly*]. Your best char—

CATHERINE [*hastily interrupting him*]. Don't be foolish, Paul. An Arabian mare will cost you 50,000 levas.

RAINA [*suddenly coming out of her picturesque revery*]. Really, mother, if you are going to take the jewellery, I don't see why you should grudge me my Arab.

[*Nicola comes back with the coat and brings it to Petkoff, who can hardly believe his eyes.*]

CATHERINE. Where was it, Nicola?

NICOLA. Hanging in the blue closet, madam.

PETKOFF. Well, I am d—

CATHERINE [*stopping him*]. Paul!

PETKOFF. I could have sworn it wasn't there. Age is beginning to tell on me. I'm getting hallucinations. [*To Nicola.*] Here: help me to change. Excuse me, Bluntschli. [*He begins changing coats, Nicola acting as valet.*] Remember: I didn't take that bet of yours, Sergius. You'd better give Raina that Arab steed yourself, since you've roused her expectations. Eh, Raina? [*He looks round at her; but she is again rapt in the landscape. With a little gush of paternal affection and pride, he points her out to them and says*] She's dreaming, as usual.

SERGIUS. Assuredly she shall not be the loser.

PETKOFF. So much the better for her. *I* shan't come off so cheap, I expect. [*The change is now complete. Nicola goes out with the discarded coat.*] Ah, now I feel at home at last. [*He sits down and takes his newspaper with a grunt of relief.*]

BLUNTSCHLI [*to Sergius, handing a paper*]. That's the last order.

PETKOFF [*jumping up*]. What! finished?

BLUNTSCHLI. Finished. [*Petkoff goes beside Sergius; looks curiously over his left shoulder as he signs; and says with childlike envy*] Haven't you anything for me to sign?

BLUNTSCHLI. Not necessary. His signature will do.

PETKOFF. Ah, well, I think we've done a thundering good day's work. [*He goes away from the table.*] Can I do anything more?

BLUNTSCHLI. You had better both see the fellows that are to take these. [*To Sergius.*] Pack them off at once; and shew them that I've marked on the orders the time they should hand them in by. Tell them that if they stop to drink or tell stories—if they're five minutes late, they'll have the skin taken off their backs.

SERGIUS [*rising indignantly*]. I'll say so. And if one of them is man enough to spit in my face for insulting him, I'll buy his discharge and give him a pension. [*He strides out, his humanity deeply outraged.*]

BLUNTSCHLI [*confidentially*]. Just see that he talks to them properly, Major, will you?

PETKOFF [*officiously*]. Quite right, Bluntschli, quite right. I'll see to it. [*He goes to the door importantly, but hesitates on the threshold.*] By the by, Catherine, you may as well come, too. They'll be far more frightened of you than of me.

CATHERINE [*putting down her embroidery*]. I daresay I had better. You will only splutter at them. [*She goes out, Petkoff holding the door for her and following her.*]

BLUNTSCHLI. What a country! They make cannons out of cherry trees; and the officers send for their wives to keep discipline! [*He begins to fold and docket the papers. Raina, who has risen from the divan, strolls down the room with her hands clasped behind her, and looks mischievously at him.*]

RAINA. You look ever so much nicer than when we last met. [*He looks up, surprised.*] What have you done to yourself?

BLUNTSCHLI. Washed; brushed; good night's sleep and breakfast. That's all.

RAINA. Did you get back safely that morning?

BLUNTSCHLI. Quite, thanks.

RAINA. Were they angry with you for running away from Sergius's charge?

BLUNTSCHLI. No, they were glad; because they'd all just run away themselves.

RAINA [*going to the table, and leaning over it towards him*]. It must have made a lovely story for them—all that about me and my room.

BLUNTSCHLI. Capital story. But I only told it to one of them—a particular friend.

RAINA. On whose discretion you could absolutely rely?

BLUNTSCHLI. Absolutely.

RAINA. Hm! He told it all to my father and Sergius

the day you exchanged the prisoners. [*She turns away and strolls carelessly across to the other side of the room.*]

BLUNTSCHLI [*deeply concerned and half incredulous*]. No! you don't mean that, do you?

RAINA [*turning, with sudden earnestness*]. I do indeed. But they don't know that it was in this house that you hid. If Sergius knew, he would challenge you and kill you in a duel.

BLUNTSCHLI. Bless me! then don't tell him.

RAINA [*full of reproach for his levity*]. Can you realize what it is to me to deceive him? I want to be quite perfect with Sergius—no meanness, no smallness, no deceit. My relation to him is the one really beautiful and noble part of my life. I hope you can understand that.

BLUNTSCHLI [*sceptically*]. You mean that you wouldn't like him to find out that the story about the ice pudding was a—a—a— You know.

RAINA [*wincing*]. Ah, don't talk of it in that flippant way. I lied: I know it. But I did it to save your life. He would have killed you. That was the second time I ever uttered a falsehood. [*Bluntschli rises quickly and looks doubtfully and somewhat severely at her.*] Do you remember the first time?

BLUNTSCHLI. I! No. Was I present?

RAINA. Yes; and I told the officer who was searching for you that you were not present.

BLUNTSCHLI. True. I should have remembered it.

RAINA [*greatly encouraged*]. Ah, it is natural that you should forget it first. It cost you nothing: it cost me a lie!—a lie!! [*She sits down on the ottoman, looking straight before her with her hands clasped on her knee. Bluntschli, quite touched, goes to the ottoman with a particularly reassuring and considerate air, and sits down beside her.*]

BLUNTSCHLI. My dear young lady, don't let this worry you. Remember: I'm a soldier. Now what are the two things that happen to a soldier so often that he comes to think nothing of them? One is hearing people tell lies [*Raina recoils*]: the other is getting his life saved in all sorts of ways by all sorts of people.

RAINA [*rising in indignant protest*]. And so he becomes a creature incapable of faith and of gratitude.

BLUNTSCHLI [*making a wry face*]. Do you like gratitude? I don't. If pity is akin to love, gratitude is akin to the other thing.

RAINA. Gratitude! [*Turning on him.*] If you are incapable of gratitude you are incapable of any noble sentiment. Even animals are grateful. Oh, I see now exactly what you think of me! You were not surprised to hear me lie. To you it was something I probably did every day—every hour. That is how men think of women. [*She walks up the room melodramatically.*]

BLUNTSCHLI [*dubiously*]. There's reason in everything. You said you'd told only two lies in your whole life. Dear young lady: isn't that rather a short allowance? I'm quite a straightforward man myself; but it wouldn't last me a whole morning.

RAINA [*staring haughtily at him*]. Do you know, sir, that you are insulting me?

BLUNTSCHLI. I can't help it. When you get into that noble attitude and speak in that thrilling voice, I admire you; but I find it impossible to believe a single word you say.

RAINA [*superbly*]. Captain Bluntschli!

BLUNTSCHLI [*unmoved*]. Yes?

RAINA [*coming a little towards him, as if she could not believe her senses*]. Do you mean what you said just now? Do you *know* what you said just now?

BLUNTSCHLI. I do.

RAINA [*gasping*]. I! I!!! [*She points to herself incredulously, meaning "I, Raina Petkoff, tell lies!" He meets her gaze unflinchingly. She suddenly sits down beside him, and adds, with a complete change of manner from the heroic to the familiar*] How did you find me out?

BLUNTSCHLI [*promptly*]. Instinct, dear young lady. Instinct, and experience of the world.

RAINA [*wonderingly*]. Do you know, you are the first man I·ever met who did not take me seriously?

BLUNTSCHLI. You mean, don't you, that I am the first man that has ever taken you quite seriously?

RAINA. Yes, I suppose I do mean that. [*Cosily, quite at her ease with him.*] How strange it is to be talked to in such a way! You know, I've always gone on like that—I mean the noble attitude and the thrilling voice. I did it when I was a tiny child to my nurse. She believed in it. I do it before my parents. They believe in it. I do it before Sergius. He believes in it.

BLUNTSCHLI. Yes: he's a little in that line himself, isn't he?

RAINA [*startled*]. Do you think so?

BLUNTSCHLI. You know him better than I do.

RAINA. I wonder—I wonder is he? If I thought that— ! [*Discouraged.*] Ah, well, what does it matter? I suppose, now that you've found me out, you despise me.

BLUNTSCHLI [*warmly, rising*]. No, my dear young lady, no, no, no a thousand times. It's part of your youth—part of your charm. I'm like all the rest of them—the nurse—your parents—Sergius: I'm your infatuated admirer.

RAINA [*pleased*]. Really?

BLUNTSCHLI [*slapping his breast smartly with his hand, German fashion*]. Hand aufs Herz! Really and truly.

RAINA [*very happy*]. But what did you think of me for giving you my portrait?

BLUNTSCHLI [*astonished*]. Your portrait! You never gave me your portrait.

RAINA [*quickly*]. Do you mean to say you never got it?

BLUNTSCHLI. No. [*He sits down beside her, with renewed interest, and says, with some complacency*] When did you send it to me?

RAINA [*indignantly*]. I did not send it to you. [*She turns her head away, and adds, reluctantly*] It was in the pocket of that coat.

BLUNTSCHLI [*pursing his lips and rounding his eyes*]. Oh-o-oh! I never found it. It must be there still.

RAINA [*springing up*]. There still!—for my father to find the first time he puts his hand in his pocket! Oh, how could you be so stupid?

BLUNTSCHLI [*rising also*]. It doesn't matter: it's only a photograph: how can he tell who it was intended for? Tell him he put it there himself.

RAINA [*impatiently*]. Yes, that is so clever—so clever! What shall I do?

BLUNTSCHLI. Ah, I see. You wrote something on it. That was rash!

RAINA [*annoyed almost to tears*]. Oh, to have done such a thing for you, who care no more—except to laugh at me—oh! Are you sure nobody has touched it?

BLUNTSCHLI. Well, I can't be quite sure. You see I couldn't carry it about with me all the time: one can't take much luggage on active service.

RAINA. What did you do with it?

BLUNTSCHLI. When I got through to Peerot I had to put it in safe keeping somehow. I thought of the railway cloak room; but that's the surest place to get looted in modern warfare. So I pawned it.

RAINA. Pawned it!!!

BLUNTSCHLI. I know it doesn't sound nice; but it was much the safest plan. I redeemed it the day before yesterday. Heaven only knows whether the pawnbroker cleared out the pockets or not.

RAINA [*furious—throwing the words right into his face*]. You have a low, shopkeeping mind. You think of things that would never come into a gentleman's head.

BLUNTSCHLI [*phlegmatically*]. That's the Swiss national character, dear lady.

RAINA. Oh, I wish I had never met you. [*She flounces away and sits at the window fuming.*]

[*Louka comes in with a heap of letters and telegrams on her salver, and crosses, with her bold, free gait, to the table. Her left sleeve is looped up to the shoulder with a brooch, shewing her naked arm, with a broad gilt bracelet covering the bruise.*]

LOUKA [*to Bluntschli*]. For you. [*She empties the salver recklessly on the table.*] The messenger is waiting. [*She is determined not to be civil to a Servian, even if she must bring him his letters.*]

BLUNTSCHLI [*to Raina*]. Will you excuse me: the last postal delivery that reached me was three weeks ago. These are the subsequent accumulations. Four telegrams—a week old. [*He opens one.*] Oho! Bad news!

RAINA [*rising and advancing a little remorsefully*]. Bad news?

BLUNTSCHLI. My father's dead. [*He looks at the tele-*

gram with his lips pursed, musing on the unexpected change in his arrangements.]

RAINA. Oh, how very sad!

BLUNTSCHLI. Yes: I shall have to start for home in an hour. He has left a lot of big hotels behind him to be looked after. [*Takes up a heavy letter in a long blue envelope.*] Here's a whacking letter from the family solicitor. [*He pulls out the enclosures and glances over them.*] Great Heavens! Seventy! Two hundred! [*In a crescendo of dismay.*] Four hundred! Four thousand!! Nine thousand six hundred!!! What on earth shall I do with them all?

RAINA [*timidly*]. Nine thousand hotels?

BLUNTSCHLI. Hotels! Nonsense. If you only knew!— oh, it's too ridiculous! Excuse me: I must give my fellow orders about starting. [*He leaves the room hastily, with the documents in his hand.*]

LOUKA [*tauntingly*]. He has not much heart, that Swiss, though he is so fond of the Servians. He has not a word of grief for his poor father.

RAINA [*bitterly*]. Grief!—a man who has been doing nothing but killing people for years! What does he care? What does any soldier care? [*She goes to the door, evidently restraining her tears with difficulty.*]

LOUKA. Major Saranoff has been fighting, too; and he has plenty of heart left. [*Raina, at the door, looks haughtily at her and goes out.*] Aha! I thought you wouldn't get much feeling out of your soldier. [*She is following Raina when Nicola enters with an armful of logs for the fire.*]

NICOLA [*grinning amorously at her*]. I've been trying all the afternoon to get a minute alone with you, my girl. [*His countenance changes as he notices her arm.*] Why, what fashion is that of wearing your sleeve, child?

LOUKA [*proudly*]. My own fashion.

NICOLA. Indeed! If the mistress catches you, she'll talk to you. [*He throws the logs down on the ottoman, and sits comfortably beside them.*]

LOUKA. Is that any reason why you should take it on yourself to talk to me?

NICOLA. Come: don't be so contrary with me. I've

some good news for you. [*He takes out some paper money. Louka, with an eager gleam in her eyes, comes close to look at it.*] See, a twenty leva bill! Sergius gave me that out of pure swagger. A fool and his money are soon parted. There's ten levas more. The Swiss gave me that for backing up the mistress's and Raina's lies about him. He's no fool, he isn't. You should have heard old Catherine downstairs as polite as you please to me, telling me not to mind the Major being a little impatient; for they knew what a good servant I was—after making a fool and a liar of me before them all! The twenty will go to our savings; and you shall have the ten to spend if you'll only talk to me so as to remind me I'm a human being. I get tired of being a servant occasionally.

LOUKA [*scornfully*]. Yes: sell your manhood for thirty levas, and buy me for ten! Keep your money. You were born to be a servant. I was not. When you set up your shop you will only be everybody's servant instead of somebody's servant.

NICOLA [*picking up his logs, and going to the stove*]. Ah, wait till you see. We shall have our evenings to ourselves; and I shall be master in my own house, I promise you. [*He throws the logs down and kneels at the stove.*]

LOUKA. You shall never be master in mine. [*She sits down on Sergius's chair.*]

NICOLA [*turning, still on his knees, and squatting down rather forlornly, on his calves, daunted by her implacable disdain*]. You have a great ambition in you, Louka. Remember: if any luck comes to you, it was I that made a woman of you.

LOUKA. You!

NICOLA [*with dogged self-assertion*]. Yes, me. Who was it made you give up wearing a couple of pounds of false black hair on your head and reddening your lips and cheeks like any other Bulgarian girl? I did. Who taught you to trim your nails, and keep your hands clean, and be dainty about yourself, like a fine Russian lady? Me! do you hear that? me! [*She tosses her head defiantly; and he rises, ill-humóredly, adding more coólly*] I've often thought that if Raina were out of the way, and you just a little less of a fool and Sergius just a little more of one, you might come to be one of my grandest customers, instead of only being my wife and costing me money.

LOUKA. I believe you would rather be my servant than my husband. You would make more out of me. Oh, I know that soul of yours.

NICOLA [*going up close to her for greater emphasis*]. Never you mind my soul; but just listen to my advice. If you want to be a lady, your present behaviour to me won't do at all, unless when we're alone. It's too sharp and impudent; and impudence is a sort of familiarity: it shews affection for me. And don't you try being high and mighty with me either. You're like all country girls: you think it's genteel to treat a servant the way I treat a stable-boy. That's only your ignorance; and don't you forget it. And don't be so ready to defy everybody. Act as if you expected to have your own way, not as if you expected to be ordered about. The way to get on as a lady is the same as the way to get on as a servant: you've got to know your place; that's the secret of it. And you may depend on me to know my place if you get promoted. Think over it, my girl. I'll stand by you: one servant should always stand by another.

LOUKA [*rising impatiently*]. Oh, I must behave in my own way. You take all the courage out of me with your cold-blooded wisdom. Go and put those logs on the fire: that's the sort of thing you understand. [*Before Nicola can retort, Sergius comes in. He checks himself a moment on seeing Louka; then goes to the stove.*]

SERGIUS [*to Nicola*]. I am not in the way of your work, I hope.

NICOLA [*in a smooth, elderly manner*]. Oh, no, sir, thank you kindly. I was only speaking to this foolish girl about her habit of running up here to the library whenever she gets a chance, to look at the books. That's the worst of her education, sir: it gives her habits above her station. [*To Louka.*] Make that table tidy, Louka, for the Major. [*He goes out sedately.*]

[*Louka, without looking at Sergius, begins to arrange the papers on the table. He crosses slowly to her, and studies the arrangement of her sleeve reflectively.*]

SERGIUS. Let me see: is there a mark there? [*He*

turns up the bracelet and sees the bruise made by his grasp. She stands motionless, not looking at him: fascinated, but on her guard.] Ffff! Does it hurt?

LOUKA. Yes.

SERGIUS. Shall I cure it?

LOUKA [*instantly withdrawing herself proudly, but still not looking at him*]. No. You cannot cure it now.

SERGIUS [*masterfully*]. Quite sure? [*He makes a movement as if to take her in his arms.*]

LOUKA. Don't trifle with me, please. An officer should not trifle with a servant.

SERGIUS [*touching the arm with a merciless stroke of his forefinger*]. That was no trifle, Louka.

LOUKA. No. [*Looking at him for the first time.*] Are you sorry?

SERGIUS [*with measured emphasis, folding his arms*]. I am never sorry.

LOUKA [*wistfully*]. I wish I could believe a man could be so unlike a woman as that. I wonder are you really a brave man?

SERGIUS [*unaffectedly, relaxing his attitude*]. Yes: I am a brave man. My heart jumped like a woman's at the first shot; but in the charge I found that I was brave. Yes: that at least is real about me.

LOUKA. Did you find in the charge that the men whose fathers are poor like mine were any less brave than the men who are rich like you?

SERGIUS [*with bitter levity*]. Not a bit. They all slashed and cursed and yelled like heroes. Psha! the courage to rage and kill is cheap. I have an English bull terrier who has as much of that sort of courage as the whole Bulgarian nation, and the whole Russian nation at its back. But he lets my groom thrash him, all the same. That's your soldier all over! No, Louka, your poor men can cut throats; but they are afraid of their officers; they put up with insults and blows; they stand by and see one another punished like children—aye, and help to do it when they are ordered. And the officers!—well [*with a short, bitter laugh*] *I* am an officer. Oh [*fervently*] give me the man who will defy to the death any power on earth or in heaven that sets itself up against his own will and conscience: he alone is the brave man.

LOUKA. How easy it is to talk! Men never seem to me to grow up: they all have schoolboy's ideas. You don't know what true courage is.

SERGIUS [*ironically*]. Indeed! I am willing to be instructed.

LOUKA. Look at me! how much am I allowed to have my own will? I have to get your room ready for you—to sweep and dust, to fetch and carry. How could that degrade me if it did not degrade you to have it done for you? But [*with subdued passion*] if I were Empress of Russia, above everyone in the world, then—ah, then, though according to you I could shew no courage at all; you should see, you should see.

SERGIUS. What would you do, most noble Empress?

LOUKA. I would marry the man I loved, which no other queen in Europe has the courage to do. If I loved you, though you would be as far beneath me as I am beneath you, I would dare to be the equal of my inferior. Would you dare as much if you loved me? No: if you felt the beginnings of love for me you would not let it grow. You dare not: you would marry a rich man's daughter because you would be afraid of what other people would say of you.

SERGIUS [*carried away*]. You lie: it is not so, by all the stars! If I loved you, and I were the Czar himself, I would set you on the throne by my side. You know that I love another woman, a woman as high above you as heaven is above earth. And you are jealous of her.

LOUKA. I have no reason to be. She will never marry you now. The man I told you of has come back. She will marry the Swiss.

SERGIUS [*recoiling*]. The Swiss!

LOUKA. A man worth ten of you. Then you can come to me; and I will refuse you. You are not good enough for me. [*She turns to the door.*]

SERGIUS [*springing after her and catching her fiercely in his arms*]. I will kill the Swiss; and afterwards I will do as I please with you.

LOUKA [*in his arms, passive and steadfast*]. The Swiss will kill you, perhaps. He has beaten you in love. He may beat you in war.

SERGIUS [*tormentedly*]. Do you think I believe that

she—she! whose worst thoughts are higher than your best ones, is capable of trifling with another man behind my back?

LOUKA. Do you think she would believe the Swiss if he told her now that I am in your arms?

SERGIUS [*releasing her in despair*]. Damnation! Oh, damnation! Mockery, mockery everywhere: everything I think is mocked by everything I do. [*He strikes himself frantically on the breast.*] Coward, liar, fool! Shall I kill myself like a man, or live and pretend to laugh at myself? [*She again turns to go.*] Louka! [*She stops near the door.*] Remember: you belong to me.

LOUKA [*quietly*]. What does that mean—an insult?

SERGIUS [*commandingly*]. It means that you love me, and that I have had you here in my arms, and will perhaps have you there again. Whether that is an insult I neither know nor care: take it as you please. But [*vehemently*] I will not be a coward and a trifler. If I choose to love you, I dare marry you, in spite of all Bulgaria. If these hands ever touch you again, they shall touch my affianced bride.

LOUKA. We shall see whether you dare keep your word. But take care. I will not wait long.

SERGIUS [*again folding his arms and standing motionless in the middle of the room*]. Yes, we shall see. And you shall wait my pleasure.

[*Bluntschli, much preoccupied, with his papers still in his hand, enters, leaving the door open for Louka to go out. He goes across to the table, glancing at her as he passes. Sergius, without altering his resolute attitude, watches him steadily. Louka goes out, leaving the door open.*]

BLUNTSCHLI [*absently, sitting at the table as before, and putting down his papers*]. That's a remarkable looking young woman.

SERGIUS [*gravely, without moving*]. Captain Bluntschli.

BLUNTSCHLI. Eh?

SERGIUS. You have deceived me. You are my rival. I brook no rivals. At six o'clock I shall be in the drilling-ground on the Klissoura road, alone, on horseback, with my sabre. Do you understand?

BLUNTSCHLI [*staring, but sitting quite at his ease*]. Oh, thank you: that's a cavalry man's proposal. I'm in the artillery; and I have the choice of weapons. If I go, I shall take a machine gun. And there shall be no mistake about the cartridges this time.

SERGIUS [*flushing, but with deadly coldness*]. Take care, sir. It is not our custom in Bulgaria to allow invitations of that kind to be trifled with.

BLUNTSCHLI [*warmly*]. Pooh! don't talk to me about Bulgaria. You don't know what fighting is. But have it your own way. Bring your sabre along. I'll meet you.

SERGIUS [*fiercely delighted to find his opponent a man of spirit*]. Well said, Switzer. Shall I lend you my best horse?

BLUNTSCHLI. No: damn your horse!—thank you all the same, my dear fellow. [*Raina comes in, and hears the next sentence.*] I shall fight you on foot. Horseback's too dangerous: I don't want to kill you if I can help it.

RAINA [*hurrying forward anxiously*]. I have heard what Captain Bluntschli said, Sergius. You are going to fight. Why? [*Sergius turns away in silence, and goes to the stove, where he stands watching her as she continues, to Bluntschli*] What about?

BLUNTSCHLI. I don't know: he hasn't told me. Better not interfere, dear young lady. No harm will be done: I've often acted as sword instructor. He won't be able to touch me; and I'll not hurt him. It will save explanations. In the morning I shall be off home; and you'll never see me or hear of me again. You and he will then make it up and live happily ever after.

RAINA [*turning away deeply hurt, almost with a sob in her voice*]. I never said I wanted to see you again.

SERGIUS [*striding forward*]. Ha! That is a confession.

RAINA [*haughtily*]. What do you mean?

SERGIUS. You love that man!

RAINA [*scandalized*]. Sergius!

SERGIUS. You allow him to make love to you behind my back, just as you accept me as your affianced husband behind his. Bluntschli: you knew our relations; and you deceived me. It is for that that I call you to account, not for having received favours that I never enjoyed.

BLUNTSCHLI [*jumping up indignantly*]. Stuff! Rubbish! I have received no favours. Why, the young lady doesn't even know whether I'm married or not.

RAINA [*forgetting herself*]. Oh! [*Collapsing on the ottoman.*] Are you?

SERGIUS. You see the young lady's concern, Captain Bluntschli. Denial is useless. You have enjoyed the privilege of being received in her own room, late at night—

BLUNTSCHLI [*interrupting him pepperily*]. Yes; you blockhead! She received me with a pistol at her head. Your cavalry were at my heels. I'd have blown out her brains if she'd uttered a cry.

SERGIUS [*taken aback*]. Bluntschli! Raina: is this true?

RAINA [*rising in wrathful majesty*]. Oh, how dare you, how dare you?

BLUNTSCHLI. Apologize, man, apologize! [*He resumes his seat at the table.*]

SERGIUS [*with the old measured emphasis, folding his arms*]. I *never* apologize.

RAINA [*passionately*]. This is the doing of that friend of yours, Captain Bluntschli. It is he who is spreading this horrible story about me. [*She walks about excitedly.*]

BLUNTSCHLI. No: he's dead—burnt alive.

RAINA [*stopping, shocked*]. Burnt alive!

BLUNTSCHLI. Shot in the hip in a wood-yard. Couldn't drag himself out. Your fellows' shells set the timber on fire and burnt him, with half a dozen other poor devils in the same predicament.

RAINA. How horrible!

SERGIUS. And how ridiculous! Oh, war! war! the dream of patriots and heroes! A fraud, Bluntschli, a hollow sham, like love.

RAINA [*outraged*]. Like love! You say that before me.

BLUNTSCHLI. Come, Saranoff: that matter is explained.

SERGIUS. A hollow sham, I say. Would you have come back here if nothing had passed between you, except at the muzzle of your pistol? Raina is mistaken about our friend who was burnt. He was not my informant.

RAINA. Who then? [*Suddenly guessing the truth.*] Ah, Louka! my maid, my servant! You were with her this morning all that time after—after— Oh, what sort of god is this I have been worshipping! [*He meets her gaze with sardonic enjoyment of her disenchantment. Angered all the more, she goes closer to him, and says, in a lower, intenser tone*] Do you know that I looked out of the window as I went upstairs, to have another sight of my hero; and I saw something that I did not understand then. I know now that you were making love to her.

SERGIUS [*with grim humor*]. You saw that?

RAINA. Only too well. [*She turns away, and throws herself on the divan under the centre window, quite overcome.*]

SERGIUS [*cynically*]. Raina: our romance is shattered. Life's a farce.

BLUNTSCHLI [*to Raina, goodhumoredly*]. You see: he's found himself out now.

SERGIUS. Bluntschli: I have allowed you to call me a blockhead. You may now call me a coward as well. I refuse to fight you. Do you know why?

BLUNTSCHLI. No; but it doesn't matter. I didn't ask the reason when you cried on; and I don't ask the reason now that you cry off. I'm a professional soldier. I fight when I have to, and am very glad to get out of it when I haven't to. You're only an amateur: you think fighting's an amusement.

SERGIUS. You shall hear the reason all the same, my professional. The reason is that it takes two men—real men—men of heart, blood and honor—to make a genuine combat. I could no more fight with you than I could make love to an ugly woman. You've no magnetism: you're not a man, you're a machine.

BLUNTSCHLI [*apologetically*]. Quite true, quite true. I always was that sort of chap. I'm very sorry. But now that you've found that life isn't a farce, but something quite sensible and serious, what further obstacle is there to your happiness?

RAINA [*rising*]. You are very solicitous about my happiness and his. Do you forget his new love—Louka? It is not you that he must fight now, but his rival, Nicola.

SERGIUS. Rival!! [*Striking his forehead.*]

RAINA. Did you not know that they are engaged?

SERGIUS. Nicola! Are fresh abysses opening! Nicola!!

RAINA [*sarcastically*]. A shocking sacrifice, isn't it? Such beauty, such intellect, such modesty, wasted on a middle-aged servant man! Really, Sergius, you cannot stand by and allow such a thing. It would be unworthy of your chivalry.

SERGIUS [*losing all self-control*]. Viper! Viper! [*He rushes to and fro, raging.*]

BLUNTSCHLI. Look here, Saranoff; you're getting the worst of this.

RAINA [*getting angrier*]. Do you realize what he has done, Captain Bluntschli? He has set this girl as a spy on us; and her reward is that he makes love to her.

SERGIUS. False! Monstrous!

RAINA. Monstrous! [*Confronting him.*] Do you deny that she told you about Captain Bluntschli being in my room?

SERGIUS. No; but—

RAINA [*interrupting*]. Do you deny that you were making love to her when she told you?

SERGIUS. No; but I tell you—

RAINA [*cutting him short contemptuously*]. It is unnecessary to tell us anything more. That is quite enough for us. [*She turns her back on him and sweeps majestically back to the window.*]

BLUNTSCHLI [*quietly, as Sergius, in an agony of mortification, sinks on the ottoman, clutching his averted head between his fists*]. I told you you were getting the worst of it, Saranoff.

SERGIUS. Tiger cat!

RAINA [*running excitedly to Bluntschli*]. You hear this man calling me names, Captain Bluntschli?

BLUNTSCHLI. What else can he do, dear lady? He must defend himself somehow. Come [*very persuasively*], don't quarrel. What good does it do? [*Raina, with a gasp, sits down on the ottoman, and after a vain effort to look vexedly at Bluntschli, she falls a victim to her sense of humor, and is attacked with a disposition to laugh.*]

SERGIUS. Engaged to Nicola! [*He rises.*] Ha! ha! [*Going to the stove and standing with his back to it.*] Ah,

well, Bluntschli, you are right to take this huge imposture of a world coolly.

RAINA [*to Bluntschli with an intuitive guess at his
state of mind*]. I daresay you think us a couple of grown
up babies, don't you?

SERGIUS [*grinning a little*]. He does, he does. Swiss
civilization nursetending Bulgarian barbarism, eh?

BLUNTSCHLI [*blushing*]. Not at all, I assure you. I'm
only very glad to get you two quieted. There now, let's
be pleasant and talk it over in a friendly way. Where is
this other young lady?

RAINA. Listening at the door, probably.

SERGIUS [*shivering as if a bullet had struck him, and
speaking with quiet but deep indignation*]. I will prove
that that, at least, is a calumny. [*He goes with dignity to
the door and opens it. A yell of fury bursts from him as
he looks out. He darts into the passage, and returns drag-
ging in Louka, whom he flings against the table, R., as he
cries*] Judge her, Bluntschli—you, the moderate, cautious
man: judge the eavesdropper.

[*Louka stands her ground, proud and silent.*]

BLUNTSCHLI [*shaking his head*]. I mustn't judge her.
I once listened myself outside a tent when there was
a mutiny brewing. It's all a question of the degree of
provocation. My life was at stake.

LOUKA. My love was at stake. [*Sergius flinches,
ashamed of her in spite of himself.*] I am not ashamed.

RAINA [*contemptuously*]. Your love! Your curiosity,
you mean.

LOUKA [*facing her and retorting her contempt with
interest*]. My love, stronger than anything you can feel,
even for your chocolate cream soldier.

SERGIUS [*with quick suspicion—to Louka*]. What
does that mean?

LOUKA [*fiercely*]. It means—

SERGIUS [*interrupting her slightingly*]. Oh, I remember, the ice pudding. A paltry taunt, girl.

[*Major Petkoff enters, in his shirtsleeves.*]

PETKOFF. Excuse my shirtsleeves, gentlemen. Raina:
somebody has been wearing that coat of mine: I'll swear
it—somebody with bigger shoulders than mine. It's all
burst open at the back. Your mother is mending it. I

wish she'd make haste. I shall catch cold. [*He looks more attentively at them.*] Is anything the matter?

RAINA. No. [*She sits down at the stove with a tranquil air.*]

SERGIUS. Oh, no! [*He sits down at the end of the table, as at first.*]

BLUNTSCHLI [*who is already seated*]. Nothing, nothing.

PETKOFF [*sitting down on the ottoman in his old place*]. That's all right. [*He notices Louka.*] Anything the matter, Louka?

LOUKA. No, sir.

PETKOFF [*genially*]. That's all right. [*He sneezes.*] Go and ask your mistress for my coat, like a good girl, will you? [*She turns to obey; but Nicola enters with the coat; and she makes a pretence of having business in the room by taking the little table with the hookah away to the wall near the windows.*]

RAINA [*rising quickly, as she sees the coat on Nicola's arm*]. Here it is, papa. Give it to me, Nicola; and do you put some more wood on the fire. [*She takes the coat, and brings it to the Major, who stands up to put it on. Nicola attends to the fire.*]

PETKOFF [*to Raina, teasing her affectionately*]. Aha! Going to be very good to poor old papa just for one day after his return from the wars, eh?

RAINA [*with solemn reproach*]. Ah, how can you say that to me, father?

PETKOFF. Well, well, only a joke, little one. Come, give me a kiss. [*She kisses him.*] Now give me the coat.

RAINA. Now, I am going to put it on for you. Turn your back. [*He turns his back and feels behind him with his arms for the sleeves. She dexterously takes the photograph from the pocket and throws it on the table before Bluntschli, who covers it with a sheet of paper under the very nose of Sergius, who looks on amazed, with his suspicions roused in the highest degree. She then helps Petkoff on with his coat.*] There, dear! Now are you comfortable?

PETKOFF. Quite, little love. Thanks. [*He sits down; and Raina returns to her seat near the stove.*] Oh, by the bye, I've found something funny. What's the meaning of this? [*He puts his hand into the picked pocket.*] Eh? Hallo! [*He tries the other pocket.*] Well, I could have sworn— [*Much puzzled, he tries the breast pocket.*] I wonder— [*Tries the original pocket.*] Where can it— [*A light flashes on him; he rises, exclaiming*] Your mother's taken it.

RAINA [*very red*]. Taken what?

PETKOFF. Your photograph, with the inscription: "Raina, to her Chocolate Cream Soldier—a souvenir." Now you know there's something more in this than meets the eye; and I'm going to find it out. [*Shouting.*] Nicola!

NICOLA [*dropping a log, and turning*]. Sir!

PETKOFF. Did you spoil any pastry of Miss Raina's this morning?

NICOLA. You heard Miss Raina say that I did, sir.

PETKOFF. I know that, you idiot. Was it true?

NICOLA. I am sure Miss Raina is incapable of saying anything that is not true, sir.

PETKOFF. Are you? Then I'm not. [*Turning to the others.*] Come: do you think I don't see it all? [*Goes to Sergius, and slaps him on the shoulder.*] Sergius: you're the chocolate cream soldier, aren't you?

SERGIUS [*starting up*]. I! a chocolate cream soldier! Certainly not.

PETKOFF. Not! [*He looks at them. They are all very serious and very conscious.*] Do you mean to tell me that Raina sends photographic souvenirs to other men?

SERGIUS [*enigmatically*]. The world is not such an innocent place as we used to think, Petkoff.

BLUNTSCHLI [*rising*]. It's all right, Major. I'm the chocolate cream soldier. [*Petkoff and Sergius are equally astonished.*] The gracious young lady saved my life by giving me chocolate creams when I was starving—shall I ever forget their flavour! My late friend Stolz told you the story at Peerot. I was the fugitive.

PETKOFF. You! [*He gasps.*] Sergius: do you remember how those two women went on this morning when we mentioned it? [*Sergius smiles cynically. Petkoff confronts Raina severely.*] You're a nice young woman, aren't you?

RAINA [*bitterly*]. Major Saranoff has changed his

mind. And when I wrote that on the photograph, I did not know that Captain Bluntschli was married.

BLUNTSCHLI [*much startled—protesting vehemently*]. I'm *not* married.

RAINA [*with deep reproach*]. You said you were.

BLUNTSCHLI. I did not. I positively did not. I never was married in my life.

PETKOFF [*exasperated*]. Raina: will you kindly inform me, if I am not asking too much, which gentleman you are engaged to?

RAINA. To neither of them. This young lady [*introducing Louka, who faces them all proudly*] is the object of Major Saranoff's affections at present.

PETKOFF. Louka! Are you mad, Sergius? Why, this girl's engaged to Nicola.

NICOLA [*coming forward*]. I beg your pardon, sir. There is a mistake. Louka is not engaged to me.

PETKOFF. Not engaged to you, you scoundrel! Why, you had twenty-five levas from me on the day of your betrothal; and she had that gilt bracelet from Miss Raina.

NICOLA [*with cool unction*]. We gave it out so, sir. But it was only to give Louka protection. She had a soul above her station; and I have been no more than her confidential servant. I intend, as you know, sir, to set up a shop later on in Sofea; and I look forward to her custom and recommendation should she marry into the nobility. [*He goes out with impressive discretion, leaving them all staring after him.*]

PETKOFF [*breaking the silence*]. Well, I am—hm!

SERGIUS. This is either the finest heroism or the most crawling baseness. Which is it, Bluntschli?

BLUNTSCHLI. Never mind whether it's heroism or baseness. Nicola's the ablest man I've met in Bulgaria. I'll make him manager of a hotel if he can speak French and German.

LOUKA [*suddenly breaking out at Sergius*]. I have been insulted by everyone here. You set them the example. You owe me an apology. [*Sergius immediately, like a repeating clock of which the spring has been touched, begins to fold his arms.*]

BLUNTSCHLI [*before he can speak*]. It's no use. He never apologizes.

LOUKA. Not to you, his equal and his enemy. To me, his poor servant, he will not refuse to apologize.

SERGIUS [*approvingly*]. You are right. [*He bends his knee in his grandest manner.*] Forgive me!

LOUKA. I forgive you. [*She timidly gives him her hand, which he kisses.*] That touch makes me your affianced wife.

SERGIUS [*springing up*]. Ah, I forgot that!

LOUKA [*coldly*]. You can withdraw if you like.

SERGIUS. Withdraw! Never! You belong to me! [*He puts his arm about her and draws her to him.*]

[*Catherine comes in and finds Louka in Sergius's arms, and all the rest gazing at them in bewildered astonishment.*]

CATHERINE. What does this mean? [*Sergius releases Louka.*]

PETKOFF. Well, my dear, it appears that Sergius is going to marry Louka instead of Raina. [*She is about to break out indignantly at him: he stops her by exclaiming testily*] Don't blame me: I've nothing to do with it. [*He retreats to the stove.*]

CATHERINE. Marry Louka! Sergius: you are bound by your word to us!

SERGIUS [*folding his arms*]. Nothing binds me.

BLUNTSCHLI [*much pleased by this piece of common sense*]. Saranoff: your hand. My congratulations. These heroics of yours have their practical side after all. [*To Louka.*] Gracious young lady: the best wishes of a good Republican! [*He kisses her hand, to Raina's great disgust.*]

CATHERINE [*threateningly*]. Louka: you have been telling stories.

LOUKA. I have done Raina no harm.

CATHERINE [*haughtily*]. Raina! [*Raina is equally indignant at the liberty.*]

LOUKA. I have a right to call her Raina: she calls me Louka. I told Major Saranoff she would never marry him if the Swiss gentleman came back.

BLUNTSCHLI [*surprised*]. Hallo!

LOUKA [*turning to Raina*]. I thought you were

fonder of him than of Sergius. You know best whether I was right.

BLUNTSCHLI. What nonsense! I assure you, my dear Major, my dear Madame, the gracious young lady simply saved my life, nothing else. She never cared two straws for me. Why, bless my heart and soul, look at the young lady and look at me. She, rich, young, beautiful, with her imagination full of fairy princes and noble natures and cavalry charges and goodness knows what! And I, a commonplace Swiss soldier who hardly knows what a decent life is after fifteen years of barracks and battles— a vagabond—a man who has spoiled all his chances in life through an incurably romantic disposition—a man—

SERGIUS [*starting as if a needle had pricked him and interrupting Bluntschli in incredulous amazement*]. Excuse me, Bluntschli: *what* did you say had spoiled your chances in life?

BLUNTSCHLI [*promptly*]. An incurably romantic disposition. I ran away from home twice when I was a boy. I went into the army instead of into my father's business. I climbed the balcony of this house when a man of sense would have dived into the nearest cellar. I came sneaking back here to have another look at the young lady when any other man of my age would have sent the coat back—

PETKOFF. My coat!

BLUNTSCHLI. —Yes: that's the coat I mean—would have sent it back and gone quietly home. Do you suppose I am the sort of fellow a young girl falls in love with? Why, look at our ages! I'm thirty-four: I don't suppose the young lady is much over seventeen. [*This estimate produces a marked sensation, all the rest turning and staring at one another. He proceeds innocently.*] All that adventure which was life or death to me, was only a schoolgirl's game to her—chocolate creams and hide and seek. Here's the proof! [*He takes the photograph from the table.*] Now, I ask you, would a woman who took the affair seriously have sent me this and written on it: "Raina, to her chocolate cream soldier—a souvenir"? [*He exhibits the photograph triumphantly, as if it settled the matter beyond all possibility of refutation.*]

PETKOFF. That's what I was looking for. How the deuce did it get there?

BLUNTSCHLI [*to Raina complacently*]. I have put everything right, I hope, gracious young lady!

RAINA [*in uncontrollable vexation*]. I quite agree with your account of yourself. You are a romantic idiot. [*Bluntschli is unspeakably taken aback.*] Next time I hope you will know the difference between a schoolgirl of seventeen and a woman of twenty-three.

BLUNTSCHLI [*stupefied*]. Twenty-three! [*She snaps the photograph contemptuously from his hand; tears it across; and throws the pieces at his feet.*]

SERGIUS [*with grim enjoyment of Bluntschli's discomfiture*]. Bluntschli: my one last belief is gone. Your sagacity is a fraud, like all the other things. You have less sense than even I have.

BLUNTSCHLI [*overwhelmed*]. Twenty-three! Twenty-three!! [*He considers.*] Hm! [*Swiftly making up his mind.*] In that case, Major Petkoff, I beg to propose formally to become a suitor for your daughter's hand, in place of Major Saranoff retired.

RAINA. You dare!

BLUNTSCHLI. If you were twenty-three ·when you said those things to me this afternoon, I shall take them seriously.

CATHERINE [*loftily polite*]. I doubt, sir, whether you quite realize either my daughter's position or that of Major Sergius Saranoff, whose place you propose to take. The Petkoffs and the Saranoffs are known as the richest and most important families in the country. Our position is almost historical: we can go back for nearly twenty years.

PETKOFF. Oh, never mind that, Catherine. [*To Bluntschli.*] We should be most happy, Bluntschli, if it were only a question of your position; but hang it, you know, Raina is accustomed to a very comfortable establishment. Sergius keeps twenty horses.

BLUNTSCHLI. But what on earth is the use of twenty horses? Why, it's a circus.

CATHERINE [*severely*]. My daughter, sir, is accustomed to a first-rate stable.

RAINA. Hush, mother, you're making me ridiculous.

BLUNTSCHLI. Oh, well, if it comes to a question of an establishment, here goes! [*He goes impetuously to the table and seizes the papers in the blue envelope.*] How many horses did you say?

SERGIUS. Twenty, noble Switzer!

BLUNTSCHLI. I have two hundred horses. [*They are amazed.*] How many carriages?

SERGIUS. Three.

BLUNTSCHLI. I have seventy. Twenty-four of them will hold twelve inside, besides two on the box, without counting the driver and conductor. How many table-cloths have you?

SERGIUS. How the deuce do I know?

BLUNTSCHLI. Have you four thousand?

SERGIUS. No.

BLUNTSCHLI. I have. I have nine thousand six hundred pairs of sheets and blankets, with two thousand four hundred eider-down quilts. I have ten thousand knives and forks, and the same quantity of dessert spoons. I have six hundred servants. I have six palatial establishments, besides two livery stables, a tea garden and a private house. I have four medals for distinguished services; I have the rank of an officer and the standing of a gentleman; and I have three native languages. Show me any man in Bulgaria that can offer as much.

PETKOFF [*with childish awe*]. Are you Emperor of Switzerland?

BLUNTSCHLI. My rank is the highest known in Switzerland: I'm a free citizen.

CATHERINE. Then Captain Bluntschli, since you are my daughter's choice, I shall not stand in the way of her happiness. [*Petkoff is about to speak.*] That is Major Petkoff's feeling also.

PETKOFF. Oh, I shall be only too glad. Two hundred horses! Whew!

SERGIUS. What says the lady?

RAINA [*pretending to sulk*]. The lady says that he can keep his tablecloths and his omnibuses. I am not here to be sold to the highest bidder.

BLUNTSCHLI. I won't take that answer. I appealed to you as a fugitive, a beggar, and a starving man. You accepted me. You gave me your hand to kiss, your bed to sleep in, and your roof to shelter me—

RAINA [*interrupting him*]. I did not give them to the Emperor of Switzerland!

BLUNTSCHLI. That's just what I say. [*He catches her hand quickly and looks her straight in the face as he adds, with confident mastery*] Now tell us who you did give them to.

RAINA [*succumbing with a shy smile*]. To my chocolate cream soldier!

BLUNTSCHLI [*with a boyish laugh of delight*]. That'll do. Thank you. [*Looks at his watch and suddenly becomes businesslike.*] Time's up, Major. You've managed those regiments so well that you are sure to be asked to get rid of some of the Infantry of the Teemok division. Send them home by way of Lom Palanka. Saranoff: don't get married until I come back: I shall be here punctually at five in the evening on Tuesday fortnight. Gracious ladies—good evening. [*He makes them a military bow, and goes.*]

SERGIUS. What a man! What a man!

Candida

ACT ONE

A *fine October morning in the north east suburbs of London, a vast district many miles away from the London of Mayfair and St. James's, much less known there than the Paris of the Rue de Rivoli and the Champs Elysées, and much less narrow, squalid, fetid and airless in its slums; strong in comfortable, prosperous middle class life; wide streeted; myriad-populated; well-served with ugly iron urinals, Radical clubs, tram lines, and a perpetual stream of yellow cars; enjoying in its main thoroughfares the luxury of grass-grown "front gardens," untrodden by the foot of man save as to the path from the gate to the hall door; but blighted by an intolerable monotony of miles and miles of graceless, characterless brick houses, black iron railings, stony pavements, slaty roofs, and respectably ill dressed or disreputably poorly dressed people, quite accustomed to the place, and mostly plodding about somebody else's work, which they would not do if they themselves could help it. The little energy and eagerness that crop up shew themselves in cockney cupidity and business "push." Even the policemen and the chapels are not infrequent enough to break the monotony. The sun is shining cheerfully; there is no fog; and though the smoke effectually prevents anything, whether faces and hands or bricks and mortar, from looking fresh and clean, it is not hanging heavily enough to trouble a Londoner.*

This desert of unattractiveness has its oasis. Near the outer end of the Hackney Road is a park of 217 acres, fenced in, not by railings, but by a wooden paling, and containing plenty of greensward, trees, a lake for bathers,

171

flower beds with the flowers arranged carefully in patterns by the admired cockney art of carpet gardening and a sandpit, imported from the seaside for the delight of the children, but speedily deserted on its becoming a natural vermin preserve for all the petty fauna of Kingsland, Hackney and Hoxton. A bandstand, an unfinished forum for religious, anti-religious and political orators, cricket pitches, a gymnasium, and an old fashioned stone kiosk are among its attractions. Wherever the prospect is bounded by trees or rising green grounds, it is a pleasant place. Where the ground stretches flat to the grey palings, with bricks and mortar, sky signs, crowded chimneys and smoke beyond, the prospect makes it desolate and sordid.

The best view of Victoria Park is from the front window of St. Dominic's Parsonage, from which not a single chimney is visible. The parsonage is a semi-detached villa with a front garden and a porch. Visitors go up the flight of steps to the porch: tradespeople and members of the family go down by a door under the steps to the basement, with a breakfast room, used for all meals, in front, and the kitchen at the back. Upstairs, on the level of the hall door, is the drawing-room, with its large plate glass window looking on the park. In this room, the only sitting-room that can be spared from the children and the family meals, the parson, the Reverend James Mavor Morell, does his work. He is sitting in a strong round backed revolving chair at the right hand end of a long table, which stands across the window, so that he can cheer himself with the view of the park at his elbow. At the opposite end of the table, adjoining it, is a little table only half the width of the other, with a typewriter on it. His typist is sitting at this machine, with her back to the window. The large table is littered with pamphlets, journals, letters, nests of drawers, an office diary, postage scales and the like. A spare chair for visitors having business with the parson is in the middle, turned to his end. Within reach of his hand is a stationery case, and a cabinet photograph in a frame. Behind him the right hand wall, recessed above the fireplace, is fitted with bookshelves, on which an adept eye can measure the parson's divinity and casuistry by a complete set of Browning's poems and Maurice's Theological Essays, *and guess at his politics from a yellow backed* Progress and Poverty, Fabian Essays, A Dream of John Ball, *Marx's* Capital, *and half a dozen other literary landmarks in Socialism. Opposite him on the left, near the typewriter, is the door. Further down the room, opposite the fireplace, a bookcase stands on a cellaret, with a sofa near it. There is a generous fire burning; and the hearth, with a comfortable armchair and a japanned flower painted coal scuttle at one side, a miniature chair for a boy or girl on the other, a nicely varnished wooden mantelpiece, with neatly moulded shelves, tiny bits of mirror let into the panels, and a travelling clock in a leather case* [the inevitable wedding present], *and on the wall above a large autotype of the chief figure in Titian's Virgin of the Assumption, is very inviting. Altogether the room is the room of a good housekeeper, vanquished, as far as the table is concerned, by an untidy man, but elsewhere mistress of the situation. The furniture, in its ornamental aspect, betrays the style of the advertised "drawing-room suite" of the pushing suburban furniture dealer; but there is nothing useless or pretentious in the room. The paper and panelling are dark, throwing the big cheery window and the park outside into strong relief.*

The Reverend James Mavor Morell is a Christian Socialist clergyman of the Church of England, and an active member of the Guild of St. Matthew and the Christian Social Union. A vigorous, genial, popular man of forty, robust and goodlooking, full of energy, with pleasant, hearty, considerate manners, and a sound, unaffected voice, which he uses with the clean, athletic articulation of a practised orator, and with a wide range and perfect command of expression. He is a first rate clergyman, able to say what he likes to whom he likes, to lecture people without setting himself up against them, to impose his authority on them without humiliating them, and to interfere in their business without impertinence. His well spring of spiritual enthusiasm and sympathetic emotion has never run dry for a moment: he still eats and sleeps heartily enough to win the daily battle between exhaustion and recuperation triumphantly. Withal, a great baby, pardonably vain of his powers and unconsciously pleased with himself. He has a healthy complexion, a good fore-

*head, with the brows somewhat blunt, and the eyes bright
and eager, a mouth resolute, but not particularly well cut,
and a substantial nose, with the mobile, spreading nostrils
of the dramatic orator, but, like all his features, void of
subtlety.*

*The typist, Miss Proserpine Garnett, is a brisk little
woman of about 30, of the lower middle class, neatly but
cheaply dressed in a black merino skirt and a blouse,
rather pert and quick of speech, and not very civil in her
manner, but sensitive and affectionate. She is clattering
away busily at her machine whilst Morell opens the last
of his morning's letters. He realizes its contents with a
comic groan of despair.*

PROSERPINE. Another lecture?

MORELL. Yes. The Hoxton Freedom Group want me
to address them on Sunday morning [*great emphasis on
"Sunday," this being the unreasonable part of the business*]. What are they?

PROSERPINE. Communist Anarchists, I think.

MORELL. Just like Anarchists not to know that they
can't have a parson on Sunday! Tell them to come to
church if they want to hear me: it will do them good.
Say I can only come on Mondays and Thursdays. Have
you the diary there?

PROSERPINE [*taking up the diary*]. Yes.

MORELL. Have I any lecture on for next Monday?

PROSERPINE [*referring to diary*]. Tower Hamlets
Radical Club.

MORELL. Well, Thursday then?

PROSERPINE. English Land Restoration League.

MORELL. What next?

PROSERPINE. Guild of St. Matthew on Monday. Independent Labor Party, Greenwich Branch, on Thursday. Monday, Social-Democratic Federation, Mile End
Branch. Thursday, first Confirmation class— [*Impatiently.*] Oh, I'd better tell them you can't come. They're
only half a dozen ignorant and conceited costermongers
without five shillings between them.

MORELL [*amused*]. Ah; but you see they're near relatives of mine, Miss Garnett.

PROSERPINE [*staring at him*]. Relatives of yours!

MORELL. Yes: we have the same father—in Heaven.

PROSERPINE [*relieved*]. Oh, is that all?

MORELL [*with a sadness which is a luxury to a man whose voice expresses it so finely*]. Ah, you don't believe it. Everybody says it: nobody believes it—nobody. [*Briskly, getting back to business.*] Well, well! Come, Miss Proserpine, can't you find a date for the costers? What about the 25th?: that was vacant the day before yesterday.

PROSERPINE [*referring to diary*]. Engaged—the Fabian Society.

MORELL. Bother the Fabian Society! Is the 28th gone, too?

PROSERPINE. City dinner. You're invited to dine with the Founder's Company.

MORELL. That'll do; I'll go to the Hoxton Group of Freedom instead. [*She enters the engagement in silence, with implacable disparagement of the Hoxton Anarchists in every line of her face. Morell bursts open the cover of a copy of* The Church Reformer, *which has come by post, and glances through Mr. Stewart Hendlam's leader and the Guild of St. Matthew news. These proceedings are presently enlivened by the appearance of Morell's curate, the Reverend Alexander Mill, a young gentleman gathered by Morell from the nearest University settlement, whither he had come from Oxford to give the east end of London the benefit of his university training. He is a conceitedly well intentioned, enthusiastic, immature person, with nothing positively unbearable about him except a habit of speaking with his lips carefully closed for half an inch from each corner, a finicking articulation, and a set of horribly corrupt vowels, notably ow for o, this being his chief means of bringing Oxford refinement to bear on Hackney vulgarity. Morell, whom he has won over by a doglike devotion, looks up indulgently from* The Church Reformer *as he enters, and remarks*] Well, Lexy! Late again, as usual.

LEXY. I'm afraid so. I wish I could get up in the morning.

MORELL [*exulting in his own energy*]. Ha! ha! [*Whimsically.*] Watch and pray, Lexy: watch and pray.

LEXY. I know. [*Rising wittily to the occasion.*] But

how can I watch and pray when I am asleep? Isn't that
so, Miss Prossy?

PROSERPINE [*sharply*]. Miss Garnett, if you please.

LEXY. I beg your pardon—Miss Garnett.

PROSERPINE. You've got to do all the work to-day.

LEXY. Why?

PROSERPINE. Never mind why. It will do you good
to earn your supper before you eat it, for once in a way,
as I do. Come: don't dawdle. You should have been off
on your rounds half an hour ago.

LEXY [*perplexed*]. Is she in earnest, Morell?

MORELL [*in the highest spirits—his eyes dancing*].
Yes. *I* am going to dawdle to-day.

LEXY. You! You don't know how.

MORELL [*heartily*]. Ha! ha! Don't I? I'm going to
have this day all to myself—or at least the forenoon. My
wife's coming back: she's due here at 11.45.

LEXY [*surprised*]. Coming back already—with the
children? I thought they were to stay to the end of the
month.

MORELL. So they are: she's only coming up for two
days, to get some flannel things for Jimmy, and to see
how we're getting on without her.

LEXY [*anxiously*]. But, my dear Morell, if what
Jimmy and Fluffy had was scarlatina, do you think it
wise—

MORELL. Scarlatina!—rubbish, German measles. I
brought it into the house myself from the Pycroft Street
School. A parson is like a doctor, my boy: he must face
infection as a soldier must face bullets. [*He rises and
claps Lexy on the shoulder.*] Catch the measles if you
can, Lexy: she'll nurse you; and what a piece of luck
that will be for you!—eh?

LEXY [*smiling uneasily*]. It's so hard to understand
you about Mrs. Morell—

MORELL [*tenderly*]. Ah, my boy, get married—get
married to a good woman; and then you'll understand.
That's a foretaste of what will be best in the Kingdom
of Heaven we are trying to establish on earth. That will
cure you of dawdling. An honest man feels that he must
pay Heaven for every hour of happiness with a good
spell of hard, unselfish work to make others happy. We

have no more right to consume happiness without producing it than to consume wealth without producing it. Get a wife like my Candida; and you'll always be in arrear with your repayment.

[*He pats Lexy affectionately on the back, and is leaving the room when Lexy calls to him.*]

LEXY. Oh, wait a bit: I forgot. [*Morell halts and turns with the door knob in his hand.*] Your father-in-law is coming round to see you. [*Morell shuts the door again, with a complete change of manner.*]

MORELL [*surprised and not pleased*]. Mr. Burgess?

LEXY. Yes. I passed him in the park, arguing with somebody. He gave me good day and asked me to let you know that he was coming.

MORELL [*half incredulous*]. But he hasn't called here for— I may almost say for years. Are you sure, Lexy? You're not joking, are you?

LEXY [*earnestly*]. No, sir, really.

MORELL [*thoughtfully*]. Hm! Time for him to take another look at Candida before she grows out of his knowledge. [*He resigns himself to the inevitable, and goes out. Lexy looks after him with beaming, foolish worship.*]

LEXY. What a good man! What a thorough, loving soul he is!

[*He takes Morell's place at the table, making himself very comfortable as he takes out a cigaret.*]

PROSERPINE [*impatiently, pulling the letter she has been working at off the typewriter and folding it*]. Oh, a man ought to be able to be fond of his wife without making a fool of himself about her.

LEXY [*shocked*]. Oh, Miss Prossy!

PROSERPINE [*rising busily and coming to the stationery case to get an envelope, in which she encloses the letter as she speaks*]. Candida here, and Candida there, and Candida everywhere! [*She licks the envelope.*] It's enough to drive anyone out of their senses [*thumping the envelope to make it stick*] to hear a perfectly commonplace woman raved about in that absurd manner merely because she's got good hair, and a tolerable figure.

LEXY [*with reproachful gravity*]. I think her extremely beautiful, Miss Garnett. [*He takes the photo-*

graph up; looks at it; and adds, with even greater impressiveness] Extremely beautiful. How fine her eyes are!

PROSERPINE. Her eyes are not a bit better than mine—now! [*He puts down the photograph and stares austerely at her.*] And you know very well that you think me dowdy and second rate enough.

LEXY [*rising majestically*]. Heaven forbid that I should think of any of God's creatures in such a way! [*He moves stiffly away from her across the room to the neighbourhood of the bookcase.*]

PROSERPINE. Thank you. That's very nice and comforting.

LEXY [*saddened by her depravity*]. I had no idea you had any feeling against Mrs. Morell.

PROSERPINE [*indignantly*]. I have no feeling against her. She's very nice, very good-hearted: I'm very fond of her and can appreciate her real qualities far better than any man can. [*He shakes his head sadly and turns to the bookcase, looking along the shelves for a volume. She follows him with intense pepperiness.*] You don't believe me? [*He turns and faces her. She pounces at him with spitfire energy.*] You think I'm jealous. Oh, what a profound knowledge of the human heart you have, Mr. Lexy Mill! How well you know the weaknesses of Woman, don't you! It must be so nice to be a man and have a fine penetrating intellect instead of mere emotions like us, and to know that the reason we don't share your amorous delusions is that we're all jealous of one another! [*She abandons him with a toss of her shoulders, and crosses to the fire to warm her hands.*]

LEXY. Ah, if you women only had the same clue to Man's strength that you have to his weakness, Miss Prossy, there would be no Woman Question.

PROSERPINE [*over her shoulder, as she stoops, holding her hands to the blaze*]. Where did you hear Morell say that? You didn't invent it yourself: you're not clever enough.

LEXY. That's quite true. I am not ashamed of owing him that, as I owe him so many other spiritual truths. He said it at the annual conference of the Women's Liberal Federation. Allow me to add that though they didn't appreciate it, I, a mere man, did. [*He turns to the book-case again, hoping that this may leave her crushed.*]

PROSERPINE [*putting her hair straight at the little panel of mirror in the mantelpiece*]. Well, when you talk to me, give me your own ideas, such as they are, and not his. You never cut a poorer figure than when you are trying to imitate him.

LEXY [*stung*]. I try to follow his example, not to imitate him.

PROSERPINE [*coming at him again on her way back to her work*]. Yes, you do: you imitate him. Why do you tuck your umbrella under your left arm instead of carrying it in your hand like anyone else? Why do you walk with your chin stuck out before you, hurrying along with that eager look in your eyes—you, who never get up before half past nine in the morning? Why do you say "knoaledge" in church, though you always say "knolledge" in private conversation! Bah! do you think I don't know? [*She goes back to the typewriter.*] Here, come and set about your work: we've wasted enough time for one morning. Here's a copy of the diary for to-day. [*She hands him a memorandum.*]

LEXY [*deeply offended*]. Thank you. [*He takes it and stands at the table with his back to her, reading it. She begins to transcribe her shorthand notes on the typewriter without troubling herself about his feelings. Mr. Burgess enters unannounced. He is a man of sixty, made coarse and sordid by the compulsory selfishness of petty commerce, and later on softened into sluggish bumptiousness by overfeeding and commercial success. A vulgar, ignorant, guzzling man, offensive and contemptuous to people whose labor is cheap, respectful to wealth and rank, and quite sincere and without rancour or envy in both attitudes. Finding him without talent, the world has offered him no decently paid work except ignoble work, and he has become, in consequence, somewhat hoggish. But he has no suspicion of this himself, and honestly regards his commercial prosperity as the inevitable and socially wholesome triumph of the ability, industry, shrewdness and experience in business of a man who in private is easygoing, affectionate and humorously convivial to a fault. Corporeally, he is a podgy man, with a square,*] *clean shaven face and a square beard under his chin, dust colored, with a patch of grey in the centre, and small watery blue eyes with a plaintively sentimental expression, which he transfers easily to his voice by his habit of pompously intoning his sentences.*]

BURGESS [*stopping on the threshold, and looking round*]. They told me Mr. Morell was here.

PROSERPINE [*rising*]. He's upstairs. I'll fetch him for you.

BURGESS [*staring boorishly at her*]. You're not the same young lady as hused to typewrite for him?

PROSERPINE. No.

BURGESS [*assenting*]. No: she was young-er. [*Miss Garnett stolidly stares at him; then goes out with great dignity. He receives this quite obtusely, and crosses to the hearth-rug, where he turns and spreads himself with his back to the fire.*] Startin' on your rounds, Mr. Mill?

LEXY [*folding his paper and pocketing it*]. Yes: I must be off presently.

BURGESS [*momentously*]. Don't let me detain you, Mr. Mill. What I come about is private between me and Mr. Morell.

LEXY [*huffily*]. I have no intention of intruding, I am sure, Mr. Burgess. Good morning.

BURGESS [*patronizingly*]. Oh, good morning to you. [*Morell returns as Lexy is making for the door.*]

MORELL [*to Lexy*]. Off to work?

LEXY. Yes, sir.

MORELL [*patting him affectionately on the shoulder*]. Take my silk handkerchief and wrap your throat up. There's a cold wind. Away with you.

[*Lexy brightens up, and goes out.*]

BURGESS. Spoilin' your curates, as usu'l, James. Good mornin'. When I pay a man, an' 'is livin' depen's on me, I keep him in his place.

MORELL [*rather shortly*]. I always keep my curates in their places as my helpers and comrades. If you get as much work out of your clerks and warehousemen as I do out of my curates, you must be getting rich pretty fast. Will you take your old chair?

[*He points with curt authority to the arm chair beside*

the fireplace; then takes the spare chair from the table and sits down in front of Burgess.]

BURGESS [*without moving*]. Just the same as hever, James!

MORELL. When you last called—it was about three years ago, I think—you said the same thing a little more frankly. Your exact words then were: "Just as big a fool as ever, James?"

BURGESS [*soothingly*]. Well, perhaps I did; but [*with conciliatory cheerfulness*] I meant no offence by it. A clorgyman is privileged to be a bit of a fool, you know: it's on'y becomin' in his profession that he should. Anyhow, I come here, not to rake up hold differences, but to let bygones be bygones. [*Suddenly becoming very solemn, and approaching Morell.*] James: three year ago, you done me a hill turn. You done me hout of a contrac'; an' when I gev you 'arsh words in my nat'ral disappointment, you turned my daughrter again me. Well, I've come to act the part of a Cherischin. [*Offering his hand.*] I forgive you, James.

MORELL [*starting up*]. Confound your impudence!

BURGESS [*retreating, with almost lachrymose deprecation of this treatment*]. Is that becomin' language for a clorgyman, James?—and you so partic'lar, too?

MORELL [*hotly*]. No, sir, it is not becoming language for a clergyman. I used the wrong word. I should have said damn your impudence: that's what St. Paul, or any honest priest, would have said to you. Do you think I have forgotten that tender of yours for the contract to supply clothing to the workhouse?

BURGESS [*in a paroxysm of public spirit*]. I acted in the interest of the ratepayers, James. It was the lowest tender: you can't deny that.

MORELL. Yes, the lowest, because you paid worse wages than any other employer—starvation wages—aye, worse than starvation wages—to the women who made the clothing. Your wages would have driven them to the streets to keep body and soul together. [*Getting angrier and angrier.*] Those women were my parishioners. I shamed the Guardians out of accepting your tender: I shamed the ratepayers out of letting them do it: I shamed everybody but you. [*Boiling over.*] How dare you, sir, come here and offer to forgive me, and talk about your daughter, and—

BURGESS. Easy, James, easy, easy. Don't git hinto a fluster about nothink. I've howned I was wrong.

MORELL [*fuming about*]. Have you? I didn't hear you.

BURGESS. Of course I did. I hown it now. Come: I harsk your pardon for the letter I wrote you. Is that enough?

MORELL [*snapping his fingers*]. That's nothing. Have you raised the wages?

BURGESS [*triumphantly*]. Yes.

MORELL [*stopping dead*]. What!

BURGESS [*unctuously*]. I've turned a moddle hemployer. I don't hemploy no women now: they're all sacked; and the work is done by machinery. Not a man 'as less than sixpence a *h*our; and the skilled 'ands gits the Trade Union rate. [*Proudly.*] What 'ave you to say to me now?

MORELL [*overwhelmed*]. Is it possible! Well, there's more joy in heaven over one sinner that repenteth— [*Going to Burgess with an explosion of apologetic cordiality.*] My dear Burgess, I most heartily beg your pardon for my hard thoughts of you. [*Grasps his hand.*] And now, don't you feel the better for the change? Come, confess, you're happier. You look happier.

BURGESS [*ruefully*]. Well, p'raps I do. I s'pose I must, since you notice it. At all events, I git my contrax asseppit [accepted] by the County Council. [*Savagely.*] They dussent 'ave nothink to do with me unless I paid fair wages—curse 'em for a parcel o' meddlin' fools!

MORELL [*dropping his hand, utterly discouraged*]. So that was why you raised the wages! [*He sits down moodily.*]

BURGESS [*severely, in spreading, mounting tones*]. Why else should I do it? What does it lead to but drink and huppishness in workin' men? [*He seats himself magisterially in the easy chair.*] It's hall very well for you, James: it gits you hinto the papers and makes a great man of you; but you never think of the 'arm you do, puttin' money into the pockets of workin' men that they don't know 'ow to spend, and takin' it from people that might be makin' a good huse on it.

MORELL [*with a heavy sigh, speaking with cold politeness*]. What is your business with me this morning? I shall not pretend to believe that you are here merely out of family sentiment.

BURGESS [*obstinately*]. Yes, I ham—just family sentiment and nothink else.

MORELL [*with weary calm*]. I don't believe you!

BURGESS [*rising threateningly*]. Don't say that to me again, James Mavor Morell.

MORELL [*unmoved*]. I'll say it just as often as may be necessary to convince you that it's true. I don't believe you.

BURGESS [*collapsing into an abyss of wounded feeling*]. Oh, well, if you're determined to be unfriendly, I s'pose I'd better go. [*He moves reluctantly towards the door. Morell makes no sign. He lingers.*] I didn't hexpect to find a hunforgivin' spirit in you, James. [*Morell still not responding, he takes a few more reluctant steps doorwards. Then he comes back whining.*] We huseter git on well enough, spite of our different opinions. Why are you so changed to me? I give you my word I come here in pyorr [*pure*] frenliness, not wishin' to be on bad terms with my hown daughrter's 'usban'. Come, James: be a Cherischin and shake 'ands. [*He puts his hand sentimentally on Morrell's shoulder.*]

MORELL [*looking up at him thoughtfully*]. Look here, Burgess. Do you want to be as welcome here as you were before you lost that contract?

BURGESS. I do, James. I do—honest.

MORELL. Then why don't you behave as you did then?

BURGESS [*cautiously removing his hand*]. 'Ow d'y'mean?

MORELL. I'll tell you. You thought me a young fool then.

BURGESS [*coaxingly*]. No, I didn't, James. I—

MORELL [*cutting him short*]. Yes, you did. And I thought you an old scoundrel.

BURGESS [*most vehemently deprecating this gross self-accusation on Morell's part*]. No, you didn't, James. Now you do yourself a hinjustice.

MORELL. Yes, I did. Well, that did not prevent our getting on very well together. God made you what I call a scoundrel as he made me what you call a fool. [*The effect of this observation on Burgess is to remove the keystone of his moral arch. He becomes bodily weak, and, with his eyes fixed on Morell in a helpless stare, puts out his hand apprehensively to balance himself, as if the floor had suddenly sloped under him. Morell proceeds in the same tone of quiet conviction.*] It was not for me to quarrel with his handiwork in the one case more than in the other. So long as you come here honestly as a self-respecting, thorough, convinced scoundrel, justifying your scoundrelism, and proud of it, you are welcome. But [*and now Morell's tone becomes formidable; and he rises and strikes the back of the chair for greater emphasis*] I won't have you here snivelling about being a model employer and a converted man when you're only an apostate with your coat turned for the sake of a County Council contract. [*He nods at him to enforce the point; then goes to the hearth-rug, where he takes up a comfortably commanding position with his back to the fire, and continues*] No: I like a man to be true to himself, even in wickedness. Come now: either take your hat and go; or else sit down and give me a good scoundrelly reason for wanting to be friends with me. [*Burgess, whose emotions have subsided sufficiently to be expressed by a dazed grin, is relieved by this concrete proposition. He ponders it for a moment, and then, slowly and very modestly, sits down in the chair Morell has just left.*] That's right. Now, out with it.

BURGESS [*chuckling in spite of himself*]. Well, you are a queer bird, James, and no mistake. But [*almost enthusiastically*] one carnt 'elp likin' you; besides, as I said afore, of course one don't take all a clorgyman says seriously, or the world couldn't go on. Could it now? [*He composes himself for graver discourse, and turning his eyes on Morell proceeds with dull seriousness*] Well, I don't mind tellin' you, since it's your wish we should be free with one another, that I did think you a bit of

a fool once; but I'm beginnin' to think that p'r'aps I was
be'ind the times a bit.

MORELL [*delighted*]. Aha! You're finding that out at
last, are you?

BURGESS [*portentously*]. Yes, times 'as changed
mor'n I could a believed. Five yorr [year] ago, no sensible man would a thought o' takin' up with your ideas. I
hused to wonder you was let preach at all. Why, I know
a clorgyman that 'as bin kep' hout of his job for yorrs
by the Bishop of London, although the pore feller's not
a bit more religious than you are. But to-day, if henyone
was to offer to bet me a thousan' poun' that you'll end
by bein' a bishop yourself, I shouldn't venture to take
the bet. You and yore crew are gettin' hinfluential: I can
see that. They'll 'ave to give you something someday, if
it's only to stop yore mouth. You 'ad the right instinc'
arter all, James: the line you took is the payin' line in
the long run fur a man o' your sort.

MORELL [*decisively—offering his hand*]. Shake hands,
Burgess. Now you're talking honestly. I don't think they'll
make me a bishop; but if they do, I'll introduce you to the
biggest jobbers I can get to come to my dinner parties.

BURGESS [*who has risen with a sheepish grin and
accepted the hand of friendship*]. You will 'ave your joke,
James. Our quarrel's made up now, isn't it?

A WOMAN'S VOICE. Say yes, James.

[*Startled, they turn quickly and find that Candida has
just come in, and is looking at them with an amused
maternal indulgence which is her characteristic expression. She is a woman of 33, well built, well nourished,
likely, one guesses, to become matronly later on, but
now quite at her best, with the double charm of youth
and motherhood. Her ways are those of a woman who
has found that she can always manage people by engaging their affection, and who does so frankly and instinctively without the smallest scruple. So far, she is
like any other pretty woman who is just clever enough
to make the most of her sexual attractions for trivially
selfish ends; but Candida's serene brow, courageous
eyes, and well set mouth and chin signify largeness of
mind and dignity of character to ennoble her cunning
in the affections. A wisehearted observer, looking at*

*her, would at once guess that whoever had placed the
Virgin of the Assumption over her hearth did so because he fancied some spiritual resemblance between
them, and yet would not suspect either her husband or
herself of any such idea, or indeed of any concern with
the art of Titian.*

*Just now she is in bonnet and mantle, laden with a
strapped rug with her umbrella stuck through it, a handbag, and a supply of illustrated papers.]*

MORELL [*shocked at his remissness*]. Candida! Why—
[*looks at his watch, and is horrified to find it so late.*] My
darling! [*Hurrying to her and seizing the rug strap, pour-
ing forth his remorseful regrets all the time.*] I intended
to meet you at the train. I let the time slip. [*Flinging the
rug on the sofa.*] I was so engrossed by—[*returning to
her*]—I forgot—oh! [*He embraces her with penitent
emotion.*]

BURGESS [*a little shamefaced and doubtful of his
reception*]. How orr you, Candy? [*She, still in Morell's
arms, offers him her cheek, which he kisses.*] James and
me is come to a unnerstandin'—a honourable
unnerstandin'. Ain' we, James?

MORELL [*impetuously*]. Oh, bother your understanding! You've kept me late for Candida. [*With compassionate fervor.*] My poor love: how did you manage about
the luggage?—how—

CANDIDA [*stopping him and disengaging herself*].
There, there, there. I wasn't alone. Eugene came down
yesterday; and we travelled up together.

MORELL [*pleased*]. Eugene!

CANDIDA. Yes: he's struggling with my luggage, poor
boy. Go out, dear, at once; or he will pay for the cab;
and I don't want that. [*Morell hurries out. Candida puts
down her handbag; then takes off her mantle and bonnet
and puts them on the sofa with the rug, chatting meanwhile.*] Well, papa, how are you getting on at home?

BURGESS. The 'ouse ain't worth livin' in since you
left it, Candy. I wish you'd come round and give the gurl
a talkin' to. Who's this Eugene that's come with you?

CANDIDA. Oh, Eugene's one of James's discoveries.
He found him sleeping on the Embankment last June.

Haven't you noticed our new picture [*pointing to the Virgin*]? He gave us that.

BURGESS [*incredulously*]. Garn! D'you mean to tell me—your hown father!—that cab touts or such like, orf the Embankment, buys pictur's like that? [*Severely.*] Don't deceive me, Candy: it's a 'Igh Church pictur; and James chose it hisself.

CANDIDA. Guess again. Eugene isn't a cab tout.

BURGESS. Then wot is he? [*Sarcastically.*] A nobleman, I s'pose.

CANDIDA [*delighted—nodding*]. Yes. His uncle's a peer—a real live earl.

BURGESS [*not daring to believe such good news*]. No!

CANDIDA. Yes. He had a seven day bill for £55 in his pocket when James found him on the Embankment. He thought he couldn't get any money for it until the seven days were up; and he was too shy to ask for credit. Oh, he's a dear boy! We are very fond of him.

BURGESS [*pretending to belittle the aristocracy, but with his eyes gleaming*]. Hm, I thort you wouldn't git a piorr's [*peer's*] nevvy visitin' in Victoria Park unless he were a bit of a flat. [*Looking again at the picture.*] Of course I don't 'old with that pictur, Candy; but still it's a 'igh class, fust rate work of art: I can see that. Be sure you hintroduce me to him. [*He looks at his watch anxiously.*] I can only stay about two minutes.

[*Morell comes back with Eugene, whom Burgess contemplates moist-eyed with enthusiasm. He is a strange, shy youth of eighteen, slight, effeminate, with a delicate childish voice, and a hunted, tormented expression and shrinking manner that shew the painful sensitiveness that very swift and acute apprehensiveness produces in youth, before the character has grown to its full strength. Yet everything that his timidity and frailty suggests is contradicted by his face. He is miserably irresolute, does not know where to stand or what to do with his hands and feet, is afraid of Burgess, and would run away into solitude if he dared; but the very intensity with which he feels a perfectly commonplace position shews great nervous force, and his nostrils and mouth shew a fiercely petulant wilfulness, as to the quality of which his great imaginative*]

*eyes and fine brow are reassuring. He is so entirely un-
common as to be almost unearthly; and to prosaic people
there is something noxious in this unearthliness, just as to
poetic people there is something angelic in it. His dress is
anarchic. He wears an old blue serge jacket, unbuttoned
over a woollen lawn tennis shirt, with a silk handkerchief
for a cravat, trousers matching the jacket, and brown canvas shoes. In these garments he has apparently lain in the
heather and waded through the waters; but there is no
evidence of his having ever brushed them.*

*As he catches sight of a stranger on entering, he stops,
and edges along the wall on the opposite side of the
room.*]

MORELL [*as he enters*]. Come along: you can spare
us quarter of an hour, at all events. This is my father-
in-law, Mr. Burgess—Mr. Marchbanks.

MARCHBANKS [*nervously backing against the bookcase*]. Glad to meet you, sir.

BURGESS [*crossing to him with great heartiness, whilst
Morell joins Candida at the fire*]. Glad to meet you, I'm
shore, Mr. Morchbanks. [*Forcing him to shake hands.*]
'Ow do you find yoreself this weather? 'Ope you ain't
lettin' James put no foolish ideas into your 'ed?

MARCHBANKS. Foolish ideas! Oh, you mean Socialism. No.

BURGESS. That's right. [*Again looking at his watch.*]
Well, I must go now: there's no 'elp for it. Yo're not
comin' my way, are you, Mr. Morchbanks?

MARCHBANKS. Which way is that?

BURGESS. Victawriar Pork Station. There's a city
train at 12:25.

MORELL. Nonsense. Eugene will stay to lunch with
us, I expect.

MARCHBANKS [*anxiously excusing himself*]. No—I—
I—

BURGESS. Well, well, I shan't press you: I bet you'd
rather lunch with Candy. Some night, I 'ope, you'll come
and dine with me at my club, the Freeman Founders in
Nortn Folgit. Come, say you will.

MARCHBANKS. Thank you, Mr. Burgess. Where is
Norton Folgate—down in Surrey, isn't it? [*Burgess, inexpressibly tickled, begins to splutter with laughter.*]

CANDIDA [*coming to the rescue*]. You'll lose your train, papa, if you don't go at once. Come back in the afternoon and tell Mr. Marchbanks where to find the club.

BURGESS [*roaring with glee*]. Down in Surrey—har, har! that's not a bad one. Well, I never met a man as didn't know Nortn Folgit before. [*Abashed at his own noisiness.*] Good-bye, Mr. Morchbanks: I know yo're too 'ighbred to take my pleasantry in bad part. [*He again offers his hand.*]

MARCHBANKS [*taking it with a nervous jerk*]. Not at all.

BURGESS. Bye, byè, Candy. I'll look in again later on. So long, James.

MORELL. Must you go?

BURGESS. Don't stir. [*He goes out with unabated heartiness.*]

MORELL. Oh, I'll see you out. [*He follows him out. Eugene stares after them apprehensively, holding his breath until Burgess disappears.*]

CANDIDA [*laughing*]. Well, Eugene. [*He turns with a start and comes eagerly towards her, but stops irresolutely as he meets her amused look.*] What do you think of my father?

MARCHBANKS. I—I hardly know him yet. He seems to be a very nice old gentleman.

CANDIDA [*with gentle irony*]. And you'll go to the Freeman Founders to dine with him, won't you?

MARCHBANKS [*miserably, taking it quite seriously*]. Yes, if it will please you.

CANDIDA [*touched*]. Do you know, you are a very nice boy, Eugene, with all your queerness. If you had laughed at my father I shouldn't have minded; but I like you ever so much better for being nice to him.

MARCHBANKS. Ought I to have laughed? I noticed that he said something funny; but I am so ill at ease with strangers; and I never can see a joke! I'm very sorry. [*He sits down on the sofa, his elbows on his knees and his temples between his fists, with an expression of hopeless suffering.*]

CANDIDA [*bustling him goodnaturedly*]. Oh, come! You great baby, you! You are worse than usual this morning. Why were you so melancholy as we came along in the cab?

MARCHBANKS. Oh, that was nothing. I was wondering how much I ought to give the cabman. I know it's utterly silly; but you don't know how dreadful such things are to me—how I shrink from having to deal with strange people. [*Quickly and reassuringly.*] But it's all right. He beamed all over and touched his hat when Morell gave him two shillings. I was on the point of offering him ten. [*Candida laughs heartily. Morell comes back with a few letters and newspapers which have come by the midday post.*]

CANDIDA. Oh, James, dear, he was going to give the cabman ten shillings—ten shillings for a three minutes' drive—oh, dear!

MORELL [*at the table, glancing through the letters*]. Never mind her, Marchbanks. The overpaying instinct is a generous one: better than the underpaying instinct, and not so common.

MARCHBANKS [*relapsing into dejection*]. No: cowardice, incompetence. Mrs. Morell's quite right.

CANDIDA. Of course she is. [*She takes up her handbag.*] And now I must leave you to James for the present. I suppose you are too much of a poet to know the state a woman finds her house in when she's been away for three weeks. Give me my rug. [*Eugene takes the strapped rug from the couch, and gives it to her. She takes it in her left hand, having the bag in her right.*] Now hang my cloak across my arm. [*He obeys.*] Now my hat. [*He puts it into the hand which has the bag.*] Now open the door for me. [*He hurries up before her and opens the door.*] Thanks. [*She goes out; and Marchbanks shuts the door.*]

MORELL [*still busy at the table*]. You'll stay to lunch, Marchbanks, of course.

MARCHBANKS [*scared*]. I mustn't. [*He glances quickly at Morell, but at once avoids his frank look, and adds, with obvious disingenuousness*] I can't.

MORELL [*over his shoulder*]. You mean you won't.

MARCHBANKS [*earnestly*]. No: I should like to, indeed. Thank you very much. But—but—

MORELL [*breezily, finishing with the letters and com-*

ing close to him]. But—but—but—but—bosh! If you'd like to stay, stay. You don't mean to persuade me you have anything else to do. If you're shy, go and take a turn in the park and write poetry until half past one; and then come in and have a good feed.

MARCHBANKS. Thank you, I should like that very much. But I really mustn't. The truth is, Mrs. Morell told me not to. She said she didn't think you'd ask me to stay to lunch, but that I was to remember, if you did, that you didn't really want me to. [*Plaintively.*] She said I'd understand; but I don't. Please don't tell her I told you.

MORELL [*drolly*]. Oh, is that all? Won't my suggestion that you should take a turn in the park meet the difficulty?

MARCHBANKS. How?

MORELL [*exploding good-humoredly*]. Why, you duffer— [*But this boisterousness jars himself as well as Eugene. He checks himself, and resumes, with affectionate seriousness*] No: I won't put it in that way. My dear lad: in a happy marriage like ours, there is something very sacred in the return of the wife to her home. [*Marchbanks looks quickly at him, half anticipating his meaning.*] An old friend or a truly noble and sympathetic soul is not in the way on such occasions; but a chance visitor is. [*The hunted, horror-stricken expression comes out with sudden vividness in Eugene's face as he understands. Morell, occupied with his own thought, goes on without noticing it.*] Candida thought I would rather not have you here; but she was wrong. I'm very fond of you, my boy, and I should like you to see for yourself what a happy thing it is to be married as I am.

MARCHBANKS. Happy!—your marriage! You think that! You believe that!

MORELL [*buoyantly*]. I know, it, my lad. La Rochefoucauld said that there are convenient marriages, but no delightful ones. You don't know the comfort of seeing through and through a thundering liar and rotten cynic like that fellow. Ha, ha! Now off with you to the park, and write your poem. Half past one, sharp, mind: we never wait for anybody.

MARCHBANKS [*wildly*]. No: stop; you shan't. I'll force it into the light.

MORELL [*puzzled*]. Eh? Force what?

MARCHBANKS. I must speak to you. There is something that must be settled between us.

MORELL [*with a whimsical glance at the clock*]. Now?

MARCHBANKS [*passionately*]. Now. Before you leave this room. [*He retreats a few steps, and stands as if to bar Morell's way to the door.*]

MORELL [*without moving, and gravely, perceiving now that there is something serious the matter*]. I'm not going to leave it, my dear boy: I thought you were. [*Eugene, baffled by his firm tone, turns his back on him, writhing with anger. Morell goes to him and puts his hand on his shoulder strongly and kindly, disregarding his attempt to shake it off.*] Come: sit down quietly; and tell me what it is. And remember: we are friends, and need not fear that either of us will be anything but patient and kind to the other, whatever we may have to say.

MARCHBANKS [*twisting himself round on him*]. Oh, I am not forgetting myself: I am only [*covering his face desperately with his hands*] full of horror. [*Then, dropping his hands, and thrusting his face forward fiercely at Morell, he goes on threateningly.*] You shall see whether this is a time for patience and kindness. [*Morell, firm as a rock, looks indulgently at him.*] Don't look at me in that self-complacent way. You think yourself stronger than I am; but I shall stagger you if you have a heart in your breast.

MORELL [*powerfully confident*]. Stagger me, my boy. Out with it.

MARCHBANKS. First—

MORELL. First?

MARCHBANKS. I love your wife.

[*Morell recoils, and, after staring at him for a moment in utter amazement, bursts into uncontrollable laughter. Eugene is taken aback, but not disconcerted; and he soon becomes indignant and contemptuous.*]

MORELL [*sitting down to have his laugh out*]. Why, my dear child, of course you do. Everybody loves her: they can't help it. I like it. But [*looking up whimsically at him*] I say, Eugene: do you think yours is a case to be talked about? You're under twenty: she's over thirty. Doesn't it look rather too like a case of calf love?

MARCHBANKS [*vehemently*]. You dare say that of

her! You think that way of the love she inspires! It is
an insult to her!

MORELL [*rising quickly, in an altered tone*]. To her!
Eugene: take care. I have been patient. I hope to remain
patient. But there are some things I won't allow. Don't
force me to shew you the indulgence I should shew to
a child. Be a man.

MARCHBANKS [*with a gesture as if sweeping something behind him*]. Oh, let us put aside all that cant. It
horrifies me when I think of the doses of it she has had
to endure in all the weary years during which you have
selfishly and blindly sacrificed her to minister to your
self-sufficiency—you [*turning on him*] who have not one
thought—one sense—in common with her.

MORELL [*philosophically*]. She seems to bear it
pretty well. [*Looking him straight in the face.*] Eugene,
my boy: you are making a fool of yourself—a very great
fool of yourself. There's a piece of wholesome plain
speaking for you.

MARCHBANKS. Oh, do you think I don't know all
that? Do you think that the things people make fools of
themselves about are any less real and true than the
things they behave sensibly about? [*Morell's gaze wavers
for the first time. He instinctively averts his face and stands
listening, startled and thoughtful.*] They are more true:
they are the only things that are true. You are very calm
and sensible and moderate with me because you can see
that I am a fool about your wife; just as no doubt that
old man who was here just now is very wise over your
socialism, because he sees that you are a fool about it.
[*Morell's perplexity deepens markedly. Eugene follows up
his advantage, plying him fiercely with questions.*] Does
that prove you wrong? Does your complacent superiority to me prove that *I* am wrong?

MORELL [*turning on Eugene, who stands his ground*].
Marchbanks: some devil is putting these words into your
mouth. It is easy—terribly easy—to shake a man's faith
in himself. To take advantage of that to break a man's
spirit is devil's work. Take care of what you are doing.
Take care.

MARCHBANKS [*ruthlessly*]. I know. I'm doing it on
purpose. I told you I should stagger you.

[*They confront one another threateningly for a moment. Then Morell recovers his dignity.*]

MORELL [*with noble tenderness*]. Eugene: listen to me. Some day, I hope and trust, you will be a happy man like me. [*Eugene chafes intolerantly, repudiating the worth of his happiness. Morell, deeply insulted, controls himself with fine forbearance, and continues steadily, with great artistic beauty of delivery*] You will be married; and you will be working with all your might and valor to make every spot on earth as happy as your own home. You will be one of the makers of the Kingdom of Heaven on earth; and—who knows?—you may be a pioneer and master builder where I am only a humble journeyman; for don't think, my boy, that I cannot see in you, young as you are, promise of higher powers than I can ever pretend to. I well know that it is in the poet that the holy spirit of man—the god within him—is most godlike. It should make you tremble to think of that— to think that the heavy burthen and great gift of a poet may be laid upon you.

MARCHBANKS [*unimpressed and remorseless, his boyish crudity of assertion telling sharply against Morell's oratory*]. It does not make me tremble. It is the want of it in others that makes me tremble.

MORELL [*redoubling his force of style under the stimulus of his genuine feeling and Eugene's obduracy*]. Then help to kindle it in them—in me—not to extinguish it. In the future—when you are as happy as I am—I will be your true brother in the faith. I will help you to believe that God has given us a world that nothing but our own folly keeps from being a paradise. I will help you to believe that every stroke of your work is sowing happiness for the great harvest that all—even the humblest—shall one day reap. And last, but trust me, not least, I will help you to believe that your wife loves you and is happy in her home. We need such help, Marchbanks: we need it greatly and always. There are so many things to make us doubt, if once we let our understanding be troubled. Even at home, we sit as if in camp, encompassed by a hostile army of doubts. Will you play the traitor and let them in on me?

MARCHBANKS [*looking round him*]. Is it like this for

her here always? A woman, with a great soul, craving
for reality, truth, freedom, and being fed on metaphors,
sermons, stale perorations, mere rhetoric. Do you think
a woman's soul can live on your talent for preaching?

MORELL [*stung*]. Marchbanks: you make it hard for
me to control myself. My talent is like yours insofar as
it has any real worth at all. It is the gift of finding words
for divine truth.

MARCHBANKS [*impetuously*]. It's the gift of the gab,
nothing more and nothing less. What has your knack of
fine talking to do with the truth, any more than playing
the organ has? I've never been in your church; but I've
been to your political meetings; and I've seen you do
what's called rousing the meeting to enthusiasm: that is,
you excited them until they behaved exactly as if they
were drunk. And their wives looked on and saw clearly
enough what fools they were. Oh, it's an old story: you'll
find it in the Bible. I imagine King David, in his fits of
enthusiasm, was very like you. [*Stabbing him with the
words.*] "But his wife despised him in her heart."

MORELL [*wrathfully*]. Leave my house. Do you hear?
[*He advances on him threateningly.*]

MARCHBANKS [*shrinking back against the couch*]. Let
me alone. Don't touch me. [*Morell grasps him powerfully by the lapel of his coat: he cowers down on the sofa
and screams passionately.*] Stop, Morell, if you strike me,
I'll kill myself: I won't bear it. [*Almost in hysterics.*] Let
me go. Take your hand away.

MORELL [*with slow, emphatic scorn*]. You little snivelling, cowardly whelp. [*Releasing him.*] Go, before you
frighten yourself into a fit.

MARCHBANKS [*on the sofa, gasping, but relieved by
the withdrawal of Morell's hand*]. I'm not afraid of you:
it's you who are afraid of me.

MORELL [*quietly, as he stands over him*]. It looks like
it, doesn't it?

MARCHBANKS [*with petulant vehemence*]. Yes, it does.
[*Morell turns away contemptuously. Eugene scrambles to
his feet and follows him.*] You think because I shrink from
being brutally handled—because [*with tears in his voice*] I
can do nothing but cry with rage when I am met with
violence—because I can't lift a heavy trunk down from

the top of a cab like you—because I can't fight you for your wife as a navvy would: all that makes you think that I'm afraid of you. But you're wrong. If I haven't got what you call British pluck, I haven't British cowardice either: I'm not afraid of a clergyman's ideas. I'll fight your ideas. I'll rescue her from their slavery to them: I'll pit my own ideas against them. You are driving me out of the house because you daren't let her choose between your ideas and mine. You are afraid to let me see her again. [*Morell, angered, turns suddenly on him. He flies to the door in involuntary dread.*] Let me alone, I say. I'm going.

MORELL [*with cold scorn*]. Wait a moment: I am not going to touch you: don't be afraid. When my wife comes back she will want to know why you have gone. And when she finds you are never going to cross our threshold again, she will want to have that explained too. Now I don't wish to distress her by telling her that you have behaved like a blackguard.

MARCHBANKS [*coming back with renewed vehemence*]. You shall—you must. If you give any explanation but the true one, you are a liar and a coward. Tell her what I said; and how you were strong and manly, and shook me as a terrier shakes a rat; and how I shrank and was terrified; and how you called me a snivelling little whelp and put me out of the house. If you don't tell her, I will: I'll write it to her.

MORELL [*taken aback*]. Why do you want her to know this?

MARCHBANKS [*with lyric rapture*]. Because she will understand me, and know that I understand her. If you keep back one word of it from her—if you are not ready to lay the truth at her feet as I am—then you will know to the end of your days that she really belongs to me and not to you. Good-bye. [*Going.*]

MORELL [*terribly disquieted*]. Stop: I will not tell her.

MARCHBANKS [*turning near the door*]. Either the truth or a lie you must tell her, if I go.

MORELL [*temporizing*]. Marchbanks: it is sometimes justifiable.

MARCHBANKS [*cutting him short*]. I know—to lie. It will be useless. Good-bye, Mr. Clergyman.

[*As he turns finally to the door, it opens and Candida enters in housekeeping attire.*]

CANDIDA. Are you going, Eugene? [*Looking more observantly at him.*] Well, dear me, just look at you, going out into the street in that state! You are a poet, certainly. Look at him, James! [*She takes him by the coat, and brings him forward to show him to Morell.*] Look at his collar! look at his tie! look at his hair! One would think somebody had been throttling you. [*The two men guard themselves against betraying their consciousness.*] Here! Stand still. [*She buttons his collar; ties his neckerchief in a bow; and arranges his hair.*] There! Now you look so nice that I think you'd better stay to lunch after all, though I told you you mustn't. It will be ready in half an hour. [*She puts a final touch to the bow. He kisses her hand.*] Don't be silly.

MARCHBANKS. I want to stay, of course—unless the reverend gentleman, your husband, has anything to advance to the contrary.

CANDIDA. Shall he stay, James, if he promises to be a good boy and to help me to lay the table? [*Marchbanks turns his head and looks steadfastly at Morell over his shoulder, challenging his answer.*]

MORELL [*shortly*]. Oh, yes, certainly: he had better. [*He goes to the table and pretends to busy himself with his papers there.*]

MARCHBANKS [*offering his arm to Candida*]. Come and lay the table. [*She takes it and they go to the door together. As they go out he adds*] I am the happiest of men.

MORELL. So was I—an hour ago.

ACT TWO

The same day. The same room. Late in the afternoon. The spare chair for visitors has been replaced at the table, which is, if possible, more untidy than before. Marchbanks, alone and idle, is trying to find out how the typewriter works. Hearing someone at the door, he steals guiltily away to the window and pretends to be absorbed in

*the view. Miss Garnett, carrying the note-book in which she
takes down Morell's letters in shorthand from his dictation,
sits down at the typewriter and sets to work transcribing
them, much too busy to notice Eugene. Unfortunately the
first key she strikes sticks.*

PROSERPINE. Bother! You've been meddling with my
typewriter, Mr. Marchbanks; and there's not the least
use in your trying to look as if you hadn't.

MARCHBANKS [*timidly*]. I'm very sorry, Miss Garnett.
I only tried to make it write.

PROSERPINE. Well, you've made this key stick.

MARCHBANKS [*earnestly*]. I assure you I didn't touch
the keys. I didn't, indeed. I only turned a little wheel.
[*He points irresolutely at the tension wheel.*]

PROSERPINE. Oh, now I understand. [*She sets the machine to rights, talking volubly all the time.*] I suppose
you thought it was a sort of barrel-organ. Nothing to do
but turn the handle, and it would write a beautiful love
letter for you straight off, eh?

MARCHBANKS [*seriously*]. I suppose a machine could
be made to write love letters. They're all the same, aren't
they?

PROSERPINE [*somewhat indignantly: any such discussion, except by way of pleasantry, being outside her code
of manners*]. How do I know? Why do you ask me?

MARCHBANKS. I beg your pardon. I thought clever
people—people who can do business and write letters,
and that sort of thing—always had love affairs.

PROSERPINE [*rising, outraged*]. Mr. Marchbanks! [*She
looks severely at him, and marches with much dignity to
the bookcase.*]

MARCHBANKS [*approaching her humbly*]. I hope I
haven't offended you. Perhaps I shouldn't have alluded
to your love affairs.

PROSERPINE [*plucking a blue book from the shelf and
turning sharply on him*]. I haven't any love affairs. How
dare you say such a thing?

MARCHBANKS [*simply*]. Really! Oh, then you are shy,
like me. Isn't that so?

PROSERPINE. Certainly I am not shy. What do you
mean?

MARCHBANKS [*secretly*]. You must be: that is the reason there are so few love affairs in the world. We all go about longing for love: it is the first need of our natures, the loudest cry of our hearts; but we dare not utter our longing: we are too shy. [*Very earnestly.*] Oh, Miss Garnett, what would you not give to be without fear, without shame—

PROSERPINE [*scandalized*]. Well, upon my word!

MARCHBANKS [*with petulant impatience*]. Ah, don't say those stupid things to me: they don't deceive me: what use are they? Why are you afraid to be your real self with me? I am just like you.

PROSERPINE. Like me! Pray, are you flattering me or flattering yourself? I don't feel quite sure which. [*She turns to go back to the typewriter.*]

MARCHBANKS [*stopping her mysteriously*]. Hush! I go about in search of love; and I find it in unmeasured stores in the bosoms of others. But when I try to ask for it, this horrible shyness strangles me; and I stand dumb, or worse than dumb, saying meaningless things— foolish lies. And I see the affection I am longing for given to dogs and cats and pet birds, because they come and ask for it. [*Almost whispering.*] It must be asked for: it is like a ghost: it cannot speak unless it is first spoken to. [*At his normal pitch, but with deep melancholy.*] All the love in the world is longing to speak; only it dare not, because it is shy, shy, shy. That is the world's tragedy. [*With a deep sigh he sits in the spare chair and buries his face in his hands.*]

PROSERPINE [*amazed, but keeping her wits about her—her point of honor in encounters with strange young men*]. Wicked people get over that shyness occasionally, don't they?

MARCHBANKS [*scrambling up almost fiercely*]. Wicked people means people who have no love: therefore they have no shame. They have the power to ask love because they don't need it: they have the power to offer it because they have none to give. [*He collapses into his seat, and adds, mournfully*] But we, who have love, and long to mingle it with the love of others: we cannot utter a word. [*Timidly.*] You find that, don't you?

PROSERPINE. Look here: if you don't stop talking

like this, I'll leave the room, Mr. Marchbanks: I really will. It's not proper.

[*She resumes her seat at the typewriter, opening the blue book and preparing to copy a passage from it.*]

MARCHBANKS [*hopelessly*]. Nothing that's worth saying is proper. [*He rises, and wanders about the room in his lost way, saying*] I can't understand you, Miss Garnett. What am I to talk about?

PROSERPINE [*snubbing him*]. Talk about indifferent things. Talk about the weather.

MARCHBANKS. Would you stand and talk about indifferent things if a child were by, crying bitterly with hunger?

PROSERPINE. I suppose not.

MARCHBANKS. Well: *I* can't talk about indifferent things with my heart crying out bitterly in its hunger.

PROSERPINE. Then hold your tongue.

MARCHBANKS. Yes: that is what it always comes to. We hold our tongues. Does that stop the cry of your heart?—for it does cry: doesn't it? It must, if you have a heart.

PROSERPINE [*suddenly rising with her hand pressed on her heart*]. Oh, it's no use trying to work while you talk like that. [*She leaves her little table and sits on the sofa. Her feelings are evidently strongly worked on.*] It's no business of yours, whether my heart cries or not; but I have a mind to tell you, for all that.

MARCHBANKS. You needn't. I know already that it must.

PROSERPINE. But mind: if you ever say I said so, I'll deny it.

MARCHBANKS [*compassionately*]. Yes, I know. And so you haven't the courage to tell him?

PROSERPINE [*bouncing up*]. Him! Who?

MARCHBANKS. Whoever he is. The man you love. It might be anybody. The curate, Mr. Mill, perhaps.

PROSERPINE [*with disdain*]. Mr. Mill!!! A fine man to break my heart about, indeed! I'd rather have you than Mr. Mill.

MARCHBANKS [*recoiling*]. No, really—I'm very sorry; but you mustn't think of that. I—

PROSERPINE [*testily, crossing to the fire and standing*]

at it with her back to him]. Oh, don't be frightened: it's not you. It's not any one particular person.

MARCHBANKS. I know. You feel that you could love anybody that offered—

PROSERPINE [*exasperated*]. Anybody that offered! No, I do not. What do you take me for?

MARCHBANKS [*discouraged*]. No use. You won't make me real answers—only those things that everybody says. [*He strays to the sofa and sits down disconsolately.*]

PROSERPINE [*nettled at what she takes to be a disparagement of her manners by an aristocrat*]. Oh, well, if you want original conversation, you'd better go and talk to yourself.

MARCHBANKS. That is what all poets do: they talk to themselves out loud; and the world overhears them. But it's horribly lonely not to hear someone else talk sometimes.

PROSERPINE. Wait until Mr. Morell comes. He'll talk to you. [*Marchbanks shudders.*] Oh, you needn't make wry faces over him: he can talk better than you. [*With temper.*] He'd talk your little head off. [*She is going back angrily to her place, when, suddenly enlightened, he springs up and stops her.*]

MARCHBANKS. Ah, I understand now!

PROSERPINE [*reddening*]. What do you understand?

MARCHBANKS. Your secret. Tell me: is it really and truly possible for a woman to love him?

PROSERPINE [*as if this were beyond all bounds*]. Well!!

MARCHBANKS [*passionately*]. No, answer me. I want to know: I must know. *I* can't understand it. I can see nothing in him but words, pious resolutions, what people call goodness. You can't love that.

PROSERPINE [*attempting to snub him by an air of cool propriety*]. I simply don't know what you're talking about. I don't understand you.

MARCHBANKS [*vehemently*]. You do. You lie—

PROSERPINE. Oh!

MARCHBANKS. You do understand; and you know. [*Determined to have an answer.*] Is it possible for a woman to love him?

PROSERPINE [*looking him straight in the face*]. Yes.

[*He covers his face with his hands.*] Whatever is the matter with you! [*He takes down his hands and looks at her. Frightened at the tragic mask presented to her, she hurries past him at the utmost possible distance, keeping her eyes on his face until he turns from her and goes to the child's chair beside the hearth, where he sits in the deepest dejection. As she approaches the door, it opens and Burgess enters. On seeing him, she ejaculates*] Praise heaven, here's somebody! [*and sits down, reassured, at her table. She puts a fresh sheet of paper into the typewriter as Burgess crosses to Eugene.*]

BURGESS [*bent on taking care of the distinguished visitor*]. Well: so this is the way they leave you to yourself, Mr. Morchbanks. I've come to keep you company. [*Marchbanks looks up at him in consternation, which is quite lost on him.*] James is receivin' a deppitation in the dinin' room; and Candy is hupstairs educatin' of a young stitcher gurl she's hinterusted in. She's settin' there learnin' her to read out of the " 'Ev'nly Twins." [*Condolingly.*] You must find it lonesome here with no one but the typist to talk to. [*He pulls round the easy chair above the fire, and sits down.*]

PROSERPINE [*highly incensed*]. He'll be all right now that he has the advantage of your polished conversation: that's one comfort, anyhow. [*She begins to typewrite with clattering asperity.*]

BURGESS [*amazed at her audacity*]. Hi was not addressin' myself to you, young woman, that I'm awerr of.

PROSERPINE [*tartly, to Marchbanks*]. Did you ever see worse manners, Mr. Marchbanks?

BURGESS [*with pompous severity*]. Mr. Morchbanks is a gentleman and knows his place, which is more than some people do.

PROSERPINE [*fretfully*]. It's well you and I are not ladies and gentlemen: I'd talk to you pretty straight if Mr. Marchbanks wasn't here. [*She pulls the letter out of the machine so crossly that it tears.*] There, now I've spoiled this letter—have to be done all over again. Oh, I can't contain myself—silly old fathead!

BURGESS [*rising, breathless with indignation*]. Ho! I'm a silly ole fat'ead, am I? Ho, indeed [*gasping*]. Hall

right, my gurl! Hall right. You just wait till I tell that to
your employer. You'll see. I'll teach you: see if I don't.

PROSERPINE. I—

BURGESS [*cutting her short*]. No, you've done it now.
No huse a-talkin' to me. I'll let you know who I am.
[*Prosperine shifts her paper carriage with a defiant bang,
and disdainfully goes on with her work.*] Don't you take
no notice of her, Mr. Morchbanks. She's beneath it. [*He
sits down again loftily.*]

MARCHBANKS [*miserably nervous and disconcerted*].
Hadn't we better change the subject. I—I don't think
Miss Garnett meant anything.

PROSERPINE [*with intense conviction*]. Oh, didn't I
though, just!

BURGESS. I wouldn't demean myself to take notice
on her.

[*An electric bell rings twice.*]

PROSERPINE [*gathering up her note-book and papers*]. That's for me. [*She hurries out.*]

BURGESS [*calling after her*]. Oh, we can spare you.
[*Somewhat relieved by the triumph of having the last
word, and yet half inclined to try to improve on it, he
looks after her for a moment; then subsides into his seat
by Eugene, and addresses him very confidentially.*] Now
we're alone, Mr. Morchbanks, let me give you a friendly
'int that I wouldn't give to everybody. 'Ow long 'ave
you known my son-in-law James here?

MARCHBANKS. I don't know. I never can remember
dates. A few months, perhaps.

BURGESS. Ever notice anything queer about him?

MARCHBANKS. I don't think so.

BURGESS [*impressively*]. No more you wouldn't.
That's the danger in it. Well, he's mad.

MARCHBANKS. Mad!

BURGESS. Mad as a Morch 'are. You take notice on
him and you'll see.

MARCHBANKS [*beginning*]. But surely that is only because his opinions—

BURGESS [*touching him with his forefinger on his
knee, and pressing it as if to hold his attention with it*].
That's wot I used ter think, Mr. Morchbanks. Hi thought

long enough that it was honly 'is opinions; though, mind
you, hopinions becomes vurry serious things when people takes to hactin on 'em as 'e does. But that's not wot
I go on. [*He looks round to make sure that they are
alone, and bends over to Eugene's ear.*] Wot do you think
he says to me this mornin' in this very room?

MARCHBANKS. What?

BURGESS. He sez to me—this is as sure as we're
settin' here now—he sez: "I'm a fool," he sez; "and
yore a scounderl"—as cool as possible. Me a scounderl,
mind you! And then shook 'ands with me on it, as if
it was to my credit! Do you mean to tell me that that
man's sane?

MORELL [*outside, calling to Proserpine, holding the
door open*]. Get all their names and addresses, Miss
Garnett.

PROSERPINE [*in the distance*]. Yes, Mr. Morell.

[*Morell comes in, with the deputation's documents in
his hands.*]

BURGESS [*aside to Marchbanks*]. Yorr he is. Just you
keep your heye on him and see. [*Rising momentously.*]
I'm sorry, James, to 'ave to make a complaint to you. I
don't want to do it; but I feel I oughter, as a matter o'
right and dooty.

MORELL. What's the matter?

BURGESS. Mr. Morchbanks will bear me out: he was
a witness. [*Very solemnly.*] Your young woman so far
forgot herself as to call me a silly ole fat'ead.

MORELL [*delighted—with tremendous heartiness*].
Oh, now, isn't that exactly like Prossy? She's so frank:
she can't contain herself! Poor Prossy! Ha! Ha!

BURGESS [*trembling with rage*]. And do you hexpec
me to put up with it from the like of 'er?

MORELL. Pooh, nonsense! you can't take any notice
of it. Never mind. [*He goes to the cellaret and puts the
papers into one of the drawers.*]

BURGESS. Oh, *I* don't mind. I'm above it. But is it
right?—that's what I want to know. Is it right?

MORELL. That's a question for the Church, not for
the laity. Has it done you any harm, that's the question
for you, eh? Of course, it hasn't. Think no more of it.

[*He dismisses the subject by going to his place at the table and setting to work at his correspondence.*]

BURGESS [*aside to Marchbanks*]. What did I tell you? Mad as a 'atter. [*He goes to the table and asks, with the sickly civility of a hungry man*] When's dinner, James?

MORELL. Not for half an hour yet.

BURGESS [*with plaintive resignation*]. Gimme a nice book to read over the fire, will you, James: thur's a good chap.

MORELL. What sort of book? A good one?

BURGESS [*with almost a yell of remonstrance*]. Nah-oo! Summat pleasant, just to pass the time. [*Morell takes an illustrated paper from the table and offers it. He accepts it humbly.*] Thank yer, James. [*He goes back to his easy chair at the fire, and sits there at his ease, reading.*]

MORELL [*as he writes*]. Candida will come to entertain you presently. She has got rid of her pupil. She is filling the lamps.

MARCHBANKS [*starting up in the wildest consternation*]. But that will soil her hands. I can't bear that, Morell: it's a shame. I'll go and fill them. [*He makes for the door.*]

MORELL. You'd better not. [*Marchbanks stops irresolutely.*] She'd only set you to clean my boots, to save me the trouble of doing it myself in the morning.

BURGESS [*with grave disapproval*]. Don't you keep a servant now, James?

MORELL. Yes; but she isn't a slave; and the house looks as if I kept three. That means that everyone has to lend a hand. It's not a bad plan: Prossy and I can talk business after breakfast whilst we're washing up. Washing up's no trouble when there are two people to do it.

MARCHBANKS [*tormentedly*]. Do you think every woman is as coarse-grained as Miss Garnett?

BURGESS [*emphatically*]. That's quite right, Mr. Morchbanks. That's quite right. She is corse-grained.

MORELL [*quietly and significantly*]. Marchbanks!

MARCHBANKS. Yes.

MORELL. How many servants does your father keep?

MARCHBANKS. Oh, I don't know. [*He comes back uneasily to the sofa, as if to get as far as possible from Morell's questioning, and sits down in great agony of mind, thinking of the paraffin.*]

MORELL [*very gravely*]. So many that you don't know. [*More aggressively.*] Anyhow, when there's anything coarse-grained to be done, you ring the bell and throw it on to somebody else, eh? That's one of the great facts in your existence, isn't it?

MARCHBANKS. Oh, don't torture me. The one great fact now is that your wife's beautiful fingers are dabbling in paraffin oil, and that you are sitting here comfortably preaching about it—everlasting preaching, preaching, words, words, words.

BURGESS [*intensely appreciating this retort*]. Ha, ha! Devil a better. [*Radiantly.*] 'Ad you there, James, straight.

[*Candida comes in, well aproned, with a reading lamp trimmed, filled, and ready for lighting. She places it on the table near Morell, ready for use.*]

CANDIDA [*brushing her finger tips together with a slight twitch of her nose*]. If you stay with us, Eugene, I think I will hand over the lamps to you.

MARCHBANKS. I will stay on condition that you hand over all the rough work to me.

CANDIDA. That's very gallant; but I think I should like to see how you do it first. [*Turning to Morell.*] James: you've not been looking after the house properly.

MORELL. What have I done—or not done—my love?

CANDIDA [*with serious vexation*]. My own particular pet scrubbing brush has been used for blackleading. [*A heartbreaking wail bursts from Marchbanks. Burgess looks round, amazed. Candida hurries to the sofa.*] What's the matter? Are you ill, Eugene?

MARCHBANKS. No, not ill. Only horror, horror, horror! [*He bows his head on his hands.*]

BURGESS [*shocked*]. What! Got the 'orrors, Mr. Morchbanks! Oh, that's bad, at your age. You must leave it off grajally.

CANDIDA [*reassured*]. Nonsense, papa. It's only poetic horror, isn't it, Eugene? [*Petting him.*]

BURGESS [*abashed*]. Oh, poetic 'orror, is it? I beg

your pordon, I'm shore. [*He turns to the fire again, depre-cating his hasty conclusion.*]

CANDIDA. What is it, Eugene—the scrubbing brush? [*He shudders.*] Well, there! never mind. [*She sits down beside him.*] Wouldn't you like to present me with a nice new one, with an ivory back inlaid with mother-of-pearl?

MARCHBANKS [*softly and musically, but sadly and longingly*]. No, not a scrubbing brush, but a boat—a tiny shallop to sail away in, far from the world, where the marble floors are washed by the rain and dried by the sun, where the south wind dusts the beautiful green and purple carpets. Or a chariot—to carry us up into the sky, where the lamps are stars, and don't need to be filled with paraffin oil every day.

MORELL [*harshly*]. And where there is nothing to do but to be idle, selfish and useless.

CANDIDA [*jarred*]. Oh, James, how could you spoil it all!

MARCHBANKS [*firing up*]. Yes, to be idle, selfish and useless: that is to be beautiful and free and happy: hasn't every man desired that with all his soul for the woman he loves? That's my ideal: what's yours, and that of all the dreadful people who live in these hideous rows of houses? Sermons and scrubbing brushes! With you to preach the sermon and your wife to scrub.

CANDIDA [*quaintly*]. He cleans the boots, Eugene. You will have to clean them to-morrow for saying that about him.

MARCHBANKS. Oh! don't talk about boots. Your feet should be beautiful on the mountains.

CANDIDA. My feet would not be beautiful on the Hackney Road without boots.

BURGESS [*scandalized*]. Come, Candy, don't be vulgar. Mr. Morchbanks ain't accustomed to it. You're givin' him the 'orrors again. I mean the poetic ones.

[*Morell is silent. Apparently he is busy with his letters: really he is puzzling with misgiving over his new and alarming experience that the surer he is of his moral thrusts, the more swiftly and effectively Eugene parries them. To find himself beginning to fear a man whom he does not respect afflicts him bitterly.*

Miss Garnett comes in with a telegram.]

PROSERPINE [*handing the telegram to Morell.*] Reply paid. The boy's waiting. [*To Candida, coming back to her machine and sitting down.*] Maria is ready for you now in the kitchen, Mrs. Morell. [*Candida rises.*] The onions have come.

MARCHBANKS [*convulsively*]. Onions!

CANDIDA. Yes, onions. Not even Spanish ones— nasty little red onions. You shall help me to slice them. Come along.

[*She catches him by the wrist and runs out, pulling him after her. Burgess rises in consternation, and stands aghast on the hearth-rug, staring after them.*]

BURGESS. Candy didn't oughter 'andle a peer's nevvy like that. It's goin' too fur with it. Lookee 'ere, James: do 'e often git taken queer like that?

MORELL [*shortly, writing a telegram*]. I don't know.

BURGESS [*sentimentally*]. He talks very pretty. I allus had a turn for a bit of potery. Candy takes arter me that-a-way: huse ter make me tell her fairy stories when she was on'y a little kiddy not that 'igh [*indicating a stature of two feet or thereabouts*].

MORELL [*preoccupied*]. Ah, indeed. [*He blots the telegram, and goes out.*]

PROSERPINE. Used you to make the fairy stories up out of your own head?

[*Burgess, not deigning to reply, strikes an attitude of the haughtiest disdain on the hearth-rug.*]

PROSERPINE [*calmly*]. I should never have supposed you had it in you. By the way, I'd better warn you, since you've taken such a fancy to Mr. Marchbanks. He's mad.

BURGESS. Mad! Wot! 'Im too!!

PROSERPINE. Mad as a March hare. He did frighten me, I can tell you, just before you came in that time. Haven't you noticed the queer things he says?

BURGESS. So that's wot the poetic 'orrors means. Blame me if it didn't come into my head once or twyst that he must be off his chump! [*He crosses the room to the door, lifting up his voice as he goes.*] Well, this is a pretty sort of asylum for a man to be in, with no one but you to take care of him!

PROSERPINE [*as he passes her*]. Yes, what a dreadful thing it would be if anything happened to you!

BURGESS [*loftily*]. Don't you address no remarks to me. Tell your hemployer that I've gone into the garden for a smoke.

PROSERPINE [*mocking*]. Oh!

[*Before Burgess can retort, Morell comes back.*]

BURGESS [*sentimentally*]. Goin' for a turn in the garden to smoke, James.

MORELL [*brusquely*]. Oh, all right, all right. [*Burgess goes out pathetically in the character of the weary old man. Morell stands at the table, turning over his papers, and adding, across to Proserpine, half humorously, half absently*] Well, Miss Prossy, why have you been calling my father-in-law names?

PROSERPINE [*blushing fiery red, and looking quickly up at him, half scared, half reproachful*]. I— [*She bursts into tears.*]

MORELL [*with tender gaiety, leaning across the table towards her, and consoling her*]. Oh, come, come, come! Never mind, Pross: he is a silly old fathead, isn't he?

[*With an explosive sob, she makes a dash at the door, and vanishes, banging it. Morell, shaking his head resignedly, sighs, and goes wearily to his chair, where he sits down and sets to work, looking old and careworn.*

Candida comes in. She has finished her household work and taken off the apron. She at once notices his dejected appearance, and posts herself quietly at the spare chair, looking down at him attentively; but she says nothing.]

MORELL [*looking up, but with his pen raised ready to resume his work*]. Well? Where is Eugene?

CANDIDA. Washing his hands in the scullery—under the tap. He will make an excellent cook if he can only get over his dread of Maria.

MORELL [*shortly*]. Ha! No doubt. [*He begins writing again.*]

CANDIDA [*going nearer, and putting her hand down softly on his to stop him, as she says*]. Come here, dear. Let me look at you. [*He drops his pen and yields himself at her disposal. She makes him rise and brings him a little away from the table, looking at him critically all the time.*] Turn your face to the light. [*She places him facing the window.*] My boy is not looking well. Has he been overworking?

MORELL. Nothing more than usual.

CANDIDA. He looks very pale, and grey, and wrinkled, and old. [*His melancholy deepens; and she attacks it with wilful gaiety.*] Here [*pulling him towards the easy chair*] you've done enough writing for to-day. Leave Prossy to finish it and come and talk to me.

MORELL. But—

CANDIDA. Yes, I must be talked to sometimes. [*She makes him sit down, and seats herself on the carpet beside his knee.*] Now [*patting his hand*] you're beginning to look better already. Why don't you give up all this tiresome overworking—going out every night lecturing and talking? Of course what you say is all very true and very right; but it does no good: they don't mind what you say to them one little bit. Of course they agree with you; but what's the use of people agreeing with you if they go and do just the opposite of what you tell them the moment your back is turned? Look at our congregation at St. Dominic's! Why do they come to hear you talking about Christianity every Sunday? Why, just because they've been so full of business and money-making for six days that they want to forget all about it and have a rest on the seventh, so that they can go back fresh and make money harder than ever! You positively help them at it instead of hindering them.

MORELL [*with energetic seriousness*]. You know very well, Candida, that I often blow them up soundly for that. But if there is nothing in their church-going but rest and diversion, why don't they try something more amusing—more self-indulgent? There must be some good in the fact that they prefer St. Dominic's to worse places on Sundays.

CANDIDA. Oh, the worst places aren't open; and even if they were, they daren't be seen going to them. Besides, James, dear, you preach so splendidly that it's as good as a play for them. Why do you think the women are so enthusiastic?

MORELL [*shocked*]. Candida!

CANDIDA. Oh, *I* know. You silly boy: you think it's your Socialism and your religion; but if it was that, they'd do what you tell them instead of only coming to look at you. They all have Prossy's complaint.

MORELL. Prossy's complaint! What do you mean, Candida?

CANDIDA. Yes, Prossy, and all the other secretaries you ever had. Why does Prossy condescend to wash up the things, and to peel potatoes and abase herself in all manner of ways for six shillings a week less than she used to get in a city office? She's in love with you, James: that's the reason. They're all in love with you. And you are in love with preaching because you do it so beautifully. And you think it's all enthusiasm for the kingdom of Heaven on earth; and so do they. You dear silly!

MORELL. Candida: what dreadful, what soul-destroying cynicism! Are you jesting? Or—can it be?—are you jealous?

CANDIDA [*with curious thoughtfulness*]. Yes, I feel a little jealous sometimes.

MORELL [*incredulously*]. What! Of Prossy!

CANDIDA [*laughing*]. No, no, no, no. Not jealous of anybody. Jealous for somebody else, who is not loved as he ought to be.

MORELL. Me!

CANDIDA. You! Why, you're spoiled with love and worship: you get far more than is good for you. No: I mean Eugene.

MORELL [*startled*]. Eugene!

CANDIDA. It seems unfair that all the love should go to you, and none to him, although he needs it so much more than you do. [*A convulsive movement shakes him in spite of himself.*] What's the matter? Am I worrying you?

MORELL [*hastily*]. Not at all. [*Looking at her with troubled intensity.*] You know that I have perfect confidence in you, Candida.

CANDIDA. You vain thing! Are you so sure of your irresistible attractions?

MORELL. Candida: you are shocking me. I never thought of my attractions. I thought of your goodness—your purity. That is what I confide in.

CANDIDA. What a nasty, uncomfortable thing to say

to me! Oh, you are a clergyman, James—a thorough clergyman.

MORELL [*turning away from her, heart-stricken*]. So Eugene says.

CANDIDA [*with lively interest, leaning over to him with her arms on his knee*]. Eugene's always right. He's a wonderful boy: I have grown fonder and fonder of him all the time I was away. Do you know, James, that though he has not the least suspicion of it himself, he is ready to fall madly in love with me?

MORELL [*grimly*]. Oh, he has no suspicion of it himself, hasn't he?

CANDIDA. Not a bit. [*She takes her arms from his knee, and turns thoughtfully, sinking into a more restful attitude with her hands in her lap.*] Some day he will know—when he is grown up and experienced, like you. And he will know that I must have known. I wonder what he will think of me then.

MORELL. No evil, Candida. I hope and trust, no evil.

CANDIDA [*dubiously*]. That will depend.

MORELL [*bewildered*]. Depend!

CANDIDA [*looking at him*]. Yes: it will depend on what happens to him. [*He looks vacantly at her.*] Don't you see? It will depend on how he comes to learn what love really is. I mean on the sort of woman who will teach it to him.

MORELL [*quite at a loss*]. Yes. No. I don't know what you mean.

CANDIDA [*explaining*]. If he learns it from a good woman, then it will be all right: he will forgive me.

MORELL. Forgive!

CANDIDA. But suppose he learns it from a bad woman, as so many men do, especially poetic men, who imagine all women are angels! Suppose he only discovers the value of love when he has thrown it away and degraded himself in his ignorance. Will he forgive me then, do you think?

MORELL. Forgive you for what?

CANDIDA [*realizing how stupid he is, and a little disappointed, though quite tenderly so*]. Don't you understand? [*He shakes his head. She turns to him again, so as to explain with the fondest intimacy.*] I mean, will he forgive me for not teaching him myself? For abandoning him to the bad women for the sake of my goodness—my purity, as you call it? Ah, James, how little you understand me, to talk of your confidence in my goodness and purity! I would give them both to poor Eugene as willingly as I would give my shawl to a beggar dying of cold, if there were nothing else to restrain me. Put your trust in my love for you, James, for if that went, I should care very little for your sermons—mere phrases that you cheat yourself and others with every day. [*She is about to rise.*]

MORELL. His words!

CANDIDA [*checking herself quickly in the act of getting up, so that she is on her knees, but upright*]. Whose words?

MORELL. Eugene's.

CANDIDA [*delighted*]. He is always right. He understands you; he understands me; he understands Prossy; and you, James—you understand nothing. [*She laughs, and kisses him to console him. He recoils as if stung, and springs up.*]

MORELL. How can you bear to do that when—oh, Candida [*with anguish in his voice*], I had rather you had plunged a grappling iron into my heart than given me that kiss.

CANDIDA [*rising, alarmed*]. My dear: what's the matter?

MORELL [*frantically waving her off*]. Don't touch me.

CANDIDA [*amazed*]. James!

[*They are interrupted by the entrance of Marchbanks, with Burgess, who stops near the door, staring, whilst Eugene hurries forward between them.*]

MARCHBANKS. Is anything the matter?

MORELL [*deadly white, putting an iron constraint on himself*]. Nothing but this: that either you were right this morning, or Candida is mad.

BURGESS [*in loudest protest*]. Wot! Candy mad too! Oh, come, come, come! [*He crosses the room to the fireplace, protesting as he goes, and knocks the ashes out of his pipe on the bars. Morell sits down desperately, leaning forward to hide his face, and interlacing his fingers rigidly to keep them steady.*]

CANDIDA [*to Morell, relieved and laughing*]. Oh, you're only shocked! Is that all? How conventional all you unconventional people are!

BURGESS. Come: be'ave yourself, Candy. What'll Mr. Morchbanks think of you?

CANDIDA. This comes of James teaching me to think for myself, and never to hold back out of fear of what other people may think of me. It works beautifully as long as I think the same things as he does. But now, because I have just thought something different!—look at him—just look! [*She points to Morell, greatly amused. Eugene looks, and instantly presses his hand on his heart, as if some deadly pain had shot through it, and sits down on the sofa like a man witnessing a tragedy.*]

BURGESS [*on the hearth-rug*]. Well, James, you certainly ain't as himpressive lookin' as usu'l.

MORELL [*with a laugh which is half a sob*]. I suppose not. I beg all your pardons: I was not conscious of making a fuss. [*Pulling himself together.*] Well, well, well, well, well! [*He goes back to his place at the table, setting to work at his papers again with resolute cheerfulness.*]

CANDIDA [*going to the sofa and sitting beside Marchbanks, still in a bantering humor*]. Well, Eugene, why are you so sad? Did the onions make you cry?

[*Morell cannot prevent himself from watching them.*]

MARCHBANKS [*aside to her*]. It is your cruelty. I hate cruelty. It is a horrible thing to see one person make another suffer.

CANDIDA [*petting him ironically*]. Poor boy, have I been cruel? Did I make it slice nasty little red onions?

MARCHBANKS [*earnestly*]. Oh, stop, stop: I don't mean myself. You have made him suffer frightfully. I feel his pain in my own heart. I know that it is not your fault—it is something that must happen; but don't make light of it. I shudder when you torture him and laugh.

CANDIDA [*incredulously*]. *I* torture James! Nonsense, Eugene: how you exaggerate! Silly! [*She looks round at Morell, who hastily resumes his writing. She goes to him and stands behind his chair, bending over him.*] Don't work any more, dear. Come and talk to us.

MORELL [*affectionately but bitterly*]. Ah no: *I* can't talk. I can only preach.

CANDIDA [*caressing him*]. Well, come and preach.

BURGESS [*strongly remonstrating*]. Aw, no, Candy. 'Ang it all!

[*Lexy Mill comes in, looking anxious and important.*]

LEXY [*hastening to shake hands with Candida*]. How do you do, Mrs. Morell? So glad to see you back again.

CANDIDA. Thank you, Lexy. You know Eugene, don't you?

LEXY. Oh, yes. How do you do, Marchbanks?

MARCHBANKS. Quite well, thanks.

LEXY [*to Morell*]. I've just come from the Guild of St. Matthew. They are in the greatest consternation about your telegram. There's nothing wrong, is there?

CANDIDA. What did you telegraph about, James?

LEXY [*to Candida*]. He was to have spoken for them to-night. They've taken the large hall in Mare Street and spent a lot of money on posters. Morell's telegram was to say he couldn't come. It came on them like a thunderbolt.

CANDIDA [*surprised, and beginning to suspect something wrong*]. Given up an engagement to speak!

BURGESS. First time in his life, I'll bet. Ain't it, Candy?

LEXY [*to Morell*]. They decided to send an urgent telegram to you asking whether you could not change your mind. Have you received it?

MORELL [*with restrained impatience*]. Yes, yes: I got it.

LEXY. It was reply paid.

MORELL. Yes, I know. I answered it. I can't go.

CANDIDA. But why, James?

MORELL [*almost fiercely*]. Because I don't choose. These people forget that I am a man: they think I am a talking machine to be turned on for their pleasure every evening of my life. May I not have one night at home, with my wife, and my friends?

[*They are all amazed at this outburst, except Eugene. His expression remains unchanged.*]

CANDIDA. Oh, James, you know you'll have an attack of bad conscience to-morrow; and *I* shall have to suffer for that.

LEXY [*intimidated, but urgent*]. I know, of course,

that they make the most unreasonable demands on you.
But they have been telegraphing all over the place for
another speaker: and they can get nobody but the President of the Agnostic League.

MORELL [*promptly*]. Well, an excellent man. What
better do they want?

LEXY. But he always insists so powerfully on the
divorce of Socialism from Christianity. He will undo all
the good we have been doing. Of course you know best;
but— [*He hesitates.*]

CANDIDA [*coaxingly*]. Oh, do go, James. We'll all go.

BURGESS [*grumbling*]. Look 'ere, Candy! I say! Let's
stay at home by the fire, comfortable. He won't need to
be more'n a couple-o'-hour away.

CANDIDA. You'll be just as comfortable at the meeting. We'll all sit on the platform and be great people.

EUGENE [*terrified*]. Oh, please don't let us go on the
platform. No—everyone will stare at us—I couldn't. I'll
sit at the back of the room.

CANDIDA. Don't be afraid. They'll be too busy looking at James to notice you.

MORELL [*turning his head and looking meaningly at
her over his shoulder*]. Prossy's complaint, Candida! Eh?

CANDIDA [*gaily*]. Yes.

BURGESS [*mystified*]. Prossy's complaint. Wot are
you talking about, James?

MORELL [*not heeding him, rises; goes to the door;
and holds it open, shouting in a commanding voice*].
Miss Garnett.

PROSERPINE [*in the distance*]. Yes, Mr. Morell. Coming. [*They all wait, except Burgess, who goes stealthily to
Lexy and draws him aside.*]

BURGESS. Listen here, Mr. Mill. Wot's Prossy's complaint? Wot's wrong with 'er?

LEXY [*confidentially*]. Well, I don't exactly know; but
she spoke very strangely to me this morning. I'm afraid
she's a little out of her mind sometimes.

BURGESS [*overwhelmed*]. Why, it must be catchin'!
Four in the same 'ouse! [*He goes back to the hearth,
quite lost before the instability of the human intellect in
a clergyman's house.*]

PROSERPINE [*appearing on the threshold*]. What is it, Mr. Morell?

MORELL. Telegraph to the Guild of St. Matthew that I am coming.

PROSERPINE [*surprised*]. Don't they expect you?

MORELL [*peremptorily*]. Do as I tell you.

[*Proserpine, frightened, sits down at her typewriter, and obeys. Morell goes across to Burgess, Candida watching his movements all the time with growing wonder and misgiving.*]

MORELL. Burgess: you don't want to come?

BURGESS [*in deprecation*]. Oh, don't put it like that, James. It's only that it ain't Sunday, you know.

MORELL. I'm sorry. I thought you might like to be introduced to the chairman. He's on the Works Committee of the County Council and has some influence in the matter of contracts. [*Burgess wakes up at once. Morell, expecting as much, waits a moment, and says*] Will you come?

BURGESS [*with enthusiasm*]. Course I'll come, James. Ain' it always a pleasure to 'ear you.

MORELL [*turning from him*]. I shall want you to take some notes at the meeting, Miss Garnett, if you have no other engagement. [*She nods, afraid to speak.*] You are coming, Lexy, I suppose.

LEXY. Certainly.

CANDIDA. We are all coming, James.

MORELL. No: you are not coming; and Eugene is not coming. You will stay here and entertain him—to celebrate your return home. [*Eugene rises, breathless.*]

CANDIDA. But James—

MORELL [*authoritatively*]. I insist. You do not want to come; and he does not want to come. [*Candida is about to protest.*] Oh, don't concern yourselves: I shall have plenty of people without you: your chairs will be wanted by unconverted people who have never heard me before.

CANDIDA [*troubled*]. Eugene: wouldn't you like to come?

MORELL. I should be afraid to let myself go before Eugene: he is so critical of sermons. [*Looking at him.*]

He knows I am afraid of him: he told me as much this morning. Well, I shall shew him how much afraid I am by leaving him here in your custody, Candida.

MARCHBANKS [*to himself, with vivid feeling*]. That's brave. That's beautiful. [*He sits down again listening with parted lips.*]

CANDIDA [*with anxious misgiving*]. But—but— Is anything the matter, James? [*Greatly troubled.*] I can't understand—

MORELL. Ah, I thought it was *I* who couldn't understand, dear. [*He takes her tenderly in his arms and kisses her on the forehead; then looks round quietly at Marchbanks.*]

ACT THREE

Late in the evening. Past ten. The curtains are drawn, and the lamps lighted. The typewriter is in its case; the large table has been cleared and tidied; everything indicates that the day's work is done.

Candida and Marchbanks are seated at the fire. The reading lamp is on the mantelshelf above Marchbanks, who is sitting on the small chair reading aloud from a manuscript. A little pile of manuscripts and a couple of volumes of poetry are on the carpet beside him. Candida is in the easy chair with the poker, a light brass one, upright in her hand. She is leaning back and looking at the point of it curiously, with her feet stretched towards the blaze and her heels resting on the fender, profoundly unconscious of her appearance and surroundings.

MARCHBANKS [*breaking off in his recitation*]. Every poet that ever lived has put that thought into a sonnet. He must: he can't help it. [*He looks to her for assent, and notices her absorption in the poker.*] Haven't you been listening? [*No response.*] Mrs. Morell!

CANDIDA [*starting*]. Eh?

MARCHBANKS. Haven't you been listening?

CANDIDA [*with a guilty excess of politeness*]. Oh, yes. It's very nice. Go on, Eugene. I'm longing to hear what happens to the angel.

MARCHBANKS [*crushed—the manuscript dropping from his hand to the floor*]. I beg your pardon for boring you.

CANDIDA. But you are not boring me, I assure you. Please go on. Do, Eugene.

MARCHBANKS. I finished the poem about the angel quarter of an hour ago. I've read you several things since.

CANDIDA [*remorsefully*]. I'm so sorry, Eugene. I think the poker must have fascinated me. [*She puts it down.*]

MARCHBANKS. It made me horribly uneasy.

CANDIDA. Why didn't you tell me? I'd have put it down at once.

MARCHBANKS. I was afraid of making you uneasy, too. It looked as if it were a weapon. If I were a hero of old, I should have laid my drawn sword between us. If Morell had come in he would have thought you had taken up the poker because there was no sword between us.

CANDIDA [*wondering*]. What? [*With a puzzled glance at him.*] I can't quite follow that. Those sonnets of yours have perfectly addled me. Why should there be a sword between us?

MARCHBANKS [*evasively*]. Oh, never mind. [*He stoops to pick up the manuscript.*]

CANDIDA. Put that down again, Eugene. There are limits to my appetite for poetry—even your poetry. You've been reading to me for more than two hours— ever since James went out. I want to talk.

MARCHBANKS [*rising, scared*]. No: I mustn't talk. [*He looks round him in his lost way, and adds, suddenly*] I think I'll go out and take a walk in the park. [*Making for the door.*]

CANDIDA. Nonsense: it's shut long ago. Come and sit down on the hearth-rug, and talk moonshine as you usually do. I want to be amused. Don't you want to?

MARCHBANKS [*in half terror, half rapture*]. Yes.

CANDIDA. Then come along. [*She moves her chair back a little to make room. He hesitates; then timidly stretches himself on the hearth-rug, face upwards, and throws back his head across her knees, looking up at her.*]

MARCHBANKS. Oh, I've been so miserable all the

evening, because I was doing right. Now I'm doing wrong; and I'm happy.

CANDIDA [*tenderly amused at him*]. Yes: I'm sure you feel a great grown up wicked deceiver—quite proud of yourself, aren't you?

MARCHBANKS [*raising his head quickly and turning a little to look round at her*]. Take care. I'm ever so much older than you, if you only knew. [*He turns quite over on his knees, with his hands clasped and his arms on her lap, and speaks with growing impulse, his blood beginning to stir.*] May I say some wicked things to you?

CANDIDA [*without the least fear or coldness, quite nobly, and with perfect respect for his passion, but with a touch of her wise-hearted maternal humor*]. No. But you may say anything you really and truly feel. Anything at all, no matter what it is. I am not afraid, so long as it is your real self that speaks, and not a mere attitude— a gallant attitude, or a wicked attitude, or even a poetic attitude. I put you on your honor and truth. Now say whatever you want to.

MARCHBANKS [*the eager expression vanishing utterly from his lips and nostrils as his eyes light up with pathetic spirituality*]. Oh, now I can't say anything: all the words I know belong to some attitude or other—all except one.

CANDIDA. What one is that?

MARCHBANKS [*softly, losing himself in the music of the name*]. Candida, Candida, Candida, Candida, Candida. I must say that now, because you have put me on my honor and truth; and I never think or feel Mrs. Morell: it is always Candida.

CANDIDA. Of course. And what have you to say to Candida?

MARCHBANKS. Nothing, but to repeat your name a thousand times. Don't you feel that every time is a prayer to you?

CANDIDA. Doesn't it make you happy to be able to pray?

MARCHBANKS. Yes, very happy.

CANDIDA. Well, that happiness is the answer to your prayer. Do you want anything more?

MARCHBANKS [*in beatitude*]. No: I have come into heaven, where want is unknown.

[*Morell comes in. He halts on the threshold, and takes in the scene at a glance.*]

MORELL [*grave and self-contained*]. I hope I don't disturb you.

[*Candida starts up violently, but without the smallest embarrassment, laughing at herself. Eugene, still kneeling, saves himself from falling by putting his hands on the seat of the chair, and remains there, staring open mouthed at Morell.*]

CANDIDA [*as she rises*]. Oh, James, how you startled me! I was so taken up with Eugene that I didn't hear your latch-key. How did the meeting go off? Did you speak well?

MORELL. I have never spoken better in my life.

CANDIDA. That was first rate! How much was the collection?

MORELL. I forgot to ask.

CANDIDA [*to Eugene*]. He must have spoken splendidly, or he would never have forgotten that. [*To Morell.*] Where are all the others?

MORELL. They left long before I could get away: I thought I should never escape. I believe they are having supper somewhere.

CANDIDA [*in her domestic business tone*]. Oh; in that case, Maria may go to bed. I'll tell her. [*She goes out to the kitchen.*]

MORELL [*looking sternly down at Marchbanks*]. Well?

MARCHBANKS [*squatting cross-legged on the hearth-rug, and actually at ease with Morell—even impishly humorous*]. Well?

MORELL. Have you anything to tell me?

MARCHBANKS. Only that I have been making a fool of myself here in private whilst you have been making a fool of yourself in public.

MORELL. Hardly in the same way, I think.

MARCHBANKS [*scrambling up—eagerly*]. The very, very, very same way. I have been playing the good man just like you. When you began your heroics about leaving me here with Candida—

MORELL [*involuntarily*]. Candida?

MARCHBANKS. Oh, yes: I've got that far. Heroics are

infectious: I caught the disease from you. I swore not to say a word in your absence that I would not have said a month ago in your presence.

MORELL. Did you keep your oath?

MARCHBANKS [*suddenly perching himself grotesquely on the easy chair*]. I was ass enough to keep it until about ten minutes ago. Up to that moment I went on desperately reading to her—reading my own poems—anybody's poems—to stave off a conversation. I was standing outside the gate of Heaven, and refusing to go in. Oh, you can't think how heroic it was, and how uncomfortable! Then—

MORELL [*steadily controlling his suspense*]. Then?

MARCHBANKS [*prosaically slipping down into a quite ordinary attitude in the chair*]. Then she couldn't bear being read to any longer.

MORELL. And you approached the gate of Heaven at last?

MARCHBANKS. Yes.

MORELL. Well? [*Fiercely.*] Speak, man: have you no feeling for me?

MARCHBANKS [*softly and musically*]. Then she became an angel; and there was a flaming sword that turned every way, so that I couldn't go in; for I saw that that gate was really the gate of Hell.

MORELL [*triumphantly*]. She repulsed you!

MARCHBANKS [*rising in wild scorn*]. No, you fool: if she had done that I should never have seen that I was in Heaven already. Repulsed me! You think that would have saved me—virtuous indignation! Oh, you are not worthy to live in the same world with her. [*He turns away contemptuously to the other side of the room.*]

MORELL [*who has watched him quietly without changing his place*]. Do you think you make yourself more worthy by reviling me, Eugene?

MARCHBANKS. Here endeth the thousand and first lesson. Morell: I don't think much of your preaching after all: I believe I could do it better myself. The man I want to meet is the man that Candida married.

MORELL. The man that—? Do you mean me?

MARCHBANKS. I don't mean the Reverend James Mavor Morell, moralist and windbag. I mean the real

man that the Reverend James must have hidden somewhere inside his black coat—the man that Candida
loved. You can't make a woman like Candida love you
by merely buttoning your collar at the back instead of
in front.

MORELL [*boldly and steadily*]. When Candida promised to marry me, I was the same moralist and windbag
that you now see. I wore my black coat; and my collar
was buttoned behind instead of in front. Do you think
she would have loved me any the better for being insin-
cere in my profession?

MARCHBANKS [*on the sofa hugging his ankles*]. Oh,
she forgave you, just as she forgives me for being a coward, and a weakling, and what you call a snivelling little
whelp and all the rest of it. [*Dreamily.*] A woman like
that has divine insight: she loves our souls, and not our
follies and vanities and illusions, or our collars and coats,
or any other of the rags and tatters we are rolled up in.
[*He reflects on this for an instant; then turns intently to
question Morell.*] What I want to know is how you got
past the flaming sword that stopped me.

MORELL [*meaningly*]. Perhaps because I was not interrupted at the end of ten minutes.

MARCHBANKS [*taken aback*]. What!

MORELL. Man can climb to the highest summits; but
he cannot dwell there long.

MARCHBANKS. It's false: there can he dwell for ever
and there only. It's in the other moments that he can
find no rest, no sense of the silent glory of life. Where
would you have me spend my moments, if not on the
summits?

MORELL. In the scullery, slicing onions and filling
lamps.

MARCHBANKS. Or in the pulpit, scrubbing cheap
earthenware souls?

MORELL. Yes, that, too. It was there that I earned
my golden moment, and the right, in that moment, to
ask her to love me. *I* did not take the moment on credit;
nor did I use it to steal another man's happiness.

MARCHBANKS [*rather disgustedly, trotting back towards
the fireplace*]. I have no doubt you conducted the trans-
action as honestly as if you were buying a pound of

cheese. [*He stops on the brink of the hearth-rug and adds, thoughtfully, to himself, with his back turned to Morell*] I could only go to her as a beggar.

MORELL [*starting*]. A beggar dying of cold—asking for her shawl?

MARCHBANKS [*turning, surprised*]. Thank you for touching up my poetry. Yes, if you like, a beggar dying of cold asking for her shawl.

MORELL [*excitedly*]. And she refused. Shall I tell you why she refused. I can tell you, on her own authority. It was because of—

MARCHBANKS. She didn't refuse.

MORELL. Not!

MARCHBANKS. She offered me all I chose to ask for, her shawl, her wings, the wreath of stars on her head, the lilies in her hand, the crescent moon beneath her feet—

MORELL [*seizing him*]. Out with the truth, man; my wife is my wife: I want no more of your poetic fripperies. I know well that if I have lost her love and you have gained it, no law will bind her.

MARCHBANKS [*quaintly, without fear or resistance*]. Catch me by the shirt collar, Morell: she will arrange it for me afterwards as she did this morning. [*With quiet rapture.*] I shall feel her hands touch me.

MORELL. You young imp, do you know how dangerous it is to say that to me? Or [*with a sudden misgiving*] has something made you brave?

MARCHBANKS. I'm not afraid now. I disliked you before: that was why I shrank from your touch. But I saw to-day—when she tortured you—that you love her. Since then I have been your friend: you may strangle me if you like.

MORELL [*releasing him*]. Eugene: if that is not a heartless lie—if you have a spark of human feeling left in you—will you tell me what has happened during my absence?

MARCHBANKS. What happened! Why, the flaming sword—[*Morell stamps with impatience.*] Well, in plain prose, I love her so exquisitely that I wanted nothing more than the happiness of being in such love. And before I had time to come down from the highest summits, you came in.

MORELL [*suffering deeply*]. So it is still unsettled—still the misery of doubt.

MARCHBANKS. Misery! I am the happiest of men. I desire nothing now but her happiness. [*With dreamy enthusiasm.*] Oh, Morell, let us both give her up. Why should she have to choose between a wretched little nervous disease like me, and a pig-headed parson like you? Let us go on a pilgrimage, you to the east and I to the west, in search of a worthy lover for her—some beautiful archangel with purple wings—

MORELL. Some fiddlestick. Oh, if she is mad enough to leave me for you, who will protect her? Who will help her? who will work for her? who will be a father to her children? [*He sits down distractedly on the sofa, with his elbows on his knees and his head propped on his clenched fists.*]

MARCHBANKS [*snapping his fingers wildly*]. She does not ask those silly questions. It is she who wants somebody to protect, to help, to work for—somebody to give her children to protect, to help and to work for. Some grown up man who has become as a little child again. Oh, you fool, you fool, you triple fool! I am the man, Morell: I am the man. [*He dances about excitedly, crying*] You don't understand what a woman is. Send for her, Morell: send for her and let her choose between— [*The door opens and Candida enters. He stops as if petrified.*]

CANDIDA [*amazed, on the threshold*]. What on earth are you at, Eugene?

MARCHBANKS [*oddly*]. James and I are having a preaching match; and he is getting the worst of it. [*Candida looks quickly round at Morell. Seeing that he is distressed, she hurries down to him, greatly vexed, speaking with vigorous reproach to Marchbanks.*]

CANDIDA. You have been annoying him. Now I won't have it, Eugene: do you hear? [*Putting her hand on Morell's shoulder and quite forgetting her wifely tact in her annoyance.*] My boy shall not be worried: I will protect him.

MORELL [*rising proudly*]. Protect!

CANDIDA [*not heeding him—to Eugene*]. What have you been saying?

MARCHBANKS [*appalled*]. Nothing—I—

CANDIDA. Eugene! Nothing?

MARCHBANKS [*piteously*]. I mean—I—I'm very sorry. I won't do it again: indeed I won't. I'll let him alone.

MORELL [*indignantly, with an aggressive movement towards Eugene*]. Let me alone! You young—

CANDIDA [*stopping him*]. Sh—no, let me deal with him, James.

MARCHBANKS. Oh, you're not angry with me, are you?

CANDIDA [*severely*]. Yes, I am—very angry. I have a great mind to pack you out of the house.

MORELL [*taken aback by Candida's vigor, and by no means relishing the sense of being rescued by her from another man*]. Gently, Candida, gently. I am able to take care of myself.

CANDIDA [*petting him*]. Yes, dear: of course you are. But you mustn't be annoyed and made miserable.

MARCHBANKS [*almost in tears, turning to the door*]. I'll go.

CANDIDA. Oh, you needn't go: I can't turn you out at this time of night. [*Vehemently.*] Shame on you! For shame!

MARCHBANKS [*desperately*]. But what have I done?

CANDIDA. I know what you have done—as well as if I had been here all the time. Oh, it was unworthy! You are like a child: you cannot hold your tongue.

MARCHBANKS. I would die ten times over sooner than give you a moment's pain.

CANDIDA [*with infinite contempt for this puerility*]. Much good your dying would do me!

MORELL. Candida, my dear: this altercation is hardly quite seemly. It is a matter between two men; and I am the right person to settle it.

CANDIDA. Two men! Do you call that a man? [*To Eugene.*] You bad boy!

MARCHBANKS [*gathering a whimsically affectionate courage from the scolding*]. If I am to be scolded like this, I must make a boy's excuse. He began it. And he's bigger than I am.

CANDIDA [*losing confidence a little as her concern*

for Morell's dignity takes the alarm]. That can't be true.
[*To Morell.*] You didn't begin it, James, did you?

MORELL [*contemptuously*]. No.

MARCHBANKS [*indignant*]. Oh!

MORELL [*to Eugene*]. You began it—this morning.
[*Candida, instantly connecting this with his mysterious
allusion in the afternoon to something told him by Eugene in the morning, looks quickly at him, wrestling
with the enigma. Morell proceeds with the emphasis of
offended superiority.*] But your other point is true. I
am certainly the bigger of the two, and, I hope, the
stronger, Candida. So you had better leave the matter
in my hands.

CANDIDA [*again soothing him*]. Yes, dear; but—
[*Troubled.*] I don't understand about this morning.

MORELL [*gently snubbing her*]. You need not understand, my dear.

CANDIDA. But, James, I— [*The street bell rings.*] Oh,
bother! Here they all come. [*She goes out to let them in.*]

MARCHBANKS [*running to Morell*]. Oh, Morell, isn't
it dreadful? She's angry with us: she hates me. What
shall I do?

MORELL [*with quaint desperation, clutching himself
by the hair*]. Eugene: my head is spinning round. I shall
begin to laugh presently. [*He walks up and down the
middle of the room.*]

MARCHBANKS [*following him anxiously*]. No, no:
she'll think I've thrown you into hysterics. Don't laugh.

[*Boisterous voices and laughter are heard approaching.
Lexy Mill, his eyes sparkling, and his bearing denoting
unwonted elevation of spirit, enters with Burgess, who is
greasy and self-complacent, but has all his wits about him.
Miss Garnett, with her smartest hat and jacket on, follows
them; but though her eyes are brighter than before, she is
evidently a prey to misgiving. She places herself with her
back to her typewriting table, with one hand on it to rest
herself, passes the other across her forehead as if she were
a little tired and giddy. Marchbanks relapses into shyness
and edges away into the corner near the window, where
Morell's books are.*]

MILL [*exhilaratedly*]. Morell: I must congratulate

you. [*Grasping his hand.*] What a noble, splendid, inspired address you gave us! You surpassed yourself.

BURGESS. So you did, James. It fair kep' me awake
to the last word. Didn't it, Miss Gornett?

PROSERPINE [*worriedly*]. Oh, I wasn't minding you: I
was trying to make notes. [*She takes out her note-book,
and looks at her stenography, which nearly makes her cry.*]

MORELL. Did I go too fast, Pross?

PROSERPINE. Much too fast. You know I can't do
more than a hundred words a minute. [*She relieves her
feelings by throwing her note-book angrily beside her machine, ready for use next morning.*]

MORELL [*soothingly*]. Oh, well, well, never mind,
never mind, never mind. Have you all had supper?

LEXY. Mr. Burgess has been kind enough to give us
a really splendid supper at the Belgrave.

BURGESS [*with effusive magnanimity*]. Don't mention
it, Mr. Mill. [*Modestly.*] You're 'arty welcome to my little treat.

PROSERPINE. We had champagne! I never tasted it
before. I feel quite giddy.

MORELL [*surprised*]. A champagne supper! That was
very handsome. Was it my eloquence that produced all
this extravagance?

MILL [*rhetorically*]. Your eloquence, and Mr. Burgess's goodness of heart. [*With a fresh burst of exhilaration.*] And what a very fine fellow the chairman is,
Morell! He came to supper with us.

MORELL [*with long drawn significance, looking at
Burgess*]. O-o-o-h, the chairman. Now I understand.

[*Burgess, covering a lively satisfaction in his diplomatic
cunning with a deprecatory cough, retires to the hearth.
Lexy folds his arms and leans against the cellaret in a
high-spirited attitude. Candida comes in with glasses, lem-
ons, and a jug of hot water on a tray.*]

CANDIDA. Who will have some lemonade? You
know our rules: total abstinence. [*She puts the tray on
the table, and takes up the lemon squeezers, looking enquiringly round at them.*]

MORELL. No use, dear. They've all had champagne.
Pross has broken her pledge.

CANDIDA [*to Proserpine*]. You don't mean to say you've been drinking champagne!

PROSERPINE [*stubbornly*]. Yes, I do. I'm only a beer teetotaller, not a champagne teetotaller. I don't like beer. Are there any letters for me to answer, Mr. Morell?

MORELL. No more to-night.

PROSERPINE. Very well. Good-night, everybody.

LEXY [*gallantly*]. Had I not better see you home, Miss Garnett?

PROSERPINE. No, thank you. I shan't trust myself with anybody to-night. I wish I hadn't taken any of that stuff. [*She walks straight out.*]

BURGESS [*indignantly*]. Stuff, indeed! That gurl dunno wot champagne is! Pommery and Greeno at twelve and six a bottle. She took two glasses a'most straight hoff.

MORELL [*a little anxious about her*]. Go and look after her, Lexy.

LEXY [*alarmed*]. But if she should really be— Suppose she began to sing in the street, or anything of that sort.

MORELL. Just so: she may. That's why you'd better see her safely home.

CANDIDA. Do, Lexy: there's a good fellow. [*She shakes his hand, and pushes him gently to the door.*]

LEXY. It's evidently my duty to go. I hope it may not be necessary. Good-night, Mrs. Morell. [*To the rest.*] Good-night. [*He goes. Candida shuts the door.*]

BURGESS. He was gushin' with hextra piety hisself arter two sips. People can't drink like they huseter. [*Dismissing the subject and bustling away from the hearth.*] Well, James: it's time to lock up. Mr. Morchbanks: shall I 'ave the pleasure of your company for a bit of the way home?

MARCHBANKS [*affrightedly*]. Yes: I'd better go. [*He hurries across to the door; but Candida places herself before it, barring his way.*]

CANDIDA [*with quiet authority*]. You sit down. You're not going yet.

MARCHBANKS [*quailing*]. No: I—I didn't mean to.

[*He comes back into the room and sits down abjectly on the sofa.*]

CANDIDA. Mr. Marchbanks will stay the night with us, papa.

BURGESS. Oh, well, I'll say good-night. So long, James. [*He shakes hands with Morell and goes on to Eugene.*] Make 'em give you a night light by your bed, Mr. Morchbanks: it'll comfort you if you wake up in the night with a touch of that complaint of yores. Good-night.

MARCHBANKS. Thank you: I will. Good-night, Mr. Burgess. [*They shake hands and Burgess goes to the door.*]

CANDIDA [*intercepting Morell, who is following Burgess*]. Stay here, dear: I'll put on papa's coat for him. [*She goes out with Burgess.*]

MARCHBANKS. Morell: there's going to be a terrible scene. Aren't you afraid?

MORELL. Not in the least.

MARCHBANKS. I never envied you your courage before. [*He rises timidly and puts his hand appealingly on Morell's forearm.*] Stand by me, won't you?

MORELL [*casting him off gently, but resolutely*]. Each for himself, Eugene. She must choose between us now. [*He goes to the other side of the room as Candida returns. Eugene sits down again on the sofa like a guilty schoolboy on his best behaviour.*]

CANDIDA [*between them, addressing Eugene*]. Are you sorry?

MARCHBANKS [*earnestly*]. Yes, heartbroken.

CANDIDA. Well, then, you are forgiven. Now go off to bed like a good little boy: I want to talk to James about you.

MARCHBANKS [*rising in great consternation*]. Oh, I can't do that, Morell. I must be here. I'll not go away. Tell her.

CANDIDA [*with quick suspicion*]. Tell me what? [*His eyes avoid hers furtively. She turns and mutely transfers the question to Morell.*]

MORELL [*bracing himself for the catastrophe*]. I have nothing to tell her, except [*here his voice deepens to a measured and mournful tenderness*] that she is my greatest treasure on earth—if she is really mine.

CANDIDA [*coldly, offended by his yielding to his orator's instinct and treating her as if she were the audience at the Guild of St. Matthew*]. I am sure Eugene can say no less, if that is all.

MARCHBANKS [*discouraged*]. Morell: she's laughing at us.

MORELL [*with a quick touch of temper*]. There is nothing to laugh at. Are you laughing at us, Candida?

CANDIDA [*with quiet anger*]. Eugene is very quick-witted, James. I hope I am going to laugh; but I am not sure that I am not going to be very angry. [*She goes to the fireplace, and stands there leaning with her arm on the mantelpiece, and her foot on the fender, whilst Eugene steals to Morell and plucks him by the sleeve.*]

MARCHBANKS [*whispering*]. Stop, Morell. Don't let us say anything.

MORELL [*pushing Eugene away without deigning to look at him*]. I hope you don't mean that as a threat, Candida.

CANDIDA [*with emphatic warning*]. Take care, James. Eugene: I asked you to go. Are you going?

MORELL [*putting his foot down*]. He shall not go. I wish him to remain.

MARCHBANKS. I'll go. I'll do whatever you want. [*He turns to the door.*]

CANDIDA. Stop! [*He obeys.*] Didn't you hear James say he wished you to stay? James is master here. Don't you know that?

MARCHBANKS [*flushing with a young poet's rage against tyranny*]. By what right is he master?

CANDIDA [*quietly*]. Tell him, James.

MORELL [*taken aback*]. My dear: I don't know of any right that makes me master. I assert no such right.

CANDIDA [*with infinite reproach*]. You don't know! Oh, James, James! [*To Eugene, musingly.*] I wonder do you understand, Eugene! No: you're too young. Well, I give you leave to stay—to stay and learn. [*She comes away from the hearth and places herself between them.*] Now, James: what's the matter? Come: tell me.

MARCHBANKS [*whispering tremulously across to him*]. Don't.

CANDIDA. Come. Out with it!

MORELL [*slowly*]. I meant to prepare your mind carefully, Candida, so as to prevent misunderstanding.

CANDIDA. Yes, dear: I am sure you did. But never mind: I shan't misunderstand.

MORELL. Well—er— [*He hesitates, unable to find the long explanation which he supposed to be available.*]

CANDIDA. Well?

MORELL [*baldly*]. Eugene declares that you are in love with him.

MARCHBANKS [*frantically*]. No, no, no, no, never. I did not, Mrs. Morell: it's not true. I said I loved you, and that he didn't. I said that I understood you, and that he couldn't. And it was not after what passed there before the fire that I spoke: it was not, on my word. It was this morning.

CANDIDA [*enlightened*]. This morning!

MARCHBANKS. Yes. [*He looks at her, pleading for credence, and then adds, simply*] That was what was the matter with my collar.

CANDIDA [*after a pause; for she does not take in his meaning at once*]. His collar! [*She turns to Morell, shocked.*] Oh, James: did you— [*she stops*]?

MORELL [*ashamed*]. You know, Candida, that I have a temper to struggle with. And he said [*shuddering*] that you despised me in your heart.

CANDIDA [*turning quickly on Eugene*]. Did you say that?

MARCHBANKS [*terrified*]. No!

CANDIDA [*severely*]. Then James has just told me a falsehood. Is that what you mean?

MARCHBANKS. No, no: I—I— [*blurting out the explanation desperately*] —it was David's wife. And it wasn't at home: it was when she saw him dancing before all the people.

MORELL [*taking the cue with a debater's adroitness*]. Dancing before all the people, Candida; and thinking he was moving their hearts by his mission when they were only suffering from—Prossy's complaint. [*She is about to protest: he raises his hand to silence her, exclaiming*] Don't try to look indignant, Candida—

CANDIDA [*interjecting*]. Try!

MORELL [*continuing*]. Eugene was right. As you told

me a few hours after, he is always right. He said nothing
that you did not say far better yourself. He is the poet,
who sees everything; and I am the poor parson, who
understands nothing.

CANDIDA [*remorsefully*]. Do you mind what is said
by a foolish boy, because I said something like it again
in jest?

MORELL. That foolish boy can speak with the inspiration of a child and the cunning of a serpent. He has
claimed that you belong to him and not to me; and,
rightly or wrongly, I have come to fear that it may be
true. I will not go about tortured with doubts and suspicions. I will not live with you and keep a secret from
you. I will not suffer the intolerable degradation of jealousy. We have agreed—he and I—that you shall choose
between us now. I await your decision.

CANDIDA [*slowly recoiling a step, her heart hardened
by his rhetoric in spite of the sincere feeling behind it*].
Oh! I am to choose, am I? I suppose it is quite settled
that I must belong to one or the other.

MORELL [*firmly*]. Quite. You must choose definitely.

MARCHBANKS [*anxiously*]. Morell: you don't understand. She means that she belongs to herself.

CANDIDA [*turning on him*]. I mean that and a good
deal more, Master Eugene, as you will both find out
presently. And pray, my lords and masters, what have
you to offer for my choice? I am up for auction, it seems.
What do you bid, James?

MORELL [*reproachfully*]. Cand— [*He breaks down:
his eyes and throat fill with tears: the orator becomes the
wounded animal.*] I can't speak—

CANDIDA [*impulsively going to him*]. Ah, dearest—

MARCHBANKS [*in wild alarm*]. Stop: it's not fair. You
mustn't show her that you suffer, Morell. I am on the
rack, too; but I am not crying.

MORELL [*rallying all his forces*]. Yes: you are right.
It is not for pity that I am bidding. [*He disengages himself from Candida.*]

CANDIDA [*retreating, chilled*]. I beg your pardon,
James; I did not mean to touch you. I am waiting to
hear your bid.

MORELL [*with proud humility*]. I have nothing to

offer you but my strength for your defence, my honesty of purpose for your surety, my ability and industry for your livelihood, and my authority and position for your dignity. That is all it becomes a man to offer to a woman.

CANDIDA [*quite quietly*]. And you, Eugene? What do you offer?

MARCHBANKS. My weakness! my desolation! my heart's need!

CANDIDA [*impressed*]. That's a good bid, Eugene. Now I know how to make my choice.

[*She pauses and looks curiously from one to the other, as if weighing them. Morell, whose lofty confidence has changed into heartbreaking dread at Eugene's bid, loses all power of concealing his anxiety. Eugene, strung to the highest tension, does not move a muscle.*]

MORELL [*in a suffocated voice—the appeal bursting from the depths of his anguish*]. Candida!

MARCHBANKS [*aside, in a flash of contempt*]. Coward!

CANDIDA [*significantly*]. I give myself to the weaker of the two.

[*Eugene divines her meaning at once: his face whitens like steel in a furnace that cannot melt it.*]

MORELL [*bowing his head with the calm of collapse*]. I accept your sentence, Candida.

CANDIDA. Do you understand, Eugene?

MARCHBANKS. Oh, I feel I'm lost. He cannot bear the burden.

MORELL [*incredulously, raising his head with prosaic abruptness*]. Do you mean me, Candida?

CANDIDA [*smiling a little*]. Let us sit and talk comfortably over it like three friends. [*To Morell.*] Sit down, dear. [*Morell takes the chair from the fireside—the children's chair.*] Bring me that chair, Eugene. [*She indicates the easy chair. He fetches it silently, even with something like cold strength, and places it next Morell, a little behind him. She sits down. He goes to the sofa and sits there, still silent and inscrutable. When they are all settled she begins, throwing a spell of quietness on them by her calm, sane, tender tone.*] You remember what you told me about yourself, Eugene: how nobody has cared for you since your old nurse died: how those clever, fashionable sisters and successful brothers of yours were your mother's and father's pets: how miserable you were at Eton: how your father is trying to starve you into returning to Oxford: how you have had to live without comfort or welcome or refuge, always lonely, and nearly always disliked and misunderstood, poor boy!

MARCHBANKS [*faithful to the nobility of his lot*]. I had my books. I had Nature. And at last I met you.

CANDIDA. Never mind that just at present. Now I want you to look at this other boy here—my boy—spoiled from his cradle. We go once a fortnight to see his parents. You should come with us, Eugene, and see the pictures of the hero of that household. James as a baby! the most wonderful of all babies. James holding his first school prize, won at the ripe age of eight! James as the captain of his eleven! James in his first frock coat! James under all sorts of glorious circumstances! You know how strong he is (I hope he didn't hurt you)—how clever he is—how happy! [*With deepening gravity.*] Ask James's mother and his three sisters what it cost to save James the trouble of doing anything but be strong and clever and happy. Ask me what it costs to be James's mother and three sisters and wife and mother to his children all in one. Ask Prossy and Maria how troublesome the house is even when we have no visitors to help us to slice the onions. Ask the tradesmen who want to worry James and spoil his beautiful sermons who it is that puts them off. When there is money to give, he gives it: when there is money to refuse, I refuse it. I build a castle of comfort and indulgence and love for him, and stand sentinel always to keep little vulgar cares out. I make him master here, though he does not know it, and could not tell you a moment ago how it came to be so. [*With sweet irony.*] And when he thought I might go away with you, his only anxiety was what should become of me! And to tempt me to stay he offered me [*leaning forward to stroke his hair caressingly at each phrase*] his strength for my defence, his industry for my livelihood, his position for my dignity, his— [*Relenting.*] Ah, I am mixing up your beautiful sentences and spoiling them, am I not, darling? [*She lays her cheek fondly against his.*]

MORELL [*quite overcome, kneeling beside her chair and embracing her with boyish ingenuousness*]. It's all true, every word. What I am you have made me with the labor of your hands and the love of your heart! You are my wife, my mother, my sisters: you are the sum of all loving care to me.

CANDIDA [*in his arms, smiling, to Eugene*]. Am I your mother and sisters to you, Eugene?

MARCHBANKS [*rising with a fierce gesture of disgust*]. Ah, never. Out, then, into the night with me!

CANDIDA [*rising quickly and intercepting him*]. You are not going like that, Eugene?

MARCHBANKS [*with the ring of a man's voice—no longer a boy's—-in the words*]. I know the hour when it strikes. I am impatient to do what must be done.

MORELL [*rising from his knee, alarmed*]. Candida: don't let him do anything rash.

CANDIDA [*confident, smiling at Eugene*]. Oh, there is no fear. He has learnt to live without happiness.

MARCHBANKS. I no longer desire happiness: life is nobler than that. Parson James: I give you my happiness with both hands: I love you because you have filled the heart of the woman I loved. Good-bye. [*He goes towards the door.*]

CANDIDA. One last word. [*He stops, but without turning to her.*] How old are you, Eugene?

MARCHBANKS. As old as the world now. This morning I was eighteen.

CANDIDA [*going to him, and standing behind him with one hand caressingly on his shoulder*]. Eighteen! Will you, for my sake, make a little poem out of the two sentences I am going to say to you? And will you promise to repeat it to yourself whenever you think of me?

MARCHBANKS [*without moving*]. Say the sentences.

CANDIDA. When I am thirty, she will be forty-five. When I am sixty, she will be seventy-five.

MARCHBANKS [*turning to her*]. In a hundred years, we shall be the same age. But I have a better secret than that in my heart. Let me go now. The night outside grows impatient.

CANDIDA. Good-bye. [*She takes his face in her hands; and as he divines her intention and bends his knee, she kisses his forehead. Then he flies out into the night. She turns to Morell, holding out her arms to him.*] Ah, James! [*They embrace. But they do not know the secret in the poet's heart.*]

Man and
Superman

TO ARTHUR BINGHAM WALKLEY

My dear Walkley

You once asked me why I did not write a Don Juan play. The levity with which you assumed this frightful responsibility has probably by this time enabled you to forget it; but the day of reckoning has arrived: here is your play! I say *your* play, because *qui facit per alium facit per se.* Its profits, like its labor, belong to me: its morals, its manners, its philosophy, its influence on the young, are for you to justify. You were of mature age when you made the suggestion; and you knew your man. It is hardly fifteen years since, as twin pioneers of the New Journalism of that time, we two, cradled in the same new sheets, made an epoch in the criticism of the theatre and the opera house by making it a pretext for a propaganda of our own views of life. So you cannot plead ignorance of the character of the force you set in motion. You meant me to *épater le bourgeois;* and if he protests, I hereby refer him to you as the accountable party.

I warn you that if you attempt to repudiate your responsibility, I shall suspect you of finding the play too decorous for your taste. The fifteen years have made me older and graver. In you I can detect no such becoming change. Your levities and audacities are like the loves and comforts prayed for by Desdemona: they increase, even as your days do grow. No mere pioneering journal dares meddle with them now: the stately *Times* itself is alone sufficiently above suspicion to act as your chaperone; and even the *Times* must sometimes thank its stars that new plays are not produced every day, since after each such event its gravity is compromised, its platitude

241

turned to epigram, its portentousness to wit, its propriety to elegance, and even its decorum into naughtiness by criticisms which the traditions of the paper do not allow you to sign at the end, but which you take care to sign with the most extravagant flourishes between the lines. I am not sure that this is not a portent of Revolution. In eighteenth-century France the end was at hand when men bought the *Encyclopedia* and found Diderot there. When I buy the *Times* and find you there, my prophetic ear catches a rattle of twentieth-century tumbrils.

However, that is not my present anxiety. The question is, will you not be disappointed with a Don Juan play in which not one of that hero's *mille e tre* adventures is brought upon the stage? To propitiate you, let me explain myself. You will retort that I never do anything else: it is your favorite jibe at me that what I call drama is nothing but explanation. But you must not expect me to adopt your inexplicable, fantastic, petulant, fastidious ways: you must take me as I am, a reasonable, patient, consistent, apologetic, laborious person, with the temperament of a schoolmaster and the pursuits of a vestryman. No doubt that literary knack of mine which happens to amuse the British public distracts attention from my character; but the character is there none the less, solid as bricks. I have a conscience; and conscience is always anxiously explanatory. You, on the contrary, feel that a man who discusses his conscience is much like a woman who discusses her modesty. The only moral force you condescend to parade is the force of your wit: the only demand you make in public is the demand of your artistic temperament for symmetry, elegance, style, grace, refinement, and the cleanliness which comes next to godliness if not before it. But my conscience is the genuine pulpit article: it annoys me to see people comfortable when they ought to be uncomfortable; and I insist on making them think in order to bring them to conviction of sin. If you don't like my preaching you must lump it. I really cannot help it.

In the preface to my *Plays for Puritans* I explained the predicament of our contemporary English drama, forced to deal almost exclusively with cases of sexual attraction, and yet forbidden to exhibit the incidents of

that attraction or even to discuss its nature. Your suggestion that I should write a Don Juan play was virtually a
challenge to me to treat this subject myself dramatically.
The challenge was difficult enough to be worth accepting, because, when you come to think of it, though
we have plenty of dramas with heroes and heroines who
are in love and must accordingly marry or perish at the
end of the play, or about people whose relations with
one another have been complicated by the marriage
laws, not to mention the looser sort of plays which trade
on the tradition that illicit love affairs are at once vicious
and delightful, we have no modern English plays in
which the natural attraction of the sexes for one another
is made the mainspring of the action. That is why we
insist on beauty in our performers, differing herein from
the countries our friend William Archer holds up as examples of seriousness to our childish theatres. There the
Juliets and Isoldes, the Romeos and Tristans, might be
our mothers and fathers. Not so the English actress. The
heroine she impersonates is not allowed to discuss the
elemental relations of men and women: all her romantic
twaddle about novelet-made love, all her purely legal
dilemmas as to whether she was married or "betrayed,"
quite miss our hearts and worry our minds. To console
ourselves we must just look at her. We do so; and her
beauty feeds our starving emotions. Sometimes we
grumble ungallantly at the lady because she does not act
as well as she looks. But in a drama which, with all its
preoccupation with sex, is really void of sexual interest,
good looks are more desired than histrionic skill.

Let me press this point on you, since you are too
clever to raise the fool's cry of paradox whenever I take
hold of a stick by the right instead of the wrong end.
Why are our occasional attempts to deal with the sex
problem on the stage so repulsive and dreary that even
those who are most determined that sex questions shall
be held open and their discussion kept free, cannot pretend to relish these joyless attempts at social sanitation?
Is it not because at bottom they are utterly sexless?
What is the usual formula for such plays? A woman has,
on some past occasion, been brought into conflict with
the law which regulates the relations of the sexes. A

man, by falling in love with her, or marrying her, is
brought into conflict with the social convention which
discountenances the woman. Now the conflicts of individuals with law and convention can be dramatized like
all other human conflicts; but they are purely judicial;
and the fact that we are much more curious about the
suppressed relations between the man and the woman
than about the relations between both and our courts of
law and private juries of matrons, produces that sensation of evasion, of dissatisfaction, of fundamental irrelevance, of shallowness, of useless disagreeableness, of
total failure to edify and partial failure to interest, which
is as familiar to you in the theatres as it was to me when
I, too, frequented those uncomfortable buildings, and
found our popular playwrights in the mind to (as they
thought) emulate Ibsen.

I take it that when you asked me for a Don Juan play
you did not want that sort of thing. Nobody does: the
successes such plays sometimes obtain are due to the
incidental conventional melodrama with which the experienced popular author instinctively saves himself from
failure. But what did you want? Owing to your unfortunate habit—you now, I hope, feel its inconvenience—of
not explaining yourself, I have had to discover this for
myself. First, then, I have had to ask myself, what is a
Don Juan? Vulgarly, a libertine. But your dislike of vulgarity is pushed to the length of a defect (universality of
character is impossible without a share of vulgarity); and
even if you could acquire the taste, you would find yourself overfed from ordinary sources without troubling me.
So I took it that you demanded a Don Juan in the philosophic sense.

Philosophically, Don Juan is a man who, though gifted
enough to be exceptionally capable of distinguishing between good and evil, follows his own instincts without
regard to the common, statute, or canon law; and therefore, whilst gaining the ardent sympathy of our rebel-
lious instincts (which are flattered by the brilliancies with
which Don Juan associates them), finds himself in mortal
conflict with existing institutions, and defends himself by
fraud and force as unscrupulously as a farmer defends
his crops by the same means against vermin. The proto-

typic Don Juan, invented early in the sixteenth century
by a Spanish monk, was presented, according to the
ideas of that time, as the enemy of God, the approach
of whose vengeance is felt throughout the drama, growing in menace from minute to minute. No anxiety is
caused on Don Juan's account by any minor antagonist:
he easily eludes the police, temporal and spiritual; and
when an indignant father seeks private redress with the
sword, Don Juan kills him without an effort. Not until
the slain father returns from heaven as the agent of God,
in the form of his own statue, does he prevail against
his slayer and cast him into hell. The moral is a monkish
one: repent and reform now; for tomorrow it may be
too. late. This is really the only point on which Don Juan
is sceptical; for he is a devout believer in an ultimate
hell, and risks damnation only because, as he is young,
it seems so far off that repentance can be postponed
until he has amused himself to his heart's content.

But the lesson intended by an author is hardly ever
the lesson the world chooses to learn from his book.
What attracts and impresses us in *El Burlador de Sevilla*
is not the immediate urgency of repentance, but the heroism of daring to be the enemy of God. From Prometheus to my own *Devil's Disciple,* such enemies have
always been popular. Don Juan became such a pet that
the world could not bear his damnation. It reconciled
him sentimentally to God in a second version, and clam-
ored for his canonization for a whole century, thus treating him as English journalism has treated that comic foe
of the gods, Punch. Molière's Don Juan casts back to
the original in point of impenitence; but in piety he falls
off greatly. True, he also proposes to repent; but in what
terms! *"Oui, ma foi! il faut s'amender. Encore vingt ou
trente ans de cette vie-ci, et puis nous songerons à nous."*
After Molière comes the artist-enchanter, the master of
masters, Mozart, who reveals the hero's spirit in magical
harmonies, elfin tones, and elate darting rhythms as of
summer lightning made audible. Here you have freedom
in love and in morality mocking exquisitely at slavery to
them, and interesting you, attracting you, tempting you,
inexplicably forcing you to range the hero with his
enemy the statue on a transcendant plane, leaving the

prudish daughter and her priggish lover on a crockery
shelf below to live piously ever after.

After these completed works Byron's fragment does
not count for much philosophically. Our vagabond libertines are no more interesting from that point of view
than the sailor who has a wife in every port; and Byron's
hero is, after all, only a vagabond libertine. And he is
dumb: he does not discuss himself with a Sganarelle-
Leporello or with the fathers or brothers of his mis-
tresses: he does not even, like Casanova, tell his own
story. In fact he is not a true Don Juan at all; for he
is no more an enemy of God than any romantic and
adventurous young sower of wild oats. Had you and I
been in his place at his age, who knows whether we
might not have done as he did, unless indeed your fastidiousness had saved you from the Empress Catherine.
Byron was as little of a philosopher as Peter the Great:
both were instances of that rare and useful, but unedi-
fying variation, an energetic genius born without the
prejudices or superstitions of his contemporaries. The
resultant unscrupulous freedom of thought made Byron
a greater poet than Wordsworth just as it made Peter a
greater king than George III; but as it was, after all,
only a negative qualification, it did not prevent Peter
from being an appalling blackguard and an arrant pol-
troon, nor did it enable Byron to become a religious
force like Shelley. Let us, then, leave Byron's Don Juan
out of account. Mozart's is the last of the true Don
Juans; for by the time he was of age, his cousin Faust
had, in the hands of Goethe, taken his place and carried
both his warfare and his reconciliation with the gods far
beyond mere lovemaking into politics, high art, schemes
for reclaiming new continents from the ocean, and recognition of an eternal womanly principle in the universe.
Goethe's *Faust* and Mozart's *Don Juan* were the last
words of the eighteenth century on the subject; and by
the time the polite critics of the nineteenth century, ignoring William Blake as superficially as the eighteenth
had ignored Hogarth or the seventeenth Bunyan, had
got past the Dickens-Macaulay-Dumas-Guizot stage and
the Stendhal-Meredith-Turgenieff stage, and were confronted with philosophic fiction by such pens as Ibsen's

and Tolstoy's, Don Juan had changed his sex and become Doña Juana, breaking out of the Doll's House and asserting herself as an individual instead of a mere item in a moral pageant.

Now it is all very well for you at the beginning of the twentieth century to ask me for a Don Juan play; but you will see from the foregoing survey that Don Juan is a full century out of date for you and for me; and if there are millions of less literate people who are still in the eighteenth century, have they not Molière and Mozart, upon whose art no human hand can improve? You would laugh at me if at this time of day I dealt in duels and ghosts and "womanly" women. As to mere libertinism, you would be the first to remind me that the *Festin de Pierre* of Molière is not a play for amorists, and that one bar of the voluptuous sentimentality of Gounod or Bizet would appear as a licentious stain on the score of *Don Giovanni.* Even the more abstract parts of the Don Juan play are dilapidated past use: for instance, Don Juan's supernatural antagonist hurled those who refuse to repent into lakes of burning brimstone, there to be tormented by devils with horns and tails. Of that antagonist, and of that conception of repentance, how much is left that could be used in a play by me dedicated to you? On the other hand, those forces of middle class public opinion which hardly existed for a Spanish nobleman in the days of the first Don Juan, are now triumphant everywhere. Civilized society is one huge bourgeoisie: no nobleman dares now shock his greengrocer. The women, *"marchesane, principesse, cameriere, cittadine"* and all, are become equally dangerous: the sex is aggressive, powerful: when women are wronged they do not group themselves pathetically to sing *"Protegga il giusto cielo":* they grasp formidable legal and social weapons, and retaliate. Political parties are wrecked and public careers undone by a single indiscretion. A man had better have all the statues in London to supper with him, ugly as they are, than be brought to the bar of the Nonconformist Conscience by Donna Elvira. Excommunication has become almost as serious a business as it was in the tenth century.

As a result, Man is no longer, like Don Juan, victor

in the duel of sex. Whether he has ever really been may be doubted: at all events the enormous superiority of Woman's natural position in this matter is telling with greater and greater force. As to pulling the Nonconformist Conscience by the beard as Don Juan plucked the beard of the Commandant's statue in the convent of San Francisco, that is out of the question nowadays: prudence and good manners alike forbid it to a hero with any mind. Besides, it is Don Juan's own beard that is in danger of plucking. Far from relapsing into hypocrisy, as Sganarelle feared, he has unexpectedly discovered a moral in his immorality. The growing recognition of his new point of view is heaping responsibility on him. His former jests he has had to take as seriously as I have had to take some of the jests of Mr. W. S. Gilbert. His scepticism, once his least tolerated quality, has now triumphed so completely that he can no longer assert himself by witty negations, and must, to save himself from cipherdom, find an affirmative position. His thousand and three affairs of gallantry, after becoming, at most, two immature intrigues leading to sordid and prolonged complications and humiliations, have been discarded altogether as unworthy of his philosophic dignity and compromising to his newly acknowledged position as the founder of a school. Instead of pretending to read Ovid he does actually read Schopenhauer and Nietzsche, studies Westermarck, and is concerned for the future of the race instead of for the freedom of his own instincts. Thus his profligacy and his dare-devil airs have gone the way of his sword and mandoline into the rag shop of anachronisms and superstitions. In fact, he is now more Hamlet than Don Juan; for though the lines put into the actor's mouth to indicate to the pit that Hamlet is a philosopher are for the most part mere harmonious platitude which, with a little debasement of the word-music, would be properer to Pecksniff, yet if you separate the real hero, inarticulate and unintelligible to himself except in flashes of inspiration, from the performer who has to talk at any cost through five acts; and if you also do what you must always do in Shakespeare's tragedies: that is, dissect out the absurd sensational incidents and physical violences of the borrowed story from the genuine Shakespearian tissue, you will get a true Promethean foe of the gods, whose instinctive attitude towards women much resembles that to which Don Juan is now driven. From this point of view Hamlet was a developed Don Juan whom Shakespeare palmed off as a reputable man just as he palmed poor Macbeth off as a murderer. Today the palming off is no longer necessary (at least on your plane and mine) because Don Juanism is no longer misunderstood as mere Casanovism. Don Juan himself is almost ascetic in his desire to avoid that misunderstanding; and so my attempt to bring him up to date by launching him as a modern Englishman into a modern English environment has produced a figure superficially quite unlike the hero of Mozart.

And yet I have not the heart to disappoint you wholly of another glimpse of the Mozartian *dissoluto punito* and his antagonist the statue. I feel sure you would like to know more of the statue—to draw him out when he is off duty, so to speak. To gratify you, I have resorted to the trick of the strolling theatrical manager who advertises the pantomime of Sinbad the Sailor with a stock of second-hand picture posters designed for Ali Baba. He simply thrusts a few oil jars into the valley of diamonds, and so fulfils the promise held out by the hoardings to the public eye. I have adapted this simple device to our occasion by thrusting into my perfectly modern three-act play a totally extraneous act in which my hero, enchanted by the air of the Sierra, has a dream in which his Mozartian ancestor appears and philosophizes at great length in a Shavio-Socratic dialogue with the lady, the statue, and the devil.

But this pleasantry is not the essence of the play. Over this essence I have no control. You propound a certain social substance, sexual attraction to wit, for dramatic distillation; and I distil it for you. I do not adulterate the product with aphrodisiacs nor dilute it with romance and water; for I am merely executing your commission, not producing a popular play for the market. You must therefore (unless, like most wise men, you read the play first and the preface afterwards) prepare yourself to face a trumpery story of modern London life, a life in which, as you know, the ordinary man's main business is to get

means to keep up the position and habits of a gentleman, and the ordinary woman's business is to get married. In 9,999 cases out of 10,000, you can count on their
doing nothing, whether noble or base, that conflicts with
these ends; and that assurance is what you rely on as
their religion, their morality, their principles, their patriotism, their reputation, their honor and so forth.

On the whole, this is a sensible and satisfactory foundation for society. Money means nourishment and marriage
means children; and that men should put nourishment
first and women children first is, broadly speaking, the
law of Nature and not the dictate of personal ambition.
The secret of the prosaic man's success, such as it is, is
the simplicity with which he pursues these ends: the secret of the artistic man's failure, such as that is, is the
versatility with which he strays in all directions after secondary ideals. The artist is either a poet or a scallawag:
as poet, he cannot see, as the prosaic man does, that
chivalry is at bottom only romantic suicide: as scallawag,
he cannot see that it does not pay to sponge and beg
and lie and brag and neglect his person. Therefore do
not misunderstand my plain statement of the fundamental constitution of London society as an Irishman's reproach to your nation. From the day I first set foot on
this foreign soil I knew the value of the prosaic qualities
of which Irishmen teach Englishmen to be ashamed as
well as I knew the vanity of the poetic qualities of which
Englishmen teach Irishmen to be proud. For the Irishman instinctively disparages the quality which makes the
Englishman dangerous to him; and the Englishman instinctively flatters the fault that makes the Irishman
harmless and amusing to him. What is wrong with the
prosaic Englishman is what is wrong with the prosaic
men of all countries: stupidity. The vitality which places
nourishment and children first, heaven and hell a somewhat remote second, and the health of society as an
organic whole nowhere, may muddle successfully
through the comparatively tribal stages of gregarious-
ness; but in nineteenth-century nations and twentieth-
century empires the determination of every man to be
rich at all costs, and of every woman to be married at
all costs, must, without a highly scientific social organiza-

tion, produce a ruinous development of poverty, celibacy, prostitution, infant mortality, adult degeneracy, and everything that wise men most dread. In short, there is no future for men, however brimming with crude vitality, who are neither intelligent nor politically educated enough to be socialists. So do not misunderstand me in the other direction either: if I appreciate the vital qualities of the Englishman as I appreciate the vital qualities of the bee, I do not guarantee the Englishman against being, like the bee (or the Canaanite), smoked out and unloaded of his honey by beings inferior to himself in simple acquisitiveness, combativeness, and fecundity, but superior to him in imagination and cunning.

The Don Juan play, however, is to deal with sexual attraction, and not with nutrition, and to deal with it in a society in which the serious business of sex is left by men to women, as the serious business of nutrition is left by women to men. That the men, to protect themselves against a too aggressive prosecution of the women's business, have set up a feeble romantic convention that the initiative in sex business must always come from the man, is true; but the pretence is so shallow that even in the theatre, that last sanctuary of unreality, it imposes only on the inexperienced. In Shakespeare's plays the woman always takes the initiative. In his problem plays and his popular plays alike the love interest is the interest of seeing the woman hunt the man down. She may do it by blandishment, like Rosalind, or by stratagem, like Mariana; but in every case the relation between the woman and the man is the same: she is the pursuer and contriver, he the pursued and disposed of. When she is baffled, like Ophelia, she goes mad and commits suicide; and the man goes straight from her funeral to a fencing match. No doubt Nature, with very young creatures, may save the woman the trouble of scheming: Prospero knows that he has only to throw Ferdinand and Miranda together and they will mate like a pair of doves; and there is no need for Perdita to capture Florizel as the lady doctor in *All's Well That Ends Well* (an early Ibsenite heroine) captures Bertram. But the mature cases all illustrate the Shakespearian law. The one apparent exception, Petruchio, is not a real one: he is most carefully characterized as a purely commercial matrimonial adventurer. Once he is assured that Katharine has money, he undertakes to marry her before he has seen her. In real life we find not only Petruchios, but Mantalinis and Dobbins who pursue women with appeals to their pity or jealousy or vanity, or cling to them in a romantically infatuated way. Such effeminates do not count in the world scheme: even Bunsby dropping like a fascinated bird into the jaws of Mrs. MacStinger is by comparison a true tragic object of pity and terror. I find in my own plays that Woman, projecting herself dramatically by my hands (a process over which I assure you I have no more real control than I have over my wife), behaves just as Woman did in the plays of Shakespeare.

And so your Don Juan has come to birth as a stage projection of the tragi-comic love chase of the man by the woman; and my Don Juan is the quarry instead of the huntsman. Yet he is a true Don Juan, with a sense of reality that disables convention, defying to the last the fate which finally overtakes him. The woman's need of him to enable her to carry on Nature's most urgent work, does not prevail against him until his resistance gathers her energy to a climax at which she dares to throw away her customary exploitations of the conventional affectionate and dutiful poses, and claim him by natural right for a purpose that far transcends their mortal personal purposes.

Among the friends to whom I have read this play in manuscript are some of our own sex who are shocked at the "unscrupulousness," meaning the total disregard of masculine fastidiousness, with which the woman pursues her purpose. It does not occur to them that if women were as fastidious as men, morally or physically, there would be an end of the race. Is there anything meaner than to throw necessary work upon other people and then disparage it as unworthy and indelicate? We laugh at the haughty American nation because it makes the Negro clean its boots and then proves the moral and physical inferiority of the Negro by the fact that he is a shoeblack; but we ourselves throw the whole drudgery of creation on one sex, and then imply that no female of any womanliness or delicacy would initiate any effort in that direction. There are no limits to male hypocrisy in this matter. No doubt there are moments when man's sexual immunities are made acutely humiliating to him. When the terrible moment of birth arrives, its supreme importance and its superhuman effort and peril, in which the father has no part, dwarf him into the meanest insignificance: he slinks out of the way of the humblest petticoat, happy if he be poor enough to be pushed out of the house to outface his ignominy by drunken rejoicings. But when the crisis is over he takes his revenge, swaggering as the breadwinner, and speaking of Woman's "sphere" with condescension, even with chivalry, as if the kitchen and the nursery were less important than the office in the city. When his swagger is exhausted he drivels into erotic poetry or sentimental uxoriousness; and the Tennysonian King Arthur posing at Guinevere becomes Don Quixote groveling before Dulcinea. You must admit that here Nature beats Comedy out of the field: the wildest hominist or feminist farce is insipid after the most commonplace "slice of life." The pretence that women do not take the initiative is part of the farce. Why, the whole world is strewn with snares, traps, gins and pitfalls for the capture of men by women. Give women the vote, and in five years there will be a crushing tax on bachelors. Men, on the other hand, attach penalties to marriage, depriving women of property, of the franchise, of the free use of their limbs, of that ancient symbol of immortality, the right to make oneself at home in the house of God by taking off the hat, of everything that he can force Woman to dispense with without compelling himself to dispense with her. All in vain. Woman must marry because the race must perish without her travail: if the risk of death and the certainty of pain, danger and unutterable discomforts cannot deter her, slavery and swaddled ankles will not. And yet we assume that the force that carries women through all these perils and hardships, stops abashed before the primnesses of our behavior for young ladies. It is assumed that the woman must wait, motionless, until she is wooed. Nay, she often does wait motionless. That is how the spider waits for the fly. But the spider spins her web. And if the fly, like my hero, shews a strength that promises to extricate him, how swiftly does she abandon her pretence of passiveness, and openly fling coil after coil about him until he is secured for ever!

If the really impressive books and other art-works of the world were produced by ordinary men, they would express more fear of women's pursuit than love of their illusory beauty. But ordinary men cannot produce really impressive art-works. Those who can are men of genius: that is, men selected by Nature to carry on the work of building up an intellectual consciousness of her own instinctive purpose. Accordingly, we observe in the man of genius all the unscrupulousness and all the "self-sacrifice" (the two things are the same) of Woman. He will risk the stake and the cross; starve, when necessary, in a garret all his life; study women and live on their work and care as Darwin studied worms and lived upon sheep; work his nerves into rags without payment, a sublime altruist in his disregard of himself, an atrocious egoist in his disregard of others. Here Woman meets a purpose as impersonal, as irresistible as her own; and the clash is sometimes tragic. When it is complicated by the genius being a woman, then the game is one for a king of critics: your George Sand becomes a mother to gain experience for the novelist and to develop her, and gobbles up men of genius, Chopins, Mussets and the like, as mere hors d'oeuvres.

I state the extreme case, of course; but what is true of the great man who incarnates the philosophic consciousness of Life and the woman who incarnates its fecundity, is true in some degree of all geniuses and all women. Hence it is that the world's books get written, its pictures painted, its statues modelled, its symphonies composed, by people who are free of the otherwise universal dominion of the tyranny of sex. Which leads us to the conclusion, astonishing to the vulgar, that art, instead of being before all things the expression of the normal sexual situation, is really the only department in which sex is a superseded and secondary power, with its consciousness so confused and its purpose so perverted, that its ideas are mere fantasy to common men. Whether the artist becomes poet or philosopher, moralist or founder of a religion, his sexual doctrine is nothing but

a barren special pleading for pleasure, excitement, and
knowledge when he is young, and for contemplative
tranquillity when he is old and satiated. Romance and
Asceticism, Amorism and Puritanism are equally unreal
in the great Philistine world. The world shewn us in
books, whether the books be confessed epics or pro-
fessed gospels, or in codes, or in political orations, or in
philosophic systems, is not the main world at all: it is
only the self-consciousness of certain abnormal people
who have the specific artistic talent and temperament. A
serious matter this for you and me, because the man
whose consciousness does not correspond to that of the
majority is a madman; and the old habit of worshipping
madmen is giving way to the new habit of locking them
up. And since what we call education and culture is for
the most part nothing but the substitution of reading for
experience, of literature for life, of the obsolete fictitious
for the contemporary real, education, as you no doubt
observed at Oxford, destroys, by supplantation, every
mind that is not strong enough to see through the imposture and to use the great Masters of Arts as what they
really are and no more: that is, patentees of highly questionable methods of thinking, and manufacturers of
highly questionable, and for the majority but half valid
representations of life. The schoolboy who uses his
Homer to throw at his fellow's head makes perhaps the
safest and most rational use of him; and I observe with
reassurance that you occasionally do the same, in your
prime, with your Aristotle.

Fortunately for us, whose minds have been so over-
whelmingly sophisticated by literature, what produces all
these treatises and poems and scriptures of one sort or
another is the struggle of Life to become divinely conscious of itself instead of blindly stumbling hither and
thither in the line of least resistance. Hence there is a
driving towards truth in all books on matters where the
writer, though exceptionally gifted, is normally consti-
tuted, and has no private axe to grind. Copernicus had
no motive for misleading his fellow-men as to the place
of the sun in the solar system: he looked for it as honestly as a shepherd seeks his path in a mist. But Copernicus would not have written love stories scientifically.

When it comes to sex relations, the man of genius does not share the common man's danger of capture, nor the woman of genius the common woman's overwhelming specialization. And that is why our scriptures and other art-works, when they deal with love, turn from honest attempts at science in physics to romantic nonsense, erotic ecstasy, or the stern asceticism of satiety ("the road of excess leads to the palace of wisdom" said William Blake; for "you never know what is enough unless you know what is more than enough").

There is a political aspect of this sex question which is too big for my comedy, and too momentous to be passed over without culpable frivolity. It is impossible to demonstrate that the initiative in sex transactions remains with Woman, and has been confirmed to her, so far, more and more by the suppression of rapine and discouragement of importunity, without being driven to very serious reflections on the fact that this initiative is politically the most important of all the initiatives, because our political experiment of democracy, the last refuge of cheap misgovernment, will ruin us if our citizens are ill bred.

When we two were born, this country was still dominated by a selected class bred by political marriages. The commercial class had not then completed the first twenty-five years of its new share of political power; and it was itself selected by money qualification, and bred, if not by political marriage, at least by a pretty rigorous class marriage. Aristocracy and plutocracy still furnish the figureheads of politics; but they are now dependent on the votes of the promiscuously bred masses. And this, if you please, at the very moment when the political problem, having suddenly ceased to mean a very limited and occasional interference, mostly by way of jobbing public appointments, in the mismanagement of a tight but parochial little island, with occasional meaningless prosecution of dynastic wars, has become the industrial reorganization of Britain, the construction of a practically international Commonwealth, and the partition of the whole of Africa and perhaps the whole of Asia by the civilized Powers. Can you believe that the people whose conceptions of society and conduct, whose power of attention and scope of interest, are measured by the British theatre as you know it today, can either handle this colossal task themselves, or understand and support the sort of mind and character that is (at least comparatively) capable of handling it? For remember: what our voters are in the pit and gallery they are also in the polling booth. We are all now under what Burke called "the hoofs of the swinish multitude." Burke's language gave great offence because the implied exceptions to its universal application made it a class insult; and it certainly was not for the pot to call the kettle black. The aristocracy he defended, in spite of the political marriages by which it tried to secure breeding for itself, had its mind undertrained by silly schoolmasters and governesses, its character corrupted by gratuitous luxury, its self-respect adulterated to complete spuriousness by flattery and flunkeyism. It is no better today and never will be any better: our very peasants have something morally hardier in them that culminates occasionally in a Bunyan, a Burns, or a Carlyle. But observe, this aristocracy, which was overpowered from 1832 to 1885 by the middle class, has come back to power by the votes of "the swinish multitude." Tom Paine has triumphed over Edmund Burke; and the swine are now courted electors. How many of their own class have these electors sent to parliament? Hardly a dozen out of 670, and these only under the persuasion of conspicuous personal qualifications and popular eloquence. The multitude thus pronounces judgment on its own units: it admits itself unfit to govern, and will vote only for a man morphologically and genetically transfigured by palatial residence and equipage, by transcendent tailoring, by the glamor of aristocratic kinship. Well, we two know these transfigured persons, these college passmen, these well groomed monocular Algys and Bobbies, these cricketers to whom age brings golf instead of wisdom, these plutocratic products of "the nail and sarspan business as he got his money by." Do you know whether to laugh or cry at the notion that they, poor devils! will drive a team of continents as they drive a four-in-hand; turn a jostling anarchy of casual trade and speculation into an ordered productivity; and federate our colonies into a world-

Power of the first magnitude? Give these people the
most perfect political constitution and the soundest political program that benevolent omniscience can devise for
them, and they will interpret it into mere fashionable
folly or canting charity as infallibly as a savage converts
the philosophical theology of a Scotch missionary into
crude African idolatry.

I do not know whether you have any illusions left on
the subject of education, progress, and so forth. I have
none. Any pamphleteer can shew the way to better
things; but when there is no will there is no way. My
nurse was fond of remarking that you cannot make a
silk purse out of a sow's ear; and the more I see of the
efforts of our churches and universities and literary sages
to raise the mass above its own level, the more convinced I am that my nurse was right. Progress can do
nothing but make the most of us all as we are, and that
most would clearly not be enough even if those who are
already raised out of the lowest abysses would allow the
others a chance. The bubble of Heredity has been
pricked: the certainty that acquirements are negligible as
elements in practical heredity has demolished the hopes
of the educationists as well as the terrors of the degeneracy mongers; and we know now that there is no hereditary "governing class" any more than a hereditary
hooliganism. We must either breed political capacity or
be ruined by Democracy, which was forced on us by the
failure of the older alternatives. Yet if Despotism failed
only for want of a capable benevolent despot, what
chance has Democracy, which requires a whole population of capable voters: that is, of political critics who, if
they cannot govern in person for lack of spare energy
or specific talent for administration, can at least recognize and appreciate capacity and benevolence in others,
and so govern through capably benevolent representa-
tives? Where are such voters to be found today? Nowhere. Promiscuous breeding has produced a weakness
of character that is too timid to face the full stringency
of a thoroughly competitive struggle for existence and
too lazy and petty to organize the commonwealth co-
operatively. Being cowards, we defeat natural selection

under cover of philanthropy: being sluggards, we neglect artificial selection under cover of delicacy and morality.

Yet we must get an electorate of capable critics or collapse as Rome and Egypt collapsed. At this moment the Roman decadent phase of *panem et circenses* is being inaugurated under our eyes. Our newspapers and melodramas are blustering about our imperial destiny; but our eyes and hearts turn eagerly to the American millionaire. As his hand goes down to his pocket, our fingers go up to the brims of our hats by instinct. Our ideal prosperity is not the prosperity of the industrial north, but the prosperity of the Isle of Wight, of Folkestone and Ramsgate, of Nice and Monte Carlo. That is the only prosperity you see on the stage, where the workers are all footmen, parlormaids, comic lodging-letters and fashionable professional men, whilst the heroes and heroines are miraculously provided with unlimited dividends, and eat gratuitously, like the knights in Don Quixote's books of chivalry. The city papers prate of the competition of Bombay with Manchester and the like. The real competition is the competition of Regent Street with the Rue de Rivoli, of Brighton and the south coast with the Riviera, for the spending money of the American Trusts. What is all this growing love of pageantry, this effusive loyalty, this officious rising and uncovering at a wave from a flag or a blast from a brass band? Imperialism? Not a bit of it. Obsequiousness, servility, cupidity roused by the prevailing smell of money. When Mr. Carnegie rattled his millions in his pockets all England became one rapacious cringe. Only, when Rhodes (who had probably been reading my *Socialism for Millionaires*) left word that no idler was to inherit his estate, the bent backs straightened mistrustfully for a moment. Could it be that the Diamond King was no gentleman after all? However, it was easy to ignore a rich man's solecism. The ungentlemanly clause was not mentioned again; and the backs soon bowed themselves back into their natural shape.

But I hear you asking me in alarm whether I have actually put all this tub thumping into a Don Juan comedy. I have not. I have only made my Don Juan a politi-

cal pamphleteer, and given you his pamphlet in full by
way of appendix. You will find it at the end of the book.
I am sorry to say that it is a common practice with romancers to announce their hero as a man of extraordinary genius, and to leave his works entirely to the reader's
imagination; so that at the end of the book you whisper
to yourself ruefully that but for the author's solemn preliminary assurance you should hardly have given the gentleman credit for ordinary good sense. You cannot accuse me
of this pitiable barrenness, this feeble evasion. I not only
tell you that my hero wrote a revolutionists' handbook: I
give you the handbook at full length for your edification
if you care to read it. And in that handbook you will
find the politics of the sex question as I conceive Don
Juan's descendant to understand them. Not that I dis-
claim the fullest responsibility for his opinions and for
those of all my characters, pleasant and unpleasant. They
are all right from their several points of view; and their
points of view are, for the dramatic moment, mine also.
This may puzzle the people who believe that there is
such a thing as an absolutely right point of view, usually
their own. It may seem to them that nobody who doubts
this can be in a state of grace. However that may be, it
is certainly true that nobody who agrees with them can
possibly be a dramatist, or indeed anything else that
turns upon a knowledge of mankind. Hence it has been
pointed out that Shakespeare had no conscience. Neither
have I, in that sense.

You may, however, remind me that this digression of
mine into politics was preceded by a very convincing
demonstration that the artist never catches the point of
view of the common man on the question of sex, because
he is not in the same predicament. I first prove that
anything I write on the relation of the sexes is sure to
be misleading; and then I proceed to write a Don Juan
play. Well, if you insist on asking me why I behave in
this absurd way, I can only reply that you asked me to,
and that in any case my treatment of the subject may
be valid for the artist, amusing to the amateur, and at
least intelligible and therefore possibly suggestive to the
Philistine. Every man who records his illusions is provid-
ing data for the genuinely scientific psychology which

the world still waits for. I plank down my view of the existing relations of men to women in the most highly civilized society for what it is worth. It is a view like any other view and no more, neither true nor false, but, I hope, a way of looking at the subject which throws into the familiar order of cause and effect a sufficient body of fact and experience to be interesting to you, if not to the playgoing public of London. I have certainly shewn little consideration for that public in this enterprise; but I know that it has the friendliest disposition towards you and me as far as it has any consciousness of our existence, and quite understands that what I write for you must pass at a considerable height over its simple romantic head. It will take my books as read and my genius for granted, trusting me to put forth work of such quality as shall bear out its verdict. So we may disport ourselves on our own plane to the top of our bent; and if any gentleman points out that neither this epistle dedicatory nor the dream of Don Juan in the third act of the ensuing comedy is suitable for immediate production at a popular theatre we need not contradict him. Napoleon provided Talma with a pit of kings, with what effect on Talma's acting is not recorded. As for me, what I have always wanted is a pit of philosophers; and this is a play for such a pit.

I should make formal acknowledgment to the authors whom I have pillaged in the following pages if I could recollect them all. The theft of the brigand-poetaster from Sir Arthur Conan Doyle is deliberate; and the metamorphosis of Leporello into Enry Straker, motor engineer and New Man, is an intentional dramatic sketch for the contemporary embryo of Mr. H. G. Wells's anticipation of the efficient engineering class which will, he hopes, finally sweep the jabberers out of the way of civilization. Mr. Barrie has also, whilst I am correcting my proofs, delighted London with a servant who knows more than his masters. The conception of Mendoza Limited I trace back to a certain West Indian colonial secretary, who, at a period when he and I and Mr. Sidney Webb were sowing our political wild oats as a sort of Fabian Three Musketeers, without any prevision of the surprising respectability of the crop that followed, recommended Webb, the encyclopedic and inexhaustible, to form himself into a company for the benefit of the shareholders. Octavius I take over unaltered from Mozart; and I hereby authorize any actor who impersonates him, to sing *"Dalla sua pace"* (if he can) at any convenient moment during the representation. Ann was suggested to me by the fifteenth-century Dutch morality called Everyman, which Mr. William Poel has lately resuscitated so triumphantly. I trust he will work that vein further, and recognize that Elizabethan Renascence fustian is no more bearable after medieval poesy than Scribe after Ibsen. As I sat watching Everyman at the Charterhouse, I said to myself Why not Everywoman? Ann was the result: every woman is not Ann; but Ann is Everywoman.

That the author of Everyman was no mere artist, but an artist-philosopher, and that the artist-philosophers are the only sort of artists I take quite seriously, will be no news to you. Even Plato and Boswell, as the dramatists who invented Socrates and Dr. Johnson, impress me more deeply than the romantic playwrights. Ever since, as a boy, I first breathed the air of the transcendental regions at a performance of Mozart's *Zauberflöte,* I have been proof against the garish splendors and alcoholic excitements of the ordinary stage combinations of Tappertitian romance with the police intelligence. Bunyan, Blake, Hogarth, and Turner (these four apart and above all the English classics), Goethe, Shelley, Schopenhauer, Wagner, Ibsen, Morris, Tolstoy, and Nietzsche are among the writers whose peculiar sense of the world I recognize as more or less akin to my own. Mark the word peculiar. I read Dickens and Shakespeare without shame or stint; but their pregnant observations and demonstrations of life are not co-ordinated into any philosophy or religion: on the contrary, Dickens's sentimental assumptions are violently contradicted by his observations; and Shakespeare's pessimism is only his wounded humanity. Both have the specific genius of the fictionist and the common sympathies of human feeling and thought in pre-eminent degree. They are often saner and shrewder than the philosophers just as Sancho Panza was often saner and shrewder than Don Quixote. They clear away vast masses of oppressive gravity by their sense of the ridiculous, which is at bottom a combination of sound moral judgment with lighthearted good humor. But they are concerned with the diversities of the world instead of with its unities: they are so irreligious that they exploit popular religion for professional purposes without delicacy or scruple (for example, Sydney Carton and the ghost in Hamlet!): they are anarchical, and cannot balance their exposures of Angelo and Dogberry, Sir Leicester Dedlock and Mr. Tite Barnacle, with any portrait of a prophet or a worthy leader: they have no constructive ideas: they regard those who have them as dangerous fanatics: in all their fictions there is no leading thought or inspiration for which any man could conceivably risk the spoiling of his hat in a shower, much less his life. Both are alike forced to borrow motives for the more strenuous actions of their personages from the common stockpot of melodramatic plots; so that Hamlet has to be stimulated by the prejudices of a policeman and Macbeth by the cupidities of a bushranger. Dickens, without the excuse of having to manufacture motives for Hamlets and Macbeths, superfluously punts his crew down the stream of his monthly parts by mechanical devices which I leave you to describe, my own memory being quite baffled by the simplest question as to Monks in *Oliver Twist,* or the long lost parentage of Smike, or the relations between the Dorrit and Clennam families so inopportunely discovered by Monsieur Rigaud Blandois. The truth is, the world was to Shakespeare a great "stage of fools" on which he was utterly bewildered. He could see no sort of sense in living at all; and Dickens saved himself from the despair of the dream in "The Chimes" by taking the world for granted and busying himself with its details. Neither of them could do anything with a serious positive character: they could place a human figure before you with perfect verisimilitude; but when the moment came for making it live and move, they found, unless it made them laugh, that they had a puppet on their hands, and had to invent some artificial external stimulus to make it work. This is what is the matter with Hamlet all through: he has no will except in his bursts of temper. Foolish Bardolaters make a virtue of this after their fashion: they declare that the play is the tragedy of irresolution; but all Shakespeare's projections of the deepest humanity he knew have the same defect: their characters and manners are lifelike; but their actions are forced on them from without, and the external force is grotesquely inappropriate except when it is quite conventional, as in the case of Henry V. Falstaff is more vivid than any of these serious reflective characters, because he is self-acting: his motives are his own appetites and instincts and humors. Richard III, too, is delightful as the whimsical comedian who stops a funeral to make love to the corpse's widow; but when, in the next act, he is replaced by a stage villain who smothers babies and offs with people's heads, we are revolted at the imposture and repudiate the changeling. Faulconbridge, Coriolanus, Leontes are admirable descriptions of instinctive temperaments: indeed the play of *Coriolanus* is the greatest of Shakespeare's comedies; but description is not philosophy; and comedy neither compromises the author nor reveals him. He must be judged by those characters into which he puts what he knows of himself, his Hamlets and Macbeths and Lears and Prosperos. If these characters are agonizing in a void about factitious melodramatic murders and revenges and the like, whilst the comic characters walk with their feet on solid ground, vivid and amusing, you know that the author has much to shew and nothing to teach. The comparison between Falstaff and Prospero is like the comparison between Micawber and David Copperfield. At the end of the book you know Micawber, whereas you only know what has happened to David, and are not interested enough in him to wonder what his politics or religion might be if anything so stupendous as a religious or political idea, or a general idea of any sort, were to occur to him. He is tolerable as a child; but he never becomes a man, and might be left out of his own biography altogether but for his usefulness as a stage confidant, a Horatio or "Charles his friend"—what they call on the stage a feeder.

Now you cannot say this of the works of the artist-philosophers. You cannot say it, for instance, of *The Pilgrim's Progress*. Put your Shakespearian hero and

coward, Henry V and Pistol or Parolles, beside Mr. Val-
iant and Mr. Fearing, and you have a sudden revelation
of the abyss that lies between the fashionable author
who could see nothing in the world but personal aims
and the tragedy of their disappointment or the comedy
of their incongruity, and the field preacher who achieved
virtue and courage by identifying himself with the purpose of the world as he understood it. The contrast is
enormous: Bunyan's coward stirs your blood more than
Shakespeare's hero, who actually leaves you cold and
secretly hostile. You suddenly see that Shakespeare, with
all his flashes and divinations, never understood virtue
and courage, never conceived how any man who was not
a fool could, like Bunyan's hero, look back from the
brink of the river of death over the strife and labor of
his pilgrimage, and say "yet do I not repent me"; or,
with the panache of a millionaire, bequeath "my sword
to him that shall succeed me in my pilgrimage, and my
courage and skill to him that can get it." This is the true
joy in life, the being used for a purpose recognized by
yourself as a mighty one; the being thoroughly worn out
before you are thrown on the scrap heap; the being a
force of Nature instead of a feverish selfish little clod of
ailments and grievances complaining that the world will
not devote itself to making you happy. And also the
only real tragedy in life is the being used by personally
minded men for purposes which you recognize to be
base. All the rest is at worst mere misfortune or mortality: this alone is misery, slavery, hell on earth; and the
revolt against it is the only force that offers a man's
work to the poor artist, whom our personally minded
rich people would so willingly employ as pander, buffoon, beauty monger, sentimentalizer and the like.

It may seem a long step from Bunyan to Nietzsche;
but the difference between their conclusions is purely
formal. Bunyan's perception that righteousness is filthy
rags, his scorn for Mr. Legality in the village of Morality,
his defiance of the Church as the supplanter of religion,
his insistence on courage as the virtue of virtues, his
estimate of the career of the conventionally respectable
and sensible Worldly Wiseman as no better at bottom
than the life and death of Mr. Badman: all this, ex-

pressed by Bunyan in the terms of a tinker's theology,
is what Nietzsche has expressed in terms of post-
Darwinian, post-Schopenhauerian philosophy; Wagner
in terms of polytheistic mythology; and Ibsen in terms
of mid-nineteenth-century Parisian dramaturgy. Nothing
is new in these matters except their novelties: for instance, it is a novelty to call Justification by Faith
"Wille," and Justification by Works "Vorstellung." The
sole use of the novelty is that you and I buy and read
Schopenhauer's treatise on Will and Representation
when we should not dream of buying a set of sermons
on Faith versus Works. At bottom the controversy is the
same, and the dramatic results are the same. Bunyan
makes no attempt to present his pilgrims as more sensible or better conducted than Mr. Worldly Wiseman. Mr.
W. W.'s worst enemies, as Mr. Embezzler, Mr. Never-
go-to-Church-on-Sunday, Mr. Bad Form, Mr. Murderer,
Mr. Burglar, Mr. Co-respondent, Mr. Blackmailer, Mr.
Cad, Mr. Drunkard, Mr. Labor Agitator and so forth,
can read the *Pilgrim's Progress* without finding a word
said against them; whereas the respectable people who
snub them and put them in prison, such as Mr. W. W.
himself and his young friend Civility; Formalist and Hypocrisy; Wildhead, Inconsiderate, and Pragmatick (who
were clearly young university men of good family and
high feeding); that brisk lad Ignorance, Talkative, By-
Ends of Fairspeech and his mother-in-law Lady
Feigning, and other reputable gentlemen and citizens,
catch it very severely. Even Little Faith, though he gets
to heaven at last, is given to understand that it served
him right to be mobbed by the brothers Faint Heart,
Mistrust, and Guilt, all three recognized members of respectable society and veritable pillars of the law. The
whole allegory is a consistent attack on morality and
respectability, without a word that one can remember
against vice and crime. Exactly what is complained of in
Nietzsche and Ibsen, is it not? And also exactly what
would be complained of in all the literature which is
great enough and old enough to have attained canonical
rank, officially or unofficially, were it not that books are
admitted to the canon by a compact which confesses
their greatness in consideration of abrogating their

meaning; so that the reverend rector can agree with the prophet Micah as to his inspired style without being committed to any complicity in Micah's furiously Radical opinions. Why, even I, as I force myself, pen in hand, into recognition and civility, find all the force of my onslaught destroyed by a simple policy of nonresistance. In vain do I redouble the violence of the language in which I proclaim my heterodoxies. I rail at the theistic credulity of Voltaire, the amoristic superstition of Shelley, the revival of tribal soothsaying and idolatrous rites which Huxley called Science and mistook for an advance on the Pentateuch, no less than at the welter of ecclesiastical and professional humbug which saves the face of the stupid system of violence and robbery which we call Law and Industry. Even atheists reproach me with infidelity and anarchists with nihilism because I cannot endure their moral tirades. And yet, instead of exclaiming "Send this inconceivable Satanist to the stake," the respectable newspapers pith me by announcing "another book by this brilliant and thoughtful writer." And the ordinary citizen, knowing that an author who is well spoken of by a respectable newspaper must be all right, reads me, as he reads Micah, with undisturbed edification from his own point of view. It is narrated that in the eighteen seventies an old lady, a very devout Methodist, moved from Colchester to a house in the neighborhood of the City Road, in London, where, mistaking the Hall of Science for a chapel, she sat at the feet of Charles Bradlaugh for many years, entranced by his eloquence, without questioning his orthodoxy or moulting a feather of her faith. I fear I shall be defrauded of my just martyrdom in the same way.

However, I am digressing, as a man with a grievance always does. And after all, the main thing in determining the artistic quality of a book is not the opinions it propagates, but the fact that the writer has opinions. The old lady from Colchester was right to sun her simple soul in the energetic radiance of Bradlaugh's genuine beliefs and disbeliefs rather than in the chill of such mere painting of light and heat as elocution and convention can achieve. My contempt for belles-lettres, and for amateurs who become the heroes of the fanciers of literary virtuosity, is not founded on any illusion of mind as to the permanence of those forms of thought (call them opinions) by which I strive to communicate my bent to my fellows. To younger men they are already outmoded; for though they have no more lost their logic than an eighteenth-century pastel has lost its drawing or its color, yet, like the pastel, they grow indefinably shabby, and will grow shabbier until they cease to count at all, when my books will either perish, or, if the world is still poor enough to want them, will have to stand, with Bunyan's, by quite amorphous qualities of temper and energy. With this conviction I cannot be a bellettrist. No doubt I must recognize, as even the Ancient Mariner did, that I must tell my story entertainingly if I am to hold the wedding guest spellbound in spite of the siren sounds of the loud bassoon. But "for art's sake" alone I would not face the toil of writing a single sentence. I know that there are men who, having nothing to say and nothing to write, are nevertheless so in love with oratory and with literature that they keep desperately repeating as much as they can understand of what others have said or written aforetime. I know that the leisurely tricks which their want of conviction leaves them free to play with the diluted and misapprehended message supply them with a pleasant parlor game which they call style. I can pity their dotage and even sympathize with their fancy. But a true original style is never achieved for its own sake: a man may pay from a shilling to a guinea, according to his means, to see, hear, or read another man's act of genius; but he will not pay with his whole life and soul to become a mere virtuoso in literature, exhibiting an accomplishment which will not even make money for him, like fiddle playing. Effectiveness of assertion is the Alpha and Omega of style. He who has nothing to assert has no style and can have none: he who has something to assert will go as far in power of style as its momentousness and his conviction will carry him. Disprove his assertion after it is made, yet its style remains. Darwin has no more destroyed the style of Job nor of Handel than Martin Luther destroyed the style of Giotto. All the assertions get disproved sooner or later; and so we find the world full of a magnificent débris of artistic fossils, with the matter-of-fact credibility gone clean out of them, but the form still splendid. And that is why the old masters play the deuce with our mere susceptibles. Your Royal Academician thinks he can get the style of Giotto without Giotto's beliefs, and correct his perspective into the bargain. Your man of letters thinks he can get Bunyan's or Shakespeare's style without Bunyan's conviction or Shakespeare's apprehension, especially if he takes care not to split his infinitives. And so with your Doctors of Music, who, with their collections of discords duly prepared and resolved or retarded or anticipated in the manner of the great composers, think they can learn the art of Palestrina from Cherubini's treatise. All this academic art is far worse than the trade in sham antique furniture; for the man who sells me an oaken chest which he swears was made in the thirteenth century, though as a matter of fact he made it himself only yesterday, at least does not pretend that there are any modern ideas in it, whereas your academic copier of fossils offers them to you as the latest outpouring of the human spirit, and, worst of all, kidnaps young people as pupils and persuades them that his limitations are rules, his observances dexterities, his timidities good taste, and his emptinesses purities. And when he declares that art should not be didactic, all the people who have nothing to teach and all the people who don't want to learn agree with him emphatically.

I pride myself on not being one of these susceptibles. If you study the electric light with which I supply you in that Bumbledonian public capacity of mine over which you make merry from time to time, you will find that your house contains a great quantity of highly susceptible copper wire which gorges itself with electricity and gives you no light whatever. But here and there occurs a scrap of intensely insusceptible, intensely resistant material; and that stubborn scrap grapples with the current and will not let it through until it has made itself useful to you as those two vital qualities of literature, light and heat. Now if I am to be no mere copper wire amateur but a luminous author, I must also be a most intensely refractory person, liable to go out and to go wrong at inconvenient moments, and with incendiary possibilities. These are the faults of my qualities; and I assure you that I sometimes dislike myself so much that when some irritable reviewer chances at that moment to pitch into me with zest, I feel unspeakably relieved and obliged. But I never dream of reforming, knowing that I must take myself as I am and get what work I can out of myself. All this you will understand; for there is community of material between us: we are both critics of life as well as of art; and you have perhaps said to yourself when I have passed your windows "There, but for the grace of God, go I." An awful and chastening reflection, which shall be the closing cadence of this immoderately long letter from yours faithfully,

—G. BERNARD SHAW
Woking, 1903

ACT ONE

*R*oebuck Ramsden *is in his study, opening the morning's letters. The study, handsomely and solidly furnished, proclaims the man of means. Not a speck of dust is visible: it is clear that there are at least two housemaids and a parlormaid downstairs, and a housekeeper upstairs who does not let them spare elbow-grease. Even the top of Roebuck's head is polished: on a sunshiny day he could heliograph his orders to distant camps by merely nodding. In no other respect, however, does he suggest the military man. It is in active civil life that men get his broad air of importance, his dignified expectation of deference, his determinate mouth disarmed and refined since the hour of his success by the withdrawal of opposition and the concession of comfort and precedence and power. He is more than a highly respectable man: he is marked out as a president of highly respectable men, a chairman among directors, an alderman among councillors, a mayor among aldermen. Four tufts of iron-grey hair, which will soon be as white as isinglass, and are in other respects not at all unlike it, grow in two symmetrical pairs above his ears and at the angles of his spreading jaws. He wears a black frock coat, a white waistcoat (it is bright spring weather), and trousers, neither black nor perceptibly blue, of one of those indefinitely mixed hues which the modern clothier has produced to harmonize with the religions of respectable men. He has not been out of doors yet to-day; so he still wears his slippers, his boots being ready for him on the hearth-rug. Surmising that he has no valet, and seeing that he has no secretary with a shorthand notebook and a typewriter, one meditates on how little our* *great burgess domesticity has been disturbed by new fashions and methods, or by the enterprise of the railway and hotel companies which sell you a Saturday to Monday of life at Folkestone as a real gentleman for two guineas, first class fares both ways included.*

How old is Roebuck? The question is important on the threshold of a drama of ideas; for under such circumstances everything depends on whether his adolescence belonged to the sixties or to the eighties. He was born, as a matter of fact, in 1839, and was a Unitarian and Free Trader from his boyhood, and an Evolutionist from the publication of the Origin of Species. *Consequently he has always classed himself as an advanced thinker and fearlessly outspoken reformer.*

Sitting at his writing table, he has on his right the windows giving on Portland Place. Through these, as through a proscenium, the curious spectator may contemplate his profile as well as the blinds will permit. On his left is the inner wall, with a stately bookcase, and the door not quite in the middle, but somewhat further from him. Against the wall opposite him are two busts on pillars: one, to his left, of John Bright; the other, to his right, of Mr. Herbert Spencer. Between them hang an engraved portrait of Richard Cobden; enlarged photographs of Martineau, Huxley, and George Eliot; autotypes of allegories by Mr. G. F. Watts (for Roebuck believes in the fine arts with all the earnestness of a man who does not understand them), and an impression of Dupont's engraving of Delaroche's Beaux Arts hemicycle, representing the great men of all ages. On the wall behind him, above the mantelshelf, is a family portrait of impenetrable obscurity.

A chair stands near the writing table for the convenience of business visitors. Two other chairs are against the wall between the busts.

A parlormaid enters with a visitor's card. Roebuck takes it, and nods, pleased. Evidently a welcome caller.

RAMSDEN. Shew him up.
[*The parlormaid goes out and returns with the visitor.*]
THE MAID. Mr. Robinson.
[*Mr. Robinson is really an uncommonly nice looking*

*young fellow. He must, one thinks, be the jeune premier;
for it is not in reason to suppose that a second such attractive
male figure should appear in one story. The slim,
shapely frame, the elegant suit of new mourning, the small
head and regular features, the pretty little moustache, the
frank clear eyes, the wholesome bloom on the youthful
complexion, the well brushed glossy hair, not curly, but
of fine texture and good dark color, the arch of good
nature in the eyebrows, the erect forehead and neatly
pointed chin, all announce the man who will love and
suffer later on. And that he will not do so without sympathy
is guaranteed by an engaging sincerity and eager modest
serviceableness which stamp him as a man of amiable
nature. The moment he appears, Ramsden's face expands
into fatherly liking and welcome, an expression which
drops into one of decorous grief as the young man approaches
him with sorrow in his face as well as in his
black clothes. Ramsden seems to know the nature of the
bereavement. As the visitor advances silently to the writing
table, the old man rises and shakes his hand across it
without a word: a long, affectionate shake which tells the
story of a recent sorrow common to both.]*

RAMSDEN [*concluding the handshake and cheering
up*] Well, well, Octavius, it's the common lot. We must
all face it some day. Sit down.

[*Octavius takes the visitor's chair. Ramsden replaces himself
in his own.*]

OCTAVIUS. Yes: we must face it, Mr. Ramsden. But
I owed him a great deal. He did everything for me that
my father could have done if he had lived.

RAMSDEN. He had no son of his own, you see.

OCTAVIUS. But he had daughters; and yet he was as
good to my sister as to me. And his death was so sudden!
I always intended to thank him—to let him know
that I had not taken all his care of me as a matter of
course, as any boy takes his father's care. But I waited
for an opportunity; and now he is dead—dropped without
a moment's warning. He will never know what I felt.
[*He takes out his handkerchief and cries unaffectedly.*]

RAMSDEN. How do we know that, Octavius? He may
know it: we cannot tell. Come! don't grieve. [*Octavius
masters himself and puts up his handkerchief.*] That's

right. Now let me tell you something to console you. The last time I saw him—it was in this very room—he said to me: "Tavy is a generous lad and the soul of honor; and when I see how little consideration other men get from their sons, I realize how much better than a son he's been to me." There! Doesn't that do you good?

OCTAVIUS. Mr. Ramsden: he used to say to me that he had met only one man in the world who was the soul of honor, and that was Roebuck Ramsden.

RAMSDEN. Oh, that was his partiality: we were very old friends, you know. But there was something else he used to say about you. I wonder whether I ought to tell you or not!

OCTAVIUS. You know best.

RAMSDEN. It was something about his daughter.

OCTAVIUS [*eagerly*] About Ann! Oh, do tell me that, Mr. Ramsden.

RAMSDEN. Well, he said he was glad, after all, you were not his son, because he thought that someday Annie and you— [*Octavius blushes vividly.*] Well, perhaps I shouldn't have told you. But he was in earnest.

OCTAVIUS. Oh, if only I thought I had a chance! You know, Mr. Ramsden, I don't care about money or about what people call position; and I can't bring myself to take an interest in the business of struggling for them. Well, Ann has a most exquisite nature; but she is so accustomed to be in the thick of that sort of thing that she thinks a man's character incomplete if he is not ambitious. She knows that if she married me she would have to reason herself out of being ashamed of me for not being a big success of some kind.

RAMSDEN [*getting up and planting himself with his back to the fireplace*]. Nonsense, my boy, nonsense! You're too modest. What does she know about the real value of men at her age? [*More seriously*] Besides, she's a wonderfully dutiful girl. Her father's wish would be sacred to her. Do you know that since she grew up to years of discretion, I don't believe she has ever once given her own wish as a reason for doing anything or not doing it. It's always "Father wishes me to," or "Mother wouldn't like it." It's really almost a fault in her. I have often told her she must learn to think for herself.

OCTAVIUS [*shaking his head*]. I couldn't ask her to marry me because her father wished it, Mr. Ramsden.

RAMSDEN. Well, perhaps not. No: of course not. I see that. No: you certainly couldn't. But when you win her on your own merits, it will be a great happiness to her to fulfil her father's desire as well as her own. Eh? Come! you'll ask her, won't you?

OCTAVIUS [*with sad gaiety*] At all events I promise you I shall never ask anyone else. .

RAMSDEN. Oh, you shan't need to. She'll accept you, my boy—although [*here he suddenly becomes very serious indeed*] you have one great drawback.

OCTAVIUS [*anxiously*] What drawback is that, Mr. Ramsden? I should rather say which of my many drawbacks?

RAMSDEN. I'll tell you, Octavius. [*He takes from the table a book bound in red cloth.*] I have in my hand a copy of the most infamous, the most scandalous, the most mischievous, the most blackguardly book that ever escaped burning at the hands of the common hangman. I have not read it: I would not soil my mind with such filth; but I have read what the papers say of it. The title is quite enough for me. [*He reads it.*] The Revolutionist's Handbook and Pocket Companion. By John Tanner, M.I.R.C., Member of the Idle Rich Class.

OCTAVIUS [*smiling*] But Jack—

RAMSDEN [*testily*]. For goodness' sake, don't call him Jack under my roof [*he throws the book violently down on the table. Then, somewhat relieved, he comes past the table to Octavius, and addresses him at close quarters with impressive gravity*]. Now, Octavius, I know that my dead friend was right when he said you were a generous lad. I know that this man was your schoolfellow, and that you feel bound to stand by him because there was a boyish friendship between you. But I ask you to consider the altered circumstances. You were treated as a son in my friend's house. You lived there; and your friends could not be turned from the door. This man Tanner was in and out there on your account almost from his childhood. He addresses Annie by her Christian name as freely as you do. Well, while her father was alive, that was her father's business, not mine. This man Tanner was only a boy to him: his opinions were something to be laughed at, like a man's hat on a child's head. But now Tanner is a grown man and Annie a grown woman. And her father is gone. We don't as yet know the exact terms of his will; but he often talked it over with me; and I have no more doubt than I have that you're sitting there that the will appoints me Annie's trustee and guardian. [*Forcibly.*] Now I tell you, once for all, I can't and I won't have Annie placed in such a position that she must, out of regard for you, suffer the intimacy of this fellow Tanner. It's not fair: it's not right: it's not kind. What are you going to do about it?

OCTAVIUS. But Ann herself has told Jack that whatever his opinions are, he will always be welcome because he knew her dear father.

RAMSDEN [*out of patience*] That girl's mad about her duty to her parents. [*He starts off like a goaded ox in the direction of John Bright, in whose expression there is no sympathy for him. As he speaks he fumes down to Herbert Spencer, who receives him still more coldly.*] Excuse me, Octavius; but there are limits to social toleration. You know that I am not a bigoted or prejudiced man. You know that I am plain Roebuck Ramsden when other men who have done less have got handles to their names, because I have stood for equality and liberty of conscience while they were truckling to the Church and to the aristocracy. Whitefield and I lost chance after chance through our advanced opinions. But I draw the line at Anarchism and Free Love and that sort of thing. If I am to be Annie's guardian, she will have to learn that she has a duty to me. I won't have it: I will not have it. She must forbid John Tanner the house; and so must you.

[*The parlormaid returns.*]

OCTAVIUS. But—

RAMSDEN [*calling his attention to the servant*] Ssh! Well?

THE MAID. Mr. Tanner wishes to see you, sir.

RAMSDEN. Mr. Tanner!

OCTAVIUS. Jack!

RAMSDEN. How dare Mr. Tanner call on me! Say I cannot see him.

OCTAVIUS [*hurt*] I am sorry you are turning my friend from your door like that.

THE MAID [*calmly*] He's not at the door, sir. He's upstairs in the drawing-room with Miss Ramsden. He came with Mrs. Whitefield and Miss Ann and Miss Robinson, sir. [*Ramsden's feelings are beyond words.*]

OCTAVIUS [*grinning*] That's very like Jack, Mr. Ramsden. You must see him, even if it's only to turn him out.

RAMSDEN [*hammering out his words with suppressed fury*] Go upstairs and ask Mr. Tanner to be good enough to step down here. [*The parlormaid goes out; and Ramsden returns to the fireplace, as to a fortified position.*] I must say that of all the confounded pieces of impertinence— well, if these are Anarchist manners, I hope you like them. And Annie with him!—Annie! A— [*He chokes.*]

OCTAVIUS. Yes: that's what surprises me. He's so desperately afraid of Ann. There must be something the matter.

[*Mr. John Tanner suddenly opens the door and enters. He is too young to be described simply as a big man with a beard. But it is already plain that middle life will find him in that category. He has still some of the slimness of youth; but youthfulness is not the effect he aims at: his frock coat would befit a prime minister; and a certain high chested carriage of the shoulders, a lofty pose of the head; and the Olympian majesty with which a mane, or rather a huge wisp, of hazel colored hair is thrown back from an imposing brow, suggest Jupiter rather than Apollo. He is prodigiously fluent of speech, restless, excitable (mark the snorting nostril and the restless blue eye, just the thirty-secondth of an inch too wide open), possibly a little mad. He is carefully dressed, not from the vanity that cannot resist finery, but from a sense of the importance of everything he does which leads him to make as much of paying a call as other men do of getting*]

*married or laying a foundation stone. A sensitive, suscep-
tible, exaggerative, earnest man: a megalomaniac, who
would be lost without a sense of humor.*

*Just at present the sense of humor is in abeyance. To
say that he is excited is nothing: all his moods are phases
of excitement. He is now in the panic-stricken phase; and
he walks straight up to Ramsden as if with the fixed intention of shooting him on his own hearth-rug. But what he
pulls from his breast pocket is not a pistol, but a foolscap
document which he thrusts under the indignant nose of
Ramsden as he exclaims—]*

TANNER. Ramsden: do you know what that is?

RAMSDEN [*loftily*] No, sir.

TANNER. It's a copy of Whitefield's will. Ann got it
this morning.

RAMSDEN. When you say Ann, you mean, I pre-
sume, Miss Whitefield.

TANNER. I mean our Ann, your Ann, Tavy's Ann,
and now, Heaven help me, my Ann!

OCTAVIUS [*rising, very pale*] What do you mean?

TANNER. Mean! [*He holds up the will.*] Do you know
who is appointed Ann's guardian by this will?

RAMSDEN [*coolly*] I believe I am.

TANNER. You! You and I, man. I! I!! I!!! Both of
us! [*He flings the will down on the writing table.*]

RAMSDEN. You! Impossible.

TANNER. It's only too hideously true. [*He throws
himself into Octavius's chair.*] Ramsden: get me out of it
somehow. You don't know Ann as well as I do. She'll
commit every crime a respectable woman can; and she'll
justify every one of them by saying that it was the wish
of her guardians. She'll put everything on us; and we
shall have no more control over her than a couple of
mice over a cat.

OCTAVIUS. Jack: I wish you wouldn't talk like that
about Ann.

TANNER. This chap's in love with her: that's another
complication. Well, she'll either jilt him and say I didn't
approve of him, or marry him and say you ordered her
to. I tell you, this is the most staggering blow that has
ever fallen on a man of my age and temperament.

RAMSDEN. Let me see that will, sir. [*He goes to the*

writing table and picks it up.] I cannot believe that my old friend Whitefield would have shewn such a want of confidence in me as to associate me with— [*His countenance falls as he reads*.]

TANNER. It's all my own doing: that's the horrible irony of it. He told me one day that you were to be Ann's guardian; and like a fool I began arguing with him about the folly of leaving a young woman under the control of an old man with obsolete ideas.

RAMSDEN [*stupended*] My ideas obsolete!!!!!!!

TANNER. Totally. I had just finished an essay called Down with Government by the Greyhaired; and I was full of arguments and illustrations. I said the proper thing was to combine the experience of an old hand with the vitality of a young one. Hang me if he didn't take me at my word and alter his will—it's dated only a fortnight after that conversation—appointing me as joint guardian with you!

RAMSDEN [*pale and determined*] I shall refuse to act.

TANNER. What's the good of that? I've been refusing all the way from Richmond; but Ann keeps on saying that of course she's only an orphan; and that she can't expect the people who were glad to come to the house in her father's time to trouble much about her now. That's the latest game. An orphan! It's like hearing an ironclad talk about being at the mercy of the winds and waves.

OCTAVIUS. This is not fair, Jack. She is an orphan. And you ought to stand by her.

TANNER. Stand by her! What danger is she in? She has the law on her side; she has popular sentiment on her side; she has plenty of money and no conscience. All she wants with me is to load up all her moral responsibilities on me, and do as she likes at the expense of my character. I can't control her; and she can compromise me as much as she likes. I might as well be her husband.

RAMSDEN. You can refuse to accept the guardianship. *I* shall certainly refuse to hold it jointly with you.

TANNER. Yes; and what will she say to that? what does she say to it? Just that her father's wishes are sacred to her, and that she shall always look up to me as her guardian whether I care to face the responsibility or not. Refuse! You might as well refuse to accept the embraces of a boa constrictor when once it gets round your neck.

OCTAVIUS. This sort of talk is not kind to me, Jack.

TANNER [*rising and going to Octavius to console him, but still lamenting*] If he wanted a young guardian, why didn't he appoint Tavy?

RAMSDEN. Ah! why indeed?

OCTAVIUS. I will tell you. He sounded me about it; but I refused the trust because I loved her. I had no right to let myself be forced on her as a guardian by her father. He spoke to her about it; and she said I was right. You know I love her, Mr. Ramsden; and Jack knows it too. If Jack loved a woman, I would not compare her to a boa constrictor in his presence, however much I might dislike her [*he sits down between the busts and turns his face to the wall*].

RAMSDEN. I do not believe that Whitefield was in his right senses when he made that will. You have admitted that he made it under your influence.

TANNER. You ought to be pretty well obliged to me for my influence. He leaves you two thousand five hundred for your trouble. He leaves Tavy a dowry for his sister and five thousand for himself.

OCTAVIUS [*his tears flowing afresh*] Oh, I can't take it. He was too good to us.

TANNER. You won't get it, my boy, if Ramsden upsets the will.

RAMSDEN. Ha! I see. You have got me in a cleft stick.

TANNER. He leaves me nothing but the charge of Ann's morals, on the ground that I have already more money than is good for me. That shews that he had his wits about him, doesn't it?

RAMSDEN [*grimly*] I admit that.

OCTAVIUS [*rising and coming from his refuge by the wall*] Mr. Ramsden: I think you are prejudiced against Jack. He is a man of honor, and incapable of abusing—

TANNER. Don't, Tavy: you'll make me ill. I am not a man of honor: I am a man struck down by a dead hand. Tavy: you must marry her after all and take her off my hands. And I had set my heart on saving you from her!

OCTAVIUS. Oh, Jack, you talk of saving me from my highest happiness.

TANNER. Yes, a lifetime of happiness. If it were only the first half hour's happiness, Tavy, I would buy it for you with my last penny. But a lifetime of happiness! No man alive could bear it: it would be hell on earth.

RAMSDEN [*violently*] Stuff, sir. Talk sense; or else go and waste someone else's time: I have something better to do than listen to your fooleries [*he positively kicks his way to his table and resumes his seat*].

TANNER. You hear him, Tavy! Not an idea in his head later than eighteen sixty. We can't leave Ann with no other guardian to turn to.

RAMSDEN. I am proud of your contempt for my character and opinions, sir. Your own are set forth in that book, I believe.

TANNER [*eagerly going to the table*]. What! You've got my book! What do you think of it?

RAMSDEN. Do you suppose I would read such a book, sir?

TANNER. Then why did you buy it?

RAMSDEN. I did not buy it, sir. It has been sent me by some foolish lady who seems to admire your views. I was about to dispose of it when Octavius interrupted me. I shall do so now, with your permission. [*He throws the book into the wastepaper basket with such vehemence that Tanner recoils under the impression that it is being thrown at his head.*]

TANNER. You have no more manners than I have myself. However, that saves ceremony between us. [*He sits down again.*] What do you intend to do about this will?

OCTAVIUS. May I make a suggestion?

RAMSDEN. Certainly, Octavius.

OCTAVIUS. Aren't we forgetting that Ann herself may have some wishes in this matter?

RAMSDEN. I quite intend that Annie's wishes shall be consulted in every reasonable way. But she is only a woman, and a young and inexperienced woman at that.

TANNER. Ramsden: I begin to pity you.

RAMSDEN [*hotly*] I don't want to know how you feel towards me, Mr. Tanner.

TANNER. Ann will do just exactly what she likes. And what's more, she'll force us to advise her to do it; and she'll put the blame on us if it turns out badly. So, as Tavy is longing to see her—

OCTAVIUS [*shyly*] I am not, Jack.

TANNER. You lie, Tavy: you are. So let's have her down from the drawing-room and ask her what she intends us to do. Off with you, Tavy, and fetch her. [*Tavy turns to go.*] And don't be long; for the strained relations between myself and Ramsden will make the interval rather painful [*Ramsden compresses his lips, but says nothing*].

OCTAVIUS. Never mind him, Mr. Ramsden. He's not serious. [*He goes out.*]

RAMSDEN [*very deliberately*] Mr. Tanner: you are the most impudent person I have ever met.

TANNER [*seriously*] I know it, Ramsden. Yet even I cannot wholly conquer shame. We live in an atmosphere of shame. We are ashamed of everything that is real about us; ashamed of ourselves, of our relatives, of our incomes, of our accents, of our opinions, of our experience, just as we are ashamed of our naked skins. Good Lord, my dear Ramsden, we are ashamed to walk, ashamed to ride in an omnibus, ashamed to hire a hansom instead of keeping a carriage, ashamed of keeping one horse instead of two and a groom-gardener instead of a coachman and footman. The more things a man is ashamed of, the more respectable he is. Why, you're ashamed to buy my book, ashamed to read it: the only thing you're not ashamed of is to judge me for it without having read it; and even that only means that you're ashamed to have heterodox opinions. Look at the effect I produce because my fairy godmother withheld from me this gift of shame. I have every possible virtue that a man can have except—

RAMSDEN. I am glad you think so well of yourself.

TANNER. All you mean by that is that you think I ought to be ashamed of talking about my virtues. You don't mean that I haven't got them: you know perfectly well that I am as sober and honest a citizen as yourself, as truthful personally, and much more truthful politically and morally.

RAMSDEN [*touched on his most sensitive point*] I deny that. I will not allow you or any man to treat me as if I were a mere member of the British public. I detest its prejudices; I scorn its narrowness; I demand the right to think for myself. You pose as an advanced man. Let me tell you that I was an advanced man before you were born.

TANNER. I knew it was a long time ago.

RAMSDEN. I am as advanced as ever I was. I defy you to prove that I have ever hauled down the flag. I am more advanced than ever I was. I grow more advanced every day.

TANNER. More advanced in years, Polonius.

RAMSDEN. Polonius! So you are Hamlet, I suppose.

TANNER. No: I am only the most impudent person you've ever met. That's your notion of a thoroughly bad character. When you want to give me a piece of your mind, you ask yourself, as a just and upright man, what is the worst you can fairly say of me. Thief, liar, forger, adulterer, perjurer, glutton, drunkard? Not one of these names fits me. You have to fall back on my deficiency in shame. Well, I admit it. I even congratulate myself; for if I were ashamed of my real self, I should cut as stupid a figure as any of the rest of you. Cultivate a little impudence, Ramsden; and you will become quite a remarkable man.

RAMSDEN. I have no—

TANNER. You have no desire for that sort of notoriety. Bless you, I knew that answer would come as well as I know that a box of matches will come out of an automatic machine when I put a penny in the slot: you would be ashamed to say anything else.

[*The crushing retort for which Ramsden has been visibly collecting his forces is lost for ever; for at this point Octavius returns with Miss Ann Whitefield and her mother; and Ramsden springs up and hurries to the door to receive them. Whether Ann is good-looking or not depends upon your taste; also and perhaps chiefly on your age and sex. To Octavius she is an enchantingly beautiful woman, in whose presence the world becomes transfig-*

ured, and the puny limits of individual consciousness are suddenly made infinite by a mystic memory of the whole life of the race to its beginnings in the east, or even back to the paradise from which it fell. She is to him the reality of romance, the inner good sense of nonsense, the unveiling of his eyes, the freeing of his soul, the abolition of time, place and circumstance, the etherealization of his blood into rapturous rivers of the very water of life itself, the revelation of all the mysteries and the sanctification of all the dogmas. To her mother she is, to put it as moderately as possible, nothing whatever of the kind. Not that Octavius's admiration is in any way ridiculous or discreditable. Ann is a well formed creature, as far as that goes; and she is perfectly ladylike, graceful, and comely, with ensnaring eyes and hair. Besides, instead of making herself an eyesore, like her mother, she has devised a mourning costume of black and violet silk which does honor to her late father and reveals the family tradition of brave unconventionality by which Ramsden sets such store.

But all this is beside the point as an explanation of Ann's charm. Turn up her nose, give a cast to her eye, replace her black and violet confection by the apron and feathers of a flower girl, strike all the aitches out of her speech, and Ann would still make men dream. Vitality is as common as humanity; but, like humanity, it sometimes rises to genius; and Ann is one of the vital geniuses. Not at all, if you please, an oversexed person: that is a vital defect, not a true excess. She is a perfectly respectable, perfectly self-controlled woman, and looks it; though her pose is fashionably frank and impulsive. She inspires confidence as a person who will do nothing she does not mean to do; also some fear, perhaps, as a woman who will probably do everything she means to do without taking more account of other people than may be necessary and what she calls right. In short, what the weaker of her own sex sometimes call a cat.

Nothing can be more decorous than her entry and her reception by Ramsden, whom she kisses. The late Mr. Whitefield would be gratified almost to impatience by the long faces of the men (except Tanner, who is fidgety), the silent handgrasps, the sympathetic placing of chairs, the sniffing of the widow, and the liquid eye of the daughter,

*whose heart, apparently, will not let her control her
tongue to speech. Ramsden and Octavius take the two
chairs from the wall, and place them for the two ladies;
but Ann comes to Tanner and takes his chair, which he
offers with a brusque gesture, subsequently relieving his
irritation by sitting down on the corner of the writing table
with studied indecorum. Octavius gives Mrs. Whitefield a
chair next Ann, and himself takes the vacant one which
Ramsden has placed under the nose of the effigy of Mr.
Herbert Spencer.*

*Mrs. Whitefield, by the way, is a little woman, whose
faded flaxen hair looks like straw on an egg. She has an
expression of muddled shrewdness, a squeak of protest in
her voice, and an odd air of continually elbowing away
some larger person who is crushing her into a corner.
One guesses her as one of those women who are conscious of being treated as silly and negligible, and who,
without having strength enough to assert themselves effectually, at any rate never submit to their fate. There is a
touch of chivalry in Octavius's scrupulous attention to
her, even whilst his whole soul is absorbed by Ann.*

*Ramsden goes solemnly back to his magisterial seat at the
writing table, ignoring Tanner, and opens the proceedings.*]

RAMSDEN. I am sorry, Annie, to force business on
you at a sad time like the present. But your poor dear
father's will has raised a very serious question. You have
read it, I believe?

[*Ann assents with a nod and a catch of her breath, too
much affected to speak.*]

I must say I am surprised to find Mr. Tanner named
as joint guardian and trustee with myself of you and
Rhoda. [*A pause. They all look portentous; but they have
nothing to say. Ramsden, a little ruffled by the lack of
any response, continues*] I don't know that I can consent
to act under such conditions. Mr. Tanner has, I understand, some objection also; but I do not profess to understand its nature: he will no doubt speak for himself. But
we are agreed that we can decide nothing until we know
your views. I am afraid I shall have to ask you to choose
between my sole guardianship and that of Mr. Tanner;
for I fear it is impossible for us to undertake a joint
arrangement.

ANN [*in a low musical voice*] Mamma—

MRS. WHITEFIELD [*hastily*] Now, Ann, I do beg you not to put it on me. I have no opinion on the subject; and if I had, it would probably not be attended to. I am quite content with whatever you three think best.

[*Tanner turns his head and looks fixedly at Ramsden, who angrily refuses to receive this mute communication.*]

ANN [*resuming in the same gentle voice, ignoring her mother's bad taste*] Mamma knows that she is not strong enough to bear the whole responsibility for me and Rhoda without some help and advice. Rhoda must have a guardian; and though I am older, I do not think any young unmarried woman should be left quite to her own guidance. I hope you agree with me, Granny?

TANNER [*starting*] Granny! Do you intend to call your guardians Granny?

ANN. Don't be foolish, Jack. Mr. Ramsden has always been Grandpapa Roebuck to me: I am Granny's Annie; and he is Annie's Granny. I christened him so when I first learned to speak.

RAMSDEN [*sarcastically*] I hope you are satisfied, Mr. Tanner. Go on, Annie: I quite agree with you.

ANN. Well, if I am to have a guardian, can I set aside anybody whom my dear father appointed for me?

RAMSDEN [*biting his lip*] You approve of your father's choice, then?

ANN. It is not for me to approve or disapprove. I accept it. My father loved me and knew best what was good for me.

RAMSDEN. Of course I understand your feeling, Annie. It is what I should have expected of you; and it does you credit. But it does not settle the question so completely as you think. Let me put a case to you. Suppose you were to discover that I had been guilty of some disgraceful action—that I was not the man your poor dear father took me for! Would you still consider it right that I should be Rhoda's guardian?

ANN. I can't imagine you doing anything disgraceful, Granny.

TANNER [*to Ramsden*] You haven't done anything of the sort, have you?

RAMSDEN [*indignantly*] No sir.

MRS. WHITEFIELD [*placidly*] Well, then, why suppose it?

ANN. You see, Granny, Mamma would not like me to suppose it.

RAMSDEN [*much perplexed*] You are both so full of natural and affectionate feeling in these family matters that it is very hard to put the situation fairly before you.

TANNER. Besides, my friend, you are not putting the situation fairly before them.

RAMSDEN [*sulkily*] Put it yourself, then.

TANNER. I will. Ann: Ramsden thinks I am not fit to be your guardian; and I quite agree with him. He considers that if your father had read my book, he wouldn't have appointed me. That book is the disgraceful action he has been talking about. He thinks it's your duty for Rhoda's sake to ask him to act alone and to make me withdraw. Say the word; and I will.

ANN. But I haven't read your book, Jack.

TANNER [*diving at the wastepaper basket and fishing the book out for her*] Then read it at once and decide.

RAMSDEN [*vehemently*] If I am to be your guardian, I positively forbid you to read that book, Annie. [*He smites the table with his fist and rises.*]

ANN. Of course not if you don't wish it. [*She puts the book on the table.*]

TANNER. If one guardian is to forbid you to read the other guardian's book, how are we to settle it? Suppose I order you to read it! What about your duty to me?

ANN [*gently*] I am sure you would never purposely force me into a painful dilemma, Jack.

RAMSDEN [*irritably*] Yes, yes, Annie: this is all very well, and, as I said, quite natural and becoming. But you must make a choice one way or the other. We are as much in a dilemma as you.

ANN. I feel that I am too young, too inexperienced, to decide. My father's wishes are sacred to me.

MRS. WHITEFIELD. If you two men won't carry them out I must say it is rather hard that you should put the responsibility on Ann. It seems to me that people are always putting things on other people in this world.

RAMSDEN. I am sorry you take it in that way.

ANN [*touchingly*] Do you refuse to accept me as your ward, Granny?

RAMSDEN. No: I never said that. I greatly object to act with Mr. Tanner: that's all.

MRS. WHITEFIELD. Why? What's the matter with poor Jack?

TANNER. My views are too advanced for him.

RAMSDEN [*indignantly*] They are not. I deny it.

ANN. Of course not. What nonsense! Nobody is more advanced than Granny. I am sure it is Jack himself who has made all the difficulty. Come, Jack! be kind to me in my sorrow. You don't refuse to accept me as your ward, do you?

TANNER [*gloomily*] No. I let myself in for it; so I suppose I must face it. [*He turns away to the bookcase, and stands there, moodily studying the titles of the volumes.*]

ANN [*rising and expanding with subdued but gushing delight*] Then we are all agreed; and my dear father's will is to be carried out. You don't know what a joy that is to me and to my mother! [*She goes to Ramsden and presses both his hands, saying*] And I shall have my dear Granny to help and advise me. [*She casts a glance at Tanner over her shoulder.*] And Jack the Giant Killer. [*She goes past her mother to Octavius*] And Jack's inseparable friend Ricky-ticky-tavy [*he blushes and looks inexpressibly foolish*].

MRS. WHITEFIELD [*rising and shaking her widow's weeds straight*] Now that you are Ann's guardian, Mr. Ramsden, I wish you would speak to her about her habit of giving people nicknames. They can't be expected to like it. [*She moves towards the door.*]

ANN. How can you say such a thing, Mamma! [*Glowing with affectionate remorse*] Oh, I wonder can you be right! Have I been inconsiderate? [*She turns to Octavius, who is sitting astride his chair with his elbows on the back of it. Putting her hand on his forehead she turns his face up suddenly.*] Do you want to be treated like a grown up man? Must I call you Mr. Robinson in future?

OCTAVIUS [*earnestly*] Oh please call me Ricky-ticky-tavy. "Mr. Robinson" would hurt me cruelly. [*She laughs and pats his cheek with her finger; then comes back to Ramsden.*] You know I'm beginning to think that Granny is rather a piece of impertinence. But I never dreamt of its hurting you.

RAMSDEN [*breezily, as he pats her affectionately on the back*] My dear Annie, nonsense. I insist on Granny. I won't answer to any other name than Annie's Granny.

ANN [*gratefully*] You all spoil me, except Jack.

TANNER [*over his shoulder, from the bookcase*] I· think you ought to call me Mr. Tanner.

ANN [*gently*] No you don't, Jack. That's like the things you say on purpose to shock people: those who know you pay no attention to them. But, if you like, I'll call you after your famous ancestor Don Juan.

RAMSDEN. Don Juan!

ANN [*innocently*] Oh, is there any harm in it? I didn't know. Then I certainly won't call you that. May I call you Jack until I can think of something else?

TANNER. Oh, for Heaven's sake don't try to invent anything worse. I capitulate. I consent to Jack. I embrace Jack. Here endeth my first and last attempt to assert my authority.

ANN. You see, Mamma, they all really like to have pet names.

MRS. WHITEFIELD. Well, I think you might at least drop them until we are out of mourning.

ANN [*reproachfully, stricken to the soul*] Oh, how could you remind me, mother? [*She hastily leaves the room to conceal her emotion.*]

MRS. WHITEFIELD. Of course. My fault as usual! [*She follows Ann.*]

TANNER [*coming from the bookcase*] Ramsden: we're beaten—smashed—nonentitized, like her mother.

RAMSDEN. Stuff, sir. [*He follows Mrs. Whitefield out of the room.*]

TANNER [*left alone with Octavius, stares whimsically at him*] Tavy: do you want to count for something in the world?

OCTAVIUS. I want to count for something as a poet: I want to write a great play.

TANNER. With Ann as the heroine?

OCTAVIUS. Yes: I confess it.

TANNER. Take care, Tavy. The play with Ann as the heroine is all right; but if you're not very careful, by Heaven she'll marry you.

OCTAVIUS [*sighing*] No such luck, Jack!

TANNER. Why, man, your head is in the lioness's mouth: you are half swallowed already—in three bites— Bite One, Ricky; Bite Two, Ticky; Bite Three, Tavy; and down you go.

OCTAVIUS. She is the same to everybody, Jack: you know her ways.

TANNER. Yes: she breaks everybody's back with the stroke of her paw; but the question is, which of us will she eat? My own opinion is that she means to eat you.

OCTAVIUS [*rising, pettishly*] It's horrible to talk like that about her when she is upstairs crying for her father. But I do so want her to eat me that I can bear your brutalities because they give me hope.

TANNER. Tavy; that's the devilish side of a woman's fascination: she makes you will your own destruction.

OCTAVIUS. But it's not destruction: it's fulfilment.

TANNER. Yes, of her purpose; and that purpose is neither her happiness nor yours, but Nature's. Vitality in a woman is a blind fury of creation. She sacrifices herself to it: do you think she will hesitate to sacrifice you?

OCTAVIUS. Why, it is just because she is self-sacrificing that she will not sacrifice those she loves.

TANNER. That is the profoundest of mistakes, Tavy. It is the self-sacrificing women that sacrifice others most recklessly. Because they are unselfish, they are kind in little things. Because they have a purpose which is not their own purpose, but that of the whole universe, a man is nothing to them but an instrument of that purpose.

OCTAVIUS. Don't be ungenerous, Jack. They take the tenderest care of us.

TANNER. Yes, as a soldier takes care of his rifle or a musician of his violin. But do they allow us any purpose or freedom of our own? Will they lend us to one another? Can the strongest man escape from them when once he is appropriated? They tremble when we are in danger, and weep when we die; but the tears are not for us, but for a father wasted, a son's breeding thrown

away. They accuse us of treating them as a mere means
to our pleasure; but how can so feeble and transient a
folly as a man's selfish pleasure enslave a woman as the
whole purpose of Nature embodied in a woman can enslave a man?

OCTAVIUS. What matter, if the slavery makes us
happy?

TANNER. No matter at all if you have no purpose of
your own, and are, like most men, a mere breadwinner.
But you, Tavy, are an artist: that is, you have a purpose
as absorbing and as unscrupulous as a woman's purpose.

OCTAVIUS. Not unscrupulous.

TANNER. Quite unscrupulous. The true artist will let
his wife starve, his children go barefoot, his mother
drudge for his living at seventy, sooner than work at
anything but his art. To women he is half vivisector, half
vampire. He gets into intimate relations with them to
study them, to strip the mask of convention from them,
to surprise their inmost secrets, knowing that they have
the power to rouse his deepest creative energies, to rescue him from his cold reason, to make him see visions
and dream dreams, to inspire him, as he calls it. He
persuades women that they may do this for their own
purpose whilst he really means them to do it for his. He
steals the mother's milk and blackens it to make print-
er's ink to scoff at her and glorify ideal women with. He
pretends to spare her the pangs of child-bearing so that
he may have for himself the tenderness and fostering
that belong of right to her children. Since marriage
began, the great artist has been known as a bad husband.
But he is worse: he is a child-robber, a blood-sucker, a
hypocrite and a cheat. Perish the race and wither a thousand women if only the sacrifice of them enable him to
act Hamlet better, to paint a finer picture, to write a
deeper poem, a greater play, a profounder philosophy!
For mark you, Tavy, the artist's work is to shew us ourselves as we really are. Our minds are nothing but this
knowledge of ourselves; and he who adds a jot to such
knowledge creates new mind as surely as any woman
creates new men. In the rage of that creation he is as
ruthless as the woman, as dangerous to her as she to
him, and as horribly fascinating. Of all human struggles

there is none so treacherous and remorseless as the struggle between the artist man and the mother woman. Which shall use up the other? that is the issue between them. And it is all the deadlier because, in your romanticist cant, they love one another.

OCTAVIUS. Even if it were so—and I don't admit it for a moment—it is out of the deadliest struggles that we get the noblest characters.

TANNER. Remember that the next time you meet a grizzly bear or a Bengal tiger, Tavy.

OCTAVIUS. I meant where there is love, Jack.

TANNER. Oh, the tiger will love you. There is no love sincerer than the love of food. I think Ann loves you that way: she patted your cheek as if it were a nicely underdone chop.

OCTAVIUS. You know, Jack, I should have to run away from you if I did not make it a fixed rule not to mind anything you say. You come out with perfectly revolting things sometimes.

[*Ramsden returns, followed by Ann. They come in quickly, with their former leisurely air of decorous grief changed to one of genuine concern, and, on Ramsden's part, of worry. He comes between the two men, intending to address Octavius, but pulls himself up abruptly as he sees Tanner.*]

RAMSDEN. I hardly expected to find you still here, Mr. Tanner.

TANNER. Am I in the way? Good morning, fellow guardian [*he goes towards the door*].

ANN. Stop, Jack. Granny: he must know, sooner or later.

RAMSDEN. Octavius: I have a very serious piece of news for you. It is of the most private and delicate nature—of the most painful nature too, I am sorry to say. Do you wish Mr. Tanner to be present whilst I explain?

OCTAVIUS [*turning pale*] I have no secrets from Jack.

RAMSDEN. Before you decide that finally, let me say that the news concerns your sister, and that it is *terrible* news.

OCTAVIUS. Violet! What has happened? Is she—dead?

RAMSDEN. I am not sure that it is not even worse than that.

OCTAVIUS. Is she badly hurt? Has there been an accident?

RAMSDEN. No: nothing of that sort.

TANNER. Ann: will you have the common humanity to tell us what the matter is?

ANN [half whispering] I can't. Violet has done something dreadful. We shall have to get her away somewhere. [She flutters to the writing table and sits in Ramsden's chair, leaving the three men to fight it out between them.]

OCTAVIUS [enlightened] Is that what you meant, Mr. Ramsden?

RAMSDEN. Yes. [Octavius sinks upon a chair, crushed.] I am afraid there is no doubt that Violet did not really go to Eastbourne three weeks ago when we thought she was with the Parry Whitefields. And she called on a strange doctor yesterday with a wedding ring on her finger. Mrs. Parry Whitefield met her there by chance; and so the whole thing came out.

OCTAVIUS [rising with his fists clenched] Who is the scoundrel?

ANN. She won't tell us.

OCTAVIUS [collapsing into the chair again] What a frightful thing!

TANNER [with angry sarcasm] Dreadful. Appalling. Worse than death, as Ramsden says. [He comes to Octavius.] What would you not give, Tavy, to turn it into a railway accident, with all her bones broken, or something equally respectable and deserving of sympathy?

OCTAVIUS. Don't be brutal, Jack.

TANNER. Brutal! Good Heavens, man, what are you crying for? Here is a woman whom we all supposed to be making bad water color sketches, practising Grieg and Brahms, gadding about to concerts and parties, wasting her life and her money. We suddenly learn that she has turned from these sillinesses to the fulfilment of her highest purpose and greatest function—to increase, multiply and replenish the earth. And instead of admiring her courage and rejoicing in her instinct; instead of crowning the completed womanhood and raising the triumphal strain of "Unto us a child is born: unto us a son is given," here you are—you who have been as merry as grigs in your mourning for the dead—all pulling long faces and looking as ashamed and disgraced as if the girl had committed the vilest of crimes.

RAMSDEN [*roaring with rage*] I will not have these abominations uttered in my house [*he smites the writing table with his fist*].

TANNER. Look here: if you insult me again I'll take you at your word and leave your house. Ann: where is Violet now?

ANN. Why? Are you going to her?

TANNER. Of course I am going to her. She wants help; she wants money; she wants respect and congratulation; she wants every chance for her child. She does not seem likely to get it from you: she shall from me. Where is she?

ANN. Don't be so headstrong, Jack. She's upstairs.

TANNER. What! Under Ramsden's sacred roof! Go and do your miserable duty, Ramsden. Hunt her out into the street. Cleanse your threshold from her contamination. Vindicate the purity of your English home. I'll go for a cab.

ANN [*alarmed*] Oh, Granny, you mustn't do that.

OCTAVIUS [*broken-heartedly, rising*] I'll take her away, Mr. Ramsden. She had no right to come to your house.

RAMSDEN [*indignantly*] But I am only too anxious to help her. [*Turning on Tanner*] How dare you, sir, impute such monstrous intentions to me? I protest against it. I am ready to put down my last penny to save her from being driven to run to you for protection.

TANNER [*subsiding*] It's all right, then. He's not going to act up to his principles. It's agreed that we all stand by Violet.

OCTAVIUS. But who is the man? He can make reparation by marrying her; and he shall, or he shall answer for it to me.

RAMSDEN. He shall, Octavius. There you speak like a man.

TANNER. Then you don't think him a scoundrel, after all?

OCTAVIUS. Not a scoundrel! He is a heartless scoundrel.

RAMSDEN. A damned scoundrel. I beg your pardon, Annie; but I can say no less.

TANNER. So we are to marry your sister to a damned scoundrel by way of reforming her character! On my soul, I think you are all mad.

ANN. Don't be absurd, Jack. Of course you are quite right, Tavy; but we don't know who he is: Violet won't tell us.

TANNER. What on earth does it matter who he is? He's done his part; and Violet must do the rest.

RAMSDEN [*beside himself*]. Stuff! lunacy! There is a rascal in our midst, a libertine, a villain worse than a murderer; and we are not to learn who he is! In our ignorance we are to shake him by the hand; to introduce him into our homes; to trust our daughters with him; to—to—

ANN [*coaxingly*] There, Granny, don't talk so loud. It's most shocking: we must all admit that; but if Violet won't tell us, what can we do? Nothing. Simply nothing.

RAMSDEN. Hmph! I'm not so sure of that. If any man has paid Violet any special attention, we can easily find that out. If there is any man of notoriously loose principles among us—

TANNER. Ahem!

RAMSDEN [*raising his voice*] Yes sir, I repeat, if there is any man of notoriously loose principles among us—

TANNER. Or any man notoriously lacking in self-control.

RAMSDEN [*aghast*] Do you dare to suggest that *I* am capable of such an act?

TANNER. My dear Ramsden, this is an act of which every man is capable. That is what comes of getting at cross purposes with Nature. The suspicion you have just flung at me clings to us all. It's a sort of mud that sticks to the judge's ermine or the cardinal's robe as fast as to the rags of the tramp. Come, Tavy: don't look so bewildered: it might have been me: it might have been Ramsden; just as it might have been anybody. If it had, what could we do but lie and protest—as Ramsden is going to protest.

RAMSDEN [*choking*] I—I—I—

TANNER. Guilt itself could not stammer more confusedly. And yet you know perfectly well he's innocent, Tavy.

RAMSDEN [*exhausted*] I am glad you admit that, sir. I admit, myself, that there is an element of truth in what you say, grossly as you may distort it to gratify your malicious humor. I hope, Octavius, no suspicion of me is possible in your mind.

OCTAVIUS. Of you! No, not for a moment.

TANNER [*drily*]. I think he suspects me just a little.

OCTAVIUS. Jack: you couldn't—you wouldn't—

TANNER. Why not?

OCTAVIUS [*appalled*]. Why not!

TANNER. Oh, well, I'll tell you why not. First, you would feel bound to quarrel with me. Second, Violet doesn't like me. Third, if I had the honor of being the father of Violet's child, I should boast of it instead of denying it. So be easy: our friendship is not in danger.

OCTAVIUS. I should have put away the suspicion with horror if only you would think and feel naturally about it. I beg your pardon.

TANNER. My pardon! nonsense! And now let's sit down and have a family council. [*He sits down. The rest follow his example, more or less under protest.*] Violet is going to do the State a service; consequently she must be packed abroad like a criminal until it's over. What's happening upstairs?

ANN. Violet is in the housekeeper's room—by herself, of course.

TANNER. Why not in the drawing-room?

ANN. Don't be absurd, Jack. Miss Ramsden is in the drawing-room with my mother, considering what to do.

TANNER. Oh! the housekeeper's room is the penitentiary, I suppose; and the prisoner is waiting to be brought before her judges. The old cats!

ANN. Oh, Jack!

RAMSDEN. You are at present a guest beneath the roof of one of the old cats, sir. My sister is the mistress of this house.

TANNER. She would put me in the housekeeper's room, too, if she dared, Ramsden. However, I withdraw cats. Cats would have more sense. Ann: as your guardian, I order you to go to Violet at once and be particularly kind to her.

ANN. I have seen her, Jack. And I am sorry to say I am afraid she is going to be rather obstinate about going abroad. I think Tavy ought to speak to her about it.

OCTAVIUS. How can I speak to her about such a thing? [*He breaks down.*]

ANN. Don't break down, Ricky. Try to bear it for all our sakes.

RAMSDEN. Life is not all plays and poems, Octavius. Come! face it like a man.

TANNER [*chafing again*] Poor dear brother! Poor dear friends of the family! Poor dear Tabbies and Grimalkins! Poor dear everybody except the woman who is going to risk her life to create another life! Tavy: don't you be a selfish ass. Away with you and talk to Violet; and bring her down here if she cares to come. [*Octavius rises.*] Tell her we'll stand by her.

RAMSDEN [*rising*] No, sir—

TANNER. [*rising also and interrupting him*] Oh, we understand: it's against your conscience; but still you'll do it.

OCTAVIUS. I assure you all, on my word, I never meant to be selfish. It's so hard to know what to do when one wishes earnestly to do right.

TANNER. My dear Tavy, your pious English habit of regarding the world as a moral gymnasium built expressly to strengthen your character in, occasionally leads you to think about your own confounded principles when you should be thinking about other people's necessities. The need of the present hour is a happy mother and a healthy baby. Bend your energies on that; and you will see your way clearly enough.

[*Octavius, much perplexed, goes out.*]

RAMSDEN [*facing Tanner impressively*] And Morality, sir? What is to become of that?

TANNER. Meaning a weeping Magdalen and an innocent child branded with her shame. Not in our circle, thank you. Morality can go to its father the devil.

RAMSDEN. I thought so, sir. Morality sent to the devil to please our libertines, male and female. That is to be the future of England, is it?

TANNER. Oh, England will survive your disapproval. Meanwhile, I understand that you agree with me as to the practical course we are to take?

RAMSDEN. Not in your spirit, sir. Not for your reasons.

TANNER. You can explain that if anybody calls you to account, here or hereafter. [*He turns away, and plants himself in front of Mr. Herbert Spencer, at whom he stares gloomily.*]

ANN [*rising and coming to Ramsden*] Granny: hadn't you better go up to the drawing-room and tell them what we intend to do?

RAMSDEN [*looking pointedly at Tanner*] I hardly like to leave you alone with this gentleman. Will you not come with me?

ANN. Miss Ramsden would not like to speak about it before me, Granny. I ought not to be present.

RAMSDEN. You are right: I should have thought of that. You are a good girl, Annie.

[*He pats her on the shoulder. She looks up at him with beaming eyes; and he goes out, much moved. Having disposed of him, she looks at Tanner. His back being turned to her, she gives a moment's attention to her personal appearance, then softly goes to him and speaks almost into his ear.*]

ANN. Jack [*he turns with a start*]: are you glad that you are my guardian? You don't mind being made responsible for me, I hope.

TANNER. The latest addition to your collection of scapegoats, eh?

ANN. Oh, that stupid old joke of yours about me! Do please drop it. Why do you say things that you know must pain me? I do my best to please you, Jack: I suppose I may tell you so now that you are my guardian. You will make me so unhappy if you refuse to be friends with me.

TANNER [*studying her as gloomily as he studied the bust*] You need not go begging for my regard. How unreal our moral judgments are! You seem to me to have absolutely no conscience—only hypocrisy; and you can't see the difference—yet there is a sort of fascination about you. I always attend to you, somehow. I should miss you if I lost you.

ANN [*tranquilly slipping her arm into his and walking about with him*] But isn't that only natural, Jack? We have known each other since we were children. Do you remember—

TANNER [*abruptly breaking loose*] Stop! I remember *everything*.

ANN. Oh, I daresay we were often very silly; but—

TANNER. I won't have it, Ann. I am no more that schoolboy now than I am the dotard of ninety I shall grow into if I live long enough. It is over: let me forget it.

ANN. Wasn't it a happy time? [*She attempts to take his arm again.*]

TANNER. Sit down and behave yourself. [*He makes her sit down in the chair next the writing table.*] No doubt it was a happy time for you. You were a good girl and never compromised yourself. And yet the wickedest child that ever was slapped could hardly have had a better time. I can understand the success with which you bullied the other girls: your virtue imposed on them. But tell me this: did you ever know a good boy?

ANN. Of course. All boys are foolish sometimes; but Tavy was always a really good boy.

TANNER [*struck by this*] Yes: you're right. For some reason you never tempted Tavy.

ANN. Tempted! Jack!

TANNER. Yes, my dear Lady Mephistopheles, tempted. You were insatiably curious as to what a boy might be capable of, and diabolically clever at getting through his guard and surprising his inmost secrets.

ANN. What nonsense! All because you used to tell me long stories of the wicked things you had done—silly boys' tricks! And you call such things inmost secrets! Boys' secrets are just like men's; and you know what they are!

TANNER [*obstinately*] No I don't. What are they, pray?

ANN. Why, the things they tell everybody, of course.

TANNER. Now I swear I told you things I told no one else. You lured me into a compact by which we were to have no secrets from one another. We were to tell one another everything. I didn't notice that you never told me anything.

ANN. You didn't want to talk about me, Jack. You wanted to talk about yourself.

TANNER. Ah, true, horribly true. But what a devil of a child you must have been to know that weakness and to play on it for the satisfaction of your own curiosity! I wanted to brag to you, to make myself interesting. And I found myself doing all sorts of mischievous things simply to have something to tell you about. I fought with boys I didn't hate; I lied about things I might just as well have told the truth about; I stole things I didn't want; I kissed little girls I didn't care for. It was all bravado: passionless and therefore unreal.

ANN. I never told of you, Jack.

TANNER. No; but if you had wanted to stop me you would have told of me. You wanted me to go on.

ANN [*flashing out*] Oh, that's not true: it's not true, Jack. I never wanted you to do those dull, disappointing, brutal, stupid, vulgar things. I always hoped that it would be something really heroic at last. [*Recovering herself*] Excuse me, Jack; but the things you did were never a bit like the things I wanted you to do. They often gave me great uneasiness; but I could not tell on you and get you into trouble. And you were only a boy. I knew you would grow out of them. Perhaps I was wrong.

TANNER [*sardonically*] Do not give way to remorse, Ann. At least nineteen twentieths of the exploits I confessed to you were pure lies. I soon noticed that you didn't like the true stories.

ANN. Of course I knew that some of the things couldn't have happened. But—

TANNER. You are going to remind me that some of the most disgraceful ones did.

ANN [*fondly, to his great terror*] I don't want to remind you of anything. But I knew the people they happened to, and heard about them.

TANNER. Yes; but even the true stories were touched up for telling. A sensitive boy's humiliations may be very good fun for ordinary thickskinned grown-ups; but to the boy himself they are so acute, so ignominious, that he cannot confess them—cannot but deny them passionately. However, perhaps it was as well for me that I romanced a bit; for, on the one occasion when I told you the truth, you threatened to tell of me.

ANN. Oh, never. Never once.

TANNER. Yes, you did. Do you remember a dark-eyed girl named Rachel Rosetree? [*Ann's brows contract for an instant involuntarily.*] I got up a love affair with her; and we met one night in the garden and walked about very uncomfortably with our arms round one another, and kissed at parting, and were most conscientiously romantic. If that love affair had gone on, it would have bored me to death; but it didn't go on; for the next thing that happened was that Rachel cut me because she found out that I had told you. How did she find it out? From you. You went to her and held the guilty secret over her head, leading her a life of abject terror and humiliation by threatening to tell on her.

ANN. And a very good thing for her, too. It was my duty to stop her misconduct; and she is thankful to me for it now.

TANNER. Is she?

ANN. She ought to be, at all events.

TANNER. It was not your duty to stop my misconduct, I suppose.

ANN. I did stop it by stopping her.

TANNER. Are you sure of that? You stopped my telling you about my adventures; but how do you know that you stopped the adventures?

ANN. Do you mean to say that you went on in the same way with other girls?

TANNER. No. I had enough of that sort of romantic tomfoolery with Rachel.

ANN [*unconvinced*] Then why did you break off our confidences and become quite strange to me?

TANNER [*enigmatically*] It happened just then that I got something that I wanted to keep all to myself instead of sharing it with you.

ANN. I am sure I shouldn't have asked for any of it if you had grudged it.

TANNER. It wasn't a box of sweets, Ann. It was something you'd never have let me call my own.

ANN [*incredulously*] What?

TANNER. My soul.

ANN. Oh, do be sensible, Jack. You know you're talking nonsense.

TANNER. The most solemn earnest, Ann. You didn't notice at that time that you were getting a soul too. But you were. It was not for nothing that you suddenly found you had a moral duty to chastise and reform Rachel. Up to that time you had traded pretty extensively in being a good child; but you had never set up a sense of duty to others. Well, I set one up too. Up to that time I had played the boy buccaneer with no more conscience than a fox in a poultry farm. But now I began to have scruples, to feel obligations, to find that veracity and honor were no longer goody-goody expressions in the mouths of grown up people, but compelling principles in myself.

ANN [*quietly*] Yes, I suppose you're right. You were beginning to be a man, and I to be a woman.

TANNER. Are you sure it was not that we were beginning to be something more? What does the beginning of manhood and womanhood mean in most people's mouths? You know: it means the beginning of love. But love began long before that for me. Love played its part in the earliest dreams and follies and romances I can remember—may I say the earliest follies and romances we can remember?—though we did not understand it at the time. No: the change that came to me was the birth in me of moral passion; and I declare that according to my experience moral passion is the only real passion.

ANN. All passions ought to be moral, Jack.

TANNER. Ought! Do you think that anything is strong enough to impose oughts on a passion except a stronger passion still?

ANN. Our moral sense controls passion, Jack. Don't be stupid.

TANNER. Our moral sense! And is that not a passion? Is the devil to have all the passions as well as all the good tunes? If it were not a passion—if it were not the mightiest of the passions, all the other passions would sweep it away like a leaf before a hurricane. It is the birth of that passion that turns a child into a man.

ANN. There are other passions, Jack. Very strong ones.

TANNER. All the other passions were in me before; but they were idle and aimless—mere childish greedinesses and cruelties, curiosities and fancies, habits and superstitions, grotesque and ridiculous to the mature intelligence. When they suddenly began to shine like newly lit flames it was by no light of their own, but by the radiance of the dawning moral passion. That passion dignified them, gave them conscience and meaning, found them a mob of appetites and organized them into an army of purposes and principles. My soul was born of that passion.

ANN. I noticed that you got more sense. You were a dreadfully destructive boy before that.

TANNER. Destructive! Stuff! I was only mischievous.

ANN. Oh Jack, you were very destructive. You ruined all the young fir trees by chopping off their leaders with a wooden sword. You broke all the cucumber frames with your catapult. You set fire to the common: the police arrested Tavy for it because he ran away when he couldn't stop you. You—

TANNER. Pooh! pooh! pooh! these were battles, bombardments, stratagems to save our scalps from the red Indians. You have no imagination, Ann. I am ten times more destructive now than I was then. The moral passion has taken my destructiveness in hand and directed it to moral ends. I have become a reformer, and, like all reformers, an iconoclast. I no longer break cucumber frames and burn gorse bushes: I shatter creeds and demolish idols.

ANN [*bored*] I am afraid I am too feminine to see any sense in destruction. Destruction can only destroy.

TANNER. Yes. That is why it is so useful. Construction cumbers the ground with institutions made by busybodies. Destruction clears it and gives us breathing space and liberty.

ANN. It's no use, Jack. No woman will agree with you there.

TANNER. That's because you confuse construction and destruction with creation and murder. They're quite different: I adore creation and abhor murder. Yes: I adore it in tree and flower, in bird and beast, even in you. [*A flush of interest and delight suddenly chases the growing perplexity and boredom from her face.*] It was the creative instinct that led you to attach me to you by bonds that have left their mark on me to this day. Yes, Ann: the old childish compact between us was an unconscious love compact—

ANN. Jack!

TANNER. Oh, don't be alarmed—

ANN. I am not alarmed.

TANNER [*whimsically*] Then you ought to be: where are your principles?

ANN. Jack: are you serious or are you not?

TANNER. Do you mean about the moral passion?

ANN. No, no; the other one. [*Confused*] Oh! you are so silly: one never knows how to take you.

TANNER. You must take me quite seriously. I am your guardian; and it is my duty to improve your mind.

ANN. The love compact is over, then, is it? I suppose you grew tired of me?

TANNER. No; but the moral passion made our childish relations impossible. A jealous sense of my new individuality arose in me—

ANN. You hated to be treated as a boy any longer. Poor Jack!

TANNER. Yes, because to be treated as a boy was to be taken on the old footing. I had become a new person; and those who knew the old person laughed at me. The only man who behaved sensibly was my tailor: he took my measure anew every time he saw me, whilst all the rest went on with their old measurements and expected them to fit me.

ANN. You became frightfully self-conscious.

TANNER. When you go to heaven, Ann, you will be frightfully conscious of your wings for the first year or so. When you meet your relatives there, and they persist in treating you as if you were still a mortal, you will not be able to bear them. You will try to get into a circle which has never known you except as an angel.

ANN. So it was only your vanity that made you run away from us after all?

TANNER. Yes, only my vanity, as you call it.

ANN. You need not have kept away from me on that account.

TANNER. From you above all others. You fought harder than anybody against my emancipation.

ANN [*earnestly*] Oh, how wrong you are! I would have done anything for you.

TANNER. Anything except let me get loose from you. Even then you had acquired by instinct that damnable woman's trick of heaping obligations on a man, of placing yourself so entirely and helplessly at his mercy that at last he dare not take a step without running to you for leave. I know a poor wretch whose one desire in life is to run away from his wife. She prevents him by threatening to throw herself in front of the engine of the train he leaves her in. That is what all women do. If we try to go where you do not want us to go there is no law to prevent us; but when we take the first step your breasts are under our foot as it descends: your bodies are under our wheels as we start. No woman shall ever enslave me in that way.

ANN. But, Jack, you cannot get through life without considering other people a little.

TANNER. Ay; but what other people? It is this consideration of other people—or rather this cowardly fear of them which we call consideration—that makes us the sentimental slaves we are. To consider you, as you call it, is to substitute your will for my own. How if it be a baser will than mine? Are women taught better than men or worse? Are mobs of voters taught better than statesmen or worse? Worse, of course, in both cases. And then what sort of world are you going to get, with its public men considering its voting mobs, and its private men considering their wives? What does Church and State mean nowadays? The Woman and the Ratepayer.

ANN [*placidly*]. I am so glad you understand politics, Jack: it will be most useful to you if you go into parliament [*he collapses like a pricked bladder*]. But I am sorry you thought my influence a bad one.

TANNER. I don't say it was a bad one. But bad or good, I didn't choose to be cut to your measure. And I won't be cut to it.

ANN. Nobody wants you to, Jack. I assure you— really on my word—I don't mind your queer opinions one little bit. You know we have all been brought up to have advanced opinions. Why do you persist in thinking me so narrow minded?

TANNER. That's the danger of it. I know you don't mind, because you've found out that it doesn't matter. The boa constrictor doesn't mind the opinions of a stag one little bit when once she has got her coils round it.

ANN [rising in sudden enlightenment] O-o-o-o-oh! now I understand why you warned Tavy that I am a boa constrictor. Granny told me. [She laughs and throws her boa round his neck.] Doesn't it feel nice and soft, Jack?

TANNER [in the toils] You scandalous woman, will you throw away even your hypocrisy?

ANN. I am never hypocritical with you, Jack. Are you angry? [She withdraws the boa and throws it on a chair.] Perhaps I shouldn't have done that.

TANNER [contemptuously] Pooh, prudery! Why should you not, if it amuses you?

ANN [shyly] Well, because—because I suppose what you really mean by the boa constrictor was this [she puts her arms round his neck].

TANNER [staring at her] Magnificent audacity! [She laughs and pats his cheeks.] Now just to think that if I mentioned this episode not a soul would believe me except the people who would cut me for telling, whilst if you accused me of it nobody would believe my denial!

ANN [taking her arms away with perfect dignity] You are incorrigible, Jack. But you should not jest about our affection for one another. Nobody could possibly misunderstand it. You do not misunderstand it, I hope.

TANNER. My blood interprets for me, Ann. Poor Ricky Ticky Tavy!

ANN [looking quickly at him as if this were a new light] Surely you are not so absurd as to be jealous of Tavy.

TANNER. Jealous! Why should I be? But I don't wonder at your grip of him. I feel the coils tightening round my very self, though you are only playing with me.

ANN. Do you think I have designs on Tavy?

TANNER. I know you have.

ANN [*earnestly*] Take care, Jack. You may make
Tavy very unhappy if you mislead him about me.

TANNER. Never fear: he will not escape you.

ANN. I wonder are you really a clever man!

TANNER. Why this sudden misgiving on the subject?

ANN. You seem to understand all the things I don't
understand; but you are a perfect baby in the things I
do understand.

TANNER. I understand how Tavy feels for you, Ann:
you may depend on that, at all events.

ANN. And you think you understand how I feel for
Tavy, don't you?

TANNER. I know only too well what is going to happen to poor Tavy.

ANN. I should laugh at you, Jack, if it were not for
poor papa's death. Mind! Tavy will be very unhappy.

TANNER. Yes; but he won't know it, poor devil. He
is a thousand times too good for you. That's why he is
going to make the mistake of his life about you.

ANN. I think men make more mistakes by being too
clever than by being too good [*she sits down, with a trace
of contempt for the whole male sex in the elegant carriage
of her shoulders*].

TANNER. Oh, I know you don't care very much
about Tavy. But there is always one who kisses and one
who only allows the kiss. Tavy will kiss; and you will
only turn the cheek. And you will throw him over if
anybody better turns up.

ANN [*offended*] You have no right to say such things,
Jack. They are not true, and not delicate. If you and
Tavy choose to be stupid about me, that is not my fault.

TANNER [*remorsefully*] Forgive my brutalities, Ann.
They are levelled at this wicked world, not at you. [*She
looks up at him, pleased and forgiving. He becomes cautious at once.*] All the same, I wish Ramsden would come
back. I never feel safe with you: there is a devilish charm—
or no: not a charm, a subtle interest [*she laughs*]—Just so:
you know it; and you triumph in it. Openly and shame-
lessly triumph in it!

ANN. What a shocking flirt you are, Jack!

TANNER. A flirt!! I!!!

ANN. Yes, a flirt. You are always abusing and offending people; but you never really mean to let go your hold of them.

TANNER. I will ring the bell. This conversation has already gone further than I intended.

[*Ramsden and Octavius come back with Miss Ramsden, a hardheaded old maiden lady in a plain brown silk gown, with enough rings, chains and brooches to shew that her plainness of dress is a matter of principle, not of poverty. She comes into the room very determinedly: the two men, perplexed and downcast, following her. Ann rises and goes eagerly to meet her. Tanner retreats to the wall between the busts and pretends to study the pictures. Ramsden goes to his table as usual; and Octavius clings to the neighborhood of Tanner.*]

MISS RAMSDEN [*almost pushing Ann aside as she comes to Mrs. Whitefield's chair and plants herself there resolutely*] I wash my hands of the whole affair.

OCTAVIUS [*very wretched*] I know you wish me to take Violet away, Miss Ramsden. I will. [*He turns irresolutely to the door.*]

RAMSDEN. No no—

MISS RAMSDEN. What is the use of saying no, Roebuck? Octavius knows that I would not turn any truly contrite and repentant woman from your doors. But when a woman is not only wicked, but intends to go on being wicked, she and I part company.

ANN. Oh, Miss Ramsden, what do you mean? What has Violet said?

RAMSDEN. Violet is certainly very obstinate. She won't leave London. I don't understand her.

MISS RAMSDEN. I do. It's as plain as the nose on your face, Roebuck, that she won't go because she doesn't want to be separated from this man, whoever he is.

ANN. Oh, surely, surely! Octavius: did you speak to her?

OCTAVIUS. She won't tell us anything. She won't make any arrangement until she has consulted somebody. It can't be anybody else than the scoundrel who has betrayed her.

TANNER [*to Octavius*] Well, let her consult him. He will be glad enough to have her sent abroad. Where is the difficulty?

MISS RAMSDEN [*taking the answer out of Octavius's mouth*] The difficulty, Mr. Jack, is that when I offered to help her I didn't offer to become her accomplice in her wickedness. She either pledges her word never to see that man again, or else she finds some new friends; and the sooner the better.

[*The parlormaid appears at the door. Ann hastily resumes her seat, and looks as unconcerned as possible. Octavius instinctively imitates her.*]

THE MAID. The cab is at the door, ma'am.

MISS RAMSDEN. What cab?

THE MAID. For Miss Robinson.

MISS RAMSDEN. Oh! [*Recovering herself*] All right. [*The maid withdraws.*] She has sent for a cab.

TANNER. *I* wanted to send for that cab half an hour ago.

MISS RAMSDEN. I am glad she understands the position she has placed herself in.

RAMSDEN. I don't like her going away in this fashion, Susan. We had better not do anything harsh.

OCTAVIUS. No: thank you again and again; but Miss Ramsden is quite right. Violet cannot expect to stay.

ANN. Hadn't you better go with her, Tavy?

OCTAVIUS. She won't have me.

MISS RAMSDEN. Of course she won't. She's going straight to that man.

TANNER. As a natural result of her virtuous reception here.

RAMSDEN [*much troubled*]. There, Susan! You hear! and there's some truth in it. I wish you could reconcile it with your principles to be a little patient with this poor girl. She's very young; and there's a time for everything.

MISS RAMSDEN. Oh, she will get all the sympathy she wants from the men. I'm surprised at you, Roebuck.

TANNER. So am I, Ramsden, most favorably.

[*Violet appears at the door. She is as impenitent and self-possessed a young lady as one would desire to see among the best behaved of her sex. Her small head and tiny resolute mouth and chin; her haughty crispness of speech and trimness of carriage; the ruthless elegance of her equipment, which includes a very smart hat with a dead bird in it, mark a personality which is as formidable as it is exquisitely pretty. She is not a siren, like Ann: admiration comes to her without any compulsion or even interest on her part; besides, there is some fun in Ann, but in this woman none, perhaps no mercy either: if anything restrains her, it is intelligence and pride, not compassion. Her voice might be the voice of a schoolmistress addressing a class of girls who had disgraced themselves, as she proceeds with complete composure and some disgust to say what she has come to say.*]

VIOLET. I have only looked in to tell Miss Ramsden that she will find her birthday present to me, the filigree bracelet, in the housekeeper's room.

TANNER. Do come in, Violet, and talk to us sensibly.

VIOLET. Thank you: I have had quite enough of the family conversation this morning. So has your mother, Ann: she has gone home crying. But at all events, I have found out what some of my pretended friends are worth. Good-bye.

TANNER. No, no: one moment. I have something to say which I beg you to hear. [*She looks at him without the slightest curiosity, but waits, apparently as much to finish getting her glove on as to hear what he has to say.*] I am altogether on your side in this matter. I congratulate you, with the sincerest respect, on having the courage to do what you have done. You are entirely in the right; and the family is entirely in the wrong.

[*Sensation. Ann and Miss Ramsden rise and turn towards the two. Violet, more surprised than any of the others, forgets her glove, and comes forward into the middle of the room, both puzzled and displeased. Octavius alone does not move or raise his head: he is overwhelmed with shame.*]

ANN [*pleading to Tanner to be sensible*] Jack!

MISS RAMSDEN [*outraged*] Well, I must say!

VIOLET [*sharply to Tanner*] Who told you?

TANNER. Why, Ramsden and Tavy of course. Why should they not?

VIOLET. But they don't know.

TANNER. Don't know what?

VIOLET. They don't know that I am in the right, I mean.

TANNER. Oh, they know it in their hearts, though

they think themselves bound to blame you by their silly superstitions about morality and propriety and so forth. But I know, and the whole world really knows, though it dare not say so, that you were right to follow your instinct; that vitality and bravery are the greatest qualities a woman can have, and motherhood her solemn initiation into womanhood; and that the fact of your not being legally married matters not one scrap either to your own worth or to our real regard for you.

VIOLET [*flushing with indignation*] Oh! You think me a wicked woman, like the rest. You think I have not only been vile, but that I share your abominable opinions. Miss Ramsden: I have borne your hard words because I knew you would be sorry for them when you found out the truth. But I won't bear such a horrible insult as to be complimented by Jack on being one of the wretches of whom he approves. I have kept my marriage a secret for my husband's sake. But now I claim my right as a married woman not to be insulted.

OCTAVIUS [*raising his head with inexpressible relief*] You are married!

VIOLET. Yes; and I think you might have guessed it. What business had you all to take it for granted that I had no right to wear my wedding ring? Not one of you even asked me: I cannot forget that.

TANNER [*in ruins*] I am utterly crushed. I meant well. I apologize—abjectly apologize.

VIOLET. I hope you will be more careful in future about the things you say. Of course one does not take them seriously; but they are very disagreeable, and rather in bad taste, I think.

TANNER [*bowing to the storm*] I have no defence: I shall know better in future than to take any woman's part. We have all disgraced ourselves in your eyes, I am afraid, except Ann. She befriended you. For Ann's sake, forgive us.

VIOLET. Yes: Ann has been very kind; but then Ann knew.

TANNER. Oh!

MISS RAMSDEN [*stiffly*] And who, pray, is the gentleman who does not acknowledge his wife?

VIOLET [*promptly*] That is my business, Miss Ramsden, and not yours. I have my reasons for keeping my marriage a secret for the present.

RAMSDEN. All I can say is that we are extremely sorry, Violet. I am shocked to think of how we have treated you.

OCTAVIUS [*awkwardly*] I beg your pardon, Violet. I can say no more.

MISS RAMSDEN [*still loth to surrender*] Of course what you say puts a very different complexion on the matter. All the same, I owe it to myself—

VIOLET [*cutting her short*] You owe me an apology, Miss Ramsden: that's what you owe both to yourself and to me. If you were a married woman you would not like sitting in the housekeeper's room and being treated like a naughty child by young girls and old ladies without any serious duties and responsibilities.

TANNER. Don't hit us when we're down, Violet. We seem to have made fools of ourselves; but really it was you who made fools of us.

VIOLET. It was no business of yours, Jack, in any case.

TANNER. No business of mine! Why, Ramsden as good as accused me of being the unknown gentleman.

[*Ramsden makes a frantic demonstration; but Violet's cool keen anger extinguishes it.*]

VIOLET. You! Oh, how infamous! how abominable! how disgracefully you have all been talking about me! If my husband knew it he would never let me speak to any of you again. [*To Ramsden*] I think you might have spared me that, at least.

RAMSDEN. But I assure you I never—at least it is a monstrous perversion of something I said that—

MISS RAMSDEN. You needn't apologize, Roebuck. She brought it all on herself. It is for her to apologize for having deceived us.

VIOLET. I can make allowances for you, Miss Ramsden: you cannot understand how I feel on this subject, though I should have expected rather better taste from people of greater experience. However, I quite feel that you have all placed yourselves in a very painful position; and the most truly considerate thing for me to do is to go at once. Good morning.

[*She goes, leaving them staring.*]

MISS RAMSDEN. Well, I must say!

RAMSDEN [*plaintively*] I don't think she is quite fair to us.

TANNER. You must cower before the wedding ring like the rest of us, Ramsden. The cup of our ignominy is full.

ACT TWO

On the carriage drive in the park of a country house near Richmond a motor car has broken down. It stands in front of a clump of trees round which the drive sweeps to the house, which is partly visible through them: indeed Tanner, standing in the drive with the car on his right hand, could get an unobstructed view of the west corner of the house on his left were he not far too much interested in a pair of supine legs in blue serge trousers which protrude from beneath the machine. He is watching them intently with bent back and hands supported on his knees. His leathern overcoat and peaked cap proclaim him one of the dismounted passengers.

THE LEGS. Aha! I got him.

TANNER. All right now?

THE LEGS. Aw right now.

[*Tanner stoops and takes the legs by the ankles, drawing their owner forth like a wheelbarrow, walking on his hands, with a hammer in his mouth. He is a young man in a neat suit of blue serge, clean shaven, dark eyed, square fingered, with short well brushed black hair and rather irregular sceptically turned eyebrows. When he is manipulating the car his movements are swift and sudden, yet attentive and deliberate. With Tanner and Tanner's friends his manner is not in the least deferential, but cool and reticent, keeping them quite effectually at a distance whilst giving them no excuse for complaining of him. Nevertheless he has a vigilant eye on them always, and that, too, rather cynically, like a man who knows the world well from its seamy side. He speaks slowly and*

*with a touch of sarcasm; and as he does not at all affect
the gentleman in his speech, it may be inferred that his
smart appearance is a mark of respect to himself and his
own class, not to that which employs him.*

*He now gets into the car to test his machinery and put
his cap and overcoat on again. Tanner takes off his leathern overcoat and pitches it into the car. The chauffeur
(or automobilist or motoreer or whatever England may
presently decide to call him) looks round inquiringly in
the act of stowing away his hammer.*]

THE CHAUFFEUR. Had enough of it, eh?

TANNER. I may as well walk to the house and stretch
my legs and calm my nerves a little. [*Looking at his
watch*] I suppose you know that we have come from
Hyde Park Corner to Richmond in twenty-one minutes.

THE CHAUFFEUR. I'd ha done it under fifteen if I'd
had a clear road all the way.

TANNER. Why do you do it? Is it for love of sport
or for the fun of terrifying your unfortunate employer?

THE CHAUFFEUR. What are you afraid of?

TANNER. The police, and breaking my neck.

THE CHAUFFEUR. Well, if you like easy going, you
can take a bus, you know. It's cheaper. You pay me to
save your time and give you the value of your thousand
pound car. [*He sits down calmly.*]

TANNER. I am the slave of that car and of you too.
I dream of the accursed thing at night.

THE CHAUFFEUR. You'll get over that. If you're
going up to the house, may I ask how long you're goin
to stay there? Because if you mean to put in the whole
morning talkin to the ladies, I'll put the car in the stables
and make myself comfortable. If not, I'll keep the car
on the go about here til you come.

TANNER. Better wait here. We shan't be long.
There's a young American gentleman, a Mr. Malone,
who is driving Mr. Robinson down in his new American
steam car.

THE CHAUFFEUR [*springing up and coming hastily
out of the car to Tanner*] American steam car! Wot! racin
us down from London!

TANNER. Perhaps they're here already.

THE CHAUFFEUR. If I'd known it! [*With deep reproach*] Why didn't you tell me, Mr. Tanner?

TANNER. Because I've been told that this car is capable of 84 miles an hour; and I already know what you are capable of when there is a rival car on the road. No, Henry: there are things it is not good for you to know; and this was one of them. However, cheer up: we are going to have a day after your own heart. The American is to take Mr. Robinson and his sister and Miss Whitefield. We are to take Miss Rhoda.

THE CHAUFFEUR [*consoled, and musing on another matter*] That's Miss Whitefield's sister, isn't it?

TANNER. Yes.

THE CHAUFFEUR. And Miss Whitefield herself is goin in the other car? Not with you?

TANNER. Why the devil should she come with me? Mr. Robinson will be in the other car. [*The Chauffeur looks at Tanner with cool incredulity, and turns to the car, whistling a popular air softly to himself. Tanner, a little annoyed, is about to pursue the subject when he hears the footsteps of Octavius on the gravel. Octavius is coming from the house, dressed for motoring, but without his overcoat.*] We've lost the race, thank Heaven: here's Mr. Robinson. Well, Tavy, is the steam car a success?

OCTAVIUS. I think so. We came from Hyde Park Corner here in seventeen minutes. [*The Chauffeur, furious, kicks the car with a groan of vexation.*] How long were you?

TANNER. Oh, about three quarters of an hour or so.

THE CHAUFFEUR [*remonstrating*] Now, now, Mr. Tanner, come now! We could ha done it easy under fifteen.

TANNER. By the way, let me introduce you. Mr. Octavius Robinson: Mr. Enry Straker.

STRAKER. Pleased to meet you, sir. Mr. Tanner is gittin at you with is Enry Straker, you know. You call it Henery. But I don't mind, bless you.

TANNER. You think it's simply bad taste in me to chaff him, Tavy. But you're wrong. This man takes more trouble to drop his aitches than ever his father did to pick them up. It's a mark of caste to him. I have never met anybody more swollen with the pride of class than Enry is.

STRAKER. Easy, easy! A little moderation, Mr. Tanner.

TANNER. A little moderation, Tavy, you observe. You would tell me to draw it mild. But this chap has been educated. What's more, he knows that we haven't. What was that Board School of yours, Straker?

STRAKER. Sherbrooke Road.

TANNER. Sherbrooke Road! Would any of us say Rugby! Harrow! Eton! in that tone of intellectual snobbery? Sherbrooke Road is a place where boys learn something: Eton is a boy farm where we are sent because we are nuisances at home, and because in after life, whenever a Duke is mentioned, we can claim him as an old schoolfellow.

STRAKER. You don't know nothing about it, Mr. Tanner. It's not the Board School that does it: it's the Polytechnic.

TANNER. His university, Octavius. Not Oxford, Cambridge, Durham, Dublin or Glasgow. Not even those Nonconformist holes in Wales. No, Tavy. Regent Street, Chelsea, the Borough—I don't know half their confounded names: these are his universities, not mere shops for selling class limitations like ours. You despise Oxford, Enry, don't you?

STRAKER. No, I don't. Very nice sort of place, Oxford, I should think, for people that like that sort of place. They teach you to be a gentleman there. In the Polytechnic they teach you to be an engineer or such like. See?

TANNER. Sarcasm, Tavy, sarcasm! Oh, if you could only see into Enry's soul, the depth of his contempt for a gentleman, the arrogance of his pride in being an engineer, would appal you. He positively likes the car to break down because it brings out my gentlemanly helplessness and his workmanlike skill and resource.

STRAKER. Never you mind him, Mr. Robinson. He likes to talk. We know him, don't we?

OCTAVIUS [*earnestly*] But there's a great truth at the bottom of what he says. I believe most intensely in the dignity of labor.

STRAKER [*unimpressed*] That's because you never done any, Mr. Robinson. My business is to do away with labor. You'll get more out of me and a machine than you will out of twenty laborers, and not so much to drink either.

TANNER. For Heaven's sake, Tavy, don't start him on political economy. He knows all about it; and we don't. You're only a poetic Socialist, Tavy: he's a scientific one.

STRAKER [*unperturbed*] Yes. Well, this conversation is very improvin; but I've got to look after the car; and you two want to talk about your ladies. *I* know. [*He retires to busy himself about the car; and presently saunters off towards the house.*]

TANNER. That's a very momentous social phenomenon.

OCTAVIUS. What is?

TANNER. Straker is. Here have we literary and cultured persons been for years setting up a cry of the New Woman whenever some unusually old fashioned female came along; and never noticing the advent of the New Man. Straker's the New Man.

OCTAVIUS. I see nothing new about him, except your way of chaffing him. But I don't want to talk about him just now. I want to speak to you about Ann.

TANNER. Straker knew even that. He learnt it at the Polytechnic, probably. Well, what about Ann? Have you proposed to her?

OCTAVIUS [*self-reproachfully*] I was brute enough to do so last night.

TANNER. Brute enough! What do you mean?

OCTAVIUS [*dithyrambically*] Jack: we men are all coarse: we never understand how exquisite a woman's sensibilities are. How could I have done such a thing!

TANNER. Done what, you maudlin idiot?

OCTAVIUS. Yes, I am an idiot. Jack: if you had heard her voice! if you had seen her tears! I have lain awake all night thinking of them. If she had reproached me, I could have borne it better.

TANNER. Tears! that's dangerous. What did she say?

OCTAVIUS. She asked me how she could think of anything now but her dear father. She stifled a sob— [*he breaks down*].

TANNER [*patting him on the back*] Bear it like a man,

Tavy, even if you feel it like an ass. It's the old game: she's not tired of playing with you yet.

OCTAVIUS [*impatiently*] Oh, don't be a fool, Jack. Do you suppose this eternal shallow cynicism of yours has any real bearing on a nature like hers?

TANNER. Hm! Did she say anything else?

OCTAVIUS. Yes; and that is why I expose myself and her to your ridicule by telling you what passed.

TANNER [*remorsefully*] No, dear Tavy, not ridicule, on my honor! However, no matter. Go on.

OCTAVIUS. Her sense of duty is so devout, so perfect, so—

TANNER. Yes: I know. Go on.

OCTAVIUS. You see, under this new arrangement, you and Ramsden are her guardians; and she considers that all her duty to her father is now transferred to you. She said she thought I ought to have spoken to you both in the first instance. Of course she is right; but somehow it seems rather absurd that I am to come to you and formally ask to be received as a suitor for your ward's hand.

TANNER. I am glad that love has not totally extinguished your sense of humor, Tavy.

OCTAVIUS. That answer won't satisfy her.

TANNER. My official answer is, obviously, Bless you, my children: may you be happy!

OCTAVIUS. I wish you would stop playing the fool about this. If it is not serious to you, it is to me, and to her.

TANNER. You know very well that she is as free to choose as you are.

OCTAVIUS. She does not think so.

TANNER. Oh, doesn't she! just! However, say what you want me to do?

OCTAVIUS. I want you to tell her sincerely and earnestly what you think about me. I want you to tell her that you can trust her to me—that is, if you feel you can.

TANNER. I have no doubt that I can trust her to you. What worries me is the idea of trusting you to her. Have you read Maeterlinck's book about the bee?

OCTAVIUS [*keeping his temper with difficulty*] I am not discussing literature at present.

TANNER. Be just a little patient with me. *I* am not

discussing literature: the book about the bee is natural
history. It's an awful lesson to mankind. You think that
you are Ann's suitor; that you are the pursuer and she
the pursued; that it is your part to woo, to persuade, to
prevail, to overcome. Fool: it is you who are the pursued,
the marked down quarry, the destined prey. You need
not sit looking longingly at the bait through the wires of
the trap: the door is open, and will remain so until it
shuts behind you for ever.

OCTAVIUS. I wish I could believe that, vilely as you
put it.

TANNER. Why, man, what other work has she in life
but to get a husband? It is a woman's business to get
married as soon as possible, and a man's to keep unmarried as long as he can. You have your poems and your
tragedies to work at: Ann has nothing.

OCTAVIUS. I cannot write without inspiration. And
nobody can give me that except Ann.

TANNER. Well, hadn't you better get it from her at
a safe distance? Petrarch didn't see half as much of
Laura, nor Dante of Beatrice, as you see of Ann now;
and yet they wrote first-rate poetry—at least so I'm told.
They never exposed their idolatry to the test of domestic
familiarity; and it lasted them to their graves. Marry
Ann; and at the end of a week you'll find no more inspiration in her than in a plate of muffins.

OCTAVIUS. You think I shall tire of her!

TANNER. Not at all: you don't get tired of muffins.
But you don't find inspiration in them; and you won't in
her when she ceases to be a poet's dream and becomes a
solid eleven stone wife. You'll be forced to dream about
somebody else; and then there will be a row.

OCTAVIUS. This sort of talk is no use, Jack. You
don't understand. You have never been in love.

TANNER. I! I have never been out of it. Why, I am
in love even with Ann. But I am neither the slave of
love nor its dupe. Go to the bee, thou poet: consider
her ways and be wise. By Heaven, Tavy, if women could
do without our work, and we ate their children's bread
instead of making it, they would kill us as the spider
kills her mate or as the bees kill the drone. And they
would be right if we were good for nothing but love.

OCTAVIUS. Ah, if we were only good enough for Love! There is nothing like Love: there is nothing else but Love: without it the world would be a dream of sordid horror.

TANNER. And this—*this* is the man who asks me to give him the hand of my ward! Tavy: I believe we were changed in our cradles, and that you are the real descendant of Don Juan.

OCTAVIUS. I beg you not to say anything like that to Ann.

TANNER. Don't be afraid. She has marked you for her own; and nothing will stop her now. You are doomed. [*Straker comes back with a newspaper.*] Here comes the New Man, demoralizing himself with a half-penny paper as usual.

STRAKER. Now would you believe it, Mr. Robinson, when we're out motoring we take in two papers, the Times for him, the Leader or the Echo for me. And do you think I ever see my paper? Not much. He grabs the Leader and leaves me to stodge myself with his Times.

OCTAVIUS. Are there no winners in the Times?

TANNER. Enry don't old with bettin, Tavy. Motor records are his weakness. What's the latest?

STRAKER. Paris to Biskra at forty mile an hour average, not countin the Mediterranean.

TANNER. How many killed?

STRAKER. Two silly sheep. What does it matter? Sheep don't cost such a lot: they were glad to ave the price without the trouble o sellin em to the butcher. All the same, d'y'see, there'll be a clamor agin it presently; and then the French Government'll stop it; an our chance'll be gone, see? That's what makes me fairly mad: Mr. Tanner won't do a good run while he can.

TANNER. Tavy: do you remember my uncle James?

OCTAVIUS. Yes. Why?

TANNER. Uncle James had a first rate cook: he couldn't digest anything except what she cooked. Well, the poor man was shy and hated society. But his cook was proud of her skill, and wanted to serve up dinners to princes and ambassadors. To prevent her from leaving him, that poor old man had to give a big dinner twice a month, and suffer agonies of awkwardness. Now here

am I; and here is this chap Enry Straker, the New Man.
I loathe travelling; but I rather like Enry. He cares for
nothing but tearing along in a leather coat and goggles,
with two inches of dust all over him, at sixty miles an
hour and the risk of his life and mine. Except, of course,
when he is lying on his back in the mud under the machine trying to find out where it has given way. Well, if
I don't give him a thousand mile run at least once a
fortnight I shall lose him. He will give me the sack and
go to some American millionaire; and I shall have to
put up with a nice respectful groom-gardener-amateur,
who will touch his hat and know his place. I am Enry's
slave, just as Uncle James was his cook's slave.

STRAKER [*exasperated*] Garn! I wish I had a car that
would go as fast as you can talk, Mr. Tanner. What I
say is that you lose money by a motor car unless you
keep it workin. Might as well ave a pram and a nussmaid
to wheel you in it as that car and me if you don't git
the last inch out of us both.

TANNER [*soothingly*] All right, Henry, all right. We'll
go out for half an hour presently.

STRAKER [*in disgust*] Arf an ahr! [*He returns to his
machine; seats himself in it; and turns up a fresh page of
his paper in search of more news.*]

OCTAVIUS. Oh, that reminds me. I have a note for
you from Rhoda. [*He gives Tanner a note.*]

TANNER [*opening it*] I rather think Rhoda is heading
for a row with Ann. As a rule there is only one person
an English girl hates more than she hates her mother;
and that's her eldest sister. But Rhoda positively prefers
her mother to Ann. She— [*indignantly*] Oh, I say!

OCTAVIUS. What's the matter?

TANNER. Rhoda was to have come with me for a
ride in the motor car. She says Ann has forbidden her
to go out with me.

[*Straker suddenly begins whistling his favorite air with
remarkable deliberation. Surprised by this burst of larklike
melody, and jarred by a sardonic note in its cheerfulness,
they turn and look inquiringly at him. But he is busy with
his paper; and nothing comes of their movement.*]

OCTAVIUS [*recovering himself*] Does she give any
reason?

TANNER. Reason! An insult is not a reason. Ann forbids her to be alone with me on any occasion. Says I am not a fit person for a young girl to be with. What do you think of your paragon now?

OCTAVIUS. You must remember that she has a very heavy responsibility now that her father is dead. Mrs. Whitefield is too weak to control Rhoda.

TANNER [*staring at him*]. In short, you agree with Ann.

OCTAVIUS. No; but I think I understand her. You must admit that your views are hardly suited for the formation of a young girl's mind and character.

TANNER. I admit nothing of the sort. I admit that the formation of a young lady's mind and character usually consists in telling her lies; but I object to the particular lie that I am in the habit of abusing the confidence of girls.

OCTAVIUS. Ann doesn't say that, Jack.

TANNER. What else does she mean?

STRAKER [*catching sight of Ann coming from the house*] Miss Whitefield, gentlemen. [*He dismounts and strolls away down the avenue with the air of a man who knows he is no longer wanted.*]

ANN [*coming between Octavius and Tanner*] Good morning, Jack. I have come to tell you that poor Rhoda has got one of her headaches and cannot go out with you to-day in the car. It is a cruel disappointment to her, poor child!

TANNER. What do you say now, Tavy?

OCTAVIUS. Surely you cannot misunderstand, Jack. Ann is shewing you the kindest consideration, even at the cost of deceiving you.

ANN. What do you mean?

TANNER. Would you like to cure Rhoda's headache, Ann?

ANN. Of course.

TANNER. Then tell her what you said just now; and add that you arrived about two minutes after I had received her letter and read it.

ANN. Rhoda has written to you!

TANNER. With full particulars.

OCTAVIUS. Never mind him, Ann. You were right—

quite right. Ann was only doing her duty, Jack; and you know it. Doing it in the kindest way, too.

ANN [*going to Octavius*] How kind you are, Tavy! How helpful! How well you understand!

[*Octavius beams.*]

TANNER. Ay: tighten the coils. You love her, Tavy, don't you?

OCTAVIUS. She knows I do.

ANN. Hush. For shame, Tavy!

TANNER. Oh, I give you leave. I am your guardian; and I commit you to Tavy's care for the next hour. I am off for a turn in the car.

ANN. No, Jack. I must speak to you about Rhoda. Ricky: will you go back to the house and entertain your American friend. He's rather on Mamma's hands so early in the morning. She wants to finish her housekeeping.

OCTAVIUS. I fly, dearest Ann [*he kisses her hand*].

ANN [*tenderly*] Ricky Ticky Tavy!

[*He looks at her with an eloquent blush, and runs off.*]

TANNER [*bluntly*] Now look here, Ann. This time you've landed yourself; and if Tavy were not in love with you past all salvation he'd have found out what an incorrigible liar you are.

ANN. You misunderstand, Jack. I didn't dare tell Tavy the truth.

TANNER. No: your daring is generally in the opposite direction. What the devil do you mean by telling Rhoda that I am too vicious to associate with her? How can I ever have any human or decent relations with her again, now that you have poisoned her mind in that abominable way?

ANN. I know you are incapable of behaving badly—

TANNER. Then why did you lie to her?

ANN. I had to.

TANNER. Had to!

ANN. Mother made me.

TANNER [*his eye flashing*] Ha! I might have known it. The mother! Always the mother!

ANN. It was that dreadful book of yours. You know how timid mother is. All timid women are conventional: we must be conventional, Jack, or we are so cruelly, so vilely misunderstood. Even you, who are a man, cannot say what you think without being misunderstood and vilified—yes: I admit it: I have had to vilify you. Do you want to have poor Rhoda misunderstood and vilified in the same way? Would it be right for mother to let her expose herself to such treatment before she is old enough to judge for herself?

TANNER. In short, the way to avoid misunderstanding is for everybody to lie and slander and insinuate and pretend as hard as they can. That is what obeying your mother comes to.

ANN. I love my mother, Jack.

TANNER [*working himself up into a sociological rage*] Is that any reason why you are not to call your soul your own? Oh, I protest against this vile abjection of youth to age! Look at fashionable society as you know it. What does it pretend to be? An exquisite dance of nymphs. What is it? A horrible procession of wretched girls, each in the claws of a cynical, cunning, avaricious, disillusioned, ignorantly experienced, foul-minded old woman whom she calls mother, and whose duty it is to corrupt her mind and sell her to the highest bidder. Why do these unhappy slaves marry anybody, however old and vile, sooner than not marry at all? Because marriage is their only means of escape from these decrepit fiends who hide their selfish ambitions, their jealous hatreds of the young rivals who have supplanted them, under the mask of maternal duty and family affection. Such things are abominable: the voice of nature proclaims for the daughter a father's care and for the son a mother's. The law for father and son and mother and daughter is not the law of love: it is the law of revolution, of emancipation, of final supersession of the old and worn-out by the young and capable. I tell you, the first duty of manhood and womanhood is a Declaration of Independence: the man who pleads his father's authority is no man: the woman who pleads her mother's authority is unfit to bear citizens to a free people.

ANN [*watching him with quiet curiosity*] I suppose you will go in seriously for politics some day, Jack.

TANNER [*heavily let down*] Eh? What? Wh—? [*Col-

lecting his scattered wits] What has that got to do with what I have been saying?

ANN. You talk so well.

TANNER. Talk! Talk! It means nothing to you but talk. Well, go back to your mother, and help her to poison Rhoda's imagination as she has poisoned yours. It is the tame elephants who enjoy capturing the wild ones.

ANN. I am getting on. Yesterday I was a boa constrictor: to-day I am an elephant.

TANNER. Yes. So pack your trunk and begone: I have no more to say to you.

ANN. You are so utterly unreasonable and impracticable. What can I do?

TANNER. Do! Break your chains. Go your way according to your own conscience and not according to your mother's. Get your mind clean and vigorous; and learn to enjoy a fast ride in a motor car instead of seeing nothing in it but an excuse for a detestable intrigue. Come with me to Marseilles and across to Algiers and to Biskra, at sixty miles an hour. Come right down to the Cape if you like. That will be a Declaration of Independence with a vengeance. You can write a book about it afterwards. That will finish your mother and make a woman of you.

ANN [*thoughtfully*]. I don't think there would be any harm in that, Jack. You are my guardian: you stand in my father's place, by his own wish. Nobody could say a word against our travelling together. It would be delightful: thank you a thousand times, Jack. I'll come.

TANNER [*aghast*] You'll come!!!

ANN. Of course.

TANNER. But— [*he stops, utterly appalled; then resumes feebly*] No: look here, Ann: if there's no harm in it there's no point in doing it.

ANN. How absurd you are! You don't want to compromise me, do you?

TANNER. Yes: that's the whole sense of my proposal.

ANN. You are talking the greatest nonsense; and you know it. You would never do anything to hurt me.

TANNER. Well, if you don't want to be compromised, don't come.

ANN [*with simple earnestness*] Yes, I will come, Jack,
since you wish it. You are my guardian; and I think we
ought to see more of one another and come to know
one another better. [*Gratefully*] It's very thoughtful and
very kind of you, Jack, to offer me this lovely holiday,
especially after what I said about Rhoda. You really are
good—much better than you think. When do we start?

TANNER. But——

[*The conversation is interrupted by the arrival of Mrs.
Whitefield from the house. She is accompanied by the American gentleman, and followed by Ramsden and Octavius.*

*Hector Malone is an Eastern American; but he is not
at all ashamed of his nationality. This makes English people of fashion think well of him, as of a young fellow
who is manly enough to confess to an obvious disadvantage without any attempt to conceal or extenuate it. They
feel that he ought not to be made to suffer for what is
clearly not his fault, and make a point of being specially
kind to him. His chivalrous manners to women, and his
elevated moral sentiments, being both gratuitous and unusual, strike them as being a little unfortunate; and though
they find his vein of easy humor rather amusing when it
has ceased to puzzle them (as it does at first), they have
had to make him understand that he really must not tell
anecdotes unless they are strictly personal and scandalous,
and also that oratory is an accomplishment which belongs
to a cruder stage of civilization than that in which his
migration has landed him. On these points Hector is not
quite convinced: he still thinks that the British are apt to
make merits of their stupidities, and to represent their
various incapacities as points of good breeding. English
life seems to him to suffer from a lack of edifying rhetoric
(which he calls moral tone); English behavior to shew a
want of respect for womanhood; English pronunciation
to fail very vulgarly in tackling such words as world, girl,
bird, etc.; English society to be plain spoken to an extent
which stretches occasionally to intolerable coarseness; and
English intercourse to need enlivening by games and stories and other pastimes; so he does not feel called upon
to acquire these defects after taking great pains to cultivate
himself in a first rate manner before venturing across the
Atlantic. To this culture he finds English people either*

totally indifferent, as they very commonly are to all culture, or else politely evasive, the truth being that Hector's culture is nothing but a state of saturation with our literary exports of thirty years ago, reimported by him to be unpacked at a moment's notice and hurled at the head of English literature, science and art, at every conversational opportunity. The dismay set up by these sallies encourages him in his belief that he is helping to educate England. When he finds people chattering harmlessly about Anatole France and Nietzsche, he devastates them with Matthew Arnold, the Autocrat of the Breakfast Table, and even Macaulay; and as he is devoutly religious at bottom, he first leads the unwary, by humorous irreverences, to leave popular theology out of account in discussing moral questions with him, and then scatters them in confusion by demanding whether the carrying out of his ideals of conduct was not the manifest object of God Almighty in creating honest men and pure women. The engaging freshness of his personality and the dumbfoundering staleness of his culture make it extremely difficult to decide whether he is worth knowing; for whilst his company is undeniably pleasant and enlivening, there is intellectually nothing new to be got out of him, especially as he despises politics, and is careful not to talk commercial shop, in which department he is probably much in advance of his English capitalist friends. He gets on best with romantic Christians of the amoristic sect: hence the friendship which has sprung up between him and Octavius.

In appearance Hector is a neatly built young man of twenty-four, with a short, smartly trimmed black beard, clear, well shaped eyes, and an ingratiating vivacity of expression. He is, from the fashionable point of view, faultlessly dressed. As he comes along the drive from the house with Mrs. Whitefield he is sedulously making himself agreeable and entertaining, and thereby placing on her slender wit a burden it is unable to bear. An Englishman would let her alone, accepting boredom and indifference as their common lot; and the poor lady wants to be either let alone or let prattle about the things that interest her.

Ramsden strolls over to inspect the motor car. Octavius joins Hector.]

ANN [*pouncing on her mother joyously*] Oh, mamma, what do you think! Jack is going to take me to Nice in his motor car. Isn't it lovely? I am the happiest person in London.

TANNER [*desperately*] Mrs. Whitefield objects. I am sure she objects. Doesn't she, Ramsden?

RAMSDEN. I should think it very likely indeed.

ANN. You don't object, do you, mother?

MRS. WHITEFIELD. *I* object! Why should I? I think it will do you good, Ann. [*Trotting over to Tanner*] I meant to ask you to take Rhoda out for a run occasionally: she is too much in the house; but it will do when you come back.

TANNER. Abyss beneath abyss of perfidy!

ANN [*hastily, to distract attention from this outburst*] Oh, I forgot: you have not met Mr. Malone. Mr. Tanner, my guardian: Mr. Hector Malone.

HECTOR. Pleased to meet you, Mr. Tanner. I should like to suggest an extension of the travelling party to Nice, if I may.

ANN. Oh, we're all coming. That's understood, isn't it?

HECTOR. I also am the modest possessor of a motor car. If Miss Robinson will allow me the privilege of taking her, my car is at her service.

OCTAVIUS. Violet!

[*General constraint.*]

ANN [*subduedly*] Come, mother: we must leave them to talk over the arrangements. I must see to my travelling kit.

[*Mrs. Whitefield looks bewildered; but Ann draws her discreetly away; and they disappear round the corner towards the house.*]

HECTOR. I think I may go so far as to say that I can depend on Miss Robinson's consent.

[*Continued embarrassment.*]

OCTAVIUS. I'm afraid we must leave Violet behind. There are circumstances which make it impossible for her to come on such an expedition.

HECTOR [*amused and not at all convinced*] Too American, eh? Must the young lady have a chaperone?

OCTAVIUS. It's not that, Malone—at least not altogether.

HECTOR. Indeed! May I ask what other objection applies?

TANNER [*impatiently*] Oh, tell him, tell him. We shall never be able to keep the secret unless everybody knows what it is. Mr. Malone: if you go to Nice with Violet, you go with another man's wife. She is married.

HECTOR [*thunderstruck*]. You don't tell me so!

TANNER. We do. In confidence.

RAMSDEN [*with an air of importance, lest Malone should suspect a misalliance*] Her marriage has not yet been made known: she desires that it shall not be mentioned for the present.

HECTOR. I shall respect the lady's wishes. Would it be indiscreet to ask who her husband is, in case I should have an opportunity of consulting him about this trip?

TANNER. We don't know who he is.

HECTOR [*retiring into his shell in a very marked manner*] In that case, I have no more to say.

[*They become more embarrassed than ever.*]

OCTAVIUS. You must think this very strange.

HECTOR. A little singular. Pardon me for saying so.

RAMSDEN [*half apologetic, half huffy*] The young lady was married secretly; and her husband has forbidden her, it seems, to declare his name. It is only right to tell you, since you are interested in Miss—er—in Violet.

OCTAVIUS [*sympathetically*] I hope this is not a disappointment to you.

HECTOR [*softened, coming out of his shell again*] Well: it is a blow. I can hardly understand how a man can leave his wife in such a position. Surely it's not customary. It's not manly. It's not considerate.

OCTAVIUS. We feel that, as you may imagine, pretty deeply.

RAMSDEN [*testily*] It is some young fool who has not enough experience to know what mystifications of this kind lead to.

HECTOR [*with strong symptoms of moral repugnance*] I hope so. A man need be very young and pretty foolish too to be excused for such conduct. You take a very lenient view, Mr. Ramsden. Too lenient to my mind. Surely marriage should ennoble a man.

TANNER [*sardonically*] Ha!

HECTOR. Am I to gather from that cacchination that you don't agree with me, Mr. Tanner?

TANNER [*drily*] Get married and try. You may find it delightful for a while: you certainly won't find it ennobling. The greatest common measure of a man and a woman is not necessarily greater than the man's single measure.

HECTOR. Well, we think in America that a woman's moral number is higher than a man's, and that the purer nature of a woman lifts a man right out of himself, and makes him better than he was.

OCTAVIUS [*with conviction*] So it does.

TANNER. No wonder American women prefer to live in Europe! It's more comfortable than standing all their lives on an altar to be worshipped. Anyhow, Violet's husband has not been ennobled. So what's to be done?

HECTOR [*shaking his head*] I can't dismiss that man's conduct as lightly as you do, Mr. Tanner. However, I'll say no more. Whoever he is, he's Miss Robinson's husband; and I should be glad for her sake to think better of him.

OCTAVIUS [*touched; for he divines a secret sorrow*] I'm very sorry, Malone. Very sorry.

HECTOR [*gratefully*] You're a good fellow, Robinson. Thank you.

TANNER. Talk about something else. Violet's coming from the house.

HECTOR. I should esteem it a very great favor, gentlemen, if you would take the opportunity to let me have a few words with the lady alone. I shall have to cry off this trip; and it's rather a delicate—

RAMSDEN [*glad to escape*] Say no more. Come, Tanner. Come, Tavy. [*He strolls away into the park with Octavius and Tanner, past the motor car.*]

[*Violet comes down the avenue to Hector.*]

VIOLET. Are they looking?

HECTOR. No.

[*She kisses him.*]

VIOLET. Have you been telling lies for my sake?

HECTOR. Lying! Lying hardly describes it. I overdo it. I get carried away in an ecstasy of mendacity. Violet: I wish you'd let me own up.

VIOLET [*instantly becoming serious and resolute*] No, no, Hector: you promised me not to.

HECTOR. I'll keep my promise until you release me from it. But I feel mean, lying to those men, and denying my wife. Just dastardly.

VIOLET. I wish your father were not so unreasonable.

HECTOR. He's not unreasonable. He's right from his point of view. He has a prejudice against the English middle class.

VIOLET. It's too ridiculous. You know how I dislike saying such things to you, Hector; but if I were to—oh, well, no matter.

HECTOR. I know. If you were to marry the son of an English manufacturer of office furniture, your friends would consider it a misalliance. And here's my silly old dad, who is the biggest office furniture man in the world, would shew me the door for marrying the most perfect lady in England merely because she has no handle to her name. Of course it's just absurd. But I tell you, Violet, I don't like deceiving him. I feel as if I was stealing his money. Why won't you let me own up?

VIOLET. We can't afford it. You can be as romantic as you please about love, Hector; but you mustn't be romantic about money.

HECTOR [*divided between his uxoriousness and his habitual elevation of moral sentiment*]. That's very English. [*Appealing to her impulsively.*] Violet: dad's bound to find us out someday.

VIOLET. Oh yes, later on of course. But don't let's go over this every time we meet, dear. You promised—

HECTOR. All right, all right, I—

VIOLET [*not to be silenced*]. It is I and not you who suffer by this concealment; and as to facing a struggle and poverty and all that sort of thing I simply will not do it. It's too silly.

HECTOR. You shall not. I'll sort of borrow the money from my dad until I get on my own feet; and then I can own up and pay up at the same time.

VIOLET [*alarmed and indignant*]. Do you mean to work? Do you want to spoil our marriage?

HECTOR. Well, I don't mean to let marriage spoil

my character. Your friend Mr. Tanner has got the laugh on me a bit already about that; and—

VIOLET. The beast! I hate Jack Tanner.

HECTOR [*magnanimously*]. Oh, he's all right: he only needs the love of a good woman to ennoble him. Besides, he's proposed a motoring trip to Nice; and I'm going to take you.

VIOLET. How jolly!

HECTOR. Yes; but how are we going to manage? You see, they've warned me off going with you, so to speak. They've told me in confidence that you're married. That's just the most overwhelming confidence I've ever been honored with.

[*Tanner returns with Straker, who goes to his car.*]

TANNER. Your car is a great success, Mr. Malone. Your engineer is showing it off to Mr. Ramsden.

HECTOR [*eagerly—forgetting himself*] Let's come, Vi.

VIOLET [*coldly, warning him with her eyes*] I beg your pardon, Mr. Malone, I did not quite catch—

HECTOR [*recollecting himself*] I ask to be allowed the pleasure of shewing you my little American steam car, Miss Robinson.

VIOLET. I shall be very pleased. [*They go off together down the avenue.*]

TANNER. About this trip, Straker.

STRAKER [*preoccupied with the car*] Yes?

TANNER. Miss Whitefield is supposed to be coming with me.

STRAKER. So I gather.

TANNER. Mr. Robinson is to be one of the party.

STRAKER. Yes.

TANNER. Well, if you can manage so as to be a good deal occupied with me, and leave Mr. Robinson a good deal occupied with Miss Whitefield, he will be deeply grateful to you.

STRAKER [*looking round at him*] Evidently.

TANNER. "Evidently"! Your grandfather would have simply winked.

STRAKER. My grandfather would have touched his at.

TANNER. And I should have given your good nice respectful grandfather a sovereign.

STRAKER. Five shillins, more likely. [*He leaves the car and approaches Tanner.*] What about the lady's views?

TANNER. She is just as willing to be left to Mr. Robinson as Mr. Robinson is to be left to her. [*Straker looks at his principal with cool scepticism; then turns to the car whistling his favorite air.*] Stop that aggravating noise. What do you mean by it? [*Straker calmly resumes the melody and finishes it. Tanner politely hears it out before he again addresses Straker, this time with elaborate seriousness.*] Enry: I have ever been a warm advocate of the spread of music among the masses; but I object to your obliging the company whenever Miss Whitefield's name is mentioned. You did it this morning, too.

STRAKER [*obstinately*] It's not a bit o use. Mr. Robinson may as well give it up first as last.

TANNER. Why?

STRAKER. Garn! You know why. Course it's not my business; but you needn't start kiddin me about it.

TANNER. I am not kidding. I don't know why.

STRAKER [*cheerfully sulky*] Oh, very well. All right. It ain't my business.

TANNER [*impressively*]. I trust, Enry, that, as between employer and engineer, I shall always know how to keep my proper distance, and not intrude my private affairs on you. Even our business arrangements are subject to the approval of your Trade Union. But don't abuse your advantages. Let me remind you that Voltaire said that what was too silly to be said could be sung.

STRAKER. It wasn't Voltaire: it was Bow Mar Shay.

TANNER. I stand corrected: Beaumarchais of course. Now you seem to think that what is too delicate to be said can be whistled. Unfortunately your whistling, though melodious, is unintelligible. Come! there's nobody listening: neither my genteel relatives nor the secretary of your confounded Union. As man to man, Enry, why do you think that my friend has no chance with Miss Whitefield?

STRAKER. Cause she's arter summun else.

TANNER. Bosh! who else?

STRAKER. You.

TANNER. Me!!!

STRAKER. Mean to tell me you didn't know? Oh, come, Mr. Tanner!

TANNER [*in fierce earnest*] Are you playing the fool, or do you mean it?

STRAKER [*with a flash of temper*] I'm not playin no fool. [*More coolly.*] Why, it's as plain as the nose on your face. If you ain't spotted that, you don't know much about these sort of things. [*Serene again*] Ex-cuse me, you know, Mr. Tanner; but you asked me as man to man; and I told you as man to man.

TANNER [*wildly appealing to the heavens*] Then I—*I* am the bee, the spider, the marked down victim, the destined prey.

STRAKER. I dunno about the bee and the spider. But the marked down victim, that's what you are and no mistake; and a jolly good job for you, too, I should say.

TANNER [*momentously*] Henry Straker: the golden moment of your life has arrived.

STRAKER. What d'y' mean?

TANNER. That record to Biskra.

STRAKER [*eagerly*] Yes?

TANNER. Break it.

STRAKER [*rising to the height of his destiny*] D'y' mean it?

TANNER. I do.

STRAKER. When?

TANNER. Now. Is that machine ready to start?

STRAKER [*quailing*] But you can't—

TANNER [*cutting him short by getting into the car*] Off we go. First to the bank for money; then to my rooms for my kit; then to your rooms for your kit; then break the record from London to Dover or Folkestone; then across the channel and away like mad to Marseilles, Gibraltar, Genoa, any port from which we can sail to a Mahometan country where men are protected from women.

STRAKER. Garn! you're kiddin.

TANNER [*resolutely*] Stay behind then. If you won't come I'll do it alone. [*He starts the motor*].

STRAKER [*running after him*] Here! Mister! arf a mo! steady on! [*He scrambles in as the car plunges forward*].

ACT THREE

Evening in the Sierra Nevada. Rolling slopes of brown, with olive trees instead of apple trees in the cultivated patches, and occasional prickly pears instead of gorse and bracken in the wilds. Higher up, tall stone peaks and precipices, all handsome and distinguished. No wild nature here: rather a most aristocratic mountain landscape made by a fastidious artist-creator. No vulgar profusion of vegetation: even a touch of aridity in the frequent patches of stones: Spanish magnificence and Spanish economy everywhere.

Not very far north of a spot at which the high road over one of the passes crosses a tunnel on the railway from Malaga to Granada, is one of the mountain amphitheatres of the Sierra. Looking at it from the wide end of the horse-shoe, one sees, a little to the right, in the face of the cliff, a romantic cave which is really an abandoned quarry, and towards the left a little hill, commanding a view of the road, which skirts the amphitheatre on the left, maintaining its higher level on embankments and an occasional stone arch. On the hill, watching the road, is a man who is either a Spaniard or a Scotchman. Probably a Spaniard, since he wears the dress of a Spanish goatherd and seems at home in the Sierra Nevada, but very like a Scotchman for all that. In the hollow, on the slope leading to the quarry-cave, are about a dozen men who, as they recline at their ease round a heap of smouldering white ashes of dead leaf and brushwood, have an air of being conscious of themselves as picturesque scoundrels honoring the Sierra by using it as an effective pictorial background. As a matter of artistic fact they are not picturesque; and the mountains tolerate them as lions tolerate lice. An English policeman or Poor Law Guardian would recognize them as a selected band of tramps and ablebodied paupers.

This description of them is not wholly contemptuous. Whoever has intelligently observed the tramp, or visited the ablebodied ward of a workhouse, will admit that our social failures are not all drunkards and weaklings. Some of them are men who do not fit the class they were born into. *Precisely the same qualities that make the educated gentleman an artist may make an uneducated manual laborer an ablebodied pauper. There are men who fall helplessly into the workhouse because they are good for nothing; but there are also men who are there because they are strongminded enough to disregard the social convention [obviously not a disinterested one on the part of the ratepayer] which bids a man live by heavy and badly paid drudgery when he has the alternative of walking into the workhouse, announcing himself as a destitute person, and legally compelling the Guardians to feed, clothe and house him better than he could feed, clothe and house himself without great exertion. When a man who is born a poet refuses a stool in a stockbroker's office, and starves in a garret, sponging on a poor landlady or on his friends and relatives sooner than work against his grain; or when a lady, because she is a lady, will face any extremity of parasitic dependence rather than take a situation as cook or parlormaid, we make large allowances for them. To such allowances the ablebodied pauper, and his nomadic variant the tramp, are equally entitled.*

Further, the imaginative man, if his life is to be tolerable to him, must have leisure to tell himself stories, and a position which lends itself to imaginative decoration. The ranks of unskilled labor offer no such positions. We misuse our laborers horribly; and when a man refuses to be misused, we have no right to say that he is refusing honest work. Let us be frank in this matter before we go on with our play; so that we may enjoy it without hypocrisy. If we were reasoning, farsighted people, four fifths of us would go straight to the Guardians for relief, and knock the whole social system to pieces with most beneficial reconstructive results. The reason we do not do this is because we work like bees or ants, by instinct or habit, not reasoning about the matter at all. Therefore when a man comes along who can and does reason, and who, applying the Kantian test to his conduct, can truly say to us, If everybody did as I do, the world would be compelled to reform itself industrially, and abolish slavery and squalor, which exist only because everybody does as you do, let us honor that man and seriously consider the advisability of following his example. Such a man is the ablebodied, able-minded pauper. Were he a gentleman doing his best to get a pension or a sinecure instead of sweeping a crossing, nobody would blame him for deciding that so long as the alternative lies between living mainly at the expense of the community and allowing the community to live mainly at his, it would be folly to accept what is to him personally the greater of the two evils.

We may therefore contemplate the tramps of the Sierra without prejudice, admitting cheerfully that our objects— briefly, to be gentlemen of fortune—are much the same as theirs, and the difference in our position and methods merely accidental. One or two of them, perhaps, it would be wiser to kill without malice in a friendly and frank manner; for there are bipeds, just as there are quadrupeds, who are too dangerous to be left unchained and unmuzzled; and these cannot fairly expect to have other men's lives wasted in the work of watching them. But as society has not the courage to kill them, and, when it catches them, simply wreaks on them some superstitious expiatory rites of torture and degradation, and then lets them loose with heightened qualifications for mischief, it is just as well that they are at large in the Sierra, and in the hands of a chief who looks as if he might possibly, on provocation, order them to be shot.

This chief, seated in the centre of the group on a squared block of stone from the quarry, is a tall strong man, with a striking cockatoo nose, glossy black hair, pointed beard, upturned moustache, and a Mephistophelean affectation which is fairly imposing, perhaps because the scenery admits of a larger swagger than Piccadilly, perhaps because of a certain sentimentality in the man which gives him that touch of grace which alone can excuse deliberate picturesqueness. His eyes and mouth are by no means rascally; he has a fine voice and a ready wit; and whether he is really the strongest man in the party or not, he looks it. He is certainly the best fed, the best dressed, and the best trained. The fact that he speaks English is not unexpected, in spite of the Spanish landscape; for with the exception of one man who might be guessed as a bullfighter ruined by drink, and one unmistakable Frenchman, they are all cockney or American; therefore, in a land of cloaks and sombreros, they mostly

wear seedy overcoats, woollen mufflers, hard hemispheri-
cal hats, and dirty brown gloves. Only a very few dress
after their leader, whose broad sombrero with a cock's
feather in the band, and voluminous cloak descending to
his high boots, are as un-English as possible. None of
them are armed; and the ungloved ones keep their hands
in their pockets because it is their national belief that it
must be dangerously cold in the open air with the night
coming on. [It is as warm an evening as any reasonable
man could desire].

Except the bullfighting inebriate there is only one per-
son in the company who looks more than, say, thirty-
three. He is a small man with reddish whiskers, weak
eyes, and the anxious look of a small tradesman in diffi-
culties. He wears the only tall hat visible: it shines in the
sunset with the sticky glow of some sixpenny patent hat
reviver, often applied and constantly tending to produce
a worse state of the original surface than the ruin it was
applied to remedy. He has a collar and cuffs of celluloid;
and his brown Chesterfield overcoat, with velvet collar, is
still presentable. He is pre-eminently the respectable man
of the party, and is certainly over forty, possibly over fifty.
He is the corner man on the leader's right, opposite three
men in scarlet ties on his left. One of these three is the
Frenchman. Of the remaining two, who are both English,
one is argumentative, solemn, and obstinate; the other
rowdy and mischievous.

The chief, with a magnificent fling of the end of his
cloak across his left shoulder, rises to address them. The
applause which greets him shews that he is a favorite
orator.

THE CHIEF. Friends and fellow brigands. I have a
proposal to make to this meeting. We have now spent
three evenings in discussing the question Have Anarchists or Social-Democrats the most personal courage?
We have gone into the principles of Anarchism and
Social-Democracy at great length. The cause of Anarchy
has been ably represented by our one Anarchist, who
doesn't know what Anarchism means [*laughter*]—

THE ANARCHIST [*rising*] A point of order, Mendoza—

MENDOZA [*forcibly*] No, by thunder: your last point

of order took half an hour. Besides, Anarchists don't believe in order.

THE ANARCHIST [*mild, polite but persistent: he is, in fact, the respectable looking elderly man in the celluloid collar and cuffs*] That is a vulgar error. I can prove—

MENDOZA. Order, order.

THE OTHERS [*shouting*] Order, order. Sit down. Chair! Shut up.

[*The Anarchist is suppressed.*]

MENDOZA. On the other hand we have three Social-Democrats among us. They are not on speaking terms; and they have put before us three distinct and incompatible views of Social-Democracy.

THE THREE MEN IN SCARLET TIES. 1. Mr. Chairman, I protest. A personal explanation. 2. It's a lie. I never said so. Be fair, Mendoza. 3. Je demande la parole. C'est absolument faux. C'est faux! faux!! faux!!! Assas-s-s-s-sin!!!!!!

MENDOZA. Order, order.

THE OTHERS. Order, order, order! Chair!

[*The Social-Democrats are suppressed.*]

MENDOZA. Now, we tolerate all opinions here. But after all, comrades, the vast majority of us are neither Anarchists nor Socialists, but gentlemen and Christians.

THE MAJORITY [*shouting assent*] Hear, hear! So we are. Right.

THE ROWDY SOCIAL-DEMOCRAT [*smarting under suppression*] You ain't no Christian. You're a Sheeny, you are.

MENDOZA [*with crushing magnanimity*] My friend: *I* am an exception to all rules. It is true that I have the honor to be a Jew; and when the Zionists need a leader to reassemble our race on its historic soil of Palestine, Mendoza will not be the last to volunteer [*sympathetic applause—hear, hear, &c.*]. But I am not a slave to any superstition. I have swallowed all the formulas, even that of Socialism; though, in a sense, once a Socialist, always a Socialist.

THE SOCIAL-DEMOCRATS. Hear, hear!

MENDOZA. But I am well aware that the ordinary man—even the ordinary brigand, who can scarcely be called an ordinary man [*Hear, hear!*]—is not a philosopher. Common sense is good enough for him; and in our business affairs common sense is good enough for me. Well, what is our business here in the Sierra Nevada, chosen by the Moors as the fairest spot in Spain? Is it to discuss abstruse questions of political economy? No: it is to hold up motor cars and secure a more equitable distribution of wealth.

THE SULKY SOCIAL-DEMOCRAT. All made by labor, mind you.

MENDOZA [*urbanely*] Undoubtedly. All made by labor, and on its way to be squandered by wealthy vagabonds in the dens of vice that disfigure the sunny shores of the Mediterranean. We intercept that wealth. We restore it to circulation among the class that produced it and that chiefly needs it—the working class. We do this at the risk of our lives and liberties, by the exercise of the virtues of courage, endurance, foresight, and abstinence—especially abstinence. I myself have eaten nothing but prickly pears and broiled rabbit for three days.

THE SULKY SOCIAL-DEMOCRAT [*stubbornly*] No more ain't we.

MENDOZA [*indignantly*] Have I taken more than my share?

THE SULKY SOCIAL-DEMOCRAT [*unmoved*] Why should you?

THE ANARCHIST. Why should he not? To each according to his needs: from each according to his means.

THE FRENCHMAN [*shaking his fist at the Anarchist*] Fumiste!

MENDOZA [*diplomatically*] I agree with both of you.

THE GENUINELY ENGLISH BRIGANDS. Hear, hear! Bravo Mendoza!

MENDOZA. What I say is, let us treat one another as gentlemen, and strive to excel in personal courage only when we take the field.

THE ROWDY SOCIAL-DEMOCRAT [*derisively*] Shikespear.

[*A whistle comes from the goatherd on the hill. He springs up and points excitedly forward along the road to the north.*]

THE GOATHERD. Automobile! Automobile! [*He rushes down the hill and joins the rest, who all scramble to their feet.*]

MENDOZA [*in ringing tones*] To arms! Who has the gun?

THE SULKY SOCIAL-DEMOCRAT [*handing a rifle to Mendoza*]. Here.

MENDOZA. Have the nails been strewn in the road?

THE ROWDY SOCIAL-DEMOCRAT. Two ahnces of em.

MENDOZA. Good! [*To the Frenchman*] With me, Duval. If the nails fail, puncture their tires with a bullet. [*He gives the rifle to Duval, who follows him up the hill. Mendoza produces an opera glass. The others hurry across to the road and disappear to the north.*]

MENDOZA [*on the hill, using his glass*] Two only, a capitalist and his chauffeur. They look English.

DUVAL. Angliche! Aoh yess. Cochons! [*Handling the rifle*] Faut tirer, n'est-ce-pas?

MENDOZA. No: the nails have gone home. Their tire is down: they stop.

DUVAL [*shouting to the others*] Fondez sur eux, nom de Dieu!

MENDOZA [*rebuking his excitement*] Du calme, Duval: keep your hair on. They take it quietly. Let us descend and receive them.

[*Mendoza descends, passing behind the fire and coming forward, whilst Tanner and Straker, in their motoring goggles, leather coats, and caps, are led in from the road by the brigands.*]

TANNER. Is this the gentleman you describe as your boss? Does he speak English?

THE ROWDY SOCIAL-DEMOCRAT. Course he does. Y' downt suppowz we Hinglishmen lets ahrselves be bossed by a bloomin Spenniard, do you?

MENDOZA [*with dignity*] Allow me to introduce myself: Mendoza, President of the League of the Sierra! [*Posing loftily*] I am a brigand: I live by robbing the rich.

TANNER [*promptly*] I am a gentleman: I live by robbing the poor. Shake hands.

THE ENGLISH SOCIAL-DEMOCRATS. Hear, hear!

[*General laughter and good humor. Tanner and Mendoza shake hands. The Brigands drop into their former places.*]

STRAKER. Ere! where do I come in?

TANNER [*introducing*] My friend and chauffeur.

THE SULKY SOCIAL-DEMOCRAT [*suspiciously*] Well,

which is he? friend or show-foor? It makes all the difference, you know.

MENDOZA [*explaining*] We should expect ransom for a friend. A professional chauffeur is free of the mountains. He even takes a trifling percentage of his principal's ransom if he will honor us by accepting it.

STRAKER. I see. Just to encourage me to come this way again. Well, I'll think about it.

DUVAL [*impulsively rushing across to Straker*] Mon frère! [*He embraces him rapturously and kisses him on both cheeks.*]

STRAKER [*disgusted*] Ere, git out: don't be silly. Who are you, pray?

DUVAL. Duval: Social-Democrat.

STRAKER. Oh, you're a Social-Democrat, are you?

THE ANARCHIST. He means that he has sold out to the parliamentary humbugs and the bourgeoisie. Compromise! that is his faith.

DUVAL [*furiously*] I understand what he say. He say Bourgeois. He say Compromise. Jamais de la vie! Misérable menteur—

STRAKER. See here, Captain Mendoza, ow much o this sort o thing do you put up with here? Are we avin a pleasure trip in the mountains, or are we at a Socialist meetin?

THE MAJORITY. Hear, hear! Shut up. Chuck it. Sit down, &c. &c. [*The Social-Democrats and the Anarchist are hustled into the background. Straker, after superintending this proceeding with satisfaction, places himself on Mendoza's left, Tanner being on his right.*]

MENDOZA. Can we offer you anything? Broiled rabbit and prickly pears—

TANNER. Thank you: we have dined.

MENDOZA [*to his followers*] Gentlemen: business is over for the day. Go as you please until morning.

[*The Brigands disperse into groups lazily. Some go into the cave. Others sit down or lie down to sleep in the open. A few produce a pack of cards and move off towards the road; for it is now starlight; and they know that motor cars have lamps which can be turned to account for lighting a card party.*]

STRAKER [*calling after them*] Don't none of you go fooling with that car, d'ye hear?

MENDOZA. No fear, Monsieur le Chauffeur. The first one we captured cured us of that.

STRAKER [*interested*] What did it do?

MENDOZA. It carried three brave comrades of ours, who did not know how to stop it, into Granada, and capsized them opposite the police station. Since then we never touch one without sending for the chauffeur. Shall we chat at our ease?

TANNER. By all means.

[*Tanner, Mendoza, and Straker sit down on the turf by the fire. Mendoza delicately waives his presidential dignity, of which the right to sit on the squared stone block is the appanage, by sitting on the ground like his guests, and using the stone only as a support for his back.*]

MENDOZA. It is the custom in Spain always to put off business until to-morrow. In fact, you have arrived out of office hours. However, if you would prefer to settle the question of ransom at once, I am at your service.

TANNER. To-morrow will do for me. I am rich enough to pay anything in reason.

MENDOZA [*respectfully, much struck by this admission*]. You are a remarkable man, sir. Our guests usually describe themselves as miserably poor.

TANNER. Pooh! Miserably poor people don't own motor cars.

MENDOZA. Precisely what we say to them.

TANNER. Treat us well: we shall not prove ungrateful.

STRAKER. No prickly pears and broiled rabbits, you know. Don't tell me you can't do us a bit better than that if you like.

MENDOZA. Wine, kids, milk, cheese and bread can be procured for ready money.

STRAKER [*graciously*] Now you're talking.

TANNER. Are you all Socialists here, may I ask?

MENDOZA [*repudiating this humiliating misconception*] Oh no, no, no: nothing of the kind, I assure you. We naturally have modern views as to the justice of the existing distribution of wealth: otherwise we should lose our self-respect. But nothing that you could take exception to, except two or three faddists.

TANNER. I had no intention of suggesting anything discreditable. In fact, I am a bit of a Socialist myself.

STRAKER [drily] Most rich men are, I notice.

MENDOZA. Quite so. It has reached us, I admit. It is in the air of the century.

STRAKER. Socialism must be looking up a bit if your chaps are taking to it.

MENDOZA. That is true, sir. A movement which is confined to philosophers and honest men can never exercise any real political influence: there are too few of them. Until a movement shews itself capable of spreading among brigands, it can never hope for a political majority.

TANNER. But are your brigands any less honest than ordinary citizens?

MENDOZA. Sir: I will be frank with you. Brigandage is abnormal. Abnormal professions attract two classes: those who are not good enough for ordinary bourgeois life and those who are too good for it. We are dregs and scum, sir: the dregs very filthy, the scum very superior.

STRAKER. Take care! some o the dregs'll hear you.

MENDOZA. It does not matter: each brigand thinks himself scum, and likes to hear the others called dregs.

TANNER. Come! you are a wit [Mendoza inclines his head, flattered]. May one ask you a blunt question?

MENDOZA. As blunt as you please.

TANNER. How does it pay a man of your talent to shepherd such a flock as this on broiled rabbit and prickly pears? I have seen men less gifted, and I'll swear less honest, supping at the Savoy on foie gras and champagne.

MENDOZA. Pooh! they have all had their turn at the broiled rabbit, just as I shall have my turn at the Savoy. Indeed, I have had a turn there already—as waiter.

TANNER. A waiter! You astonish me!

MENDOZA [reflectively] Yes: I, Mendoza of the Sierra, was a waiter. Hence, perhaps, my cosmopolitanism. [With sudden intensity] Shall I tell you the story of my life?

STRAKER [apprehensively] If it ain't too long, old chap—

TANNER [interrupting him] Tsh-sh: you are a Philis-

tine, Henry: you have no romance in you. [*To Mendoza*]
You interest me extremely, President. Never mind
Henry: he can go to sleep.

MENDOZA. The woman I loved—

STRAKER. Oh, this is a love story, is it? Right you
are. Go on: I was only afraid you were going to talk
about yourself.

MENDOZA. Myself! I have thrown myself away for
her sake: that is why I am here. No matter: I count the
world well lost for her. She had, I pledge you my word,
the most magnificent head of hair I ever saw. She had
humor; she had intellect; she could cook to perfection;
and her highly strung temperament made her uncertain,
incalculable, variable, capricious, cruel, in a word,
enchanting.

STRAKER. A six shillin novel sort o woman, all but
the cookin. Er name was Lady Gladys Plantagenet,
wasn't it?

MENDOZA. No, sir: she was not an earl's daughter.
Photography, reproduced by the half-tone process, has
made me familiar with the appearance of the daughters
of the English peerage; and I can honestly say that I
would have sold the lot, faces, dowries, clothes, titles,
and all, for a smile from this woman. Yet she was a
woman of the people, a worker: otherwise—let me recip-
rocate your bluntness—I should have scorned her.

TANNER. Very properly. And did she respond to
your love?

MENDOZA. Should I be here if she did? She objected
to marry a Jew.

TANNER. On religious grounds?

MENDOZA. No: she was a freethinker. She said that
every Jew considers in his heart that English people are
dirty in their habits.

TANNER [*surprised*] Dirty!

MENDOZA. It shewed her extraordinary knowledge
of the world; for it is undoubtedly true. Our elaborate
sanitary code makes us unduly contemptuous of the
Gentile.

TANNER. Did you ever hear that, Henry?

STRAKER. I've heard my sister say so. She was cook
in a Jewish family once.

MENDOZA. I could not deny it; neither could I eradicate the impression it made on her mind. I could have got round any other objection; but no woman can stand a suspicion of indelicacy as to her person. My entreaties were in vain: she always retorted that she wasn't good enough for me, and recommended me to marry an accursed barmaid named Rebecca Lazarus, whom I loathed. I talked of suicide: she offered me a packet of beetle poison to do it with. I hinted at murder: she went into hysterics; and as I am a living man I went to America so that she might sleep without dreaming that I was stealing upstairs to cut her throat. In America I went out west and fell in with a man who was wanted by the police for holding up trains. It was he who had the idea of holding up motors cars in the South of Europe: a welcome idea to a desperate and disappointed man. He gave me some valuable introductions to capitalists of the right sort. I formed a syndicate; and the present enterprise is the result. I became leader, as the Jew always becomes leader, by his brains and imagination. But with all my pride of race I would give everything I possess to be an Englishman. I am like a boy: I cut her name on the trees and her initials on the sod. When I am alone I lie down and tear my wretched hair and cry Louisa—

STRAKER [*startled*] Louisa!

MENDOZA. It is her name—Louisa—Louisa Straker—

TANNER. Straker!

STRAKER [*scrambling up on his knees most indignantly*] Look here: Louisa Straker is my sister, see? Wot do you mean by gassin about her like this? Wotshe got to do with you?

MENDOZA. A dramatic coincidence! You are Enry, her favorite brother!

STRAKER. Oo are you callin Enry? What call have you to take a liberty with my name or with hers? For two pins I'd punch your fat ed, so I would.

MENDOZA [*with grandiose calm*] If I let you do it, will you promise to brag of it afterwards to her? She will be reminded of her Mendoza: that is all I desire.

TANNER. This is genuine devotion, Henry. You should respect it.

STRAKER [*fiercely*] Funk, more likely.

MENDOZA [*springing to his feet*] Funk! Young man: I come of a famous family of fighters; and as your sister well knows, you would have as much chance against me as a perambulator against your motor car.

STRAKER [*secretly daunted, but rising from his knees with an air of reckless pugnacity*] I ain't afraid of you. With your Louisa! Louisa! Miss Straker is good enough for you, I should think.

MENDOZA. I wish you could persuade her to think so.

STRAKER [*exasperated*] Here—

TANNER [*rising quickly and interposing*] Oh come, Henry: even if you could fight the President you can't fight the whole League of the Sierra. Sit down again and be friendly. A cat may look at a king; and even a President of brigands may look at your sister. All this family pride is really very old fashioned.

STRAKER [*subdued, but grumbling*] Let him look at her. But wot does he mean by makin out that she ever looked at im? [*Reluctantly resuming his couch on the turf*] Ear him talk, one ud think she was keepin company with him. [*He turns his back on them and composes himself to sleep.*]

MENDOZA [*to Tanner, becoming more confidential as he finds himself virtually alone with a sympathetic listener in the still starlight of the mountains; for all the rest are asleep by this time*] It was just so with her, sir. Her intellect reached forward into the twentieth century: her social prejudices and family affections reached back into the dark ages. Ah, sir, how the words of Shakespeare seem to fit every crisis in our emotions!

> I loved Louisa: 40,000 brothers
> Could not with all their quantity of love
> Make up my sum.

And so on. I forget the rest. Call it madness if you will—infatuation. I am an able man, a strong man: in ten years I should have owned a first-class hotel. I met her; and—you see!—I am a brigand, an outcast. Even Shakespeare cannot do justice to what I feel for Louisa. Let me read you some lines that I have written about her myself. However slight their literary merit may be, they express what I feel better than any casual words can. [*He produces a packet of hotel bills scrawled with manuscript, and kneels at the fire to decipher them, poking it with a stick to make it glow.*]

TANNER [*slapping him rudely on the shoulder*] Put them in the fire, President.

MENDOZA [*startled*] Eh?

TANNER. You are sacrificing your career to a monomania.

MENDOZA. I know it.

TANNER. No you don't. No man would commit such a crime against himself if he really knew what he was doing. How can you look round at these august hills, look up at this divine sky, taste this finely tempered air, and then talk like a literary hack on a second floor in Bloomsbury?

MENDOZA [*shaking his head*] The Sierra is no better than Bloomsbury when once the novelty has worn off. Besides, these mountains make you dream of women— of women with magnificent hair.

TANNER. Of Louisa, in short. They will not make me dream of women, my friend: I am heartwhole.

MENDOZA. Do not boast until morning, sir. This is a strange country for dreams.

TANNER. Well, we shall see. Good-night. [*He lies down and composes himself to sleep*].

[*Mendoza, with a sigh, follows his example; and for a few moments there is peace in the Sierra. Then Mendoza sits up suddenly and says pleadingly to Tanner—*]

MENDOZA. Just allow me to read a few lines before you go to sleep. I should really like your opinion of them.

TANNER [*drowsily*] Go on. I am listening.

MENDOZA. I saw thee first in Whitsun week
                    Louisa, Louisa—

TANNER [*rousing himself*] My dear President, Louisa is a very pretty name; but it really doesn't rhyme well to Whitsun week.

MENDOZA. Of course not. Louisa is not the rhyme, but the refrain.

TANNER [*subsiding*] Ah, the refrain. I beg your pardon. Go on.

MENDOZA. Perhaps you do not care for that one: I think you will like this better. [*He recites, in rich soft tones, and in slow time*]

> Louisa, I love thee.
> I love thee, Louisa.
> Louisa, Louisa, Louisa, I love thee.
> One name and one phrase make my music, Louisa.
> Louisa, Louisa, Louisa, I love thee.
>
> Mendoza thy lover,
> Thy lover, Mendoza,
> Mendoza adoringly lives for Louisa.
> There's nothing but that in the world for Mendoza.
> Louisa, Louisa, Mendoza adores thee.

[*Affected*] There is no merit in producing beautiful lines upon such a name. Louisa is an exquisite name, is it not?

TANNER [*all but asleep, responds with a faint groan*].

MENDOZA.

> O wert thou, Louisa,
> The Wife of Mendoza,
> Mendoza's Louisa, Louisa Mendoza,
> How blest were the life of Louisa's Mendoza!
> How painless his longing of love for Louisa!

That is real poetry—from the heart—from the heart of hearts. Don't you think it will move her?

[*No answer.*]

[*Resignedly*] Asleep, as usual. Doggerel to all the world: heavenly music to me! Idiot that I am to wear my heart on my sleeve! [*He composes himself to sleep, murmuring*] Louisa, I love thee; I love thee, Louisa; Louisa, Louisa, Louisa, I—

[*Straker snores; rolls over on his side; and relapses into sleep. Stillness settles on the Sierra; and the darkness deepens. The fire has again buried itself in white ash and ceased to glow. The peaks shew unfathomably dark*

*against the starry firmament; but now the stars dim and
vanish; and the sky seems to steal away out of the universe. Instead of the Sierra there is nothing; omnipresent
nothing. No sky, no peaks, no light, no sound, no time
nor space, utter void. Then somewhere the beginning of
a pallor, and with it a faint throbbing buzz as of a ghostly
violoncello palpitating on the same note endlessly. A couple of ghostly violins presently take advantage of this bass
and therewith the pallor reveals a man in the void,]*

*an incorporeal but visible man, seated, absurdly enough,
on nothing. For a moment he raises his head as the music
passes him by. Then, with a heavy sigh, he droops in
utter dejection; and the violins, discouraged, retrace their
melody in despair and at last give it up, extinguished by
wailings from uncanny wind instruments, thus:—*

It is all very odd. One recognizes the Mozartian strain;
and on this hint, and by the aid of certain sparkles of
violet light in the pallor, the man's costume explains itself
as that of a Spanish nobleman of the XV–XVI century.
Don Juan, of course; but where? why? how? Besides, in
the brief lifting of his face, now hidden by his hat brim,
there was a curious suggestion of Tanner. A more critical,
fastidious, handsome face, paler and colder, without Tanner's impetuous credulity and enthusiasm, and without
a touch of his modern plutocratic vulgarity, but still a
resemblance, even an identity. The name too: Don Juan
Tenorio, John Tanner. Where on earth—or elsewhere—
have we got to from the XX century and the Sierra?

Another pallor in the void, this time not violet, but a

disagreeable smoky yellow. With it, the whisper of a ghostly clarionet turning this tune into infinite sadness:

The yellowish pallor moves: there is an old crone wandering in the void, bent and toothless; draped, as well as one can guess, in the coarse brown frock of some religious order. She wanders and wanders in her slow hopeless way, much as a wasp flies in its rapid busy way, until she blunders against the thing she seeks: companionship. With a sob of relief the poor old creature clutches at the presence of the man and addresses him in her dry unlovely voice, which can still express pride and resolution as well as suffering.]

THE OLD WOMAN. Excuse me; but I am so lonely; and this place is so awful.

DON JUAN. A new comer?

THE OLD WOMAN. Yes: I suppose I died this morning. I confessed; I had extreme unction; I was in bed with my family about me and my eyes fixed on the cross. Then it grew dark; and when the light came back it was this light by which I walk seeing nothing. I have wandered for hours in horrible loneliness.

DON JUAN [*sighing*] Ah! you have not yet lost the sense of time. One soon does, in eternity.

THE OLD WOMAN. Where are we?

DON JUAN. In hell.

THE OLD WOMAN [*proudly*] Hell! I in hell! How dare you?

DON JUAN [*unimpressed*] Why not, Señora?

THE OLD WOMAN. You do not know to whom you are speaking. I am a lady, and a faithful daughter of the Church.

DON JUAN. I do not doubt it.

THE OLD WOMAN. But how then can I be in hell? Purgatory, perhaps: I have not been perfect: who has? But hell! oh, you are lying.

DON JUAN. Hell, Señora, I assure you; hell at its best: that is, its most solitary—though perhaps you would prefer company.

THE OLD WOMAN. But I have sincerely repented; I have confessed—

DON JUAN. How much?

THE OLD WOMAN. More sins than I really committed. I loved confession.

DON JUAN. Ah, that is perhaps as bad as confessing too little. At all events, Señora, whether by oversight or intention, you are certainly damned, like myself; and there is nothing for it now but to make the best of it.

THE OLD WOMAN [indignantly] Oh! and I might have been so much wickeder! All my good deeds wasted! It is unjust.

DON JUAN. No: you were fully and clearly warned. For your bad deeds, vicarious atonement, mercy without justice. For your good deeds, justice without mercy. We have many good people here.

THE OLD WOMAN. Were you a good man?

DON JUAN. I was a murderer.

THE OLD WOMAN. A murderer! Oh, how dare they send me to herd with murderers! I was not as bad as that: I was a good woman. There is some mistake: where can I have it set right?

DON JUAN. I do not know whether mistakes can be corrected here. Probably they will not admit a mistake even if they have made one.

THE OLD WOMAN. But whom can I ask?

DON JUAN. I should ask the Devil, Señora: he understands the ways of this place, which is more than I ever could.

THE OLD WOMAN. The Devil! I speak to the Devil!

DON JUAN. In hell, Señora, the Devil is the leader of the best society.

THE OLD WOMAN. I tell you, wretch, I know I am not in hell.

DON JUAN. How do you know?

THE OLD WOMAN. Because I feel no pain.

DON JUAN. Oh, then there is no mistake: you are intentionally damned.

THE OLD WOMAN. Why do you say that?

DON JUAN. Because hell, Señora, is a place for the wicked. The wicked are quite comfortable in it: it was made for them. You tell me you feel no pain. I conclude you are one of those for whom hell exists.

THE OLD WOMAN. Do you feel no pain?

DON JUAN. I am not one of the wicked, Señora; therefore it bores me, bores me beyond description, beyond belief.

THE OLD WOMAN. Not one of the wicked! You said you were a murderer.

DON JUAN. Only a duel. I ran my sword through an old man who was trying to run his through me.

THE OLD WOMAN. If you were a gentleman, that was not a murder.

DON JUAN. The old man called it murder, because he was, he said, defending his daughter's honor. By this he meant that because I foolishly fell in love with her and told her so, she screamed; and he tried to assassinate me after calling me insulting names.

THE OLD WOMAN. You were like all men. Libertines and murderers all, all, all!

DON JUAN. And yet we meet here, dear lady.

THE OLD WOMAN. Listen to me. My father was slain by just such a wretch as you, in just such a duel, for just such a cause. I screamed: it was my duty. My father drew on my assailant: his honor demanded it. He fell: that was the reward of honor. I am here: in hell, you tell me: that is the reward of duty. Is there justice in heaven?

DON JUAN. No; but there is justice in hell: heaven is far above such idle human personalities. You will be welcome in hell, Señora. Hell is the home of honor, duty, justice, and the rest of the seven deadly virtues. All the wickedness on earth is done in their name: where else but in hell should they have their reward? Have I not told you that the truly damned are those who are happy in hell?

THE OLD WOMAN. And are you happy here?

DON JUAN [springing to his feet] No; and that is the enigma on which I ponder in darkness. Why am I here? I, who repudiated all duty, trampled honor underfoot, and laughed at justice!

THE OLD WOMAN. Oh, what do I care why you are here? Why am I here? I, who sacrificed all my inclinations to womanly virtue and propriety!

DON JUAN. Patience, lady: you will be perfectly happy and at home here. As saith the poet, "Hell is a city much like Seville."

THE OLD WOMAN. Happy! here! where I am nothing! where I am nobody!

DON JUAN. Not at all: you are a lady; and wherever ladies are is hell. Do not be surprised or terrified: you will find everything here that a lady can desire, including devils who will serve you from sheer love of servitude, and magnify your importance for the sake of dignifying their service—the best of servants.

THE OLD WOMAN. My servants will be devils!

DON JUAN. Have you ever had servants who were not devils?

THE OLD WOMAN. Never: they were devils, perfect devils, all of them. But that is only a manner of speaking. I thought you meant that my servants here would be real devils.

DON JUAN. No more real devils than you will be a real lady. Nothing is real here. That is the horror of damnation.

THE OLD WOMAN. Oh, this is all madness. This is worse than fire and the worm.

DON JUAN. For you, perhaps, there are consolations. For instance: how old were you when you changed from time to eternity?

THE OLD WOMAN. Do not ask me how old I was— as if I were a thing of the past. I am 77.

DON JUAN. A ripe age, Señora. But in hell old age is not tolerated. It is too real. Here we worship Love and Beauty. Our souls being entirely damned, we cultivate our hearts. As a lady of 77, you would not have a single acquaintance in hell.

THE OLD WOMAN. How can I help my age, man?

DON JUAN. You forget that you have left your age behind you in the realm of time. You are no more 77 than you are 7 or 17 or 27.

THE OLD WOMAN. Nonsense!

DON JUAN. Consider, Señora: was not this true even when you lived on earth? When you were 70, were you really older underneath your wrinkles and your grey hairs than when you were 30?

THE OLD WOMAN. No, younger: at 30 I was a fool. But of what use is it to feel younger and look older?

DON JUAN. You see, Señora, the look was only an illusion. Your wrinkles lied, just as the plump smooth skin of many a stupid girl of 17, with heavy spirits and decrepit ideas, lies about her age. Well, here we have no bodies: we see each other as bodies only because we learnt to think about one another under that aspect when we were alive; and we still think in that way, knowing no other. But we can appear to one another at what age we choose. You have but to will any of your old looks back, and back they will come.

THE OLD WOMAN. It cannot be true.

DON JUAN. Try.

THE OLD WOMAN. Seventeen!

DON JUAN. Stop. Before you decide, I had better tell you that these things are a matter of fashion. Occasionally we have a rage for 17; but it does not last long. Just at present the fashionable age is 40—or say 37; but there are signs of a change. If you were at all good-looking at 27, I should suggest your trying that, and setting a new fashion.

THE OLD WOMAN. I do not believe a word you are saying. However, 27 be it. [*Whisk! the old woman becomes a young one, and so handsome that in the radiance into which her dull yellow halo has suddenly lightened one might almost mistake her for Ann Whitefield.*]

DON JUAN. Doña Ana de Ulloa!

ANA. What? You know me!

DON JUAN. And you forget me!

ANA. I cannot see your face. [*He raises his hat.*] Don Juan Tenorio! Monster! You who slew my father! even here you pursue me.

DON JUAN. I protest I do not pursue you. Allow me to withdraw [*going*].

ANA [*seizing his arm*] You shall not leave me alone in this dreadful place.

DON JUAN. Provided my staying be not interpreted as pursuit.

ANA [*releasing him*] You may well wonder how I can endure your presence. My dear, dear father!

DON JUAN. Would you like to see him?

ANA. My father here!!!

DON JUAN. No: he is in heaven.

ANA. I knew it. My noble father! He is looking down on us now. What must he feel to see his daughter in this place, and in conversation with his murderer!

DON JUAN. By the way, if we should meet him—

ANA. How can we meet him? He is in heaven.

DON JUAN. He condescends to look in upon us here from time to time. Heaven bores him. So let me warn you that if you meet him he will be mortally offended if you speak of me as his murderer! He maintains that he was a much better swordsman than I, and that if his foot had not slipped he would have killed me. No doubt he is right: I was not a good fencer. I never dispute the point; so we are excellent friends.

ANA. It is no dishonor to a soldier to be proud of his skill in arms.

DON JUAN. You would rather not meet him, probably.

ANA. How dare you say that?

DON JUAN. Oh, that is the usual feeling here. You may remember that on earth—though of course we never confessed it—the death of anyone we knew, even those we liked best, was always mingled with a certain satisfaction at being finally done with them.

ANA. Monster! Never, never.

DON JUAN [placidly] I see you recognize the feeling. Yes: a funeral was always a festivity in black, especially the funeral of a relative. At all events, family ties are rarely kept up here. Your father is quite accustomed to this: he will not expect any devotion from you.

ANA. Wretch: I wore mourning for him all my life.

DON JUAN. Yes: it became you. But a life of mourning is one thing: an eternity of it quite another. Besides, here you are as dead as he. Can anything be more ridiculous than one dead person mourning for another? Do not look shocked, my dear Ana; and do not be alarmed: there is plenty of humbug in hell (indeed there is hardly anything else); but the humbug of death and age and change is dropped because here we are all dead and all eternal. You will pick up our ways soon.

ANA. And will all the men call me their dear Ana?

DON JUAN. No. That was a slip of the tongue. I beg your pardon.

ANA [*almost tenderly*] Juan: did you really love me when you behaved so disgracefully to me?

DON JUAN [*impatiently*] Oh, I beg you not to begin talking about love. Here they talk of nothing else but love—its beauty, its holiness, its spirituality, its devil knows what!—excuse me; but it does so bore me. They don't know what they're talking about. I do. They think they have achieved the perfection of love because they have no bodies. Sheer imaginative debauchery! Faugh!

ANA. Has even death failed to refine your soul, Juan? Has the terrible judgment of which my father's statue was the minister taught you no reverence?

DON JUAN. How is that very flattering statue, by the way? Does it still come to supper with naughty people and cast them into this bottomless pit?

ANA. It has been a great expense to me. The boys in the monastery school would not let it alone: the mischievous ones broke it; and the studious ones wrote their names on it. Three new noses in two years, and fingers without end. I had to leave it to its fate at last; and now I fear it is shockingly mutilated. My poor father!

DON JUAN. Hush! Listen! [*Two great chords rolling on syncopated waves of sound break forth: D minor and its dominant: a sound of dreadful joy to all musicians.*] Ha! Mozart's statue music. It is your father. You had better disappear until I prepare him. [*She vanishes.*]

[*From the void comes a living statue of white marble, designed to represent a majestic old man. But he waives his majesty with infinite grace; walks with a featherlike step; and makes every wrinkle in his war worn visage brim over with holiday joyousness. To his sculptor he owes a perfectly trained figure, which he carries erect and trim; and the ends of his moustache curl up, elastic as watchsprings, giving him an air which, but for its Spanish dignity, would be called jaunty. He is on the pleasantest terms with Don Juan. His voice, save for a much more distinguished intonation, is so like the voice of Roebuck Ramsden that it calls attention to the fact that they are not unlike one another in spite of their very different fashions of shaving.*]

DON JUAN. Ah, here you are, my friend. Why don't you learn to sing the splendid music Mozart has written for you?

THE STATUE. Unluckily he has written it for a bass voice. Mine is a counter tenor. Well: have you repented yet?

DON JUAN. I have too much consideration for you to repent, Don Gonzalo. If I did, you would have no excuse for coming from heaven to argue with me.

THE STATUE. True. Remain obdurate, my boy. I wish I had killed you, as I should have done but for an accident. Then I should have come here; and you would have had a statue and a reputation for piety to live up to. Any news?

DON JUAN. Yes: your daughter is dead.

THE STATUE [*puzzled*] My daughter? [*Recollecting*] Oh! the one you were taken with. Let me see: what was her name?

DON JUAN. Ana.

THE STATUE. To be sure: Ana. A goodlooking girl, if I recollect aright. Have you warned Whatshisname— her husband?

DON JUAN. My friend Ottavio? No: I have not seen him since Ana arrived.

[*Ana comes indignantly to light.*]

ANA. What does this mean? Ottavio here and your friend! And you, father, have forgotten my name. You are indeed turned to stone.

THE STATUE. My dear: I am so much more admired in marble than I ever was in my own person that I have retained the shape the sculptor gave me. He was one of the first men of his day: you must acknowledge that.

ANA. Father! Vanity! personal vanity! from you!

THE STATUE. Ah, you outlived that weakness, my daughter: you must be nearly 80 by this time. I was cut off (by an accident) in my 64th year, and am considerably your junior in consequence. Besides, my child, in this place, what our libertine friend here would call the farce of parental wisdom is dropped. Regard me, I beg, as a fellow creature, not as a father.

ANA. You speak as this villain speaks.

THE STATUE. Juan is a sound thinker, Ana. A bad fencer, but a sound thinker.

ANA [*horror creeping upon her*] I begin to understand. These are devils, mocking me. I had better pray.

THE STATUE [*consoling her*] No, no, no, my child: do not pray. If you do, you will throw away the main advantage of this place. Written over the gate here are the words "Leave every hope behind, ye who enter." Only think what a relief that is! For what is hope? A form of moral responsibility. Here there is no hope, and consequently no duty, no work, nothing to be gained by praying, nothing to be lost by doing what you like. Hell, in short, is a place where you have nothing to do but amuse yourself. [*Don Juan sighs deeply.*] You sigh, friend Juan; but if you dwelt in heaven, as I do, you would realize your advantages.

DON JUAN. You are in good spirits to-day, Commander. You are positively brilliant. What is the matter?

THE STATUE. I have come to a momentous decision, my boy. But first, where is our friend the Devil? I must consult him in the matter. And Ana would like to make his acquaintance, no doubt.

ANA. You are preparing some torment for me.

DON JUAN. All that is superstition, Ana. Reassure yourself. Remember: the devil is not so black as he is painted.

THE STATUE. Let us give him a call.

[*At the wave of the statue's hand the great chords roll out again; but this time Mozart's music gets grotesquely adulterated with Gounod's. A scarlet halo begins to glow; and into it the Devil rises, very Mephistophelean, and not at all unlike Mendoza, though not so interesting. He looks older; is getting prematurely bald; and, in spite of an effusion of goodnature and friendliness, is peevish and sensitive when his advances are not reciprocated. He does not inspire much confidence in his powers of hard work or endurance, and is, on the whole, a disagreeably self-indulgent looking person; but he is clever and plausible, though perceptibly less well bred than the two other men, and enormously less vital than the woman.*]

THE DEVIL [*heartily*] Have I the pleasure of again

receiving a visit from the illustrious Commander of Cala-
trava? [*Coldly*] Don Juan, your servant. [*Politely*] And
a strange lady? My respects, Señora.

ANA. Are you—

THE DEVIL [*bowing*] Lucifer, at your service.

ANA. I shall go mad.

THE DEVIL [*gallantly*] Ah, Señora, do not be anxious.
You come to us from earth, full of the prejudices and
terrors of that priest-ridden place. You have heard me
ill spoken of; and yet, believe me, I have hosts of
friends there.

ANA. Yes: you reign in their hearts.

THE DEVIL [*shaking his head*] You flatter me, Señora; but you are mistaken. It is true that the world
cannot get on without me; but it never gives me credit
for that: in its heart it mistrusts and hates me. Its sympathies are all with misery, with poverty, with starvation
of the body and of the heart. I call on it to sympathize
with joy, with love, with happiness, with beauty—

DON JUAN [*nauseated*] Excuse me: I am going. You
know I cannot stand this.

THE DEVIL [*angrily*] Yes: I know that you are no
friend of mine.

THE STATUE. What harm is he doing you, Juan? It
seems to me that he was talking excellent sense when
you interrupted him.

THE DEVIL [*warmly shaking the statue's hand*] Thank
you, my friend: thank you. You have always understood
me: he has always disparaged and avoided me.

DON JUAN. I have treated you with perfect courtesy.

THE DEVIL. Courtesy! What is courtesy? I care nothing for mere courtesy. Give me warmth of heart, true
sincerity, the bond of sympathy with love and joy—

DON JUAN. You are making me ill.

THE DEVIL. There! [*Appealing to the statue*] You
hear, sir! Oh, by what irony of fate was this cold selfish
egotist sent to my kingdom, and you taken to the icy
mansions of the sky!

THE STATUE. I can't complain. I was a hypocrite; and
it served me right to be sent to heaven.

THE DEVIL. Why, sir, do you not join us, and leave
a sphere for which your temperament is too sympathetic,

your heart too warm, your capacity for enjoyment too generous?

THE STATUE. I have this day resolved to do so. In future, excellent Son of the Morning, I am yours. I have left heaven for ever.

THE DEVIL [*again grasping his hand*] Ah, what an honor for me! What a triumph for our cause! Thank you, thank you. And now, my friend—I may call you so at last—could you not persuade him to take the place you have left vacant above?

THE STATUE [*shaking his head*] I cannot conscientiously recommend anybody with whom I am on friendly terms to deliberately make himself dull and uncomfortable.

THE DEVIL. Of course not; but are you sure he would be uncomfortable? Of course you know best: you brought him here originally; and we had the greatest hopes of him. His sentiments were in the best taste of our best people. You remember how he sang? [*He begins to sing in a nasal operatic baritone, tremulous from an eternity of misuse in the French manner.*]

> Vivan le femmine!
> Viva il buon vino!

THE STATUE [*taking up the tune an octave higher in his counter tenor*]

> Sostegno e gloria
> D'umanità.

THE DEVIL. Precisely. Well, he never sings for us now.

DON JUAN. Do you complain of that? Hell is full of musical amateurs: music is the brandy of the damned. May not one lost soul be permitted to abstain?

THE DEVIL. You dare blaspheme against the sublimest of the arts!

DON JUAN [*with cold disgust*] You talk like a hysterical woman fawning on a fiddler.

THE DEVIL. I am not angry. I merely pity you. You have no soul; and you are unconscious of all that you lose. Now you, Señor Commander, are a born musician.

How well you sing! Mozart would be delighted if he were still here; but he moped and went to heaven. Curious how these clever men, whom you would have supposed born to be popular here, have turned out social failures, like Don Juan!

DON JUAN. I am really very sorry to be a social failure.

THE DEVIL. Not that we don't admire your intellect, you know. We do. But I look at the matter from your own point of view. You don't get on with us. The place doesn't suit you. The truth is, you have—I won't say no heart; for we know that beneath all your affected cynicism you have a warm one—

DON JUAN [shrinking] Don't, please don't.

THE DEVIL [nettled] Well, you've no capacity for enjoyment. Will that satisfy you?

DON JUAN. It is a somewhat less insufferable form of cant than the other. But if you'll allow me, I'll take refuge, as usual, in solitude.

THE DEVIL. Why not take refuge in heaven? That's the proper place for you. [To Ana] Come, Señora! could you not persuade him for his own good to try a change of air?

ANA. But can he go to heaven if he wants to?

THE DEVIL. What's to prevent him?

ANA. Can anybody—can I go to heaven if I want to?

THE DEVIL [rather contemptuously] Certainly, if your taste lies that way.

ANA. But why doesn't everybody go to heaven, then?

THE STATUE [chuckling] I can tell you that, my dear. It's because heaven is the most angelically dull place in all creation: that's why.

THE DEVIL. His excellency the Commander puts it with military bluntness; but the strain of living in heaven is intolerable. There is a notion that I was turned out of it; but as a matter of fact nothing could have induced me to stay there. I simply left it and organized this place.

THE STATUE. I don't wonder at it. Nobody could stand an eternity of heaven.

THE DEVIL. Oh, it suits some people. Let us be just, Commander: it is a question of temperament. I don't admire the heavenly temperament: I don't understand it:

I don't know that I particularly want to understand it; but it takes all sorts to make a universe. There is no accounting for tastes: there are people who like it. I think Don Juan would like it.

DON JUAN. But—pardon my frankness—could you really go back there if you desired to; or are the grapes sour?

THE DEVIL. Back there! I often go back there. Have you never read the book of Job? Have you any canonical authority for assuming that there is any barrier between our circle and the other one?

ANA. But surely there is a great gulf fixed.

THE DEVIL. Dear lady: a parable must not be taken literally. The gulf is the difference between the angelic and the diabolic temperament. What more impassable gulf could you have? Think of what you have seen on earth. There is no physical gulf between the philosopher's class room and the bull ring; but the bull fighters do not come to the class room for all that. Have you ever been in the country where I have the largest following—England? There they have great racecourses, and also concert rooms where they play the classical compositions of his Excellency's friend Mozart. Those who go to the racecourses can stay away from them and go to the classical concerts instead if they like: there is no law against it; for Englishmen never will be slaves: they are free to do whatever the Government and public opinion allow them to do. And the classical concert is admitted to be a higher, more cultivated, poetic, intellectual, ennobling place than the racecourse. But do the lovers of racing desert their sport and flock to the concert room? Not they. They would suffer there all the weariness the Commander has suffered in heaven. There is the great gulf of the parable between the two places. A mere physical gulf they could bridge; or at least I could bridge it for them (the earth is full of Devil's Bridges); but the gulf of dislike is impassable and eternal. And that is the only gulf that separates my friends here from those who are invidiously called the blest.

ANA. I shall go to heaven at once.

THE STATUE. My child: one word of warning first. Let me complete my friend Lucifer's similitude of the classical concert. At every one of those concerts in England you will find rows of weary people who are there, not because they really like classical music, but because they think they ought to like it. Well, there is the same thing in heaven. A number of people sit there in glory, not because they are happy, but because they think they owe it to their position to be in heaven. They are almost all English.

THE DEVIL. Yes: the Southerners give it up and join me just as you have done. But the English really do not seem to know when they are thoroughly miserable. An Englishman thinks he is moral when he is only uncomfortable.

THE STATUE. In short, my daughter, if you go to heaven without being naturally qualified for it, you will not enjoy yourself there.

ANA. And who dares say that I am not naturally qualified for it? The most distinguished princes of the Church have never questioned it. I owe it to myself to leave this place at once.

THE DEVIL [offended] As you please, Señora. I should have expected better taste from you.

ANA. Father: I shall expect you to come with me. You cannot stay here. What will people say?

THE STATUE. People! Why, the best people are here—princes of the church and all. So few go to heaven, and so many come here, that the blest, once called a heavenly host, are a continually dwindling minority. The saints, the fathers, the elect of long ago are the cranks, the faddists, the outsiders of to-day.

THE DEVIL. It is true. From the beginning of my career I knew that I should win in the long run by sheer weight of public opinion, in spite of the long campaign of misrepresentation and calumny against me. At bottom the universe is a constitutional one; and with such a majority as mine I cannot be kept permanently out of office.

DON JUAN. I think, Ana, you had better stay here.

ANA [jealously] You do not want me to go with you.

DON JUAN. Surely you do not want to enter heaven in the company of a reprobate like me.

ANA. All souls are equally precious. You repent, do you not?

DON JUAN. My dear Ana, you are silly. Do you suppose heaven is like earth, where people persuade themselves that what is done can be undone by repentance; that what is spoken can be unspoken by withdrawing it; that what is true can be annihilated by a general agreement to give it the lie? No: heaven is the home of the masters of reality: that is why I am going thither.

ANA. Thank you: I am going to heaven for happiness. I have had quite enough of reality on earth.

DON JUAN. Then you must stay here; for hell is the home of the unreal and of the seekers for happiness. It is the only refuge from heaven, which is, as I tell you, the home of the masters of reality, and from earth, which is the home of the slaves of reality. The earth is a nursery in which men and women play at being heroes and heroines, saints and sinners; but they are dragged down from their fool's paradise by their bodies: hunger and cold and thirst, age and decay and disease, death above all, make them slaves of reality: thrice a day meals must be eaten and digested: thrice a century a new generation must be engendered: ages of faith, of romance, and of science are all driven at last to have but one prayer "Make me a healthy animal." But here you escape this tyranny of the flesh; for here you are not an animal at all: you are a ghost, an appearance, an illusion, a convention, deathless, ageless: in a word, bodiless. There are no social questions here, no political questions, no religious questions, best of all, perhaps, no sanitary questions. Here you call your appearance beauty, your emotions love, your sentiments heroism, your aspirations virtue, just as you did on earth; but here there are no hard facts to contradict you, no ironic contrast of your needs with your pretensions, no human comedy, nothing but a perpetual romance, a universal melodrama. As our German friend put it in his poem, "the poetically nonsensical here is good sense; and the Eternal Feminine draws us ever upward and on"—without getting us a step farther. And yet you want to leave this paradise!

ANA. But if hell be so beautiful as this, how glorious must heaven be!

[The Devil, the Statue, and Don Juan all begin to speak at once in violent protest; then stop, abashed.]

DON JUAN. I beg your pardon.

THE DEVIL. Not at all. I interrupted you.

THE STATUE. You were going to say something.

DON JUAN. After you, gentlemen.

THE DEVIL [*to Don Juan*] You have been so eloquent on the advantages of my dominions that I leave you to do equal justice to the drawbacks of the alternative establishment.

DON JUAN. In heaven, as I picture it, dear lady, you live and work instead of playing and pretending. You face things as they are; you escape nothing but glamor; and your steadfastness and your peril are your glory. If the play still goes on here and on earth, and all the world is a stage, heaven is at least behind the scenes. But heaven cannot be described by metaphor. Thither I shall go presently, because there I hope to escape at last from lies and from the tedious, vulgar pursuit of happiness, to spend my eons in contemplation—

THE STATUE. Ugh!

DON JUAN. Señor Commander: I do not blame your disgust: a picture gallery is a dull place for a blind man. But even as you enjoy the contemplation of such roman-tic mirages as beauty and pleasure; so would I enjoy the contemplation of that which interests me above all things: namely, Life: the force that ever strives to attain greater power of contemplating itself. What made this brain of mine, do you think? Not the need to move my limbs; for a rat with half my brains moves as well as I. Not merely the need to do, but the need to know what I do, lest in my blind efforts to live I should be slaying myself.

THE STATUE. You would have slain yourself in your blind efforts to fence but for my foot slipping, my friend.

DON JUAN. Audacious ribald: your laughter will fin-ish in hideous boredom before morning.

THE STATUE. Ha ha! Do you remember how I fright-ened you when I said something like that to you from my pedestal in Seville? It sounds rather flat without my trombones.

DON JUAN. They tell me it generally sounds flat with them, Commander.

ANA. Oh, do not interrupt with these frivolities, father. Is there nothing in heaven but contemplation, Juan?

DON JUAN. In the heaven I seek, no other joy. But there is the work of helping life in its struggle upward. Think of how it wastes and scatters itself, how it raises up obstacles to itself and destroys itself in its ignorance and blindness. It needs a brain, this irresistible force, lest in its ignorance it should resist itself. What a piece of work is man! says the poet. Yes: but what a blunderer! Here is the highest miracle of organization yet attained by life, the most intensely alive thing that exists, the most conscious of all the organisms; and yet, how wretched are his brains! Stupidity made sordid and cruel by the realities learnt from toil and poverty: Imagination resolved to starve sooner than face these realities, piling up illusions to hide them, and calling itself cleverness, genius! And each accusing the other of its own defect: Stupidity accusing Imagination of folly, and Imagination accusing Stupidity of ignorance: whereas, alas! Stupidity has all the knowledge, and Imagination all the intelligence.

THE DEVIL. And a pretty kettle of fish they make of it between them. Did I not say, when I was arranging that affair of Faust's, that all Man's reason has done for him is to make him beastlier than any beast. One splendid body is worth the brains of a hundred dyspeptic, flatulent philosophers.

DON JUAN. You forget that brainless magnificence of body has been tried. Things immeasurably greater than man in every respect but brain have existed and perished. The megatherium, the icthyosaurus have paced the earth with seven-league steps and hidden the day with cloud vast wings. Where are they now? Fossils in museums, and so few and imperfect at that, that a knuckle bone or a tooth of one of them is prized beyond the lives of a thousand soldiers. These things lived and wanted to live; but for lack of brains they did not know how to carry out their purpose, and so destroyed themselves.

THE DEVIL. And is Man any the less destroying himself for all this boasted brain of his? Have you walked up and down upon the earth lately? I have; and I have examined Man's wonderful inventions. And I tell you that in the arts of life man invents nothing; but in the

arts of death he outdoes Nature herself, and produces
by chemistry and machinery all the slaughter of plague,
pestilence and famine. The peasant I tempt to-day eats
and drinks what was eaten and drunk by the peasants
of ten thousand years ago; and the house he lives in has
not altered as much in a thousand centuries as the fashion of a lady's bonnet in a score of weeks. But when he
goes out to slay, he carries a marvel of mechanism that
lets loose at the touch of his finger all the hidden molec-
ular energies, and leaves the javelin, the arrow, the blow-
pipe of his fathers far behind. In the arts of peace Man
is a bungler. I have seen his cotton factories and the like,
with machinery that a greedy dog could have invented if
it had wanted money instead of food. I know his clumsy
typewriters and bungling locomotives and tedious bicycles:
they are toys compared to the Maxim gun, the submarine
torpedo boat. There is nothing in Man's industrial machinery but his greed and sloth: his heart is in his weapons.
This marvellous force of Life of which you boast is a
force of Death: Man measures his strength by his destructiveness. What is his religion? An excuse for hating
me. What is his law? An excuse for hanging you. What is
his morality? Gentility! an excuse for consuming without
producing. What is his art? An excuse for gloating over
pictures of slaughter. What are his politics? Either the
worship of a despot because a despot can kill, or parliamentary cockfighting. I spent an evening lately in a certain celebrated legislature, and heard the pot lecturing
the kettle for its blackness, and ministers answering
questions. When I left I chalked up on the door the old
nursery saying "Ask no questions and you will be told
no lies." I bought a sixpenny family magazine, and found
it full of pictures of young men shooting and stabbing
one another. I saw a man die: he was a London bricklay-
er's laborer with seven children. He left seventeen
pounds club money; and his wife spent it all on his funeral and went into the workhouse with the children
next day. She would not have spent sevenpence on her
children's schooling: the law had to force her to let them
be taught gratuitously; but on death she spent all she
had. Their imagination glows, their energies rise up at
the idea of death, these people: they love it; and the

more horrible it is the more they enjoy it. Hell is a place
far above their comprehension: they derive their notion
of it from two of the greatest fools that ever lived, an
Italian and an Englishman. The Italian described it as a
place of mud, frost, filth, fire, and venomous serpents:
all torture. This ass, when he was not lying about me,
was maundering about some woman whom he saw once
in the street. The Englishman described me as being expelled from Heaven by cannons and gunpowder; and to
this day every Briton believes that the whole of his silly
story is in the Bible. What else he says I do not know;
for it is all in a long poem which neither I nor anyone
else ever succeeded in wading through. It is the same in
everything. The highest form of literature is the tragedy,
a play in which everybody is murdered at the end. In the
old chronicles you read of earthquakes and pestilences,
and are told that these shewed the power and majesty of
God and the littleness of Man. Nowadays the chronicles
describe battles. In a battle two bodies of men shoot at
one another with bullets and explosive shells until one
body runs away, when the others chase the fugitives on
horseback and cut them to pieces as they fly. And this,
the chronicle concludes, shews the greatness and majesty
of empires, and the littleness of the vanquished. Over
such battles the people run about the streets yelling with
delight, and egg their Governments on to spend hun-
dreds of millions of money in the slaughter, whilst the
strongest Ministers dare not spend an extra penny in the
pound against the poverty and pestilence through which
they themselves daily walk. I could give you a thousand
instances; but they all come to the same thing: the power
that governs the earth is not the power of Life but of
Death; and the inner need that has nerved Life to the
effort of organizing itself into the human being is not
the need for higher life but for a more efficient engine
of destruction. The plague, the famine, the earthquake,
the tempest were too spasmodic in their action; the tiger
and crocodile were too easily satiated and not cruel
enough: something more constantly, more ruthlessly,
more ingeniously destructive was needed; and that something was Man, the inventor of the rack, the stake, the
gallows, and the electrocutor; of the sword and gun;

above all, of justice, duty, patriotism and all the other isms by which even those who are clever enough to be humanely disposed are persuaded to become the most destructive of all the destroyers.

DON JUAN. Pshaw! all this is old. Your weak side, my diabolic friend, is that you have always been a gull: you take Man at his own valuation. Nothing would flatter him more than your opinion of him. He loves to think of himself as bold and bad. He is neither one nor the other: he is only a coward. Call him tyrant, murderer, pirate, bully; and he will adore you, and swagger about with the consciousness of having the blood of the old sea kings in his veins. Call him liar and thief; and he will only take an action against you for libel. But call him coward; and he will go mad with rage: he will face death to outface that stinging truth. Man gives every reason for his conduct save one, every excuse for his crimes save one, every plea for his safety save one; and that one is his cowardice. Yet all his civilization is founded on his cowardice, on his abject tameness, which he calls his respectability. There are limits to what a mule or an ass will stand: but Man will suffer himself to be degraded until his vileness becomes so loathsome to his oppressors that they themselves are forced to reform it.

THE DEVIL. Precisely. And these are the creatures in whom you discover what you call a Life Force!

DON JUAN. Yes; for now comes the most surprising part of the whole business.

THE STATUE. What's that?

DON JUAN. Why, that you can make any of these cowards brave by simply putting an idea into his head.

THE STATUE. Stuff! As an old soldier I admit the cowardice: it's as universal as sea sickness, and matters just as little. But that about putting an idea into a man's head is stuff and nonsense. In a battle all you need to make you fight is a little hot blood and the knowledge that it's more dangerous to lose than to win.

DON JUAN. That is perhaps why battles are so useless. But men never really overcome fear until they imagine they are fighting to further a universal purpose—fighting for an idea, as they call it. Why was the Crusader braver than the pirate? Because he fought, not for himself, but for the Cross. What force was it that met him with a valor as reckless as his own? The force of men who fought, not for themselves, but for Islam. They took Spain from us, though we were fighting for our very hearths and homes; but when we, too, fought for that mighty idea, a Catholic Church, we swept them back to Africa.

THE DEVIL [*ironically*] What! you a Catholic, Señor Don Juan! A devotee! My congratulations.

THE STATUE [*seriously*] Come come! as a soldier, I can listen to nothing against the Church.

DON JUAN. Have no fear, Commander: this idea of a Catholic Church will survive Islam, will survive the Cross, will survive even that vulgar pageant of incompetent schoolboyish gladiators which you call the Army.

THE STATUE. Juan: you will force me to call you to account for this.

DON JUAN. Useless: I cannot fence. Every idea for which Man will die will be a Catholic idea. When the Spaniard learns at last that he is no better than the Saracen, and his prophet no better than Mahomet, he will arise, more Catholic than ever, and die on a barricade across the filthy slum he starves in, for universal liberty and equality.

THE STATUE. Bosh!

DON JUAN. What you call bosh is the only thing men dare die for. Later on, Liberty will not be Catholic enough: men will die for human perfection, to which they will sacrifice all their liberty gladly.

THE DEVIL. Ay: they will never be at a loss for an excuse for killing one another.

DON JUAN. What of that? It is not death that matters, but the fear of death. It is not killing and dying that degrades us, but base living, and accepting the wages and profits of degradation. Better ten dead men than one live slave or his master. Men shall yet rise up, father against son and brother against brother, and kill one another for the great Catholic idea of abolishing slavery.

THE DEVIL. Yes, when the Liberty and Equality of which you prate shall have made free white Christians cheaper in the labor market than black heathen slaves sold by auction at the block.

DON JUAN. Never fear! the white laborer shall have his turn too. But I am not now defending the illusory forms the great ideas take. I am giving you examples of the fact that this creature Man, who in his own selfish affairs is a coward to the backbone, will fight for an idea like a hero. He may be abject as a citizen; but he is dangerous as a fanatic. He can only be enslaved whilst he is spiritually weak enough to listen to reason. I tell you, gentlemen, if you can shew a man a piece of what he now calls God's work to do, and what he will later on call by many new names, you can make him entirely reckless of the consequences to himself personally.

ANA. Yes: he shirks all his responsibilities, and leaves his wife to grapple with them.

THE STATUE. Well said, daughter. Do not let him talk you out of your common sense.

THE DEVIL. Alas! Señor Commander, now that we have got on to the subject of Woman, he will talk more than ever. However, I confess it is for me the one supremely interesting subject.

DON JUAN. To a woman, Señora, man's duties and responsibilities begin and end with the task of getting bread for her children. To her, Man is only a means to the end of getting children and rearing them.

ANA. Is that your idea of a woman's mind? I call it cynical and disgusting materialism.

DON JUAN. Pardon me, Ana: I said nothing about a woman's whole mind. I spoke of her view of Man as a separate sex. It is no more cynical than her view of herself as above all things a Mother. Sexually, Woman is Nature's contrivance for perpetuating its highest achievement. Sexually, Man is Woman's contrivance for fulfilling Nature's behest in the most economical way. She knows by instinct that far back in the evolutional process she invented him, differentiated him, created him in order to produce something better than the single-sexed process can produce. Whilst he fulfils the purpose for which she made him, he is welcome to his dreams, his follies, his ideals, his heroisms, provided that the keystone of them all is the worship of woman, of motherhood, of the family, of the hearth. But how rash and dangerous it was to invent a separate creature whose sole function was her own impregnation! For mark what has happened. First, Man has multiplied on her hands until there are as many men as women; so that she has been unable to employ for her purposes more than a fraction of the immense energy she has left at his disposal by saving him the exhausting labor of gestation. This superfluous energy has gone to his brain and to his muscle. He has become too strong to be controlled by her bodily, and too imaginative and mentally vigorous to be content with mere self-reproduction. He has created civilization without consulting her, taking her domestic labor for granted as the foundation of it.

ANA. That is true, at all events.

THE DEVIL. Yes; and this civilization! what is it, after all?

DON JUAN. After all, an excellent peg to hang your cynical commonplaces on; but before all, it is an attempt on Man's part to make himself something more than the mere instrument of Woman's purpose. So far, the result of Life's continual effort not only to maintain itself, but to achieve higher and higher organization and completer self-consciousness, is only, at best, a doubtful campaign between its forces and those of Death and Degeneration. The battles in this campaign are mere blunders, mostly won, like actual military battles, in spite of the commanders.

THE STATUE. That is a dig at me. No matter: go on, go on.

DON JUAN. It is a dig at a much higher power than you, Commander. Still, you must have noticed in your profession that even a stupid general can win battles when the enemy's general is a little stupider.

THE STATUE [*very seriously*] Most true, Juan, most true. Some donkeys have amazing luck.

DON JUAN. Well, the Life Force is stupid; but it is not so stupid as the forces of Death and Degeneration. Besides, these are in its pay all the time. And so Life wins, after a fashion. What mere copiousness of fecundity can supply and mere greed preserve, we possess. The survival of whatever form of civilization can produce the best rifle and the best fed riflemen is assured.

THE DEVIL. Exactly! the survival, not of the most effective means of Life but of the most effective means of Death. You always come back to my point, in spite of your wrigglings and evasions and sophistries, not to mention the intolerable length of your speeches.

DON JUAN. Oh come! who began making long speeches? However, if I overtax your intellect, you can leave us and seek the society of love and beauty and the rest of your favorite boredoms.

THE DEVIL [much offended] This is not fair, Don Juan, and not civil. I am also on the intellectual plane. Nobody can appreciate it more than I do. I am arguing fairly with you, and, I think, utterly refuting you. Let us go on for another hour if you like.

DON JUAN. Good: let us.

THE STATUE. Not that I see any prospect of your coming to any point in particular, Juan. Still, since in this place, instead of merely killing time we have to kill eternity, go ahead by all means.

DON JUAN [somewhat impatiently] My point, you marble-headed old masterpiece, is only a step ahead of you. Are we agreed that Life is a force which has made innumerable experiments in organizing itself; that the mammoth and the man, the mouse and the megatherium, the flies and the fleas and the Fathers of the Church, are all more or less successful attempts to build up that raw force into higher and higher individuals, the ideal individual being omnipotent, omniscient, infallible, and withal completely, unilludedly self-conscious: in short, a god?

THE DEVIL. I agree, for the sake of argument.

THE STATUE. I agree, for the sake of avoiding argument.

ANA. I most emphatically disagree as regards the Fathers of the Church; and I must beg you not to drag them into the argument.

DON JUAN. I did so purely for the sake of alliteration, Ana; and I shall make no further allusion to them. And now, since we are, with that exception, agreed so far, will you not agree with me further that Life has not measured the success of its attempts at godhead by the beauty or bodily perfection of the result, since in both these respects the birds, as our friend Aristophanes long ago pointed out, are so extraordinarily superior, with their power of flight and their lovely plumage, and, may I add, the touching poetry of their loves and nestings, that it is inconceivable that Life, having once produced them, should, if love and beauty were her object, start off on another line and labor at the clumsy elephant and the hideous ape, whose grandchildren we are?

ANA. Aristophanes was a heathen; and you, Juan, I am afraid, are very little better.

THE DEVIL. You conclude, then, that Life was driving at clumsiness and ugliness?

DON JUAN. No, perverse devil that you are, a thousand times no. Life was driving at brains—at its darling object: an organ by which it can attain not only self-consciousness but self-understanding.

THE STATUE. This is metaphysics, Juan. Why the devil should— [to The Devil] I beg your pardon.

THE DEVIL. Pray don't mention it. I have always regarded the use of my name to secure additional emphasis as a high compliment to me. It is quite at your service, Commander.

THE STATUE. Thank you: that's very good of you. Even in heaven, I never quite got out of my old military habits of speech. What I was going to ask Juan was why Life should bother itself about getting a brain. Why should it want to understand itself? Why not be content to enjoy itself?

DON JUAN. Without a brain, Commander, you would enjoy yourself without knowing it, and so lose all the fun.

THE STATUE. True, most true. But I am quite content with brain enough to know that I'm enjoying myself. I don't want to understand why. In fact, I'd rather not. My experience is that one's pleasures don't bear thinking about.

DON JUAN. That is why intellect is so unpopular. But to Life, the force behind the Man, intellect is a necessity, because without it he blunders into death. Just as Life, after ages of struggle, evolved that wonderful bodily organ the eye, so that the living organism could see where it was going and what was coming to help or threaten it, and thus avoid a thousand dangers that formerly slew it, so it is evolving today a mind's eye that shall see, not the physical world, but the purpose of Life, and thereby enable the individual to work for that purpose instead of thwarting and baffling it by setting up shortsighted personal aims as at present. Even as it is, only one sort of man has ever been happy, has ever been universally respected among all the conflicts of interests and illusions.

THE STATUE. You mean the military man.

DON JUAN. Commander: I do not mean the military man. When the military man approaches, the world locks up its spoons and packs off its womankind. No: I sing, not arms and the hero, but the philosophic man: he who seeks in contemplation to discover the inner will of the world, in invention to discover the means of fulfilling that will, and in action to do that will by the so-discovered means. Of all other sorts of men I declare myself tired. They are tedious failures. When I was on earth, professors of all sorts prowled round me feeling for an unhealthy spot in me on which they could fasten. The doctors of medicine bade me consider what I must do to save my body, and offered me quack cures for imaginary diseases. I replied that I was not a hypochondriac; so they called me Ignoramus and went their way. The doctors of divinity bade me consider what I must do to save my soul; but I was not a spiritual hypochondriac any more than a bodily one, and would not trouble myself about that either; so they called me Atheist and went their way. After them came the politician, who said there was only one purpose in Nature, and that was to get him into parliament. I told him I did not care whether he got into parliament or not; so he called me Mugwump and went his way. Then came the romantic man, the Artist, with his love songs and his paintings and his poems; and with him I had great delight for many years, and some profit; for I cultivated my senses for his sake; and his songs taught me to hear better, his paintings to see better, and his poems to feel more deeply. But he led me at last into the worship of Woman.

ANA. Juan!

DON JUAN. Yes: I came to believe that in her voice was all the music of the song, in her face all the beauty of the painting, and in her soul all the emotion of the poem.

ANA. And you were disappointed, I suppose. Well, was it her fault that you attributed all these perfections to her?

DON JUAN. Yes, partly. For with a wonderful instinctive cunning, she kept silent and allowed me to glorify her; to mistake my own visions, thoughts, and feelings for hers. Now my friend the romantic man was often too poor or too timid to approach those women who were beautiful or refined enough to seem to realize his ideal; and so he went to his grave believing in his dream. But I was more favored by nature and circumstance. I was of noble birth and rich; and when my person did not please, my conversation flattered, though I generally found myself fortunate in both.

THE STATUE. Coxcomb!

DON JUAN. Yes; but even my coxcombry pleased. Well, I found that when I had touched a woman's imagination, she would allow me to persuade myself that she loved me; but when my suit was granted she never said "I am happy: my love is satisfied": she always said, first, "At last, the barriers are down," and second, "When will you come again?"

ANA. That is exactly what men say.

DON JUAN. I protest I never said it. But all women say it. Well, these two speeches always alarmed me; for the first meant that the lady's impulse had been solely to throw down my fortifications and gain my citadel; and the second openly announced that henceforth she regarded me as her property, and counted my time as already wholly at her disposal.

THE DEVIL. That is where your want of heart came in.

THE STATUE [*shaking his head*] You shouldn't repeat what a woman says, Juan.

ANA [*severely*] It should be sacred to you.

THE STATUE. Still, they certainly do always say it. I

never minded the barriers; but there was always a slight shock about the other, unless one was very hard hit indeed.

DON JUAN. Then the lady, who had been happy and idle enough before, became anxious, preoccupied with me, always intriguing, conspiring, pursuing, watching, waiting, bent wholly on making sure of her prey—I being the prey, you understand. Now this was not what I had bargained for. It may have been very proper and very natural; but it was not music, painting, poetry and joy incarnated in a beautiful woman. I ran away from it. I ran away from it very often: in fact I became famous for running away from it.

ANA. Infamous, you mean.

DON JUAN. I did not run away from you. Do you blame me for running away from the others?

ANA. Nonsense, man. You are talking to a woman of 77 now. If you had had the chance, you would have run away from me too—if I had let you. You would not have found it so easy with me as with some of the others. If men will not be faithful to their home and their duties, they must be made to be. I daresay you all want to marry lovely incarnations of music and painting and poetry. Well, you can't have them, because they don't exist. If flesh and blood is not good enough for you you must go without: that's all. Women have to put up with flesh-and-blood husbands—and little enough of that too, sometimes; and you will have to put up with flesh-and-blood wives. [*The Devil looks dubious. The Statue makes a wry face.*] I see you don't like that, any of you; but it's true, for all that; so if you don't like it you can lump it.

DON JUAN. My dear lady, you have put my whole case against romance into a few sentences. That is just why I turned my back on the romantic man with the artist nature, as he called his infatuation. I thanked him for teaching me to use my eyes and ears; but I told him that his beauty worshipping and happiness hunting and woman idealizing was not worth a dump as a philosophy of life; so he called me Philistine and went his way.

ANA. It seems that Woman taught you something, too, with all her defects.

DON JUAN. She did more: she interpreted all the other teaching for me. Ah, my friends, when the barriers were down for the first time, what an astounding illumination! I had been prepared for infatuation, for intoxication, for all the illusions of love's young dream; and lo! never was my perception clearer, nor my criticism more ruthless. The most jealous rival of my mistress never saw every blemish in her more keenly than I. I was not duped: I took her without chloroform.

ANA. But you did take her.

DON JUAN. That was the revelation. Up to that moment I had never lost the sense of being my own master; never consciously taken a single step until my reason had examined and approved it. I had come to believe that I was a purely rational creature: a thinker! I said, with the foolish philosopher, "I think; therefore I am." It was Woman who taught me to say "I am; therefore I think." And also "I would think more; therefore I must be more."

THE STATUE. This is extremely abstract and metaphysical, Juan. If you would stick to the concrete, and put your discoveries in the form of entertaining anecdotes about your adventures with women, your conversation would be easier to follow.

DON JUAN. Bah! what need I add? Do you not understand that when I stood face to face with Woman, every fibre in my clear critical brain warned me to spare her and save myself. My morals said No. My conscience said No. My chivalry and pity for her said No. My prudent regard for myself said No. My ear, practised on a thousand songs and symphonies; my eye, exercised on a thousand paintings; tore her voice, her features, her color to shreds. I caught all those tell-tale resemblances to her father and mother by which I knew what she would be like in thirty years time. I noted the gleam of gold from a dead tooth in the laughing mouth: I made curious observations of the strange odors of the chemistry of the nerves. The visions of my romantic reveries, in which I had trod the plains of heaven with a deathless, ageless creature of coral and ivory, deserted me in that supreme hour. I remembered them and desperately strove to recover their illusion; but they now seemed the emptiest of inventions: my judgment was not to be corrupted: my brain still said No on every issue. And whilst I was in the act of framing my excuse to the lady, Life seized me and threw me into her arms as a sailor throws a scrap of fish into the mouth of a seabird.

THE STATUE. You might as well have gone without thinking such a lot about it, Juan. You are like all the clever men: you have more brains than is good for you.

THE DEVIL. And were you not the happier for the experience, Señor Don Juan?

DON JUAN. The happier, no: the wiser, yes. That moment introduced me for the first time to myself, and, through myself, to the world. I saw then how useless it is to attempt to impose conditions on the irresistible force of Life; to preach prudence, careful selection, virtue, honor, chastity—

ANA. Don Juan: a word against chastity is an insult to me.

DON JUAN. I say nothing against your chastity, Señora, since it took the form of a husband and twelve children. What more could you have done had you been the most abandoned of women?

ANA. I could have had twelve husbands and no children: that's what I could have done, Juan. And let me tell you that that would have made all the difference to the earth which I replenished.

THE STATUE. Bravo Ana! Juan: you are floored, quelled, annihilated.

DON JUAN. No; for though that difference is the true essential difference—Doña Ana has, I admit, gone straight to the real point—yet it is not a difference of love or chastity, or even constancy; for twelve children by twelve different husbands would have replenished the earth perhaps more effectively. Suppose my friend Ottavio had died when you were thirty, you would never have remained a widow: you were too beautiful. Suppose the successor of Ottavio had·died when you were forty, you would still have been irresistible; and a woman who marries twice marries three times if she becomes free to do so. Twelve lawful children borne by one highly respectable lady to three different fathers is not impossible nor condemned by public opinion. That such a lady may be more law abiding than the poor girl whom we used to spurn into the gutter for bearing one unlawful infant is no doubt true; but dare you say she is less self-indulgent?

ANA. She is less virtuous: that is enough for me.

DON JUAN. In that case, what is virtue but the Trade Unionism of the married? Let us face the facts, dear Ana. The Life Force respects marriage only because marriage is a contrivance of its own to secure the greatest number of children and the closest care of them. For honor, chastity and all the rest of your moral figments it cares not a rap. Marriage is the most licentious of human institutions—

ANA. Juan!

THE STATUE [*protesting*] Really!—

DON JUAN [*determinedly*] I say the most licentious of human institutions: that is the secret of its popularity. And a woman seeking a husband is the most unscrupulous of all the beasts of prey. The confusion of marriage with morality has done more to destroy the conscience of the human race than any other single error. Come, Ana! do not look shocked: you know better than any of us that marriage is a mantrap baited with simulated accomplishments and delusive idealizations. When your sainted mother, by dint of scoldings and punishments, forced you to learn how to play half a dozen pieces on the spinet—which she hated as much as you did—had she any other purpose than to delude your suitors into the belief that your husband would have in his home an angel who would fill it with melody, or at least play him to sleep after dinner? You married my friend Ottavio: well, did you ever open the spinet from the hour when the Church united him to you?

ANA. You are a fool, Juan. A young married woman has something else to do than sit at the spinet without any support for her back; so she gets out of the habit of playing.

DON JUAN. Not if she loves music. No: believe me, she only throws away the bait when the bird is in the net.

ANA [*bitterly*] And men, I suppose, never throw off the mask when *their* bird is in the net. The husband never becomes negligent, selfish, brutal—oh never!

DON JUAN. What do these recriminations prove, Ana? Only that the hero is as gross an imposture as the heroine.

ANA. It is all nonsense: most marriages are perfectly comfortable.

DON JUAN. "Perfectly" is a strong expression, Ana. What you mean is that sensible people make the best of one another. Send me to the galleys and chain me to the felon whose number happens to be next before mine; and I must accept the inevitable and make the best of the companionship. Many such companionships, they tell me, are touchingly affectionate; and most are at least tolerably friendly. But that does not make a chain a desirable ornament nor the galleys an abode of bliss. Those who talk most about the blessings of marriage and the constancy of its vows are the very people who declare that if the chain were broken and the prisoners left free to choose, the whole social fabric would fly asunder. You cannot have the argument both ways. If the prisoner is happy, why lock him in? If he is not, why pretend that he is?

ANA. At all events, let me take an old woman's privilege again, and tell you flatly that marriage peoples the world and debauchery does not.

DON JUAN. How if a time come when this shall cease to be true? Do you not know that where there is a will there is a way—that whatever Man really wishes to do he will finally discover a means of doing? Well, you have done your best, you virtuous ladies, and others of your way of thinking, to bend Man's mind wholly towards honorable love as the highest good, and to understand by honorable love romance and beauty and happiness in the possession of beautiful, refined, delicate, affectionate women. You have taught women to value their own youth, health, shapeliness, and refinement above all things. Well, what place have squalling babies and household cares in this exquisite paradise of the senses and emotions? Is it not the inevitable end of it all that the human will shall say to the human brain: Invent me a means by which I can have love, beauty, romance, emotion, passion without their wretched penalties, their expenses, their worries, their trials, their illnesses and agonies and risks of death, their retinue of servants and nurses and doctors and schoolmasters.

THE DEVIL. All this, Señor Don Juan, is realized here in my realm.

DON JUAN. Yes, at the cost of death. Man will not take it at that price: he demands the romantic delights of your hell whilst he is still on earth. Well, the means will be found: the brain will not fail when the will is in earnest. The day is coming when great nations will find their numbers dwindling from census to census; when the six roomed villa will rise in price above the family mansion; when the viciously reckless poor and the stupidly pious rich will delay the extinction of the race only by degrading it; whilst the boldly prudent, the thriftily selfish and ambitious, the imaginative and poetic, the lovers of money and solid comfort, the worshippers of success, of art, and of love, will all oppose to the Force of Life the device of sterility.

THE STATUE. That is all very eloquent, my young friend; but if you had lived to Ana's age, or even to mine, you would have learned that the people who get rid of the fear of poverty and children and all the other family troubles, and devote themselves to having a good time of it, only leave their minds free for the fear of old age and ugliness and impotence and death. The childless laborer is more tormented by his wife's idleness and her constant demands for amusement and distraction than he could be by twenty children; and his wife is more wretched than he. I have had my share of vanity; for as a young man I was admired by women; and as a statue I am praised by art critics. But I confess that had I found nothing to do in the world but wallow in these delights I should have cut my throat. When I married Ana's mother—or perhaps, to be strictly correct, I should rather say when I at last gave in and allowed Ana's mother to marry me—I knew that I was planting thorns in my pillow, and that marriage for me, a swaggering young officer thitherto unvanquished, meant defeat and capture.

ANA [scandalized] Father!

THE STATUE. I am sorry to shock you, my love; but since Juan has stripped every rag of decency from the discussion I may as well tell the frozen truth.

ANA. Hmf! I suppose I was one of the thorns.

THE STATUE. By no means: you were often a rose. You see, your mother had most of the trouble you gave.

DON JUAN. Then may I ask, Commander, why you have left Heaven to come here and wallow, as you express it, in sentimental beatitudes which you confess would once have driven you to cut your throat?

THE STATUE [struck by this] Egad, that's true.

THE DEVIL [alarmed] What! You are going back from your word! [To Don Juan] And all your philosophizing has been nothing but a mask for proselytizing! [To the Statue] Have you forgotten already the hideous dulness from which I am offering you a refuge here? [To Don Juan] And does your demonstration of the approaching sterilization and extinction of mankind lead to anything better than making the most of those pleasures of art and love which you yourself admit refined you, elevated you, developed you?

DON JUAN. I never demonstrated the extinction of mankind. Life cannot will its own extinction either in its blind amorphous state or in any of the forms into which it has organized itself. I had not finished when His Excellency interrupted me.

THE STATUE. I begin to doubt whether you ever will finish, my friend. You are extremely fond of hearing yourself talk.

DON JUAN. True; but since you have endured so much, you may as well endure to the end. Long before this sterilization which I described becomes more than a clearly foreseen possibility, the reaction will begin. The great central purpose of breeding the race, ay, breeding it to heights now deemed superhuman: that purpose which is now hidden in a mephitic cloud of love and romance and prudery and fastidiousness, will break through into clear sunlight as a purpose no longer to be confused with the gratification of personal fancies, the impossible realization of boys' and girls' dreams of bliss, or the need of older people for companionship or money. The plain-spoken marriage services of the ver-

nacular Churches will no longer be abbreviated and half
suppressed as indelicate. The sober decency, earnestness
and authority of their declaration of the real purpose
of marriage will be honored and accepted, whilst their
romantic vowings and pledgings and until-death-do-us-
partings and the like will be expunged as unbearable
frivolities. Do my sex the justice to admit, Señora, that
we have always recognized that the sex relation is not a
personal or friendly relation at all.

ANA. Not a personal or friendly relation! What relation is more personal? more sacred? more holy?

DON JUAN. Sacred and holy, if you like, Ana, but
not personally friendly. Your relation to God is sacred
and holy: dare you call it personally friendly? In the sex
relation the universal creative energy, of which the parties are both the helpless agents, over-rides and sweeps
away all personal considerations and dispenses with all
personal relations. The pair may be utter strangers to
one another, speaking different languages, differing in
race and color, in age and disposition, with no bond
between them but a possibility of that fecundity for the
sake of which the Life Force throws them into one another's arms at the exchange of a glance. Do we not
recognize this by allowing marriages to be made by parents without consulting the woman? Have you not often
expressed your disgust at the immorality of the English
nation, in which women and men of noble birth become
acquainted and court each other like peasants? And how
much does even the peasant know of his bride or she of
him before he engages himself? Why, you would not
make a man your lawyer or your family doctor on so
slight an acquaintance as you would fall in love with and
marry him!

ANA. Yes, Juan: we know the libertine's philosophy.
Always ignore the consequences to the woman.

DON JUAN. The consequences, yes: they justify her
fierce grip of the man. But surely you do not call that
attachment a sentimental one. As well call the policeman's attachment to his prisoner a love relation.

ANA. You see you have to confess that marriage is
necessary, though, according to you, love is the slightest
of all the relations.

DON JUAN. How do you know that it is not the greatest of all the relations? far too great to be a personal matter. Could your father have served his country if he had refused to kill any enemy of Spain unless he personally hated him? Can a woman serve her country if she refuses to marry any man she does not personally love? You know it is not so: the woman of noble birth marries as the man of noble birth fights, on political and family grounds, not on personal ones.

THE STATUE [impressed] A very clever point that, Juan: I must think it over. You are really full of ideas. How did you come to think of this one?

DON JUAN. I learnt it by experience. When I was on earth, and made those proposals to ladies which, though universally condemned, have made me so interesting a hero of legend, I was not infrequently met in some such way as this. The lady would say that she would countenance my advances, provided they were honorable. On inquiring what that proviso meant, I found that it meant that I proposed to get possession of her property if she had any, or to undertake her support for life if she had not; that I desired her continual companionship, counsel and conversation to the end of my days, and would bind myself under penalties to be always enraptured by them; and, above all, that I would turn my back on all other women for ever for her sake. I did not object to these conditions because they were exorbitant and inhuman: it was their extraordinary irrelevance that prostrated me. I invariably replied with perfect frankness that I had never dreamt of any of these things; that unless the lady's character and intellect were equal or superior to my own, her conversation must degrade and her counsel mislead me; that her constant companionship might, for all I knew, become intolerably tedious to me; that I could not answer for my feelings for a week in advance, much less to the end of my life; that to cut me off from all natural and unconstrained relations with the rest of my fellow creatures would narrow and warp me if I submitted to it, and, if not, would bring me under the curse of clandestinity; that, finally, my proposals to her were wholly unconnected with any of these matters, and were the outcome of a perfectly simple impulse of my manhood towards her womanhood.

ANA. You mean that it was an immoral impulse.

DON JUAN. Nature, my dear lady, is what you call immoral. I blush for it; but I cannot help it. Nature is a pander, Time a wrecker, and Death a murderer. I have always preferred to stand up to those facts and build institutions on their recognition. You prefer to propitiate the three devils by proclaiming their chastity, their thrift, and their loving kindness; and to base your institutions on these flatteries. Is it any wonder that the institutions do not work smoothly?

THE STATUE. What used the ladies to say, Juan?

DON JUAN. Oh come! Confidence for confidence. First tell me what you used to say to the ladies.

THE STATUE. I! Oh, I swore that I would be faithful to the death; that I should die if they refused me; that no woman could ever be to me what she was—

ANA. She! Who?

THE STATUE. Whoever it happened to be at the time, my dear. I had certain things I always said. One of them was that even when I was eighty, one white hair of the woman I loved would make me tremble more than the thickest gold tress from the most beautiful young head. Another was that I could not bear the thought of anyone else being the mother of my children.

DON JUAN [revolted] You old rascal!

THE STATUE [stoutly] Not a bit; for I really believed it with all my soul at the moment. I had a heart: not like you. And it was this sincerity that made me successful.

DON JUAN. Sincerity! To be fool enough to believe a ramping, stamping, thumping lie: that is what you call sincerity! To be so greedy for a woman that you deceive yourself in your eagerness to deceive her: sincerity, you call it!

THE STATUE. Oh, damn your sophistries! I was a man in love, not a lawyer. And the women loved me for it, bless them!

DON JUAN. They made you think so. What will you say when I tell you that though I played the lawyer so callously, they made me think so too? I also had my moments of infatuation in which I gushed nonsense and believed it. Sometimes the desire to give pleasure by saying beautiful things so rose in me on the flood of emotion that I said them recklessly. At other times I argued against myself with a devilish coldness that drew tears. But I found it just as hard to escape in the one case as in the others. When the lady's instinct was set on me, there was nothing for it but lifelong servitude or flight.

ANA. You dare boast, before me and my father, that every woman found you irresistible.

DON JUAN. Am I boasting? It seems to me that I cut the most pitiable of figures. Besides, I·said "when the lady's instinct was set on me." It was not always so; and then, heavens! what transports of virtuous indignation! what overwhelming defiance to the dastardly seducer! what scenes of Imogen and Iachimo!

ANA. I made no scenes. I simply called my father.

DON JUAN. And he came, sword in hand, to vindicate outraged honor and morality by murdering me.

THE STATUE. Murdering! What do you mean? Did I kill you or did you kill me?

DON JUAN. Which of us was the better fencer?

THE STATUE. I was.

DON JUAN. Of course you were. And yet you, the hero of those scandalous adventures you have just been relating to us, you had the effrontery to pose as the avenger of outraged morality and condemn me to death! You would have slain me but for an accident.

THE STATUE. I was expected to, Juan. That is how things were arranged on earth. I was not a social reformer; and I always did what it was customary for a gentleman to do.

DON JUAN. That may account for your attacking me, but not for the revolting hypocrisy of your subsequent proceedings as a statue.

THE STATUE. That all came of my going to heaven.

THE DEVIL. I still fail to see, Señor Don Juan, that these episodes in your earthly career and in that of the Señor Commander in any way discredit my view of life. Here, I repeat, you have all that you sought without anything that you shrank from.

DON JUAN. On the contrary, here I have everything that disappointed me without anything that I have not already tried and found wanting. I tell you that as long as I can conceive something better than myself I cannot be easy unless I am striving to bring it into existence or clearing the way for it. That is the law of my life. That is the working within me of Life's incessant aspiration to higher organization, wider, deeper, intenser self-consciousness, and clearer self-understanding. It was the supremacy of this purpose that reduced love for me to the mere pleasure of a moment, art for me to the mere schooling of my faculties, religion for me to a mere excuse for laziness, since it had set up a God who looked at the world and saw that it was good, against the instinct in me that looked through my eyes at the world and saw that it could be improved. I tell you that in the pursuit of my own pleasure, my own health, my own fortune, I have never known happiness. It was not love for Woman that delivered me into her hands: it was fatigue, exhaustion. When I was a child, and bruised my head against a stone, I ran to the nearest woman and cried away my pain against her apron. When I grew up, and bruised my soul against the brutalities and stupidities with which I had to strive, I did again just what I had done as a child. I have enjoyed, too, my rests, my recuperations, my breathing times, my very prostrations after strife; but rather would I be dragged through all the circles of the foolish Italian's Inferno than through the pleasures of Europe. That is what has made this place of eternal pleasures so deadly to me. It is the absence of this instinct in you that makes you that strange monster called a Devil. It is the success with which you have diverted the attention of men from their real purpose, which in one degree or another is the same as mine, to yours, that has earned you the name of The Tempter. It is the fact that they are doing your will, or rather drifting with your want of will, instead of doing their own, that makes them the uncomfortable, false, restless, artificial, petulant, wretched creatures they are.

THE DEVIL [*mortified*] Señor Don Juan: you are uncivil to my friends.

DON JUAN. Pooh! why should I be civil to them or

to you? In this Palace of Lies a truth or two will not
hurt you. Your friends are all the dullest dogs I know.
They are not beautiful: they are only decorated. They
are not clean: they are only shaved and starched. They
are not dignified: they are only fashionably dressed.
They are not educated: they are only college passmen.
They are not religious: they are only pewrenters. They
are not moral: they are only conventional. They are not
virtuous: they are only cowardly. They are not even vicious: they are only "frail." They are not artistic: they
are only lascivious. They are not prosperous: they are
only rich. They are not loyal, they are only servile; not
dutiful, only sheepish; not public spirited, only patriotic;
not courageous, only quarrelsome; not determined, only
obstinate; not masterful, only domineering; not self-
controlled, only obtuse; not self-respecting, only vain;
not kind, only sentimental; not social, only gregarious;
not considerate, only polite; not intelligent, only opinion-
ated; not progressive, only factious; not imaginative, only
superstitious; not just, only vindictive; not generous, only
propitiatory; not disciplined, only cowed; and not truthful at all—liars every one of them, to the very backbone
of their souls.

THE STATUE. Your flow of words is simply amazing,
Juan. How I wish I could have talked like that to my soldiers.

THE DEVIL. It is mere talk, though. It has all been
said before; but what change has it ever made? What
notice has the world ever taken of it?

DON JUAN. Yes, it is mere talk. But why is it mere
talk? Because, my friend, beauty, purity, respectability,
religion, morality, art, patriotism, bravery and the rest
are nothing but words which I or anyone else can turn
inside out like a glove. Were they realities, you would
have to plead guilty to my indictment; but fortunately
for your self-respect, my diabolical friend, they are not
realities. As you say, they are mere words, useful for
duping barbarians into adopting civilization, or the civilized poor into submitting to be robbed and enslaved.
That is the family secret of the governing caste; and if
we who are of that caste aimed at more Life for the
world instead of at more power and luxury for our mis-

erable selves, that secret would make us great. Now, since I, being a nobleman, am in the secret too, think how tedious to me must be your unending cant about all these moralistic figments, and how squalidly disastrous your sacrifice of your lives to them! If you even believed in your moral game enough to play it fairly, it would be interesting to watch; but you don't: you cheat at every trick; and if your opponent outcheats you, you upset the table and try to murder him.

THE DEVIL. On earth there may be some truth in this, because the people are uneducated and cannot appreciate my religion of love and beauty; but here—

DON JUAN. Oh yes: I know. Here there is nothing but love and beauty. Ugh! it is like sitting for all eternity at the first act of a fashionable play, before the complications begin. Never in my worst moments of superstitious terror on earth did I dream that Hell was so horrible. I live, like a hairdresser, in the continual contemplation of beauty, toying with silken tresses. I breathe an atmosphere of sweetness, like a confectioner's shopboy. Commander: are there any beautiful women in heaven?

THE STATUE. None. Absolutely none. All dowdies. Not two pennorth of jewellery among a dozen of them. They might be men of fifty.

DON JUAN. I am impatient to get there. Is the word beauty ever mentioned; and are there any artistic people?

THE STATUE. I give you my word they won't admire a fine statue even when it walks past them.

DON JUAN. I go.

THE DEVIL. Don Juan: shall I be frank with you?

DON JUAN. Were you not so before?

THE DEVIL. As far as I went, yes. But I will now go further, and confess to you that men get tired of everything, of heaven no less than of hell; and that all history is nothing but a record of the oscillations of the world between these two extremes. An epoch is but a swing of the pendulum; and each generation thinks the world is progressing because it is always moving. But when you are as old as I am; when you have a thousand times wearied of heaven, like myself and the Commander, and a thousand times wearied of hell, as you are wearied now, you will no longer imagine that every swing from heaven to hell is an emancipation, every swing from hell to heaven an evolution. Where you now see reform, progress, fulfilment of upward tendency, continual ascent by Man on the stepping stones of his dead selves to higher things, you will see nothing but an infinite comedy of illusion. You will discover the profound truth of the saying of my friend Koheleth, that there is nothing new under the sun. Vanitas vanitatum—

DON JUAN [*out of all patience*] By heaven, this is worse than your cant about love and beauty. Clever dolt that you are, is a man no better than a worm, or a dog than a wolf, because he gets tired of everything? Shall he give up eating because he destroys his appetite in the act of gratifying it? Is a field idle when it is fallow? Can the Commander expend his hellish energy here without accumulating heavenly energy for his next term of blessedness? Granted that the great Life Force has hit on the device of the clockmaker's pendulum, and uses the earth for its bob; that the history of each oscillation, which seems so novel to us the actors, is but the history of the last oscillation repeated; nay more, that in the unthinkable infinitude of time the sun throws off the earth and catches it again a thousand times as a circus rider throws up a ball, and that the total of all our epochs is but the moment between the toss and the catch, has the colossal mechanism no purpose?

THE DEVIL. None, my friend. You think, because you have a purpose, Nature must have one. You might as well expect it to have fingers and toes because you have them.

DON JUAN. But I should not have them if they served no purpose. And I, my friend, am as much a part of Nature as my own finger is a part of me. If my finger is the organ by which I grasp the sword and the mandoline, my brain is the organ by which Nature strives to understand itself. My dog's brain serves only my dog's purposes; but my brain labors at a knowledge which does nothing for me personally but make my body bitter to me and my decay and death a calamity. Were I not possessed with a purpose beyond my own I had better be a ploughman than a philosopher; for the ploughman lives as long as the philosopher, eats more, sleeps better, and rejoices in the wife of his bosom with less misgiving. This is because the philosopher is in the grip of the Life Force. This Life Force says to him "I have done a thousand wonderful things unconsciously by merely willing to live and following the line of least resistance: now I want to know myself and my destination, and choose my path; so I have made a special brain—a philosopher's brain—to grasp this knowledge for me as the husbandman's hand grasps the plough for me. And this" says the Life Force to the philosopher "must thou strive to do for me until thou diest, when I will make another brain and another philosopher to carry on the work."

THE DEVIL. What is the use of knowing?

DON JUAN. Why, to be able to choose the line of greatest advantage instead of yielding in the direction of the least resistance. Does a ship sail to its destination no better than a log drifts nowhither? The philosopher is Nature's pilot. And there you have our difference: to be in hell is to drift: to be in heaven is to steer.

THE DEVIL. On the rocks, most likely.

DON JUAN. Pooh! which ship goes oftenest on the rocks or to the bottom—the drifting ship or the ship with a pilot on board?

THE DEVIL. Well, well, go your way, Señor Don Juan. I prefer to be my own master and not the tool of any blundering universal force. I know that beauty is good to look at; that music is good to hear; that love is good to feel; and that they are all good to think about and talk about. I know that to be well exercised in these sensations, emotions, and studies is to be a refined and cultivated being. Whatever they may say of me in churches on earth, I know that it is universally admitted in good society that the Prince of Darkness is a gentleman; and that is enough for me. As to your Life Force, which you think irresistible, it is the most resistible thing in the world for a person of any character. But if you are naturally vulgar and credulous, as all reformers are, it will thrust you first into religion, where you will sprinkle water on babies to save their souls from me; then it will drive you from religion into science, where you will snatch the babies from the water sprinkling and inoculate them with disease to save them from catching it accidentally; then you will take to politics, where you will become the catspaw of corrupt functionaries and the henchman of ambitious humbugs; and the end will be despair and decrepitude, broken nerve and shattered hopes, vain regrets for that worst and silliest of wastes and sacrifices, the waste and sacrifice of the power of enjoyment: in a word, the punishment of the fool who pursues the better before he has secured the good.

DON JUAN. But at least I shall not be bored. The service of the Life Force has that advantage, at all events. So fare you well, Señor Satan.

THE DEVIL [amiably] Fare you well, Don Juan. I shall often think of our interesting chats about things in general. I wish you every happiness: heaven, as I said before, suits some people. But if you should change your mind, do not forget that the gates are always open here to the repentant prodigal. If you feel at any time that warmth of heart, sincere unforced affection, innocent enjoyment, and warm, breathing, palpitating reality—

DON JUAN. Why not say flesh and blood at once, though we have left those two greasy commonplaces behind us?

THE DEVIL [angrily] You throw my friendly farewell back in my teeth, then, Don Juan?

DON JUAN. By no means. But though there is much to be learnt from a cynical devil, I really cannot stand a sentimental one. Señor Commander: you know the way to the frontier of hell and heaven. Be good enough to direct me.

THE STATUE. Oh, the frontier is only the difference between two ways of looking at things. Any road will take you across it if you really want to get there.

DON JUAN. Good. [Saluting Doña Ana.] Señora: your servant.

ANA. But I am going with you.

DON JUAN. I can find my own way to heaven, Ana; but I cannot find yours [he vanishes].

ANA. How annoying!

THE STATUE [calling after him] Bon voyage, Juan! [He wafts a final blast of his great rolling chords after him as a parting salute. A faint echo of the first ghostly *melody comes back in acknowledgment.*] Ah! there he goes. [*Puffing a long breath out through his lips*] Whew! How he does talk! They'll never stand it in heaven.

THE DEVIL [*gloomily*] His going is a political defeat. I cannot keep these Life Worshippers: they all go. This is the greatest loss I have had since that Dutch painter went—a fellow who would paint a hag of 70 with as much enjoyment as a Venus of 20.

THE STATUE. I remember: he came to heaven. Rembrandt.

THE DEVIL. Ay, Rembrandt. There is something unnatural about these fellows. Do not listen to their gospel, Señor Commander: it is dangerous. Beware of the pursuit of the Superhuman: it leads to an indiscriminate contempt for the Human. To a man, horses and dogs and cats are mere species, outside the moral world. Well, to the Superman, men and women are a mere species too, also outside the moral world. This Don Juan was kind to women and courteous to men as your daughter here was kind to her pet cats and dogs; but such kindness is a denial of the exclusively human character of the soul.

THE STATUE. And who the deuce is the Superman?

THE DEVIL. Oh, the latest fashion among the Life Force fanatics. Did you not meet in heaven, among the new arrivals, that German Polish madman—what was his name? Nietzsche?

THE STATUE. Never heard of him.

THE DEVIL. Well, he came here first, before he recovered his wits. I had some hopes of him; but he was a confirmed Life Force worshipper. It was he who raked up the Superman, who is as old as Prometheus; and the twentieth century will run after this newest of the old crazes when it gets tired of the world, the flesh, and your humble servant.

THE STATUE. Superman is a good cry; and a good cry is half the battle. I should like to see this Nietzsche.

THE DEVIL. Unfortunately he met Wagner here, and had a quarrel with him.

THE STATUE. Quite right, too. Mozart for me!

THE DEVIL. Oh, it was not about music. Wagner once drifted into Life Force worship, and invented a Superman called Siegfried. But he came to his senses afterwards. So when they met here, Nietzsche denounced him as a renegade; and Wagner wrote a pamphlet to prove that Nietzsche was a Jew; and it ended in Nietzsche's going to heaven in a huff. And a good riddance too. And now, my friend, let us hasten to my palace and celebrate your arrival with a grand musical service.

THE STATUE. With pleasure: you're most kind.

THE DEVIL. This way, Commander. We go down the old trap [*he places himself on the grave trap*].

THE STATUE. Good. [*Reflectively*] All the same, the Superman is a fine conception. There is something statuesque about it. [*He places himself on the grave trap beside The Devil. It begins to descend slowly. Red glow from the abyss.*] Ah, this reminds me of old times.

THE DEVIL. And me also.

ANA. Stop! [*The trap stops.*]

THE DEVIL. You, Señora, cannot come this way. You will have an apotheosis. But you will be at the palace before us.

ANA. That is not what I stopped you for. Tell me: where can I find the Superman?

THE DEVIL. He is not yet created, Señora.

THE STATUE. And never will be, probably. Let us proceed: the red fire will make me sneeze. [*They descend.*]

ANA. Not yet created! Then my work is not yet done. [*Crossing herself devoutly*] I believe in the Life to Come. [*Crying to the universe*] A father—a father for the Superman!

[*She vanishes into the void; and again there is nothing: all existence seems suspended infinitely. Then, vaguely, there is a live human voice crying somewhere. One sees, with a shock, a mountain peak shewing faintly against a lighter background. The sky has returned from afar; and we suddenly remember where we were. The cry becomes distinct and urgent: it says* Automobile, Automobile. *The complete reality comes back with a rush: in a moment it is full morning in the Sierra; and the brigands are scrambling to their feet and making for the road as the goatherd runs down from the hill, warning them of the approach of another motor. Tanner and Mendoza rise amazedly and stare at one another with scattered wits. Straker sits*]

*up to yawn for a moment before he gets on his feet, mak-
ing it a point of honor not to shew any undue interest in
the excitement of the bandits. Mendoza gives a quick look
to see that his followers are attending to the alarm; then
exchanges a private word with Tanner.*]

MENDOZA. Did you dream?

TANNER. Damnably. Did you?

MENDOZA. Yes. I forget what. You were in it.

TANNER. So were you. Amazing!

MENDOZA. I warned you. [*A shot is heard from the
road.*] Dolts! they will play with that gun. [*The brigands
come running back scared*]. Who fired that shot? [*to
Duval*] Was it you?

DUVAL [*breathless*] I have not shoot. Dey shoot first.

ANARCHIST. I told you to begin by abolishing the
State. Now we are all lost.

THE ROWDY SOCIAL-DEMOCRAT [*stampeding across
the amphitheatre*] Run, everybody.

MENDOZA [*collaring him; throwing him on his back;
and drawing a knife*] I stab the man who stirs. [*He blocks
the way. The stampede is checked.*] What has happened?

THE SULKY SOCIAL-DEMOCRAT. A motor—

THE ANARCHIST. Three men—

DUVAL. Deux femmes—

MENDOZA. Three men and two women! Why have
you not brought them here? Are you afraid of them?

THE ROWDY ONE [*getting up*] Thyve a hescort. Ow,
de-ooh lut's ook it, Mendoza.

THE SULKY ONE. Two armored cars full o soldiers at
the ed o the valley.

ANARCHIST. The shot was fired in the air. It was
a signal.

[*Straker whistles his favorite air, which falls on the ears
of the brigands like a funeral march.*]

TANNER. It is not an escort, but an expedition to
capture you. We were advised to wait for it; but I was
in a hurry.

THE ROWDY ONE [*in an agony of apprehension*] And
Ow my good Lord, ere we are, wytin for em! Lut's tike
to the mahntns.

MENDOZA. Idiot, what do you know about the
mountains? Are you a Spaniard? You would be given

up by the first shepherd you met. Besides, we are already within range of their rifles.

THE ROWDY ONE. Bat—

MENDOZA. Silence. Leave this to me. [*To Tanner*] Comrade: you will not betray us.

STRAKER. Oo are you callin comrade?

MENDOZA. Last night the advantage was with me. The robber of the poor was at the mercy of the robber of the rich. You offered your hand: I took it.

TANNER. I bring no charge against you, comrade. We have spent a pleasant evening with you: that is all.

STRAKER. I gev my and to nobody, see?

MENDOZA [*turning on him impressively*] Young man, if I am tried, I shall plead guilty, and explain what drove me from England, home and duty. Do you wish to have the respectable name of Straker dragged through the mud of a Spanish criminal court? The police will search me. They will find Louisa's portrait. It will be published in the illustrated papers. You blench. It will be your doing, remember.

STRAKER [*with baffled rage*] I don't care about the court. It's avin our name mixed up with yours that I object to, you blackmailin swine, you.

MENDOZA. Language unworthy of Louisa's brother! But no matter: you are muzzled: that is enough for us. [*He turns to face his own men, who back uneasily across the amphitheatre towards the cave to take refuge behind him, as a fresh party, muffled for motoring, comes from the road in riotous spirits. Ann, who makes straight for Tanner, comes first; then Violet, helped over the rough ground by Hector holding her right hand and Ramsden her left. Mendoza goes to his presidential block and seats himself calmly with his rank and file grouped behind him, and his Staff, consisting of Duval and the Anarchist on his right and the two Social-Democrats on his left, supporting him in flank.*]

ANN. It's Jack!

TANNER. Caught!

HECTOR. Why, certainly it is. I said it was you, Tanner. We've just been stopped by a puncture: the road is full of nails.

VIOLET. What are you doing here with all these men?

ANN. Why did you leave us without a word of warning?

HECTOR. I want that bunch of roses, Miss Whitefield. [*To Tanner*] When we found you were gone, Miss Whitefield bet me a bunch of roses my car would not overtake yours before you reached Monte Carlo.

TANNER. But this is not the road to Monte Carlo.

HECTOR. No matter. Miss Whitefield tracked you at every stopping place: she is a regular Sherlock Holmes.

TANNER. The Life Force! I am lost.

OCTAVIUS [*bounding gaily down from the road into the amphitheatre, and coming between Tanner and Straker*] I am so glad you are safe, old chap. We were afraid you had been captured by brigands.

RAMSDEN [*who has been staring at Mendoza*] I seem to remember the face of your friend here. [*Mendoza rises politely and advances with a smile between Ann and Ramsden.*]

HECTOR. Why, so do I.

OCTAVIUS. I know you perfectly well, sir; but I can't think where I have met you.

MENDOZA [*to Violet*] Do you remember me, madam?

VIOLET. Oh, quite well; but I am so stupid about names.

MENDOZA. It was at the Savoy Hotel. [*To Hector*] You, sir, used to come with this lady [*Violet*] to lunch. [*To Octavius*] You, sir, often brought this lady [*Ann*] and her mother to dinner on your way to the Lyceum Theatre. [*To Ramsden*] You, sir, used to come to supper, with [*dropping his voice to a confidential, but perfectly audible whisper*] several different ladies.

RAMSDEN [*angrily*] Well, what is that to you, pray?

OCTAVIUS. Why, Violet, I thought you hardly knew one another before this trip, you and Malone!

VIOLET [*vexed*] I suppose this person was the manager.

MENDOZA. The waiter, madam. I have a grateful recollection of you all. I gathered from the bountiful way in which you treated me that you all enjoyed your visits very much.

VIOLET. What impertinence! [*She turns her back on him, and goes up the hill with Hector.*]

RAMSDEN. That will do, my friend. You do not expect these ladies to treat you as an acquaintance, I suppose, because you have waited on them at table.

MENDOZA. Pardon me: it was you who claimed my acquaintance. The ladies followed your example. However, this display of the unfortunate manners of your class closes the incident. For the future, you will please address me with the respect due to a stranger and fellow traveller. [*He turns haughtily away and resumes his presidential seat.*]

TANNER. There! I have found one man on my journey capable of reasonable conversation; and you all instinctively insult him. Even the New Man is as bad as any of you. Enry: you have behaved just like a miserable gentleman.

STRAKER. Gentleman! Not me.

RAMSDEN. Really, Tanner, this tone—

ANN. Don't mind him, Granny: you ought to know him by this time. [*She takes his arm and coaxes him away to the hill to join Violet and Hector. Octavius follows her, doglike.*]

VIOLET [*calling from the hill*] Here are the soldiers. They are getting out of their motors.

DUVAL [*panic stricken*] Oh, nom de Dieu!

THE ANARCHIST. Fools: the State is about to crush you because you spared it at the prompting of the political hangers-on of the bourgeoisie.

THE SULKY SOCIAL-DEMOCRAT [*argumentative to the last*] On the contrary, only by capturing the State machine—

THE ANARCHIST. It is going to capture you.

THE ROWDY SOCIAL-DEMOCRAT [*his anguish culminating*] Ow, chack it. Wot are we ere for? Wot are we wytin for?

MENDOZA [*between his teeth*] Go on. Talk politics, you idiots: nothing sounds more respectable. Keep it up, I tell you.

[*The soldiers line the road, commanding the amphitheatre with their rifles. The brigands, struggling with an overwhelming impulse to hide behind one another, look as unconcerned as they can. Mendoza rises superbly, with undaunted front. The officer in command steps down*] *from the road into the amphitheatre; looks hard at the brigands; and then inquiringly at Tanner.*]

THE OFFICER. Who are these men, Señor Ingles?

TANNER. My escort.

[*Mendoza, with a Mephistophelean smile, bows profoundly. An irrepressible grin runs from face to face among the brigands. They touch their hats, except the Anarchist, who defies the State with folded arms.*]

ACT FOUR

The garden of a villa in Granada. Whoever wishes to know what it is like must go to Granada and see. One may prosaically specify a group of hills dotted with villas, the Alhambra on the top of one of the hills, and a considerable town in the valley, approached by dusty white roads in which the children, no matter what they are doing or thinking about, automatically whine for half-pence and reach out little clutching brown palms for them; but there is nothing in this description except the Alhambra, the begging, and the color of the roads, that does not fit Surrey as well as Spain. The difference is that the Surrey hills are comparatively small and ugly, and should properly be called the Surrey Protuberances; but these Spanish hills are of mountain stock: the amenity which conceals their size does not compromise their dignity.

This particular garden is on a hill opposite the Alhambra; and the villa is as expensive and pretentious as a villa must be if it is to be let furnished by the week to opulent American and English visitors. If we stand on the lawn at the foot of the garden and look uphill, our horizon is the stone balustrade of a flagged platform on the edge of the infinite space at the top of the hill. Between us and this platform is a flower garden with a circular basin and fountain in the centre, surrounded by geometrical flower beds, gravel paths, and clipped yew trees in the genteelest order. The garden is higher than our lawn; so we reach it by a few steps in the middle of its embankment. The platform is higher again than the garden, from which we mount a couple more steps to look over the balustrade at a fine view of the town up the valley and of the hills that stretch away beyond it to where, in the remotest distance, they become mountains. On our left is the villa, accessible by steps from the left hand corner of the garden. Returning from the platform through the garden and down again to the lawn [a movement which leaves the villa behind us on our right] we find evidence of literary interests on the part of the tenants in the fact that there is no tennis net nor set of croquet hoops, but, on our left, a little iron garden table with books on it, mostly yellow-backed, and a chair beside it. A chair on the right has also a couple of open books upon it. There are no newspapers, a circumstance which, with the absence of games, might lead an intelligent spectator to the most far reaching conclusions as to the sort of people who live in the villa. Such speculations are checked, however, on this delightfully fine afternoon, by the appearance at a little gate in a paling on our left, of Henry Straker in his professional costume. He opens the gate for an elderly gentleman, and follows him on to the lawn.

This elderly gentleman defies the Spanish sun in a black frock coat, tall silk hat, trousers in which narrow stripes of dark grey and lilac blend into a highly respectable color, and a black necktie tied into a bow over spotless linen. Probably therefore a man whose social position needs constant and scrupulous affirmation without regard to climate: one who would dress thus for the middle of the Sahara or the top of Mont Blanc. And since he has not the stamp of the class which accepts as its life-mission the advertising and maintenance of first rate tailoring and millinery, he looks vulgar in his finery, though in a working dress of any kind he would look dignified enough. He is a bullet cheeked man with a red complexion, stubbly hair, smallish eyes, a hard mouth that folds down at the corners, and a dogged chin. The looseness of skin that comes with age has attacked his throat and the laps of his cheeks; but he is still hard as an apple above the mouth; so that the upper half of his face looks younger than the lower. He has the self-confidence of one who has made money, and something of the truculence of one who has made it in a brutalizing struggle, his civility having under it a perceptible menace that he has other methods in reserve if necessary. Withal, a man to be rather pitied when he is not to be feared; for there is something pathetic about him at times, as if the huge commercial machine which has worked him into his frock coat had allowed him very little of his own way and left his affections hungry and baffled. At the first word that falls from him it is clear that he is an Irishman whose native intonation has clung to him through many changes of place and rank. One can only guess that the original material of his speech was perhaps the surly Kerry brogue; but the degradation of speech that occurs in London, Glasgow, Dublin and big cities generally has been at work on it so long that nobody but an arrant cockney would dream of calling it a brogue now; for its music is almost gone, though its surliness is still perceptible. Straker, as a very obvious cockney, inspires him with implacable contempt, as a stupid Englishman who cannot even speak his own language properly. Straker, on the other hand, regards the old gentleman's accent as a joke thoughtfully provided by Providence expressly for the amusement of the British race, and treats him normally with the indulgence due to an inferior and unlucky species, but occasionally with indignant alarm when the old gentleman shews signs of intending his Irish nonsense to be taken seriously.

STRAKER. I'll go tell the young lady. She said you'd prefer to stay here [*he turns to go up through the garden to the villa*].

MALONE [*who has been looking round him with lively curiosity*] The young lady? That's Miss Violet, eh?

STRAKER [*stopping on the steps with sudden suspicion*] Well, you know, don't you?

MALONE. Do I?

STRAKER [*his temper rising*] Well, do you or don't you?

MALONE. What business is that of yours?

[*Straker, now highly indignant, comes back from the steps and confronts the visitor.*]

STRAKER. I'll tell you what business it is of mine. Miss Robinson—

MALONE [*interrupting*] Oh, her name is Robinson, is it? Thank you.

STRAKER. Why, you don't know even her name?

MALONE. Yes I do, now that you've told me.

STRAKER [*after a moment of stupefaction at the old man's readiness in repartee*] Look here: what do you mean by gittin into my car and lettin me bring you here if you're not the person I took that note to?

MALONE. Who else did you take it to, pray?

STRAKER. I took it to Mr. Ector Malone, at Miss Robinson's request, see? Miss Robinson is not my principal: I took it to oblige her. I know Mr. Malone; and he ain't you, not by a long chalk. At the hotel they told me that your name is Ector Malone—

MALONE. *H*ector Malone.

STRAKER [*with calm superiority*] Hector in your own country: that's what comes o livin in provincial places like Ireland and America. Over here you're Ector: if you aven't noticed it before you soon will.

[*The growing strain of the conversation is here relieved by Violet, who has sallied from the villa and through the garden to the steps, which she now descends, coming very opportunely between Malone and Straker.*]

VIOLET [*to Straker*] Did you take my message?

STRAKER. Yes, miss. I took it to the hotel and sent it up, expecting to see young Mr. Malone. Then out walks this gent, and says it's all right and he'll come with me. So as the hotel people said he was Mr. Ector Malone, I fetched him. And now he goes back on what he said. But if he isn't the gentleman you meant, say the word: it's easy enough to fetch him back again.

MALONE. I should esteem it a great favor if I might have a short conversation with you, madam. I am Hector's father, as this bright Britisher would have guessed in the course of another hour or so.

STRAKER [*coolly defiant*] No, not in another year or so. When we've ad you as long to polish up as we've ad im, perhaps you'll begin to look a little bit up to is mark. At present you fall a long way short. You've got too many aitches, for one thing. [*To Violet, amiably*] All right, Miss: you want to talk to him: I shan't intrude. [*He nods affably to Malone and goes out through the little gate in the paling.*]

VIOLET [*very civilly*] I am so sorry, Mr. Malone, if

that man has been rude to you. But what can we do? He is our chauffeur.

MALONE. Your what?

VIOLET. The driver of our automobile. He can drive a motor car at seventy miles an hour, and mend it when it breaks down. We are dependent on our motor cars; and our motor cars are dependent on him; so of course we are dependent on him.

MALONE. I've noticed, madam, that every thousand dollars an Englishman gets seems to add one to the number of people he's dependent on. However, you needn't apologize for your man: I made him talk on purpose. By doing so I learnt that you're staying here in Grannida with a party of English, including my son Hector.

VIOLET [*conversationally*] Yes. We intended to go to Nice; but we had to follow a rather eccentric member of our party who started first and came here. Won't you sit down? [*She clears the nearest chair of the two books on it.*]

MALONE [*impressed by this attention*] Thank you. [*He sits down, examining her curiously as she goes to the iron table to put down the books. When she turns to him again, he says*] Miss Robinson, I believe?

VIOLET [*sitting down*] Yes.

MALONE [*taking a letter from his pocket*] Your note to Hector runs as follows [*Violet is unable to repress a start. He pauses quietly to take out and put on his spectacles, which have gold rims*]: "Dearest: they have all gone to the Alhambra for the afternoon. I have shammed headache and have the garden all to myself. Jump into Jack's motor: Straker will rattle you here in a jiffy. Quick, quick, quick. Your loving Violet." [*He looks at her; but by this time she has recovered herself, and meets his spectacles with perfect composure. He continues slowly*] Now I don't know on what terms young people associate in English society; but in America that note would be considered to imply a very considerable degree of affectionate intimacy between the parties.

VIOLET. Yes: I know your son very well, Mr. Malone. Have you any objection?

MALONE [*somewhat taken aback*] No, no objection exactly. Provided it is understood that my son is altogether dependent on me, and that I have to be consulted in any important step he may propose to take.

VIOLET. I am sure you would not be unreasonable with him, Mr. Malone.

MALONE. I hope not, Miss Robinson; but at your age you might think many things unreasonable that don't seem so to me.

VIOLET [*with a little shrug*] Oh well, I suppose there's no use our playing at cross purposes, Mr. Malone. Hector wants to marry me.

MALONE. I inferred from your note that he might. Well, Miss Robinson, he is his own master; but if he marries you he shall not have a rap from me. [*He takes off his spectacles and pockets them with the note.*]

VIOLET [*with some severity*] That is not very complimentary to me, Mr. Malone.

MALONE. I say nothing against you, Miss Robinson: I daresay you are an amiable and excellent young lady. But I have other views for Hector.

VIOLET. Hector may not have other views for himself, Mr. Malone.

MALONE. Possibly not. Then he does without me: that's all. I daresay you are prepared for that. When a young lady writes to a young man to come to her quick, quick, quick, money seems nothing and love seems everything.

VIOLET. [*sharply*] I beg your pardon, Mr. Malone: I do not think anything so foolish. Hector must have money.

MALONE [*staggered*] Oh, very well, very well. No doubt he can work for it.

VIOLET. What is the use of having money if you have to work for it? [*She rises impatiently*]. It's all nonsense, Mr. Malone: you must enable your son to keep up his position. It is his right.

MALONE [*grimly*] I should not advise you to marry him on the strength of that right, Miss Robinson.

[*Violet, who has almost lost her temper, controls herself with an effort; unclenches her fingers; and resumes her seat with studied tranquillity and reasonableness.*]

VIOLET. What objection have you to me, pray? My

social position is as good as Hector's, to say the least. He admits it.

MALONE [*shrewdly*] You tell him so from time to time, eh? Hector's social position in England, Miss Robinson, is just what I choose to buy for him. I have made him a fair offer. Let him pick out the most historic house, castle or abbey that England contains. The day that he tells me he wants it for a wife worthy of its traditions, I buy it for him, and give him the means of keeping it up.

VIOLET. What do you mean by a wife worthy of its traditions? Cannot any well bred woman keep such a house for him?

MALONE. No: she must be born to it.

VIOLET. Hector was not born to it, was he?

MALONE. His grandmother was a barefooted Irish girl that nursed me by a turf fire. Let him marry another such, and I will not stint her marriage portion. Let him raise himself socially with my money or raise somebody else: so long as there is a social profit somewhere, I'll regard my expenditure as justified. But there must be a profit for someone. A marriage with you would leave things just where they are.

VIOLET. Many of my relations would object very much to my marrying the grandson of a common woman, Mr. Malone. That may be prejudice; but so is your desire to have him marry a title prejudice.

MALONE [*rising, and approaching her with a scrutiny in which there is a good deal of reluctant respect*] You seem a pretty straightforward, downright sort of a young woman.

VIOLET. I do not see why I should be made miserably poor because I cannot make profits for you. Why do you want to make Hector unhappy?

MALONE. He will get over it all right enough. Men thrive better on disappointments in love than on disappointments in money. I daresay you think that sordid; but I know what I'm talking about. My father died of starvation in Ireland in the black 47. Maybe you've heard of it.

VIOLET. The Famine?

MALONE [*with smouldering passion*] No, the starvation. When a country is full of food, and exporting it, there can be no famine. My father was starved dead; and I was starved out to America in my mother's arms. English rule drove me and mine out of Ireland. Well, you can keep Ireland. I and my like are coming back to buy England; and we'll buy the best of it. I want no middle class properties and no middle class women for Hector. That's straightforward, isn't it, like yourself?

VIOLET [*icily pitying his sentimentality*] Really, Mr. Malone, I am astonished to hear a man of your age and good sense talking in that romantic way. Do you suppose English noblemen will sell their places to you for the asking?

MALONE. I have the refusal of two of the oldest family mansions in England. One historic owner can't afford to keep all the rooms dusted: the other can't afford the death duties. What do you say now?

VIOLET. Of course it is very scandalous; but surely you know that the Government will sooner or later put a stop to all these Socialistic attacks on property.

MALONE [*grinning*] D'y' think they'll be able to get that done before I buy the house—or rather the abbey? They're both abbeys.

VIOLET [*putting that aside rather impatiently*] Oh, well, let us talk sense, Mr. Malone. You must feel that we haven't been talking sense so far.

MALONE. I can't say I do. I mean all I say.

VIOLET. Then you don't know Hector as I do. He is romantic and faddy—he gets it from you, I fancy—and he wants a certain sort of wife to take care of him. Not a faddy sort of person, you know.

MALONE. Somebody like you, perhaps?

VIOLET [*quietly*] Well, yes. But you cannot very well ask me to undertake this with absolutely no means of keeping up his position.

MALONE [*alarmed*] Stop a bit, stop a bit. Where are we getting to? I'm not aware that I'm asking you to undertake anything.

VIOLET. Of course, Mr. Malone, you can make it very difficult for me to speak to you if you choose to misunderstand me.

MALONE [*half bewildered*] I don't wish to take any

unfair advantage; but we seem to have got off the straight track somehow.

[*Straker, with the air of a man who has been making haste, opens the little gate, and admits Hector, who, snorting with indignation, comes upon the lawn, and is making for his father when Violet, greatly dismayed, springs up and intercepts him. Straker does not wait; at least he does not remain visibly within earshot.*]

VIOLET. Oh, how unlucky! Now please, Hector, say nothing. Go away until I have finished speaking to your father.

HECTOR [*inexorably*] No, Violet: I mean to have this thing out, right away. [*He puts her aside; passes her by; and faces his father, whose cheeks darken as his Irish blood begins to simmer.*] Dad: you've not played this hand straight.

MALONE. Hwat d'y'mean?

HECTOR. You've opened a letter addressed to me. You've impersonated me and stolen a march on this lady. That's dishonorable.

MALONE [*threateningly*] Now you take care what you're saying, Hector. Take care, I tell you.

HECTOR. I have taken care. I am taking care. I'm taking care of my honor and my position in English society.

MALONE [*hotly*] Your position has been got by my money: do you know that?

HECTOR. Well, you've just spoiled it all by opening that letter. A letter from an English lady, not addressed to you—a confidential letter! a delicate letter! a private letter! opened by my father! That's a sort of thing a man can't struggle against in England. The sooner we go back together the better. [*He appeals mutely to the heavens to witness the shame and anguish of two·outcasts.*]

VIOLET [*snubbing him with an instinctive dislike for scene making*] Don't be unreasonable, Hector. It was quite natural of Mr. Malone to open my letter: his name was on the envelope.

MALONE. There! You've no common sense, Hector. I thank you, Miss Robinson,

HECTOR. I thank you, too. It's very kind of you. My father knows no better.

MALONE [*furiously clenching his fists*] Hector—

HECTOR [*with undaunted moral force*] Oh, it's no use hectoring me. A private letter's a private letter, dad: you can't get over that.

MALONE [*raising his voice*] I won't be talked back to by you, d'y'hear?

VIOLET. Ssh! please, please. Here they all come.

[*Father and son, checked, glare mutely at one another as Tanner comes in through the little gate with Ramsden, followed by Octavius and Ann.*]

VIOLET. Back already!

TANNER. The Alhambra is not open this afternoon.

VIOLET. What a sell!

[*Tanner passes on, and presently finds himself between Hector and a strange elder, both apparently on the verge of personal combat. He looks from one to the other for an explanation. They sulkily avoid his eye, and nurse their wrath in silence.*]

RAMSDEN. Is it wise for you to be out in the sunshine with such a headache, Violet?

TANNER. Have you recovered too, Malone?

VIOLET. Oh, I forgot. We have not all met before. Mr. Malone: won't you introduce your father?

HECTOR [*with Roman firmness*] No I will not. He is no father of mine.

MALONE [*very angry*] You disown your dad before your English friends, do you?

VIOLET. Oh please don't make a scene.

[*Ann and Octavius, lingering near the gate, exchange an astonished glance, and discreetly withdraw up the steps to the garden, where they can enjoy the disturbance without intruding. On their way to the steps Ann sends a little grimace of mute sympathy to Violet, who is standing with her back to the little table, looking on in helpless annoyance as her husband soars to higher and higher moral eminences without the least regard to the old man's millions.*]

HECTOR. I'm very sorry, Miss Robinson; but I'm contending for a principle. I am a son, and, I hope, a dutiful one; but before everything I'm a Man!!! And when dad treats my private letters as his own, and takes it on himself to say that I shan't marry you if I am happy

and fortunate enough to gain your consent, then I just
snap my fingers and go my own way.

TANNER. Marry Violet!

RAMSDEN. Are you in your senses?

TANNER. Do you forget what we told you?

HECTOR [*recklessly*] I don't care what you told me.

RAMSDEN [*scandalized*] Tut tut, sir! Monstrous! [*he
flings away towards the gate, his elbows quivering with
indignation.*]

TANNER. Another madman! These men in love
should be locked up. [*He gives Hector up as hopeless,
and turns away towards the garden; but Malone, taking
offence in a new direction, follows him and compels him,
by the aggressiveness of his tone, to stop.*]

MALONE. I don't understand this. Is Hector not good
enough for this lady, pray?

TANNER. My dear sir, the lady is married already.
Hector knows it; and yet he persists in his infatuation.
Take him home and lock him up.

MALONE [*bitterly*] So this is the high-born social tone
I've spoilt by me ignorant, uncultivated behavior! Makin
love to a married woman! [*He comes angrily between
Hector and Violet, and almost bawls into Hector's left
ear*] You've picked up that habit of the British aristocracy, have you?

HECTOR. That's all right. Don't you trouble yourself
about that. I'll answer for the morality of what I'm
doing.

TANNER [*coming forward to Hector's right hand with
flashing eyes*] Well said, Malone! You also see that mere
marriage laws are not morality! I agree with you; but
unfortunately Violet does not.

MALONE. I take leave to doubt that, sir. [*Turning on
Violet*] Let me tell you, Mrs. Robinson, or whatever your
right name is, you had no right to send that letter to my
son when you were the wife of another man.

HECTOR [*outraged*] This is the last straw. Dad: you
have insulted my wife.

MALONE. *Your* wife!

TANNER. *You* the missing husband! Another moral
impostor! [*He smites his brow, and collapses into Malone's chair*].

MALONE. You've married without my consent!

RAMSDEN. You have deliberately humbugged us, sir!

HECTOR. Here: I have had just about enough of being badgered. Violet and I are married: that's the long and the short of it. Now what have you got to say—any of you?

MALONE. I know what I've got to say. She's married a beggar.

HECTOR. No; she's married a Worker [*his American pronunciation imparts an overwhelming intensity to this simple and unpopular word*]. I start to earn my own living this very afternoon.

MALONE [*sneering angrily*] Yes: you're very plucky now, because you got your remittance from me yesterday or this morning, I reckon. Wait til it's spent. You won't be so full of cheek then.

HECTOR [*producing a letter from his pocketbook*] Here it is [*thrusting it on his father*]. Now you just take your remittance and yourself out of my life. I'm done with remittances; and I'm done with you. I don't sell the privilege of insulting my wife for a thousand dollars.

MALONE [*deeply wounded and full of concern*] Hector: you don't know what poverty is.

HECTOR [*fervidly*] Well, I want to know what it is. I want'be a Man. Violet: you come along with me, to your own home: I'll see you through.

OCTAVIUS [*jumping down from the garden to the lawn and running to Hector's left hand*] I hope you'll shake hands with me before you go, Hector. I admire and respect you more than I can say. [*He is affected almost to tears as they shake hands.*]

VIOLET [*also almost in tears, but of vexation*] Oh don't be an idiot, Tavy. Hector's about as fit to become a workman as you are.

TANNER [*rising from his chair on the other side of Hector*] Never fear: there's no question of his becoming a navvy, Mrs. Malone. [*To Hector*] There's really no difficulty about capital to start with. Treat me as a friend: draw on me.

OCTAVIUS [*impulsively*] Or on me.

MALONE [*with fierce jealousy*] Who wants your durty money? Who should he draw on but his own father?

[*Tanner and Octavius recoil, Octavius rather hurt, Tanner consoled by the solution of the money difficulty. Violet looks up hopefully.*] Hector: don't be rash, my boy. I'm sorry for what I said: I never meant to insult Violet: I take it all back. She's just the wife you want: there!

HECTOR [*patting him on the shoulder*] Well, that's all right, dad. Say no more: we're friends again. Only, I take no money from anybody.

MALONE [*pleading abjectly*] Don't be hard on me, Hector. I'd rather you quarrelled and took the money than made friends and starved. You don't know what the world is: I do.

HECTOR. No, no, NO. That's fixed: that's not going to change. [*He passes his father inexorably by, and goes to Violet.*] Come, Mrs. Malone: you've got to move to the hotel with me, and take your proper place before the world.

VIOLET. But I must go in, dear, and tell Davis to pack. Won't you go on and make them give you a room overlooking the garden for me? I'll join you in half an hour.

HECTOR. Very well. You'll dine with us, dad, won't you?

MALONE [*eager to conciliate him*] Yes, yes.

HECTOR. See you all later. [*He waves his hand to Ann, who has now been joined by Tanner, Octavius, and Ramsden in the garden, and goes out through the little gate, leaving his father and Violet together on the lawn.*]

MALONE. You'll try to bring him to his senses, Violet: I know you will.

VIOLET. I had no idea he could be so headstrong. If he goes on like that, what can I do?

MALONE. Don't be discurridged: domestic pressure may be slow; but it's sure. You'll wear him down. Promise me you will.

VIOLET. I will do my best. Of course I think it's the greatest nonsense deliberately making us poor like that.

MALONE. Of course it is.

VIOLET [*after a moment's reflection*] You had better give me the remittance. He will want it for his hotel bill. I'll see whether I can induce him to accept it. Not now, of course, but presently.

MALONE [*eagerly*] Yes, yes, yes: that's just the thing [*He hands her the thousand dollar bill, and adds cunningly*] Y'understand that this is only a bachelor allowance.

VIOLET [*coolly*] Oh, quite. [*She takes it*]. Thank you. By the way, Mr. Malone, those two houses you mentioned—the abbeys.

MALONE. Yes?

VIOLET. Don't take one of them until I've seen it. One never knows what may be wrong with these places.

MALONE. I won't. I'll do nothing without consulting you, never fear.

VIOLET [*politely, but without a ray of gratitude*] Thanks: that will be much the best way. [*She goes calmly back to the villa, escorted obsequiously by Malone to the upper end of the garden.*]

TANNER [*drawing Ramsden's attention to Malone's cringing attitude as he takes leave of Violet*] And that poor devil is a billionaire! one of the master spirits of the age! Led on a string like a pug dog by the first girl who takes the trouble to despise him. I wonder will it ever come to that with me. [*He comes down to the lawn.*]

RAMSDEN [*following him*] The sooner the better for you.

MALONE [*slapping his hands as he returns through the garden*] That'll be a grand woman for Hector. I wouldn't exchange her for ten duchesses. [*He descends to the lawn and comes between Tanner and Ramsden.*]

RAMSDEN [*very civil to the billionaire*] It's an unexpected pleasure to find you in this corner of the world, Mr. Malone. Have you come to buy up the Alhambra?

MALONE. Well, I don't say I mightn't. I think I could do better with it than the Spanish government. But that's not what I came about. To tell you the truth, about a month ago I overheard a deal between two men over a bundle of shares. They differed about the price: they were young and greedy, and didn't know that if the shares were worth what was bid for them they must be worth what was asked, the margin being too small to be of any account, you see. To amuse meself, I cut in and bought the shares. Well, to this day I haven't found out what the business is. The office is in this town; and the name is Mendoza, Limited. Now whether Mendoza's a mine, or a steamboat line, or a bank, or a patent article—

TANNER. He's a man. I know him: his principles are thoroughly commercial. Let us take you round the town in our motor, Mr. Malone, and call on him on the way.

MALONE. If you'll be so kind, yes. And may I ask who—

TANNER. Mr. Roebuck Ramsden, a very old friend of your daughter-in-law.

MALONE. Happy to meet you, Mr. Ramsden.

RAMSDEN. Thank you. Mr. Tanner is also one of our circle.

MALONE. Glad to know you also, Mr. Tanner.

TANNER. Thanks. [*Malone and Ramsden go out very amicably through the little gate. Tanner calls to Octavius, who is wandering in the garden with Ann.*] Tavy! [*Tavy comes to the steps, Tanner whispers loudly to him*] Violet has married a financier of brigands. [*Tanner hurries away to overtake Malone and Ramsden. Ann strolls to the steps with an idle impulse to torment Octavius.*]

ANN. Won't you go with them, Tavy?

OCTAVIUS [*tears suddenly flushing his eyes*] You cut me to the heart, Ann, by wanting me to go [*he comes down on the lawn to hide his face from her. She follows him caressingly*].

ANN. Poor Ricky Ticky Tavy! Poor heart!

OCTAVIUS. It belongs to you, Ann. Forgive me: I must speak of it. I love you. You know I love you.

ANN. What's the good, Tavy? You know that my mother is determined that I shall marry Jack.

OCTAVIUS [*amazed*] Jack!

ANN. It seems absurd, doesn't it?

OCTAVIUS [*with growing resentment*] Do you mean to say that Jack has been playing with me all this time? That he has been urging me not to marry you because he intends to marry you himself?

ANN [*alarmed*] No no: you mustn't lead him to believe that I said that: I don't for a moment think that Jack knows his own mind. But it's clear from my father's will that he wished me to marry Jack. And my mother is set on it.

OCTAVIUS. But you are not bound to sacrifice your-self always to the wishes of your parents.

ANN. My father loved me. My mother loves me. Surely their wishes are a better guide than my own selfishness.

OCTAVIUS. Oh, I know how unselfish you are, Ann. But believe me—though I know I am speaking in my own interest—there is another side to this question. Is it fair to Jack to marry him if you do not love him? Is it fair to destroy my happiness as well as your own if you can bring yourself to love me?

ANN [*looking at him with a faint impulse of pity*] Tavy, my dear, you are a nice creature—a good boy.

OCTAVIUS [*humiliated*] Is that all?

ANN [*mischievously in spite of her pity*] That's a great deal, I assure you. You would always worship the ground I trod on, wouldn't you?

OCTAVIUS. I do. It sounds ridiculous; but it's no ex-aggeration. I do; and I always shall.

ANN. Always is a long word, Tavy. You see, I shall have to live up always to your idea of my divinity; and I don't think I could do that if we were married. But if I marry Jack, you'll never be disillusioned—at least not until I grow too old.

OCTAVIUS. I too shall grow old, Ann. And when I am eighty, one white hair of the woman I love will make me tremble more than the thickest gold tress from the most beautiful young head.

ANN [*quite touched*] Oh, that's poetry, Tavy, real poetry. It gives me that strange sudden sense of an echo from a former existence which always seems to me such a striking proof that we have immortal souls.

OCTAVIUS. Do you believe that it is true?

ANN. Tavy: if it is to come true, you must lose me as well as love me.

OCTAVIUS. Oh! [*He hastily sits down at the little table and covers his face with his hands.*]

ANN [*with conviction*] Tavy: I wouldn't for worlds destroy your illusions. I can neither take you nor let you go. I can see exactly what will suit you. You must be a sentimental old bachelor for my sake.

OCTAVIUS [*desperately*] Ann: I'll kill myself.

ANN. Oh no you won't: that wouldn't be kind. You won't have a bad time. You will be very nice to women; and you will go a good deal to the opera. A broken heart is a very pleasant complaint for a man in London if he has a comfortable income.

OCTAVIUS [*considerably cooled, but believing that he is only recovering his self-control*] I know you mean to be kind Ann. Jack has persuaded you that cynicism is a good tonic for me. [*He rises with quiet dignity.*]

ANN [*studying him slyly*] You see, I'm disillusionizing you already. That's what I dread.

OCTAVIUS. You do not dread disillusionizing Jack.

ANN [*her face lighting up with mischievous ecstasy— whispering*] I can't: he has no illusions about me. I shall surprise Jack the other way. Getting over an unfavorable impression is ever so much easier than living up to an ideal. Oh, I shall enrapture Jack sometimes!

OCTAVIUS [*resuming the calm phase of despair, and beginning to enjoy his broken heart and delicate attitude without knowing it*] I don't doubt that. You will enrapture him always. And he—the fool!—thinks you would make him wretched.

ANN. Yes: that's the difficulty, so far.

OCTAVIUS [*heroically*] Shall *I* tell him that you love him?

ANN [*quickly*] Oh no: he'd run away again.

OCTAVIUS [*shocked*] Ann: would you marry an unwilling man?

ANN. What a queer creature you are, Tavy! There's no such thing as a willing man when you really go for him [*She laughs naughtily*]. I'm shocking you, I suppose. But you know you are really getting a sort of satisfaction already in being out of danger yourself.

OCTAVIUS [*startled*] Satisfaction! [*Reproachfully*] You say that to me!

ANN. Well, if it were really agony, would you ask for more of it?

OCTAVIUS. Have I asked for more of it?

ANN. You have offered to tell Jack that I love him. That's self-sacrifice, I suppose; but there must be some satisfaction in it. Perhaps it's because you're a poet. You are like the bird that presses its breast against the sharp thorn to make itself sing.

OCTAVIUS. It's quite simple. I love you; and I want you to be happy. You don't love me; so I can't make you happy myself; but I can help another man to do it.

ANN. Yes: it seems quite simple. But I doubt if we ever know why we do things. The only really simple thing is to go straight for what you want and grab it. I suppose I don't love you, Tavy; but sometimes I feel as if I should like to make a man of you somehow. You are very foolish about women.

OCTAVIUS [*almost coldly*] I am content to be what I am in that respect.

ANN. Then you must keep away from them, and only dream about them. I wouldn't marry you for worlds, Tavy.

OCTAVIUS. I have no hope, Ann: I accept my ill luck. But I don't think you quite know how much it hurts.

ANN. You are so softhearted! It's queer that you should be so different from Violet. Violet's as hard as nails.

OCTAVIUS. Oh no. I am sure Violet is thoroughly womanly at heart.

ANN [*with some impatience*] Why do you say that? Is it unwomanly to be thoughtful and businesslike and sensible? Do you want Violet to be an idiot—or something worse, like me?

OCTAVIUS. Something worse—like you! What do you mean, Ann?

ANN. Oh well, I don't mean that, of course. But I have a great respect for Violet. She gets her own way always.

OCTAVIUS [*sighing*] So do you.

ANN. Yes; but somehow she gets it without coaxing—without having to make people sentimental about her.

OCTAVIUS [*with brotherly callousness*] Nobody could get very sentimental about Violet, I think, pretty as she is.

ANN. Oh yes they could, if she made them.

OCTAVIUS. But surely no really nice woman would deliberately practise on men's instincts in that way.

ANN [*throwing up her hands*] Oh Tavy, Tavy, Ricky Ticky Tavy, heaven help the woman who marries you!

OCTAVIUS [*his passion reviving at the name*] Oh why, why, why do you say that? Don't torment me. I don't understand.

ANN. Suppose she were to tell fibs, and lay snares for men?

OCTAVIUS. Do you think I could marry such a woman—I, who have known and loved you?

ANN. Hm! Well, at all events, she wouldn't let you if she were wise. So that's settled. And now I can't talk any more. Say you forgive me, and that the subject is closed.

OCTAVIUS. I have nothing to forgive; and the subject is closed. And if the wound is open, at least you shall never see it bleed.

ANN. Poetic to the last, Tavy. Good-bye, dear. [*She pats his cheek; has an impulse to kiss him and then another impulse of distaste which prevents her; finally runs away through the garden and into the villa.*]

[*Octavius again takes refuge at the table, bowing his head on his arms and sobbing softly. Mrs. Whitefield, who has been pottering round the Granada shops, and has a net full of little parcels in her hand, comes in through the gate and sees him.*]

MRS. WHITEFIELD [*running to him and lifting his head*]. What's the matter, Tavy? Are you ill?

OCTAVIUS. No, nothing, nothing.

MRS. WHITEFIELD [*still holding his head, anxiously*] But you're crying. Is it about Violet's marriage?

OCTAVIUS. No, no. Who told you about Violet?

MRS. WHITEFIELD [*restoring the head to its owner*] I met Roebuck and that awful old Irishman. Are you sure you're not ill? What's the matter?

OCTAVIUS [*affectionately*] It's nothing—only a man's broken heart. Doesn't that sound ridiculous?

MRS. WHITEFIELD. But what is it all about? Has Ann been doing anything to you?

OCTAVIUS. It's not Ann's fault. And don't think for a moment that I blame you.

MRS. WHITEFIELD [*startled*] For what?

OCTAVIUS [*pressing her hand consolingly*] For nothing. I said I didn't blame you.

MRS. WHITEFIELD. But I haven't done anything. What's the matter?

OCTAVIUS [*smiling sadly*] Can't you guess? I daresay you are right to prefer Jack to me as a husband for Ann; but I love Ann; and it hurts rather. [*He rises and moves away from her towards the middle of the lawn.*]

MRS. WHITEFIELD [*following him hastily*] Does Ann say that I want her to marry Jack?

OCTAVIUS. Yes: she has told me.

MRS. WHITEFIELD [*thoughtfully*] Then I'm very sorry for you, Tavy. It's only her way of saying *she* wants to marry Jack. Little she cares what *I* say or what *I* want!

OCTAVIUS. But she would not say it unless she believed it. Surely you don't suspect Ann of—of deceit!!

MRS. WHITEFIELD. Well, never mind, Tavy. I don't know which is best for a young man: to know too little, like you, or too much, like Jack.

[*Tanner returns.*]

TANNER. Well, I've disposed of old Malone. I've introduced him to Mendoza, Limited; and left the two brigands together to talk it out. Hullo, Tavy! anything wrong?

OCTAVIUS. I must go wash my face, I see. [*To Mrs. Whitefield*] Tell him what you wish. [*To Tanner*] You may take it from me, Jack, that Ann approves of it.

TANNER [*puzzled by his manner*] Approves of what?

OCTAVIUS. Of what Mrs. Whitefield wishes. [*He goes his way with sad dignity to the villa.*]

TANNER [*to Mrs. Whitefield*] This is very mysterious. What is it you wish? It shall be done, whatever it is.

MRS. WHITEFIELD [*with snivelling gratitude*] Thank you, Jack. [*She sits down. Tanner brings the other chair from the table and sits close to her with his elbows on his knees, giving her his whole attention.*] I don't know why it is that other people's children are so nice to me, and that my own have so little consideration for me. It's no wonder I don't seem able to care for Ann and Rhoda as I do for you and Tavy and Violet. It's a very queer world. It used to be so straightforward and simple; and now nobody seems to think and feel as they ought.

Nothing has been right since that speech that Professor Tyndall made at Belfast.

TANNER. Yes: life is more complicated than we used to think. But what am I to do for you?

MRS. WHITEFIELD. That's just what I want to tell you. Of course you'll marry Ann whether I like it or not—

TANNER [*starting*] It seems to me that I shall presently be married to Ann whether I like it myself or not.

MRS. WHITEFIELD [*peacefully*] Oh, very likely you will: you know what she is when she has set her mind on anything. But don't put it on me: that's all I ask. Tavy has just let out that she's been saying that I am making her marry you; and the poor boy is breaking his heart about it; for he is in love with her himself, though what he sees in her so wonderful, goodness knows: *I* don't. It's no use telling Tavy that Ann puts things into people's heads by telling them that I want them when the thought of them never crossed my mind. It only sets Tavy against me. But you know better than that. So if you marry her, don't put the blame on me.

TANNER [*emphatically*] I haven't the slightest intention of marrying her.

MRS. WHITEFIELD [*slyly*] She'd suit you better than Tavy. She'd meet her match in you, Jack. I'd like to see her meet her match.

TANNER. No man is a match for a woman, except with a poker and a pair of hobnailed boots. Not always even then. Anyhow, *I* can't take the poker to her. I should be a mere slave.

MRS. WHITEFIELD. No: she's afraid of you. At all events, you would tell her the truth about herself. She wouldn't be able to slip out of it as she does with me.

TANNER. Everybody would call me a brute if I told Ann the truth about herself in terms of her own moral code. To begin with, Ann says things that are not strictly true.

MRS. WHITEFIELD. I'm glad somebody sees she is not an angel.

TANNER. In short—to put it as a husband would put it when exasperated to the point of speaking out—she is a liar. And since she has plunged Tavy head over ears in love with her without any intention of marrying him, she is a coquette, according to the standard definition of a coquette as a woman who rouses passions she has no intention of gratifying. And as she has now reduced you to the point of being willing to sacrifice me at the altar for the mere satisfaction of getting me to call her a liar to her face, I may conclude that she is a bully as well. She can't bully men as she bullies women; so she habitually and unscrupulously uses her personal fascination to make men give her whatever she wants. That makes her almost something for which I know no polite name.

MRS. WHITEFIELD [*in mild expostulation*] Well, you can't expect perfection, Jack.

TANNER. I don't. But what annoys me is that Ann does. I know perfectly well that all this about her being a liar and a bully and a coquette and so forth is a trumped-up moral indictment which might be brought against anybody. We all lie; we all bully as much as we dare; we all bid for admiration without the least intention of earning it; we all get as much rent as we can out of our powers of fascination. If Ann would admit this I shouldn't quarrel with her. But she won't. If she has children she'll take advantage of their telling lies to amuse herself by whacking them. If another woman makes eyes at me, she'll refuse to know a coquette. She will do just what she likes herself whilst insisting on everybody else doing what the conventional code prescribes. In short, I can stand everything except her confounded hypocrisy. That's what beats me.

MRS. WHITEFIELD [*carried away by the relief of hearing her own opinion so eloquently expressed*] Oh, she is a hypocrite. She is: she is. Isn't she?

TANNER. Then why do you want to marry me to her?

MRS. WHITEFIELD [*querulously*] There now! put it on me, of course. I never thought of it until Tavy told me she said I did. But, you know, I'm very fond of Tavy: he's a sort of son to me; and I don't want him to be trampled on and made wretched.

TANNER. Whereas I don't matter, I suppose.

MRS. WHITEFIELD. Oh, you are different, somehow: you are able to take care of yourself. You'd serve her out. And anyhow, she must marry somebody.

TANNER. Aha! there speaks the life instinct. You detest her; but you feel that you must get her married.

MRS. WHITEFIELD [*rising, shocked*] Do you mean that I detest my own daughter! Surely you don't believe me to be so wicked and unnatural as that, merely because I see her faults.

TANNER [*cynically*] You love her, then?

MRS. WHITEFIELD. Why, of course I do. What queer things you say, Jack! We can't help loving our own blood relations.

TANNER. Well, perhaps it saves unpleasantness to say so. But for my part, I suspect that the tables of consanguinity have a natural basis in a natural repugnance [*he rises*].

MRS. WHITEFIELD. You shouldn't say things like that, Jack. I hope you won't tell Ann that I have been speaking to you. I only wanted to set myself right with you and Tavy. I couldn't sit mumchance and have everything put on me.

TANNER [*politely*] Quite so.

MRS. WHITEFIELD [*dissatisfied*] And now I've only made matters worse. Tavy's angry with me because I don't worship Ann. And when it's been put into my head that Ann ought to marry you, what can I say except that it would serve her right?

TANNER. Thank you.

MRS. WHITEFIELD. Now don't be silly and twist what I say into something I don't mean. I ought to have fair play—

[*Ann comes from the villa, followed presently by Violet, who is dressed for driving.*]

ANN [*coming to her mother's right hand with threatening suavity*] Well, mamma darling, you seem to be having a delightful chat with Jack. We can hear you all over the place.

MRS. WHITEFIELD [*appalled*] Have you overheard—

TANNER. Never fear: Ann is only—well, we were discussing that habit of hers just now. She hasn't heard a word.

MRS. WHITEFIELD [*stoutly*] I don't care whether she has or not: I have a right to say what I please.

VIOLET [*arriving on the lawn and coming between Mrs. Whitefield and Tanner*] I've come to say good-bye. I'm off for my honeymoon.

MRS. WHITEFIELD [*crying*] Oh don't say that, Violet. And no wedding, no breakfast, no clothes, nor anything.

VIOLET [*petting her*] It won't be for long.

MRS. WHITEFIELD. Don't let him take you to America. Promise me that you won't.

VIOLET [*very decidedly*] I should think not, indeed. Don't cry, dear: I'm only going to the hotel.

MRS. WHITEFIELD. But going in that dress, with your luggage, makes one realize— [*she chokes, and then breaks out again*] How I wish you were my daughter, Violet!

VIOLET [*soothing her*] There, there: so I am. Ann will be jealous.

MRS. WHITEFIELD. Ann doesn't care a bit for me.

ANN. Fie, mother! Come, now: you mustn't cry any more: you know Violet doesn't like it. [*Mrs. Whitefield dries her eyes, and subsides.*]

VIOLET. Good-bye, Jack.

TANNER. Good-bye, Violet

VIOLET. The sooner you get married too, the better. You will be much less misunderstood.

TANNER [*restively*] I quite expect to get married in the course of the afternoon. You all seem to have set your minds on it.

VIOLET. You might do worse. [*To Mrs. Whitefield: putting her arm round her*] Let me take you to the hotel with me: the drive will do you good. Come in and get a wrap. [*She takes her towards the villa.*]

MRS. WHITEFIELD [*as they go up through the garden*] I don't know what I shall do when you are gone, with no one but Ann in the house; and she always occupied with the men! It's not to be expected that your husband will care to be bothered with an old woman like me. Oh, you needn't tell me: politeness is all very well; but I know what people think— [*She talks herself and Violet out of sight and hearing.*]

[*Ann, musing on Violet's opportune advice, approaches Tanner; examines him humorously for a moment from toe to top; and finally delivers her opinion.*]

ANN. Violet is quite right. You ought to get married.

TANNER [*explosively*] Ann: I will not marry you. Do you hear? I won't, won't, won't, won't, WON'T marry you.

ANN [*placidly*] Well, nobody axd you, sir she said, sir she said, sir she said. So that's settled.

TANNER. Yes, nobody has asked me; but everybody treats the thing as settled. It's in the air. When we meet, the others go away on absurd pretexts to leave us alone together. Ramsden no longer scowls at me: his eye beams, as if he were already giving you away to me in church. Tavy refers me to your mother and gives me his blessing. Straker openly treats you as his future employer: it was he who first told me of it.

ANN. Was that why you ran-away?

TANNER. Yes, only to be stopped by a lovesick brigand and run down like a truant schoolboy.

ANN. Well, if you don't want to be married, you needn't be [*she turns away from him and sits down, much at her ease*].

TANNER [*following her*]. Does any man want to be hanged? Yet men let themselves be hanged without a struggle for life, though they could at least give the chaplain a black eye. We do the world's will, not our own. I have a frightful feeling that I shall let myself be married because it is the world's will that you should have a husband.

ANN. I daresay I shall, someday.

TANNER. But why me—me of all men? Marriage is to me apostasy, profanation of the sanctuary of my soul, violation of my manhood, sale of my birthright, shameful surrender, ignominious capitulation, acceptance of defeat. I shall decay like a thing that has served its purpose and is done with; I shall change from a man with a future to a man with a past; I shall see in the greasy eyes of all the other husbands their relief at the arrival of a new prisoner to share their ignominy. The young men will scorn me as one who has sold out: to the young women I, who have always been an enigma and a possibility, shall be merely somebody else's property—and damaged goods at that: a secondhand man at best.

ANN. Well, your wife can put on a cap and make

herself ugly to keep you in countenance, like my grandmother.

TANNER. So that she may make her triumph more insolent by publicly throwing away the bait the moment the trap snaps on the victim!

ANN. After all, though, what difference would it make? Beauty is all very well at first sight; but who ever looks at it when it has been in the house three days? I thought our pictures very lovely when papa bought them; but I haven't looked at them for years. You never bother about my looks: you are too well used to me. I might be the umbrella stand.

TANNER. You lie, you vampire: you lie.

ANN. Flatterer. Why are you trying to fascinate me, Jack, if you don't want to marry me?

TANNER. The Life Force. I am in the grip of the Life Force.

ANN. I don't understand in the least: it sounds like the Life Guards.

TANNER. Why don't you marry Tavy? He is willing. Can you not be satisfied unless your prey struggles?

ANN [turning to him as if to let him into a secret] Tavy will never marry. Haven't you noticed that that sort of man never marries?

TANNER. What! a man who idolizes women! who sees nothing in nature but romantic scenery for love duets! Tavy, the chivalrous, the faithful, the tender-hearted and true! Tavy never marry! Why, he was born to be swept up by the first pair of blue eyes he meets in the street.

ANN. Yes, I know. All the same, Jack, men like that always live in comfortable bachelor lodgings with broken hearts, and are adored by their landladies, and never get married. Men like you always get married.

TANNER [smiting his brow] How frightfully, horribly true! It has been staring me in the face all my life; and I never saw it before.

ANN. Oh, it's the same with women. The poetic temperament's a very nice temperament, very amiable, very harmless and poetic, I daresay; but it's an old maid's temperament.

TANNER. Barren. The Life Force passes it by.

ANN. If that's what you mean by the Life Force, yes.

TANNER. You don't care for Tavy?

ANN [*looking round carefully to make sure that Tavy is not within earshot*] No.

TANNER. And you do care for me?

ANN [*rising quietly and shaking her finger at him*] Now Jack! Behave yourself.

TANNER. Infamous, abandoned woman! Devil!

ANN. Boa-constrictor! Elephant!

TANNER. Hypocrite!

ANN [*softly*] I must be, for my future husband's sake.

TANNER. For mine! [*Correcting himself savagely*] I mean for his.

ANN [*ignoring the correction*] Yes, for yours. You had better marry what you call a hypocrite, Jack. Women who are not hypocrites go about in rational dress and are insulted and get into all sorts of hot water. And then their husbands get dragged in too, and live in continual dread of fresh complications. Wouldn't you prefer a wife you could depend on?

TANNER. No, a thousand times no: hot water is the revolutionist's element. You clean men as you clean milk-pails, by scalding them.

ANN. Cold water has its uses too. It's healthy.

TANNER [*despairingly*] Oh, you are witty: at the supreme moment the Life Force endows you with every quality. Well, I too can be a hypocrite. Your father's will appointed me your guardian, not your suitor. I shall be faithful to my trust.

ANN [*in low siren tones*] He asked me who would I have as my guardian before he made that will. I chose you!

TANNER. The will is yours then! The trap was laid from the beginning.

ANN [*concentrating all her magic*] From the beginning—from our childhood—for both of us—by the Life Force.

TANNER. I will not marry you. I will not marry you.

ANN. Oh, you will, you will.

TANNER. I tell you, no, no, no.

ANN. I tell you, yes, yes, yes.

TANNER. No.

ANN [*coaxing—imploring—almost exhausted*] Yes. Before it is too late for repentance. Yes.

TANNER [*struck by the echo from the past*] When did all this happen to me before? Are we two dreaming?

ANN [*suddenly losing her courage, with an anguish that she does not conceal*] No. We are awake; and you have said no: that is all.

TANNER [*brutally*] Well?

ANN. Well, I made a mistake: you do not love me.

TANNER [*seizing her in his arms*] It is false: I love you. The Life Force enchants me: I have the whole world in my arms when I clasp you. But I am fighting for my freedom: for my honor, for my self, one and indivisible.

ANN. Your happiness will be worth them all.

TANNER. You would sell freedom and honor and self for happiness?

ANN. It will not be all happiness for me. Perhaps death.

TANNER [*groaning*] Oh, that clutch holds and hurts. What have you grasped in me? Is there a father's heart as well as a mother's?

ANN. Take care, Jack: if anyone comes while we are like this, you will have to marry me.

TANNER. If we two stood now on the edge of a precipice, I would hold you tight and jump.

ANN [*panting, failing more and more under the strain*] Jack: let me go. I have dared so frightfully—it is lasting longer than I thought. Let me go: I can't bear it.

TANNER. Nor I. Let it kill us.

ANN. Yes: I don't care. I am at the end of my forces. I don't care. I think I am going to faint.

[*At this moment Violet and Octavius come from the villa with Mrs. Whitefield, who is wrapped up for driving. Simultaneously Malone and Ramsden, followed by Mendoza and Straker, come in through the little gate in the paling. Tanner shamefacedly releases Ann, who raises her hand giddily to her forehead.*]

MALONE. Take care. Something's the matter with the lady.

RAMSDEN. What does this mean?

VIOLET. [*running between Ann and Tanner*] Are you ill?

ANN [*reeling, with a supreme effort*] I have promised to marry Jack. [*She swoons. Violet kneels by her and chafes her hand. Tanner runs round to her other hand, and tries to lift her head. Octavius goes to Violet's assistance, but does not know what to do. Mrs. Whitefield hurries back into the villa. Octavius, Malone and Ramsden run to Ann and crowd round her, stooping to assist. Straker coolly comes to Ann's feet, and Mendoza to her head, both upright and self-possessed.*]

STRAKER. Now then, ladies and gentlemen: she don't want a crowd round her: she wants air—all the air she can git. If you please, gents— [*Malone and Ramsden allow him to drive them gently past Ann and up the lawn towards the garden, where Octavius, who has already become conscious of his uselessness, joins them. Straker, following them up, pauses for a moment to instruct Tanner.*] Don't lift er ed, Mr Tanner: let it go flat so's the blood can run back into it.

MENDOZA. He is right, Mr. Tanner. Trust to the air of the Sierra. [*He withdraws delicately to the garden steps.*]

TANNER [*rising*] I yield to your superior knowledge of physiology, Henry. [*He withdraws to the corner of the lawn; and Octavius immediately hurries down to him.*]

TAVY [*aside to Tanner, grasping his hand*] Jack: be very happy.

TANNER [*aside to Tavy*] I never asked her. It is a trap for me. [*He goes up the lawn towards the garden. Octavius remains petrified.*]

MENDOZA [*intercepting Mrs. Whitefield, who comes from the villa with a glass of brandy*] What is this, madam? [*He takes it from her.*]

MRS. WHITEFIELD. A little brandy.

MENDOZA. The worst thing you could give her. Allow me. [*He swallows it.*] Trust to the air of the Sierra, madam.

[*For a moment the men all forget Ann and stare at Mendoza.*]

ANN [*in Violet's ear clutching her round the neck*]. Violet: did Jack say anything when I fainted?

VIOLET. No.

ANN. Ah! [*with a sigh of intense relief she relapses*].

MRS. WHITEFIELD. Oh, she's fainted again.

[*They are about to rush back to her; but Mendoza stops them with a warning gesture.*]

ANN [*supine*] No I haven't. I'm quite happy.

TANNER [*suddenly walking determinedly to her, and snatching her hand from Violet to feel her pulse*] Why, her pulse is positively bounding. Come, get up. What nonsense! Up with you. [*He gets her up summarily.*]

ANN. Yes: I feel strong enough now. But you very nearly killed me, Jack, for all that.

MALONE. A rough wooer, eh? They're the best sort, Miss Whitefield. I congratulate Mr. Tanner; and I hope to meet you and him as frequent guests at the Abbey.

ANN. Thank you. [*She goes past Malone to Octavius*] Ricky Ticky Tavy: congratulate me. [*Aside to him*] I want to make you cry for the last time.

TAVY [*steadfastly*] No more tears. I am happy in your happiness. And I believe in you in spite of everything.

RAMSDEN [*coming between Malone and Tanner*] You are a happy man, Jack Tanner. I envy you.

MENDOZA [*advancing between Violet and Tanner*] Sir: there are two tragedies in life. One is not to get your heart's desire. The other is to get it. Mine and yours, sir.

TANNER. Mr. Mendoza: I have no heart's desires. Ramsden: it is very easy for you to call me a happy man: you are only a spectator. I am one of the principals; and I know better. Ann: stop tempting Tavy, and come back to me.

ANN [*complying*] You are absurd, Jack. [*She takes his proffered arm.*]

TANNER [*continuing*] I solemnly say that I am not a happy man. Ann looks happy; but she is only triumphant, successful, victorious. That is not happiness, but the price for which the strong sell their happiness. What we have both done this afternoon is to renounce happiness, renounce freedom, renounce tranquillity, above all, renounce the romantic possibilities of an unknown future, for the cares of a household and a family. I beg

that no man may seize the occasion to get half drunk
and utter imbecile speeches and coarse pleasantries at
my expense. We propose to furnish our own house according to our own taste; and I hereby give notice that
the seven or eight travelling clocks, the four or five
dressing cases, the salad bowls, the carvers and fish
slices, the copy of Tennyson in extra morocco, and all
the other articles you are preparing to heap upon us,
will be instantly sold, and the proceeds devoted to circu-
lating free copies of the Revolutionist's Handbook. The
wedding will take place three days after our return to
England, by special license, at the office of the district
superintendent registrar, in the presence of my solicitor
and his clerk, who, like his clients, will be in ordinary
walking dress—

VIOLET [*with intense conviction*] You are a brute, Jack.

ANN [*looking at him with fond pride and caressing
his arm*] Never mind her, dear. Go on talking.

TANNER. Talking!

[*Universal laughter.*]

THE REVOLUTIONIST'S HANDBOOK AND POCKET COMPANION
BY John Tanner, M.I.R.C.
(Member of the Idle Rich Class).

PREFACE TO THE REVOLUTIONIST'S HANDBOOK

"No one can contemplate the present condition of the masses of the people without desiring something like a revolution for the better." *Sir Robert Giffen.* Essays in Finance, vol. ii. p. 393.

FOREWORD

A REVOLUTIONIST is one who desires to discard the existing social order and try another.

The constitution of England is revolutionary. To a Russian or Anglo-Indian bureaucrat, a general election is as much a revolution as a referendum or plebiscite in which the people fight instead of voting. The French Revolution overthrew one set of rulers and substituted another with different interests and different views. That is what a general election enables the people to do in England every seven years if they choose. Revolution is therefore a national institution in England; and its advocacy by an Englishman needs no apology.

Every man is a revolutionist concerning the thing he understands. For example, every person who has mastered a profession is a sceptic concerning it, and consequently a revolutionist.

Every genuinely religious person is a heretic and therefore a revolutionist.

All who achieve real distinction in life begin as revolutionists. The most distinguished persons become more revolutionary as they grow older, though they are commonly supposed to become more conservative owing to their loss of faith in conventional methods of reform.

Any person under the age of thirty, who, having any knowledge of the existing social order, is not a revolutionist, is an inferior.

AND YET

Revolutions have never lightened the burden of tyranny: they have only shifted it to another shoulder.

John Tanner.

THE REVOLUTIONIST'S HANDBOOK

I. ON GOOD BREEDING

IF THERE were no God, said the eighteenth century Deist, it would be necessary to invent Him. Now this eighteenth century god was *deus ex machina,* the god who helped those who could not help themselves, the god of the lazy and incapable. The nineteenth century decided that there is indeed no such god; and now Man must take in hand all the work that he used to shirk with an idle prayer. He must, in effect, change himself into the political Providence which he formerly conceived as god; and such change is not only possible, but the only sort of change that is real. The mere transfigurations of institutions, as from military and priestly dominance to commercial and scientific dominance, from commercial dominance to proletarian democracy, from slavery to serfdom, from serfdom to capitalism, from monarchy to republicanism, from polytheism to monotheism, from monotheism to atheism, from atheism to pantheistic humanitarianism, from general illiteracy to general literacy, from romance to realism, from realism to mysticism, from metaphysics to physics, are all but changes from Tweedledum to Tweedledee: *"plus ça change, plus c'est la même chose."* But the changes from the crab apple to the pippin, from the wolf and fox to the house dog, from the charger of Henry V to the brewer's draught horse and the race horse, are real; for here Man has played the god, subduing Nature to his intention, and ennobling or debasing Life for a set purpose. And what can be done with a wolf can be done with a man. If such monsters as the tramp and the gentleman can appear as mere by-products of Man's individual greed and folly, what might we not hope for as a main product of his universal aspiration?

This is no new conclusion. The despair of institutions, and the inexorable "ye must be born again," with Mrs. Poyser's stipulation, "and born different," recurs in every generation. The cry for the Superman did not begin with Nietzsche, nor will it end with his vogue. But it has always been silenced by the same question: what kind of person is this Superman to be? You do not ask for a super-apple, but for an eatable apple; nor for a super-horse, but for a horse of greater draught or velocity. Neither is it of any use to ask for a Superman: you must furnish a specification of the sort of man you want. Unfortunately you do not know what sort of man you want. Some sort of goodlooking philosopher-athlete, with a handsome healthy woman for his mate, perhaps.

Vague as this is, it is a great advance on the popular demand for a perfect gentleman and a perfect lady. And, after all, no market demand in the world takes the form of exact technical specification of the article required. Excellent poultry and potatoes are produced to satisfy the demand of housewives who do not know the technical differences between a tuber and a chicken. They will tell you that the proof of the pudding is in the eating; and they are right. The proof of the Superman will be in the living; and we shall find out how to produce him by the old method of trial and error, and not by waiting for a completely convincing prescription of his ingredients.

Certain common and obvious mistakes may be ruled

out from the beginning. For example, we agree that we want superior mind; but we need not fall into the football club folly of counting on this as a product of superior body. Yet if we recoil so far as to conclude that superior mind consists in being the dupe of our ethical classifications of virtues and vices, in short, of conventional morality, we shall fall out of the frying pan of the football club into the fire of the Sunday School. If we must choose between a race of athletes and a race of "good" men, let us have the athletes: better Samson and Milo than Calvin and Robespierre. But neither alternative is worth changing for: Samson is no more a Superman than Calvin. What then are we to do?

II. PROPERTY AND MARRIAGE

LET US hurry over the obstacles set up by property and marriage. Revolutionists make too much of them. No doubt it is easy to demonstrate that property will destroy society unless society destroys it. No doubt, also, property has hitherto held its own and destroyed all the empires. But that was because the superficial objection to it (that it distributes social wealth and the social labor burden in a grotesquely inequitable manner) did not threaten the existence of the race, but only the individual happiness of its units, and finally the maintenance of some irrelevant political form or other, such as a nation, an empire, or the like. Now as happiness never matters to Nature, as she neither recognizes flags and frontiers nor cares a straw whether the economic system adopted by a society is feudal, capitalistic or collectivist, provided it keeps the race afoot (the hive and the anthill being as acceptable to her as Utopia), the demonstrations of Socialists, though irrefutable, will never make any serious impression on property. The knell of that overrated institution will not sound until it is felt to conflict with some more vital matter than mere personal inequities in industrial economy. No such conflict was perceived whilst society had not yet grown beyond national communities too small and simple to disastrously overtax Man's limited political capacity. But we have now reached the stage of international organization. Man's political capacity and magnanimity are clearly beaten by the vastness and complexity of the problems forced on him. And it is at this anxious moment that he finds, when he looks upward for a mightier mind to help him, that the heavens are empty. He will presently see that his discarded formula that Man is the Temple of the Holy Ghost happens to be precisely true, and that it is only through his own brain and hand that this Holy Ghost, formerly the most nebulous person in the Trinity, and now become its sole survivor as it has always been its real Unity, can help him in any way. And so, if the Superman is to come, he must be born of Woman by Man's intentional and well-considered contrivance. Conviction of this will smash everything that opposes it. Even Property and Marriage, which laugh at the laborer's petty complaint that he is defrauded of "surplus value," and at the domestic miseries of the slaves of the wedding ring, will themselves be laughed aside as the lightest of trifles if they cross this conception when it becomes a fully realized vital purpose of the race.

That they must cross it becomes obvious the moment we acknowledge the futility of breeding men for special qualities as we breed cocks for game, greyhounds for speed, or sheep for mutton. What is really important in Man is the part of him that we do not yet understand. Of much of it we are not even conscious, just as we are not normally conscious of keeping up our circulation by our heart-pump, though if we neglect it we die. We are therefore driven to the conclusion that when we have carried selection as far as we can by rejecting from the list of eligible parents all persons who are uninteresting, unpromising, or blemished without any set-off, we shall still have to trust to the guidance of fancy (*alias* Voice of Nature), both in the breeders and the parents, for that superiority in the unconscious self which will be the true characteristic of the Superman.

At this point we perceive the importance of giving fancy the widest possible field. To cut humanity up into small cliques, and effectively limit the selection of the individual to his own clique, is to postpone the Superman for eons, if not for ever. Not only should every person be nourished and trained as a possible parent, but there should be no possibility of such an obstacle to natural selection as the objection of a countess to a navvy or of a duke to a charwoman. Equality is essential to good breeding; and equality, as all economists know, is incompatible with property.

Besides, equality is an essential condition of bad breeding also; and bad breeding is indispensable to the weeding out of the human race. When the conception of heredity took hold of the scientific imagination in the middle of last century, its devotees announced that it was a crime to marry the lunatic to the lunatic or the consumptive to the consumptive. But pray are we to try to correct our diseased stocks by infecting our healthy stocks with them? Clearly the attraction which disease has for diseased people is beneficial to the race. If two really unhealthy people get married, they will, as likely as not, have a great number of children who will all die before they reach maturity. This is a far more satisfactory arrangement than the tragedy of a union between a healthy and an unhealthy person. Though more costly than sterilization of the unhealthy, it has the enormous advantage that in the event of our notions of health and unhealth being erroneous (which to some extent they most certainly are), the error will be corrected by experience instead of confirmed by evasion.

One fact must be faced resolutely, in spite of the shrieks of the romantic. There is no evidence that the best citizens are the offspring of congenial marriages, or that a conflict of temperament is not a highly important part of what breeders call crossing. On the contrary, it is quite sufficiently probable that good results may be obtained from parents who would be extremely unsuitable companions and partners, to make it certain that the experiment of mating them will sooner or later be tried purposely almost as often as it is now tried accidentally. But mating such couples must clearly not involve marrying them. In conjugation two complementary persons may supply one another's deficiencies: in the domestic partnership of marriage they only feel them and suffer from them. Thus the son of a robust, cheerful, eupeptic British country squire, with the tastes and range of his class, and of a clever, imaginative, intellectual, highly civilized Jewess, might be very superior to both his parents; but it is not likely that the Jewess would find the squire an interesting companion, or his habits, his friends, his place and mode of life congenial to her. Therefore marriage, whilst it is made an indispensable condition of mating, will delay the advent of the Superman as effectually as Property, and will be modified by the impulse towards him just as effectually.

The practical abrogation of Property and Marriage as they exist at present will occur without being much noticed. To the mass of men, the intelligent abolition of property would mean nothing except an increase in the quantity of food, clothing, housing and comfort at their personal disposal, as well as a greater control over their time and circumstances. Very few persons now make any distinction between virtually complete property and property held on such highly developed public conditions as to place its income on the same footing as that of a propertyless clergyman, officer, or civil servant. A landed proprietor may still drive men and women off his land, demolish their dwellings, and replace them with sheep or deer; and in the unregulated trades the private trader may still sponge on the regulated trades and sacrifice the life and health of the nation as lawlessly as the Manchester cotton manufacturers did at the beginning of last century. But though the Factory Code on the one hand, and Trade Union organization on the other, have, within the lifetime of men still living, converted the old unrestricted property of the cotton manufacturer in his mill and the cotton spinner in his labor into a mere permission to trade or work on stringent public or collective conditions, imposed in the interest of the general welfare without any regard for individual hard cases, people in Lancashire still speak of their "property" in the old terms, meaning nothing more by it than the things a thief can be punished for stealing. The total abolition of property, and the conversion of every citizen into a salaried functionary in the public service, would leave much more than 99 per cent of the nation quite unconscious of any greater change than now takes place when the son of a shipowner goes into the navy. They would still call their watches and umbrellas and back gardens their property.

Marriage also will persist as a name attached to a general custom long after the custom itself will have altered. For example, modern English marriage, as modified by divorce and by Married Women's Property Acts, differs more from early nineteenth century marriage than Byron's marriage did from Shakespeare's. At the present moment marriage in England differs not only from marriage in France, but from marriage in Scotland. Marriage as modified by the divorce laws in South Dakota would be called mere promiscuity in Clapham. Yet the Americans, far from taking a profligate and cynical view of marriage, do homage to its ideals with a seriousness that seems old fashioned in Clapham. Neither in England nor America would a proposal to abolish marriage be tolerated for a moment; and yet nothing is more certain than that in both countries the progressive modification of the marriage contract will be continued until it is no more onerous nor irrevocable than any ordinary commercial deed of partnership. Were even this dispensed with, people would still call themselves husbands and wives; describe their companionships as marriages; and be for the most part unconscious that they were any less married than Henry VIII. For though a glance at the legal conditions of marriage in different Christian countries shews that marriage varies legally from frontier to frontier, domesticity varies so little that most people believe their own marriage laws to be universal. Consequently here again, as in the case of Property, the absolute confidence of the public in the stability of the institution's name, makes it all the easier to alter its substance.

However, it cannot be denied that one of the changes in public opinion demanded by the need for the Superman is a very unexpected one. It is nothing less than the dissolution of the present necessary association of marriage with conjugation, which most unmarried people regard as the very diagnostic of marriage. They are wrong, of course: it would be quite as near the truth to say that conjugation is the one purely accidental and incidental condition of marriage. Conjugation is essential to nothing but the propagation of the race; and the moment that paramount need is provided for otherwise than by marriage, conjugation, from Nature's creative point of view, ceases to be essential in marriage. But marriage does not thereupon cease to be so economical, convenient, and comfortable, that the Superman might safely bribe the matrimonomaniacs by offering to revive all the old inhuman stringency and irrevocability of marriage, to abolish divorce, to confirm the horrible bond which still chains decent people to drunkards, criminals and wasters, provided only the complete extrication of conjugation from it were conceded to him. For if people could form domestic companionships on no easier terms than these, they would still marry. The Roman Catholic, forbidden by his Church to avail himself of the divorce laws, marries as freely as the South Dakotan Presbyterians who can change partners with a facility that scandalizes the old world; and were his Church to dare a further step towards Christianity and enjoin celibacy on its laity as well as on its clergy, marriages would still be contracted for the sake of domesticity by perfectly obedient sons and daughters of the Church. One need not further pursue these hypotheses: they are only suggested here to help the reader to analyze marriage into its two functions of regulating conjugation and supplying a form of domesticity. These two functions are quite separable; and domesticity is the only one of the two which is essential to the existence of marriage, because conjugation without domesticity is not marriage at all, whereas domesticity without conjugation is still marriage: in fact it is necessarily the actual condition of all fertile marriages during a great part of their duration, and of some marriages during the whole of it.

Taking it, then, that Property and Marriage, by destroying Equality and thus hampering sexual selection with irrelevant conditions, are hostile to the evolution of the Superman, it is easy to understand why the only generally known modern experiment in breeding the human race took place in a community which discarded both institutions.

III. THE PERFECTIONIST EXPERIMENT AT ONEIDA CREEK

In 1848 the Oneida Community was founded in America to carry out a resolution arrived at by a handful of Perfectionist Communists "that we will devote ourselves exclusively to the establishment of the Kingdom of God." Though the American nation declared that this sort of thing was not to be tolerated in a Christian country, the Oneida Community held its own for over thirty years, during which period it seems to have produced healthier children and done and suffered less evil than any Joint Stock Company on record. It was, however, a highly selected community; for a genuine communist (roughly definable as an intensely proud person who proposes to enrich the common fund instead of to sponge on it) is superior to an ordinary joint stock capitalist precisely as an ordinary joint stock capitalist is superior to a pirate. Further, the Perfectionists were mightily shepherded by their chief Noyes, one of those chance attempts at the Superman which occur from time to time in spite of the interference of Man's blundering institutions. The existence of Noyes simplified the breeding problem for the Communists, the question as to what sort of man they should strive to breed being settled at once by the obvious desirability of breeding another Noyes.

But an experiment conducted by a handful of people, who, after thirty years of immunity from the unintentional child slaughter that goes on by ignorant parents in private homes, numbered only 300, could do very little except prove that the Communists, under the guidance of a Superman "devoted exclusively to the establishment of the Kingdom of God," and caring no more for property and marriage than a Camberwell minister cares for Hindoo Caste or Suttee, might make a much better job of their lives than ordinary folk under the harrow of both these institutions. Yet their Superman himself admitted that this apparent success was only part of the abnormal phenomenon of his own occurrence; for when he came to the end of his powers through age, he himself guided and organized the voluntary relapse of the Communists into marriage, capitalism, and customary private life, thus admitting that the real social solution was not what a casual Superman could persuade a picked company to do for him, but what a whole community of Supermen would do spontaneously. If Noyes had had to organize, not a few dozen Perfectionists, but the whole

United States, America would have beaten him as completely as England beat Oliver Cromwell, France Napoleon, or Rome Julius Caesar. Cromwell learnt by bitter experience that God himself cannot raise a people above its own level, and that even though you stir a nation to sacrifice all its appetites to its conscience, the result will still depend wholly on what sort of conscience the nation has got. Napoleon seems to have ended by regarding mankind as a troublesome pack of hounds only worth keeping for the sport of hunting with them. Caesar's capacity for fighting without hatred or resentment was defeated by the determination of his soldiers to kill their enemies in the field instead of taking them prisoners to be spared by Caesar; and his civil supremacy was purchased by colossal bribery of the citizens of Rome. What great rulers cannot do, codes and religions cannot do. Man reads his own nature into every ordinance: if you devise a superhuman commandment so cunningly that it cannot be misinterpreted in terms of his will, he will denounce it as seditious blasphemy, or else disregard it as either crazy or totally unintelligible. Parliaments and synods may tinker as much as they please with their codes and creeds as circumstances alter the balance of classes and their interests; and, as a result of the tinkering, there may be an occasional illusion of moral evolution, as when the victory of the commercial caste over the military caste leads to the substitution of social boycotting and pecuniary damages for duelling. At certain moments there may even be a considerable material advance, as when the conquest of political power by the working class produces a better distribution of wealth through the simple action of the selfishness of the new masters; but all this is mere readjustment and reformation: until the heart and mind of the people is changed the very greatest man will no more dare to govern on the assumption that all are as great as he than a drover dare leave his flock to find its way through the streets as he himself would. Until there is an England in which every man is a Cromwell, a France in which every man is a Napoleon, a Rome in which every man is a Caesar, a Germany in which every man is a Luther plus a Goethe, the world will be no more improved by its heroes than a Brixton villa is improved by the pyramid of Cheops. The production of such nations is the only real change possible to us.

IV. MAN'S OBJECTION TO HIS OWN IMPROVEMENT

BUT WOULD such a change be tolerated if Man must rise above himself to desire it? It would, through his misconception of its nature. Man does desire an ideal Superman with such energy as he can spare from his nutrition, and has in every age magnified the best living substitute for it he can find. His least incompetent general is set up as an Alexander; his king is the first gentleman in the world; his Pope is a saint. He is never without an array of human idols who are all nothing but sham Supermen. That the real Superman will snap his superfingers at all Man's present trumpery ideals of right, duty, honor, justice, religion, even decency, and accept moral obligations beyond present human endurance, is a thing that contemporary Man does not foresee: in fact he does not notice it when our casual Supermen do it in his very face. He actually does it himself every day without knowing it. He will therefore make no objection to the production of a race of what he calls Great Men or Heroes, because he will imagine them, not as true Supermen, but as himself endowed with infinite brains, infinite courage, and infinite money.

The most troublesome opposition will arise from the general fear of mankind that any interference with our conjugal customs will be an interference with our pleasures and our romance. This fear, by putting on airs of offended morality, has always intimidated people who have not measured its essential weakness; but it will prevail with those degenerates only in whom the instinct of fertility has faded into a mere itching for pleasure. The modern devices for combining pleasure with sterility, now universally known and accessible, enable these persons to weed themselves out of the race, a process already vigorously at work; and the consequent survival of the intelligently fertile means the survival of the partizans of the Superman; for what is proposed is nothing but the replacement of the old unintelligent, inevitable, almost unconscious fertility by an intelligently controlled, conscious fertility, and the elimination of the mere voluptuary from the evolutionary process.* Even if this selective agency had not been invented, the purpose of the race would still shatter the opposition of individual instincts. Not only do the bees and the ants satisfy their reproductive and parental instincts vicariously; but marriage itself successfully imposes celibacy on millions of unmarried normal men and women. In short, the individual instinct in this matter, overwhelming as it is thoughtlessly supposed to be, is really a finally negligible one.

V. THE POLITICAL NEED FOR THE SUPERMAN

THE NEED for the Superman is, in its most imperative aspect, a political one. We have been driven to Proletarian Democracy by the failure of all the alternative systems; for these depended on the existence of Supermen acting as despots or oligarchs; and not only were these Supermen not always or even often forthcoming at the right moment and in an eligible social position, but when they were forthcoming they could not, except for a short time and by morally suicidal coercive methods, impose superhumanity on those whom they governed; so, by mere force of "human nature," government by consent of the governed has supplanted the old plan of governing the citizen as a public-schoolboy is governed.

---

* The part played in evolution by the voluptuary will be the same as that already played by the glutton. The glutton, as the man with the strongest motive for nourishing himself, will always take more pains than his fellows to get food. When food is so difficult to get that only great exertions can secure a sufficient supply of it, the glutton's appetite develops his cunning and enterprise to the utmost; and he becomes not only the best fed but the ablest man in the community. But in more hospitable climates, or where the social organization of the food supply makes it easy for a man to overeat, then the glutton eats himself out of health and finally out of existence. All other voluptuaries prosper and perish in the same way; and this is why the survival of the fittest means finally the survival of the self-controlled, because they alone can adapt themselves to the perpetual shifting of conditions produced by industrial progress.

Now we have yet to see the man who, having any practical experience of Proletarian Democracy, has any belief in its capacity for solving great political problems, or even for doing ordinary parochial work intelligently and economically. Only under despotism and oligarchies has the Radical faith in "universal suffrage" as a political panacea arisen. It withers the moment it is exposed to practical trial, because Democracy cannot rise above the level of the human material of which its voters are made. Switzerland seems happy in comparison with Russia; but if Russia were as small as Switzerland, and had her social problems simplified in the same way by impregnable natural fortifications and a population educated by the same variety and intimacy of international intercourse, there might be little to choose between them. At all events Australia and Canada, which are virtually protected democratic republics, and France and the United States, which are avowedly independent democratic republics, are neither healthy, wealthy nor wise; and they would be worse instead of better if their popular ministers were not experts in the art of dodging popular enthusiasms and duping popular ignorance. The politician who once had to learn how to flatter kings has now to learn how to fascinate, amuse, coax, humbug, frighten or otherwise strike the fancy of the electorate; and though in advanced modern States, where the artisan is better educated than the king, it takes a much bigger man to be a successful demagogue than to be a successful courtier, yet he who holds popular convictions with prodigious energy is the man for the mob, whilst the frailer sceptic who is cautiously feeling his way towards the next century has no chance unless he happens by accident to have the specific artistic talent of the mountebank as well, in which case it is as a mountebank that he catches votes, and not as a meliorist. Consequently the demagogue, though he professes (and fails) to readjust matters in the interests of the majority of the electors, yet stereotypes mediocrity, organizes intolerance, disparages exhibitions of uncommon qualities, and glorifies conspicuous exhibitions of common ones. He manages a small job well: he muddles rhetorically through a large one. When a great political movement takes place, it is not consciously led or organized: the unconscious self in mankind breaks its way through the problem as an elephant breaks through a jungle; and the politicians make speeches about whatever happens in the process, which, with the best intentions, they do all in their power to prevent. Finally, when social aggregation arrives at a point demanding international organization before the demagogues and electorates have learnt how to manage even a country parish properly much less internationalize Constantinople, the whole political business goes to smash; and presently we have Ruins of Empires, New Zealanders sitting on a broken arch of London Bridge, and so forth.

To that recurrent catastrophe we shall certainly come again unless we can have a Democracy of Supermen; and the production of such a Democracy is the only change that is now hopeful enough to nerve us to the effort that Revolution demands.

VI. PRUDERY EXPLAINED

WHY THE BEES should pamper their mothers whilst we pamper only our operatic prima donnas is a question worth reflecting on. Our notion of treating a mother is, not to increase her supply of food, but to cut it off by forbidding her to work in a factory for a month after her confinement. Everything that can make birth a misfortune to the parents as well as a danger to the mother is conscientiously done. When a great French writer, Emile Zola, alarmed at the sterilization of his nation, wrote an eloquent and powerful book to restore the prestige of parentage, it was at once assumed in England that a work of this character, with such a title as *Fecundity,* was too abominable to be translated, and that any attempt to deal with the relations of the sexes from any other than the voluptuary or romantic point of view must be sternly put down. Now if this assumption were really founded on public opinion, it would indicate an attitude of disgust and resentment towards the Life Force that could only arise in a diseased and moribund community in which Ibsen's Hedda Gabler would be the typical woman. But it has no vital foundation at all. The prudery of the newspapers is, like the prudery of the dinner table, a mere difficulty of education and language.

We are not taught to think decently on these subjects, and consequently we have no language for them except indecent language. We therefore have to declare them unfit for public discussion, because the only terms in which we can conduct the discussion are unfit for public use. Physiologists, who have a technical vocabulary at their disposal, find no difficulty; and masters of language who think decently can write popular stories like Zola's *Fecundity* or Tolstoy's *Resurrection* without giving the smallest offence to readers who can also think decently. But the ordinary modern journalist, who has never discussed such matters except in ribaldry, cannot write a simple comment on a divorce case without a conscious shamefulness or a furtive facetiousness that makes it impossible to read the comment aloud in company. All this ribaldry and prudery (the two are the same) does not mean that people do not feel decently on the subject: on the contrary, it is just the depth and seriousness of our feeling that makes its desecration by vile language and coarse humor intolerable; so that at last we cannot bear to have it spoken of at all because only one in a thousand can speak of it without wounding our self-respect, especially the self-respect of women. Add to the horrors of popular language the horrors of popular poverty. In crowded populations poverty destroys the possibility of cleanliness; and in the absence of cleanliness many of the natural conditions of life become offensive and noxious, with the result that at last the association of uncleanliness with these natural conditions becomes so overpowering that among civilized people (that is, people massed in the labyrinths of slums we call cities), half their bodily life becomes a guilty secret, unmentionable except to the doctor in emergencies; and Hedda Gabler shoots herself because maternity is so unladylike. In short, popular prudery is only a mere incident of popular squalor: the subjects which it taboos remain the most interesting and earnest of subjects in spite of it.

VII. PROGRESS AN ILLUSION

UNFORTUNATELY the earnest people get drawn off the track of evolution by the illusion of progress. Any So-

cialist can convince us easily that the difference between
Man as he is and Man as he might become, without
further evolution, under millennial conditions of nutrition, environment, and training, is enormous. He can
shew that inequality and iniquitous distribution of wealth
and allotment of labor have arisen through an unscien-
tific economic system, and that Man, faulty as he is, no
more intended to establish any such ordered disorder
than a moth intends to be burnt when it flies into a
candle flame. He can shew that the difference between
the grace and strength of the acrobat and the bent back
of the rheumatic field laborer is a difference produced
by conditions, not by nature. He can shew that many
of the most detestable human vices are not radical, but
are mere reactions of our institutions on our very virtues. The Anarchist, the Fabian, the Salvationist, the
Vegetarian, the doctor, the lawyer, the parson, the professor of ethics, the gymnast, the soldier, the sportsman, the inventor, the political program-maker, all
have some prescription for bettering us; and almost all
their remedies are physically possible and aimed at admitted evils. To them the limit of progress is, at worst,
the completion of all the suggested reforms and the
levelling up of all men to the point attained already
by the most highly nourished and cultivated in mind
and body.

Here, then, as it seems to them, is an enormous field
for the energy of the reformer. Here are many noble
goals attainable by many of those paths up the Hill Difficulty along which great spirits love to aspire. Unhap-
pily, the hill will never be climbed by Man as we know
him. It need not be denied that if we all struggled
bravely to the end of the reformer's paths we should
improve the world prodigiously. But there is no more
hope in that If than in the equally plausible assurance
that if the sky falls we shall all catch larks. We are not
going to tread those paths: we have not sufficient energy.
We do not desire the end enough: indeed in most cases
we do not effectively desire it at all. Ask any man would
he like to be a better man; and he will say yes, most
piously. Ask him would he like to have a million of
money; and he will say yes, most sincerely. But the pious

citizen who would like to be a better man goes on behaving just as he did before. And the tramp who would like the million does not take the trouble to earn ten shillings: multitudes of men and women, all eager to accept a legacy of a million, live and die without having ever possessed five pounds at one time, although beggars have died in rags on mattresses stuffed with gold which they accumulated because they desired it enough to nerve them to get it and keep it. The economists who discovered that demand created supply soon had to limit the proposition to "effective demand," which turned out, in the final analysis, to mean nothing more than supply itself; and this holds good in politics, morals, and all other departments as well: the actual supply is the measure of the effective demand; and the mere aspirations and professions produce nothing. No community has ever yet passed beyond the initial phases in which its pugnacity and fanaticism enabled it to found a nation, and its cupidity to establish and develop a commercial civilization. Even these stages have never been attained by public spirit, but always by intolerant wilfulness and brute force. Take the Reform Bill of 1832 as an example of a conflict between two sections of educated Englishmen concerning a political measure which was as obviously necessary and inevitable as any political measure has ever been or is ever likely to be. It was not passed until the gentlemen of Birmingham had made arrangements to cut the throats of the gentlemen of St. James's parish in due military form. It would not have been passed to this day if there had been no force behind it except the logic and public conscience of the Utilitarians. A despotic ruler with as much sense as Queen Elizabeth would have done better than the mob of grown-up Eton boys who governed us then by privilege, and who, since the introduction of practically Manhood Suffrage in 1884, now govern us at the request of proletarian Democracy.

At the present time we have, instead of the Utilitarians, the Fabian Society, with its peaceful, constitutional, moral, economical policy of Socialism, which needs nothing for its bloodless and benevolent realization except that the English people shall understand it and approve of it. But why are the Fabians well spoken of in circles where thirty years ago the word Socialist was understood as equivalent to cutthroat and incendiary? Not because the English have the smallest intention of studying or adopting the Fabian policy, but because they believe that the Fabians, by eliminating the element of intimidation from the Socialist agitation, have drawn the teeth of insurgent poverty and saved the existing order from the only method of attack it really fears. Of course, if the nation adopted the Fabian policy, it would be carried out by brute force exactly as our present property system is. It would become the law; and those who resisted it would be fined, sold up, knocked on the head by policemen, thrown into prison, and in the last resort "executed" just as they are when they break the present law. But as our proprietary class has no fear of that conversion taking place, whereas it does fear sporadic cutthroats and gunpowder plots, and strives with all its might to hide the fact that there is no moral difference whatever between the methods by which it enforces its proprietary rights and the method by which the dynamitard asserts his conception of natural human rights, the Fabian Society is patted on the back just as the Christian Social Union is, whilst the Socialist who says bluntly that a Social revolution can be made only as all other revolutions have been made, by the people who want it killing, coercing and intimidating the people who don't want it, is denounced as a misleader of the people, and imprisoned with hard labor to shew him how much sincerity there is in the objection of his captors to physical force.

Are we then to repudiate Fabian methods, and return to those of the barricader, or adopt those of the dynamitard and the assassin? On the contrary, we are to recognize that both are fundamentally futile. It seems easy for the dynamitard to say "Have you not just admitted that nothing is ever conceded except to physical force? Did not Gladstone admit that the Irish Church was disestablished, not by the spirit of Liberalism, but by the explosion which wrecked Clerkenwell prison?" Well, we need not foolishly and timidly deny it. Let it be fully granted. Let us grant, further, that all this lies in the nature of things; that the most ardent Socialist, if he owns property, can by no means do otherwise than Conservative proprietors until property is forcibly abolished by the whole nation; nay, that ballots and parliamentary divisions, in spite of their vain ceremony of discussion, differ from battles only as the bloodless surrender of an outnumbered force in the field differs from Waterloo or Trafalgar. I make a present of all these admissions to the Fenian who collects money from thoughtless Irishmen in America to blow up Dublin Castle; to the detective who persuades foolish young workmen to order bombs from the nearest ironmonger and then delivers them up to penal servitude; to our military and naval commanders who believe, not in preaching, but in an ultimatum backed by plenty of lyddite; and, generally, to all whom it may concern. But of what use is it to substitute the will of reckless and bloody-minded Progressives for cautious and humane ones? Is England any the better for the wreck of Clerkenwell prison, or Ireland for the disestablishment of the Irish Church? Is there the smallest reason to suppose that the nation which sheepishly let Charles and Laud and Strafford coerce it, gained anything because it afterwards, still more sheepishly, let a few strongminded Puritans, inflamed by the masterpieces of Jewish revolutionary literature, cut off the heads of the three? Suppose the Gunpowder plot had succeeded, and a Fawkes dynasty were at present on the throne, would it have made any difference to the present state of the nation? The guillotine was used in France up to the limit of human endurance, both on Girondins and Jacobins. Fouquier Tinville followed Marie Antoinette to the scaffold; and Marie Antoinette might have asked the crowd, just as pointedly as Fouquier did, whether their bread would be any cheaper when her head was off. And what came of it all? The Imperial France of the Rougon Macquart family, and the Republican France of the Panama scandal and the Dreyfus case. Was the difference worth the guillotining of all those unlucky ladies and gentlemen, useless and mischievous as many of them were? Would any sane man guillotine a mouse to bring about such a result? Turn to Republican America. America has no Star Chamber, and no feudal barons. But it has Trusts; and it has millionaires whose factories,

fenced in by live electric wires and defended by Pinker-
ton retainers with magazine rifles, would have made a
Radical of Reginald Front de Boeuf. Would Washington
or Franklin have lifted a finger in the cause of American
Independence if they had foreseen its reality?

No: what Caesar, Cromwell and Napoleon could not
do with all the physical force and moral prestige of the
State in their mighty hands, cannot be done by enthusiastic criminals and lunatics. Even the Jews, who, from
Moses to Marx and Lassalle, have inspired all the revolutions, have had to confess that, after all, the dog will
return to his vomit and the sow that was washed to her
wallowing in the mire; and we may as well make up our
minds that Man will return to his idols and his cupidities,
in spite of all "movements" and all revolutions, until his
nature is changed. Until then, his early successes in
building commercial civilizations (and such civilizations,
Good Heavens!) are but preliminaries to the inevitable
later stage, now threatening us, in which the passions
which built the civilization become fatal instead of pro-
ductive, just as the same qualities which make the lion
king in the forest ensure his destruction when he enters
a city. Nothing can save society then except the clear
head and the wide purpose: war and competition, potent
instruments of selection and evolution in one epoch, become ruinous instruments of degeneration in the next.
In the breeding of animals and plants, varieties which
have arisen by selection through many generations relapse precipitously into the wild type in a generation or
two when selection ceases; and in the same way a civilization in which lusty pugnacity and greed have ceased
to act as selective agents and have begun to obstruct
and destroy, rushes downwards and backwards with a
suddenness that enables an observer to see with consternation the upward steps of many centuries retraced in a
single lifetime. This has often occurred even within the
period covered by history; and in every instance the
turning point has been reached long before the attain-
ment, or even the general advocacy on paper, of the
levelling-up of the mass to the highest point attainable
by the best nourished and cultivated normal individuals.
We must therefore frankly give up the notion that

Man as he exists is capable of net progress. There will always be an illusion of progress, because wherever we are conscious of an evil we remedy it, and therefore always seem to ourselves to be progressing, forgetting that most of the evils we see are the effects, finally become acute, of long-unnoticed retrogressions, that our compromising remedies seldom fully recover the lost ground; above all, that on the lines along which we are degenerating, good has become evil in our eyes, and is being undone in the name of progress precisely as evil is undone and replaced by good on the lines along which we are evolving. This is indeed the Illusion of Illusions; for it gives us infallible and appalling assurance that if our political ruin is to come, it will be effected by ardent reformers and supported by enthusiastic patriots as a series of necessary steps in our progress. Let the Reformer, the Progressive, the Meliorist then reconsider himself and his eternal ifs and ans which never become pots and pans. Whilst Man remains what he is, there can be no progress beyond the point already attained and fallen headlong from at every attempt at civilization; and since even that point is but a pinnacle to which a few people cling in giddy terror above an abyss of squalor, mere progress should no longer charm us.

VIII. THE CONCEIT OF CIVILIZATION

AFTER ALL, the progress illusion is not so very subtle. We begin by reading the satires of our fathers' contemporaries; and we conclude (usually quite ignorantly) that the abuses exposed by them are things of the past. We see also that reforms of crying evils are frequently produced by the sectional shifting of political power from oppressors to oppressed. The poor man is given a vote by the Liberals in the hope that he will cast it for his emancipators. The hope is not fulfilled; but the lifelong imprisonment of penniless men for debt ceases; Factory Acts are passed to mitigate sweating; schooling is made free and compulsory; sanitary by-laws are multiplied; public steps are taken to house the masses decently; the bare-footed get boots; rags become rare; and bathrooms and pianos, smart tweeds and starched collars, reach

numbers of people who once, as "the unsoaped," played
the Jew's harp or the accordion in moleskins and belch-
ers. Some of these changes are gains: some of them are
losses. Some of them are not changes at all: all of them
are merely the changes that money makes. Still, they
produce an illusion of bustling progress; and the reading
class infers from them that the abuses of the early Victorian period no longer exist except as amusing pages in
the novels of Dickens. But the moment we look for a
reform due to character and not to money, to statesman-
ship and not to interest or mutiny, we are disillusioned.
For example, we remembered the maladministration and
incompetence revealed by the Crimean War as part of
a bygone state of things until the South African war
shewed that the nation and the War Office, like those
poor Bourbons who have been so impudently blamed
for a universal characteristic, had learnt nothing and forgotten nothing. We had hardly recovered from the fruit-
less irritation of this discovery when it transpired that
the officers' mess of our most select regiment included
a flogging club presided over by the senior subaltern.
The disclosure provoked some disgust at the details of
this schoolboyish debauchery, but no surprise at the apparent absence of any conception of manly honor and
virtue, of personal courage and self-respect, in the front
rank of our chivalry. In civil affairs we had assumed that
the sycophancy and idolatry which encouraged Charles
I to undervalue the Puritan revolt of the seventeenth
century had been long outgrown; but it has needed nothing but favorable circumstances to revive, with added
abjectness to compensate for its lost piety. We have re-
lapsed into disputes about transubstantiation at the very
moment when the discovery of the wide prevalence of
theophagy as a tribal custom has deprived us of the last
excuse for believing that our official religious rites differ
in essentials from those of barbarians. The Christian doctrine of the uselessness of punishment and the wickedness of revenge has not, in spite of its simple common
sense, found a single convert among the nations: Christianity means nothing to the masses but a sensational
public execution which is made an excuse for other exe-
cutions. In its name we take ten years of a thief's life

corpses preserved in alcohol, and to steal birds' eggs and keep them as the red Indian used to keep scalps. Coercion with the lash is as natural to an Englishman as it was to Solomon spoiling Rehoboam: indeed, the comparison is unfair to the Jews in view of the facts that the Mosaic law forbade more than forty lashes in the name of humanity, and that floggings of a thousand lashes were inflicted on English soldiers in the eighteenth and nineteenth centuries, and would be inflicted still but for the change in the balance of political power between the military caste and the commercial classes and the proletariat. In spite of that change, flogging is still an institution in the public school, in the military prison, on the training ship, and in that school of littleness called the home. The lascivious clamor of the flagellomaniac for more of it, constant as the clamor for more insolence, more war, and lower rates, is tolerated and even gratified because, having no moral ends in view, we have sense enough to see that nothing but brute coercion can impose our selfish will on others. Cowardice is universal: patriotism, public opinion, parental duty, discipline, religion, morality, are only fine names for intimidation; and cruelty, gluttony, and credulity keep cowardice in countenance. We cut the throat of a calf and hang it up by the heels to bleed to death so that our veal cutlet may be white; we nail geese to a board and cram them with food because we like the taste of liver disease; we tear birds to pieces to decorate our women's hats; we mutilate domestic animals for no reason at all except to follow an instinctively cruel fashion; and we connive at the most abominable tortures in the hope of discovering some magical cure for our own diseases by them.

Now please observe that these are not exceptional developments of our admitted vices, deplored and prayed against by all good men. Not a word has been said here of the excesses of our Neros, of whom we have the full usual percentage. With the exception of the few military examples, which are mentioned mainly to shew that the education and standing of a gentleman, reinforced by the strongest conventions of honor, *esprit de corps,* publicity and responsibility, afford no better guarantees of conduct than the passions of a mob, the illustrations given above are commonplaces taken from the daily practices of our best citizens, vehemently defended in our newspapers and in our pulpits. The very humanitarians who abhor them are stirred to murder by them: the dagger of Brutus and Ravaillac is still active in the hands of Caserio and Luccheni; and the pistol has come to its aid in the hands of Guiteau and Czolgosz. Our remedies are still limited to endurance or assassination; and the assassin is still judicially assassinated on the principle that two blacks make a white. The only novelty is in our methods: through the discovery of dynamite the overloaded musket of Hamilton of Bothwellhaugh has been superseded by the bomb; but Ravachol's heart burns just as Hamilton's did. The world will not bear thinking of to those who know what it is, even with the largest discount for the restraints of poverty on the poor and cowardice on the rich.

All that can be said for us is that people must and do live and let live up to a certain point. Even the horse, with his docked tail and bitted jaw, finds his slavery mitigated by the fact that a total disregard of his need for food and rest would put his master to the expense of buying a new horse every second day; for you cannot work a horse to death and then pick up another one for nothing, as you can a laborer. But this natural check on inconsiderate selfishness is itself checked, partly by our shortsightedness, and partly by deliberate calculation; so that beside the man who, to his own loss, will shorten his horse's life in mere stinginess, we have the tramway company which discovers actuarially that though a horse may live from 24 to 40 years, yet it pays better to work him to death in 4 and then replace him by a fresh victim. And human slavery, which has reached its worst recorded point within our own time in the form of free wage labor, has encountered the same personal and commercial limits to both its aggravation and its mitigation. Now that the freedom of wage labor has produced a scarcity of it, as in South Africa, the leading English newspaper and the leading English weekly review have openly and without apology demanded a return to compulsory labor: that is, to the methods by which, as we believe, the Egyptians built the pyramids. We know now that the crusade against chattel slavery in the nineteenth century succeeded solely because chattel slavery was neither the most effective nor the least humane method of labor exploitation; and the world is now feeling its way towards a still more effective system which shall abolish the freedom of the worker without again making his exploiter responsible for him as a chattel.

Still, there is always some mitigation: there is the fear of revolt; and there are the effects of kindliness and affection. Let it be repeated therefore that no indictment is here laid against the world on the score of what its criminals and monsters do. The fires of Smithfield and of the Inquisition were lighted by earnestly pious people, who were kind and good as kindness and goodness go. And when a Negro is dipped in kerosene and set on fire in America at the present time, he is not a good man lynched by ruffians: he is a criminal lynched by crowds of respectable, charitable, virtuously indignant, high-minded citizens, who, though they act outside the law, are at least more merciful than the American legislators and judges who not so long ago condemned men to solitary confinement for periods, not of five months, as our own practice is, but of five years and more. The things that our moral monsters do may be left out of account with St. Bartholomew massacres and other momentary outbursts of social disorder. Judge us by the admitted and respected practice of our most reputable circles; and, if you know the facts and are strong enough to look them in the face, you must admit that unless we are replaced by a more highly evolved animal—in short, by the Superman—the world must remain a den of dangerous animals among whom our few accidental supermen, our Shakespeares, Goethes, Shelleys and their like, must live as precariously as lion tamers do, taking the humor of their situation, and the dignity of their superiority, as a set-off to the horror of the one and the loneliness of the other.

IX. THE VERDICT OF HISTORY

IT MAY BE SAID that though the wild beast breaks out in Man and casts him back momentarily into barbarism under the excitement of war and crime, yet his normal life is higher than the normal life of his forefathers. This view is very acceptable to Englishmen, who always lean sincerely to virtue's side as long as it costs them nothing either in money or in thought. They feel deeply the injustice of foreigners, who allow them no credit for this conditional highmindedness. But there is no reason to suppose that our ancestors were less capable of it than we are. To all such claims for the existence of a progressive moral evolution operating visibly from grandfather to grandson, there is the conclusive reply that a thousand years of such evolution would have produced enormous social changes, of which the historical evidence would be overwhelming. But not Macaulay himself, the most confident of Whig meliorists, can produce any such evidence that will bear cross-examination. Compare our conduct and our codes with those mentioned contemporarily in such ancient scriptures and classics as have come down to us, and you will find no jot of ground for the belief that any moral progress whatever has been made in historic time, in spite of all the romantic attempts of historians to reconstruct the past on that assumption. Within that time it has happened to nations as to private families and individuals that they have flourished and decayed, repented and hardened their hearts, submitted and protested, acted and reacted, oscillated between natural and artificial sanitation (the oldest house in the world, unearthed the other day in Crete, has quite modern sanitary arrangements), and rung a thousand changes on the different scales of income and pressure of population, firmly believing all the time that mankind was advancing by leaps and bounds because men were constantly busy. And the mere chapter of accidents has left a small accumulation of chance discoveries, such as the wheel, the arch, the safety pin, gunpowder, the magnet, the Voltaic pile and so forth: things which, unlike the gospels and philosophic treatises of the sages, can be usefully understood and applied by common men; so that steam locomotion is possible without a nation of Stephensons, although national Christianity is impossible without a nation of Christs. But does any man seriously believe that the *chauffeur* who drives a motor car from

Paris to Berlin is a more highly evolved man than the charioteer of Achilles, or that a modern Prime Minister is a more enlightened ruler than Caesar because he rides a tricycle, writes his dispatches by the electric light, and instructs his stockbroker through the telephone?

Enough, then, of this goose-cackle about Progress: Man, as he is, never will nor can add a cubit to his stature by any of its quackeries, political, scientific, educational, religious, or artistic. What is likely to happen when this conviction gets into the minds of the men whose present faith in these illusions is the cement of our social system, can be imagined only by those who know how suddenly a civilization which has long ceased to think (or in the old phrase, to watch and pray) can fall to pieces when the vulgar belief in its hypocrisies and impostures can no longer hold out against its failures and scandals. When religious and ethical formulae become so obsolete that no man of strong mind can believe them, they have also reached the point at which no man of high character will profess them; and from that moment until they are formally disestablished, they stand at the door of every profession and every public office to keep out every able man who is not a sophist or a liar. A nation which revises its parish councils once in three years, but will not revise its articles of religion once in three hundred, even when those articles avowedly began as a political compromise dictated by Mr. Facing-Both-Ways, is a nation that needs remaking.

Our only hope, then, is in evolution. We must replace the Man by the Superman. It is frightful for the citizen, as the years pass him, to see his own contemporaries so exactly reproduced by the younger generation, that his companions of thirty years ago have their counterparts in every city crowd; so that he has to check himself repeatedly in the act of saluting as an old friend some young man to whom he is only an elderly stranger. All hope of advance dies in his bosom as he watches them: he knows that they will do just what their fathers did, and that the few voices which will still, as always before, exhort them to do something else and be something better, might as well spare their breath to cool their porridge (if they can get any). Men like Ruskin and Carlyle will preach to Smith and Brown for the sake of preaching, just as St. Francis preached to the birds and St. Anthony to the fishes. But Smith and Brown, like the fishes and birds, remain as they are; and poets who plan Utopias and prove that nothing is necessary for their realization but that Man should will them, perceive at last, like Richard Wagner, that the fact to be faced is that Man does not effectively will them. And he never will until he becomes Superman.

And so we arrive at the end of the Socialist's dream of "the socialization of the means of production and exchange," of the Positivist's dream of moralizing the capitalist, and of the ethical professor's, legislator's, educator's dream of putting commandments and codes and lessons and examination marks on a man as harness is put on a horse, ermine on a judge, pipeclay on a soldier, or a wig on an actor, and pretending that his nature has been changed. The only fundamental and possible Socialism is the socialization of the selective breeding of Man: in other terms, of human evolution. We must eliminate the Yahoo, or his vote will wreck the commonwealth.

X. THE METHOD

As to the method, what can be said as yet except that where there is a will, there is a way? If there be no will, we are lost. That is a possibility for our crazy little empire, if not for the universe; and as such possibilities are not to be entertained without despair, we must, whilst we survive, proceed on the assumption that we have still energy enough to not only will to live, but to will to live better. That may mean that we must establish a State Department of Evolution, with a seat in the Cabinet for its chief, and a revenue to defray the cost of direct State experiments and provide inducements to private persons to achieve successful results. It may mean a private society or a chartered company for the improvement of human live stock. But for the present it is far more likely to mean a blatant repudiation of such proposals as indecent and immoral, with, nevertheless, a general secret pushing of the human will in the repudiated direction; so that all sorts of institutions and public authorities will under some pretext or other feel their way furtively towards the Superman. Mr. Graham Wallas has already ventured to suggest, as Chairman of the School Management Committee of the London School Board, that the accepted policy of the Sterilization of the Schoolmistress, however administratively convenient, is open to criticism from the national stock-breeding point of view; and this is as good an example as any of the way in which the drift towards the Superman may operate in spite of all our hypocrisies. One thing at least is clear to begin with. If a woman can, by careful selection of a father, and nourishment of herself, produce a citizen with efficient senses, sound organs and a good digestion, she should clearly be secured a sufficient reward for that natural service to make her willing to undertake and repeat it. Whether she be financed in the undertaking by herself, or by the father, or by a speculative capitalist, or by a new department of, say, the Royal Dublin Society, or (as at present) by the War Office maintaining her "on the strength" and authorizing a particular soldier to marry her, or by a local authority under a by-law directing that women may under certain circumstances have a year's leave of absence on full salary, or by the central government, does not matter provided the result be satisfactory.

It is a melancholy fact that as the vast majority of women and their husbands have, under existing circumstances, not enough nourishment, no capital, no credit, and no knowledge of science or business, they would, if the State would pay for birth as it now pays for death, be exploited by joint stock companies for dividends, just as they are in ordinary industries. Even a joint stock human stud farm (piously disguised as a reformed Foundling Hospital or something of that sort) might well, under proper inspection and regulation, produce better results than our present reliance on promiscuous marriage. It may be objected that when an ordinary contractor produces stores for sale to the Government, and the Government rejects them as not up to the required standard, the condemned goods are either sold for what they will fetch or else scrapped: that is, treated as waste material; whereas if the goods consisted of human beings, all that could be done

would be to let them loose or send them to the nearest
workhouse. But there is nothing new in private enterprise
throwing its human refuse on the cheap labor market and
the workhouse; and the refuse of the new industry would
presumably be better bred than the staple product of ordinary poverty. In our present happy-go-lucky industrial disorder, all the human products, successful or not, would
have to be thrown on the labor market; but the unsuccessful ones would not entitle the company to a bounty and
so would be a dead loss to it. The practical commercial
difficulty would be the uncertainty and the cost in time
and money of the first experiments. Purely commercial
capital would not touch such heroic operations during the
experimental stage; and in any case the strength of mind
needed for so momentous a new departure could not be
fairly expected from the Stock Exchange. It will have to
be handled by statesmen with character enough to tell our
democracy and plutocracy that statecraft does not consist
in flattering their follies or applying their suburban stan-
dards of propriety to the affairs of four continents. The
matter must be taken up either by the State or by some
organization strong enough to impose respect upon the
State.

The novelty of any such experiment, however, is only
in the scale of it. In one conspicuous case, that of royalty, the State does already select the parents on purely
political grounds; and in the peerage, though the heir to
a dukedom is legally free to marry a dairymaid, yet the
social pressure on him to confine his choice to politically
and socially eligible mates is so overwhelming that he is
really no more free to marry the dairymaid than George
IV was to marry Mrs. Fitzherbert; and such a marriage
could only occur as a result of extraordinary strength
of character on the part of the dairymaid acting upon
extraordinary weakness on the part of the duke. Let
those who think the whole conception of intelligent breeding absurd and scandalous ask themselves why George IV
was not allowed to choose his own wife whilst any tinker
could marry whom he pleased? Simply because it did not
matter a rap politically whom the tinker married, whereas
it mattered very much whom the king married. The way
in which all considerations of the king's personal rights,

of the claims of the heart, of the sanctity of the marriage oath, and of romantic morality crumpled up before this political need shews how negligible all these apparently irresistible prejudices are when they come into conflict with the demand for quality in our rulers. We learn the same lesson from the case of the soldier, whose marriage, when it is permitted at all, is despotically controlled with a view solely to military efficiency.

Well, nowadays it is not the king that rules, but the tinker. Dynastic wars are no longer feared, dynastic alliances no longer valued. Marriages in royal families are becoming rapidly less political, and more popular, domestic and romantic. If all the kings in Europe were made as free tomorrow as King Cophetua, nobody but their aunts and chamberlains would feel a moment's anxiety as to the consequences. On the other hand a sense of the social importance of the tinker's marriage has been steadily growing. We have made a public matter of his wife's health in the month after her confinement. We have taken the minds of his children out of his hands and put them into those of our State schoolmaster. We shall presently make their bodily nourishment independent of him. But they are still riff-raff; and to hand the country over to riff-raff is national suicide, since riff-raff can neither govern nor will let anyone else govern except the highest bidder of bread and circuses. There is no public enthusiast alive of twenty years practical democratic experience who believes in the political adequacy of the electorate or of the bodies it elects. The overthrow of the aristocrat has created the necessity for the Superman.

Englishmen hate Liberty and Equality too much to understand them. But every Englishman loves and desires a pedigree. And in that he is right. King Demos must be bred like all other kings; and with Must there is no arguing. It is idle for an individual writer to carry so great a matter farther in a pamphlet. A conference on the subject is the next step needed. It will be attended by men and women who, no longer believing that they can live for ever, are seeking for some immortal work into which they can build the best of themselves before their refuse is thrown into that arch dust destructor, the cremation furnace.

MAXIMS FOR REVOLUTIONISTS

THE GOLDEN RULE

Do not do unto others as you would that they should do unto you. Their tastes may not be the same.

Never resist temptation: prove all things: hold fast that which is good.

Do not love your neighbor as yourself. If you are on good terms with yourself it is an impertinence: if on bad, an injury.

The golden rule is that there are no golden rules.

IDOLATRY

The art of government is the organization of idolatry.

The bureaucracy consists of functionaries; the aristocracy, of idols; the democracy, of idolaters.

The populace cannot understand the bureaucracy: it can only worship the national idols.

The savage bows down to idols of wood and stone: the civilized man to idols of flesh and blood.

A limited monarchy is a device for combining the inertia of a wooden idol with the credibility of a flesh and blood one.

When the wooden idol does not answer the peasant's prayer, he beats it: when the flesh and blood idol does not satisfy the civilized man, he cuts its head off.

He who slays a king and he who dies for him are alike idolaters.

ROYALTY

Kings are not born: they are made by artificial hallucination. When the process is interrupted by adversity at a critical age, as in the case of Charles II, the subject becomes sane and never completely recovers his kingliness.

The Court is the servant's hall of the sovereign.

Vulgarity in a king flatters the majority of the nation.

The flunkeyism propagated by the throne is the price we pay for its political convenience.

DEMOCRACY

If the lesser mind could measure the greater as a foot-rule can measure a pyramid, there would be finality in universal suffrage. As it is, the political problem remains unsolved.

Democracy substitutes election by the incompetent many for appointment by the corrupt few.

Democratic republics can no more dispense with national idols than monarchies with public functionaries.

Government presents only one problem: the discovery of a trustworthy anthropometric method.

IMPERIALISM

Excess of insularity makes a Briton an Imperialist.

Excess of local self-assertion makes a colonist an Imperialist.

A colonial Imperialist is one who raises colonial troops, equips a colonial squadron, claims a Federal Parliament sending its measures to the Throne instead of to the Colonial Office, and, being finally brought by this means into insoluble conflict with the insular British Imperialist, "cuts the painter" and breaks up the Empire.

LIBERTY AND EQUALITY

He who confuses political liberty with freedom and political equality with similarity has never thought for five minutes about either.

Nothing can be unconditional: consequently nothing can be free.

Liberty means responsibility. That is why most men dread it.

The duke inquires contemptuously whether his game-keeper is the equal of the Astronomer Royal; but he insists that they shall both be hanged equally if they murder him.

The notion that the colonel need be a better man than the private is as confused as the notion that the keystone need be stronger than the coping stone.

Where equality is undisputed, so also is subordination.

Equality is fundamental in every department of social organization.

The relation of superior to inferior excludes good manners.

EDUCATION

When a man teaches something he does not know to somebody else who has no aptitude for it, and gives him a certificate of proficiency, the latter has completed the education of a gentleman.

A fool's brain digests philosophy into folly, science into superstition, and art into pedantry. Hence University education.

The best brought-up children are those who have seen their parents as they are. Hypocrisy is not the parent's first duty.

The vilest abortionist is he who attempts to mould a child's character.

At the University every great treatise is postponed until its author attains impartial judgment and perfect knowledge. If a horse could wait as long for its shoes and would pay for them in advance, our blacksmiths would all be college dons.

He who can, does. He who cannot, teaches.

A learned man is an idler who kills time with study. Beware of his false knowledge: it is more dangerous than ignorance.

Activity is the only road to knowledge.

Every fool believes what his teachers tell him, and calls his credulity science or morality as confidently as his father called it divine revelation.

No man fully capable of his own language ever masters another.

No man can be a pure specialist without being in the strict sense an idiot.

Do not give your children moral and religious instruction unless you are quite sure they will not take it too seriously. Better be the mother of Henri Quatre and Nell Gwynne than of Robespierre and Queen Mary Tudor.

MARRIAGE

Marriage is popular because it combines the maximum of temptation with the maximum of opportunity.

Marriage is the only legal contract which abrogates as between the parties all the laws that safeguard the particular relation to which it refers.

The essential function of marriage is the continuance of the race, as stated in the Book of Common Prayer.

The accidental function of marriage is the gratification of the amoristic sentiment of mankind.

The artificial sterilization of marriage makes it possible for marriage to fulfil its accidental function whilst neglecting its essential one.

The most revolutionary invention of the nineteenth century was the artificial sterilization of marriage.

Any marriage system which condemns a majority of the population to celibacy will be violently wrecked on the pretext that it outrages morality.

Polygamy, when tried under modern democratic conditions, as by the Mormons, is wrecked by the revolt of the mass of inferior men who are condemned to celibacy by it; for the maternal instinct leads a woman to prefer a tenth share in a first rate man to the exclusive possession of a third rate one. Polyandry has not been tried under these conditions.

The minimum of national celibacy (ascertained by dividing the number of males in the community by the number of females, and taking the quotient as the number of wives or husbands permitted to each person) is secured in England (where the quotient is 1) by the institution of monogamy.

The modern sentimental term for the national minimum of celibacy is Purity.

Marriage, or any other form of promiscuous amoristic monogamy, is fatal to large States because it puts its ban on the deliberate breeding of man as a political animal.

CRIME AND PUNISHMENT

All scoundrelism is summed up in the phrase *"Que Messieurs les Assassins commencent!"*

The man who has graduated from the flogging block at Eton to the bench from which he sentences the garotter to be flogged is the same social product as the garotter who has been kicked by his father and cuffed by his mother until he has grown strong enough to throttle and rob the rich citizen whose money he desires.

Imprisonment is as irrevocable as death.

Criminals do not die by the hands of the law. They die by the hands of other men.

The assassin Czolgosz made President McKinley a hero by assassinating him. The United States of America made Czolgosz a hero by the same process.

Assassination on the scaffold is the worst form of assassination, because there it is invested with the approval of society.

It is the deed that teaches, not the name we give it. Murder and capital punishment are not opposites that cancel one another, but similars that breed their kind.

Crime is only the retail department of what, in wholesale, we call penal law.

When a man wants to murder a tiger he calls it sport: when the tiger wants to murder him he calls it ferocity. The distinction between Crime and Justice is no greater.

Whilst we have prisons it matters little which of us occupy the cells. The most anxious man in a prison is the governor.

It is not necessary to replace a guillotined criminal: it is necessary to replace a guillotined social system.

TITLES

Titles distinguish the mediocre, embarrass the superior, and are disgraced by the inferior.

Great men refuse titles because they are jealous of them.

HONOR

There are no perfectly honorable men; but every true man has one main point of honor and a few minor ones.

You cannot believe in honor until you have achieved it. Better keep yourself clean and bright: you are the window through which you must see the world.

Your word can never be as good as your bond, because your memory can never be as trustworthy as your honor.

PROPERTY

Property, said Proudhon, is theft. This is the only perfect truism that has been uttered on the subject.

SERVANTS

When domestic servants are treated as human beings it is not worth while to keep them.

The relation of master and servant is advantageous only to masters who do not scruple to abuse their authority, and to servants who do not scruple to abuse their trust.

The perfect servant, when his master makes humane advances to him, feels that his existence is threatened, and hastens to change his place.

Masters and servants are both tyrannical; but the masters are the more dependent of the two.

A man enjoys what he uses, not what his servants use.

Man is the only animal which esteems itself rich in proportion to the number and voracity of its parasites.

Ladies and gentlemen are permitted to have friends in the kennel, but not in the kitchen.

Domestic servants, by making spoiled children of their masters, are forced to intimidate them in order to be able to live with them.

In a slave state, the slaves rule: in Mayfair, the tradesman rules.

HOW TO BEAT CHILDREN

If you strike a child, take care that you strike it in anger, even at the risk of maiming it for life. A blow in cold blood neither can nor should be forgiven.

If you beat children for pleasure, avow your object frankly, and play the game according to the rules, as a foxhunter does; and you will do comparatively little harm. No foxhunter is such a cad as to pretend that he hunts the fox to teach it not to steal chickens, or that he suffers more acutely than the fox at the death. Remember that even in childbeating there is the sportsman's way and the cad's way.

RELIGION

Beware of the man whose god is in the skies.

What a man believes may be ascertained, not from his creed, but from the assumptions on which he habitually acts.

VIRTUES AND VICES

No specific virtue or vice in a man implies the existence of any other specific virtue or vice in him, however closely the imagination may associate them.

Virtue consists, not in abstaining from vice, but in not desiring it.

Self-denial is not a virtue: it is only the effect of prudence on rascality.

Obedience simulates subordination as fear of the police simulates honesty.

Disobedience, the rarest and most courageous of the virtues, is seldom distinguished from neglect, the laziest and commonest of the vices.

Vice is waste of life. Poverty, obedience and celibacy are the canonical vices.

Economy is the art of making the most of life.

The love of economy is the root of all virtue.

FAIRPLAY

The love of fairplay is a spectator's virtue, not a principal's.

GREATNESS

Greatness is only one of the sensations of littleness.

In heaven an angel is nobody in particular.

Greatness is the secular name for Divinity: both mean simply what lies beyond us.

If a great man could make us understand him, we should hang him.

We admit that when the divinity we worshipped made itself visible and comprehensible we crucified it.

To a mathematician the eleventh means only a single unit: to the bushman who cannot count further than his ten fingers it is an incalculable myriad.

The difference between the shallowest routineer and the deepest thinker appears, to the latter, trifling; to the former, infinite.

In a stupid nation the man of genius becomes a god: everybody worships him and nobody does his will.

BEAUTY AND HAPPINESS, ART AND RICHES

Happiness and Beauty are by-products.

Folly is the direct pursuit of Happiness and Beauty.

Riches and Art are spurious receipts for the production of Happiness and Beauty.

He who desires a lifetime of happiness with a beautiful woman desires to enjoy the taste of wine by keeping his mouth always full of it.

The most intolerable pain is produced by prolonging the keenest pleasure.

The man with toothache thinks everyone happy whose teeth are sound. The poverty-stricken man makes the same mistake about the rich man.

The more a man possesses over and above what he uses, the more careworn he becomes.

The tyranny that forbids you to make the road with pick and shovel is worse than that which prevents you from lolling along it in a carriage and pair.

In an ugly and unhappy world the richest man can purchase nothing but ugliness and unhappiness.

In his efforts to escape from ugliness and unhappiness the rich man intensifies both. Every new yard of West End creates a new acre of East End.

The nineteenth century was the Age of Faith in Fine Art. The results are before us.

THE PERFECT GENTLEMAN

The fatal reservation of the gentleman is that he sacrifices everything to his honor except his gentility.

A gentleman of our days is one who has money enough to do what every fool would do if he could afford it: that is, consume without producing.

The true diagnostic of modern gentility is parasitism.

No elaboration of physical or moral accomplishment can atone for the sin of parasitism.

A modern gentleman is necessarily the enemy of his country. Even in war he does not fight to defend it, but to prevent his power of preying on it from passing to a foreigner. Such combatants are patriots in the same sense as two dogs fighting for a bone are lovers of animals.

The North American Indian was a type of the sportsman warrior gentleman. The Periclean Athenian was a type of the intellectually and artistically cultivated gentleman. Both were political failures. The modern gentleman, without the hardihood of the one or the culture of the other, has the appetite of both put together. He will not succeed where they failed.

He who believes in education, criminal law, and sport, needs only property to make him a perfect modern gentleman.

MODERATION

Moderation is never applauded for its own sake.

A moderately honest man with a moderately faithful wife, moderate drinkers both, in a moderately healthy house: that is the true middle class unit.

THE UNCONSCIOUS SELF

The unconscious self is the real genius. Your breathing goes wrong the moment your conscious self meddles with it.

Except during the nine months before he draws his first breath, no man manages his affairs as well as a tree does.

REASON

The reasonable man adapts himself to the world: the unreasonable one persists in trying to adapt the world to himself. Therefore all progress depends on the unreasonable man.

The man who listens to Reason is lost: Reason enslaves all whose minds are not strong enough to master her.

DECENCY

Decency is Indecency's Conspiracy of Silence.

EXPERIENCE

Men are wise in proportion, not to their experience, but to their capacity for experience.

If we could learn from mere experience, the stones of London would be wiser than its wisest men.

TIME'S REVENGES

Those whom we called brutes had their revenge when Darwin shewed us that they were our cousins.

The thieves had their revenge when Marx convicted the bourgeoisie of theft.

GOOD INTENTIONS

Hell is paved with good intentions, not with bad ones. All men mean well.

NATURAL RIGHTS

The Master of Arts, by proving that no man has any natural rights, compels himself to take his own for granted.

The right to live is abused whenever it is not constantly challenged.

FAUTE DE MIEUX

In my childhood I demurred to the description of a certain young lady as "the pretty Miss So and So." My aunt rebuked me by saying "Remember always that the least homely sister is the family beauty."

No age or condition is without its heroes. The least incapable general in a nation is its Caesar, the least imbecile statesman its Solon, the least confused thinker its Socrates, the least commonplace poet its Shakespeare.

CHARITY

Charity is the most mischievous sort of pruriency.

Those who minister to poverty and disease are accomplices in the two worst of all the crimes.

He who gives money he has not earned is generous with other people's labor.

Every genuinely benevolent person loathes almsgiving and mendicity.

FAME

Life levels all men: death reveals the eminent.

DISCIPLINE

Mutiny Acts are needed only by officers who command without authority. Divine right needs no whip.

WOMEN IN THE HOME

Home is the girl's prison and the woman's workhouse.

CIVILIZATION

Civilization is a disease produced by the practice of building societies with rotten material.

Those who admire modern civilization usually identify it with the steam engine and the electric telegraph.

Those who understand the steam engine and the electric telegraph spend their lives in trying to replace them with something better.

The imagination cannot conceive a viler criminal than he who should build another London like the present one, nor a greater benefactor than he who should destroy it.

GAMBLING

The most popular method of distributing wealth is the method of the roulette table.

The roulette table pays nobody except him who keeps it. Nevertheless a passion for gaming is common, though a passion for keeping roulette tables is unknown.

Gambling promises the poor what Property performs for the rich: that is why the bishops dare not denounce it fundamentally.

THE SOCIAL QUESTION

Do not waste your time on Social Questions. What is the matter with the poor is Poverty: what is the matter with the Rich is Uselessness.

STRAY SAYINGS

We are told that when Jehovah created the world he saw that it was good. What would he say now?

The conversion of a savage to Christianity is the conversion of Christianity to savagery.

No man dares say so much of what he thinks as to appear to himself an extremist.

Mens sana in corpore sano is a foolish saying. The sound body is a product of the sound mind.

Decadence can find agents only when it wears the mask of progress.

In moments of progress the noble succeed, because things are going their way: in moments of decadence the base succeed for the same reason: hence the world is never without the exhilaration of contemporary success.

The reformer for whom the world is not good enough finds himself shoulder to shoulder with him that is not good enough for the world.

Every man over forty is a scoundrel.

Youth, which is forgiven everything, forgives itself nothing: age, which forgives itself everything, is forgiven nothing.

When we learn to sing that Britons never will be masters we shall make an end of slavery.

Do not mistake your objection to defeat for an objection to fighting, your objection to being a slave for an objection to slavery, your objection to not being as rich as your neighbor for an objection to poverty. The cowardly, the insubordinate, and the envious share your objections.

Take care to get what you like or you will be forced to like what you get. Where there is no ventilation fresh air is declared unwholesome. Where there is no religion hypocrisy becomes good taste. Where there is no knowledge ignorance calls itself science.

If the wicked flourish and the fittest survive, Nature must be the God of rascals.

If history repeats itself, and the unexpected always happens, how incapable must Man be of learning from experience!

Compassion is the fellow-feeling of the unsound.

Those who understand evil pardon it: those who resent it destroy it.

Acquired notions of propriety are stronger than natural instincts. It is easier to recruit for monasteries and convents than to induce an Arab woman to uncover her mouth in public, or a British officer to walk through Bond Street in a golfing cap on an afternoon in May.

It is dangerous to be sincere unless you are also stupid.

The Chinese tame fowls by clipping their wings, and women by deforming their feet. A petticoat round the ankles serves equally well.

Political Economy and Social Economy are amusing intellectual games; but Vital Economy is the Philosopher's Stone.

When a heretic wishes to avoid martyrdom he speaks of "Orthodoxy, True and False" and demonstrates that the True is his heresy.

Beware of the man who does not return your blow: he neither forgives you nor allows you to forgive yourself.

If you injure your neighbor, better not do it by halves.

Sentimentality is the error of supposing that quarter can be given or taken in moral conflicts.

Two starving men cannot be twice as hungry as one; but two rascals can be ten times as vicious as one.

Make your cross your crutch; but when you see another man do it, beware of him.

SELF-SACRIFICE

Self-sacrifice enables us to sacrifice other people without blushing.

If you begin by sacrificing yourself to those you love, you will end by hating those to whom you have sacrificed yourself.

AFTERWORD:
G.B.S.: AN ACTOR'S APPRECIATION

In a lampoon on G. K. Chesterton and Hilaire Belloc called "Chesterbelloc," George Bernard Shaw wrote about himself as follows:

> I have never pretended that G.B.S. was real: I have over and over again taken him to pieces before the audience to show the trick of him. And even those who cannot escape the illusion regard G.B.S. as a fraud. The whole point of the creature is that he is unique, fantastic, unrepresentative, inimitable, impossible, undesirable on any large scale, unlike anybody that ever existed before, hopelessly unnatural and void of any real passion. Clearly such a monster could do no harm, even were his example evil (which it never is).

After encountering Shaw's description of himself, one must immediately assert the joys of Shaw, that is, the joys of *playing* Shaw. His brilliant use of language gives the actor the feeling of being a person of enormous intelligence. Sometimes this truly is the case, sometimes not—but no matter what, the actor speaking Shaw's words feels confident that the audience will think he possesses vast brainpower and an extraordinary ability to express himself on all subjects. Thus Shaw contributes to the easily stimulated vanity of the actor.

Further joys in playing Shaw reside in his ability to create characters. What a gallery! They are a cast of characters both idiosyncratic and energetic, filled with Shavian charm. To play them is enormously rewarding because the members of the audience have a grand time being in on the fun and they, too, feel vastly intelligent.

Shaw loved vaudeville, and there runs through his theater work a line of humor that permits him to make his most serious points with great levity or, as he has written, "to chasten morals with ridicule." When playing Shaw, one feels oneself in a rarefied atmosphere where the brain is working not just at its fullest power but with wit and humor. And passion. And anger.

Thus his writing that he is "void of any real passion" can only be taken as mocking the cliché others had coined about him. Read the speech in *Major Barbara* that Undershaft delivers to his daughter: "I moralized and starved until one day I swore that I would be a full-fed free man at all costs; that nothing should stop me except a bullet, neither reason or morals nor the lives of other men." Read this speech and realize that when Shaw says he is void of passion he jests and awaits the reply. And what a speech to deliver: the words, the rhythm, the truth. One is aware when delivering it that one is giving something of great value to the audience. It is exhilarating. One feels there is a reason for dedicating one's life to the theater.

The occupation Shaw raised to its highest level—that of critic—has few practitioners who even approach his level. If, dear reader, you wish to determine this for yourself, read G.B.S. on *Our Theatres in the Nineties*—the 1890s, of course. Actors especially would do well to study Shaw's *Dramatic Opinions and Essays*, which remain a high point of dramatic criticism. When asked the key to acting, Spencer Tracy replied "Hit the marks." James Cagney said, "Stand on the balls of your feet and tell the truth." Salvini, when Stanislavsky asked what was required to play Othello, answered, "Three things: voice, voice, and voice." But Shaw requires more: attitude.

What Shaw wanted in an actor can best be found in his criticism, and especially in his writing about Eleonora Duse:

> The multitude of ideas which find physical expression in her movements are all of that high quality which marks off humanity from the animals. . . . Where it is remembered that the majority of tragic actors excel only in those passions which are common to man and brute, there will be no difficulty in understanding the indescribable distinction which Duse's acting acquires from the fact that behind every stroke of it is a distinctively human idea. . . . Duse's interpretation of the stage poem of Marguerite Gauthier is unspeakably touching because it is exquisitely considerate: that is, exquisitely sympathetic. No physical charm is noble as well as beautiful unless it is the expression of moral charm.

These are words for actors to mull over, in all generations of performers. In trying to achieve this exalted state lies the test and trial of acting. Recognition of it creates attitude.

Shaw's characters have, virtually all of them, an attitude that changes our ordinary way of looking at things. Although these characters are seemingly stylized with his heightened speech, Shaw has touched the deepest roots of human behavior. His work is always modern. In order to rise to Shaw's demands, actors must achieve, in his words, "an unfailing hold and yet exquisitely delicate touch upon their parts, their sleeplessly vigilant sense of beauty of thought, feeling, and action, and their prodigious industry." It isn't easy. The approach to text these days is somewhat lax if not downright insulting to the author. With Shaw the actor must not only be note perfect but skilled in delivery, so that the elegance of his writing is not reduced to sloppy naturalism.

Consider his letter to John Barrymore after seeing Barrymore's truncated *Hamlet* in London:

> I write plays that play for three hours and a half even with instantaneous changes and only one short interval. There is no time for silences or pauses; the actor must play on the line and not between the lines, and must do nine-tenths of his acting with his voice. *Hamlet*—Shakespeare's *Hamlet*—can be done from end to end in four hours in that way; and it never flags or bores. Done in any other way, Shakespeare is the worst of bores because he has to be chopped into a mere cold stew. I prefer my way. I wish you would try it, and concentrate on acting rather than authorship at which, believe me, Shakespeare can write your head off.

He signs the letter "yours perhaps too candidly."

At the time Shaw was a playwright and drama critic, of course, there were no microphones or other devices to carry the voice, so an actor's voice and diction were of paramount importance. It was also a time when theater was part of everyone's life. Not so today. Motion pictures and television now hold center stage. Where is Shaw's place in this change? Interestingly, some of his plays do very well in films and provide actors with rich parts. *Pygmalion*, *Caesar and Cleopatra*, *Major Barbara*, *The Devil's Disciple* and *My Fair Lady* come to mind.

Where can the modern actor fit in? Most of them cannot "speak the speech, I pray you, as I pronounced it to you, trippingly on the tongue." Nor are they dedicated to social theater, as in the 1930s, when for many actors it was a mission to improve the world—something Shaw does with every stroke of his pen. More now than then we see the truth of Shaw's complaint about actors whose choices have "very evidently been dictated by love of fame or money rather than by any

yearning for emotional discourse with fellow creatures." Today, a time of immediate stardom and
astronomic salaries, the old progression from walk-ons
to bit player to supporting actor to lead is gone. And
as for the necessities of training—especially speech, so
necessary to playing Shaw—there is a woeful lack
thereof. Shaw once indicated that it took twenty years
for an actor to reach that stage where he could play
leads.

And so it is up to actors to master the language
so that they can continue to play Shaw along with
Shakespeare and Molière. For in the words of his
friend St. John Ervine, "His heart was large; it con-
tained multitudes. His courage, his candor, his unfailing faith, and his fearless announcement of the truth as
he saw it made him a beacon in the time of intellectual
darkness. And that flame still brightly flares."

—NORMAN LLOYD

SELECTED
BIBLIOGRAPHY

Bloom, Harold, ed. *George Bernard Shaw's* Pygmalion: Modern Critical Interpretations. New York: Chelsea, 1988.

Chesterton, G. K. *George Bernard Shaw*. London: House of Stratus, 2000.

Gainor, J. E. *Shaw's Daughters: Dramatic and Narrative Constructions of Gender*. Ann Arbor: University of Michigan Press, 1991.

Gibbs, A. M. *A Bernard Shaw Chronology*. London: Palgrave McMillan, 2001.

Gordon, David. *Bernard Shaw and the Comic Sublime*. New York: St. Martin's Press, 1990.

Grene, Nicholas. *Bernard Shaw: A Critical View*. New York: St. Martin's Press, 1984.

Griffith, Gareth. *Soialism and Superior Brains: The Political Thought of Bernard Shaw*. London: Routledge, 1993.

Holroyd, Michael. *Bernard Shaw: The One-Volume Definitive Edition* [Abridged]. New York: Random House, 2001.

Innes, Christopher. *The Cambridge Companion to George Bernard Shaw*. Cambridge: Cambridge University Press, 1998.

Meisel, Martin. *Shaw and the Nineteenth-Century Theater*. Westport, CT: Greenwood, 1963.

Morrison, Harry. *The Socialism of Bernard Shaw*. London: McFarland, 1989.

Peters, Sally. *Bernard Shaw: The Ascent of Superman*. New Haven, CT: Yale University Press, 1996.

Silver, Arnold. *Bernard Shaw: The Darker Side*. Stanford, CA: Stanford University Press, 1982.

Weintraub, Stanley. *Bernard Shaw: A Guide to Research*. University Park: Pennsylvania State University Press, 1992.

Wisenthal, Jonathan L. *Shaw's Sense of History*. Oxford: Clarendon Press, 1988.

Signet Classics

The World's Best Drama

Four Major Plays by Ibsen: Volume One
Translated with a Foreword by Rolf Fjelde
Includes *A Doll House, The Wild Duck,*
Hedda Gabler, and *The Master Builder*

Four Major Plays by Ibsen: Volume Two
Translated by Rolf Fjelde with Afterword by Terry Otten
Includes *Ghosts, An Enemy of the People,*
The Lady from the Sea, and *John Gabriel Bookman*

Four Plays by Eugene O'Neill
Introduction by A. R. Gurney
Includes *Anna Christie, The Hairy Ape,*
The Emperor Jones, and *Beyond the Horizon*

Three by Tennessee Williams
Includes *Sweet Bird of Youth, The Rose Tattoo,*
and *The Night of the Iguana*

Available wherever books are sold or at
signetclassics.com

Classic Works by
Oscar Wilde

THE PICTURE OF DORIAN GRAY: & Other Stories

Perhaps one of the most famous stories in English, this classic
tale of good and evil has sent chills down the spines of readers
for over one hundred years. This volume also contains the well
known allegories *Lord Arthur Savile's Crime, The Happy
Prince,* and *The Birthday of the Infanta.*

TWO PLAYS BY OSCAR WILDE:
An Ideal Husband & A Woman of No Importance

From the premier dramatist of the nineteenth century, these
two plays are peppered with the unmistakable wit and satire
that made Wilde one of the most famous literary figures
of his era.

COMPLETE FAIRY TALES OF OSCAR WILDE

As Wilde explained, these tales were written "partly for
children, and partly for those who have kept the childlike
faculties of wonder and joy." This volume brings together all of
Wilde's lovely, gemlike tales filled with princes, mermaids,
giants, and kings. It also retains the wonderful and evocative
illustrations done for the original editions.

READ THE TOP 20
SIGNET CLASSICS

ANIMAL FARM by GEORGE ORWELL

1984 by GEORGE ORWELL

NARRATIVE OF THE LIFE OF FREDERICK DOUGLASS
    by FREDERICK DOUGLASS

BEOWULF (BURTON RAFFEL, TRANSLATOR)

FRANKENSTEIN by MARY SHELLEY

ALICE'S ADVENTURES IN WONDERLAND &
    THROUGH THE LOOKING GLASS by LEWIS CARROLL

THE INFERNO by DANTE

COMMON SENSE, RIGHTS OF MAN, AND OTHER
    ESSENTIAL WRITINGS by THOMAS PAINE

HAMLET by WILLIAM SHAKESPEARE

A TALE OF TWO CITIES by CHARLES DICKENS

THE HUNCHBACK OF NOTRE DAME by VICTOR HUGO

THE FEDERALIST PAPERS by ALEXANDER HAMILTON

THE SCARLET LETTER by NATHANIEL HAWTHORNE

DRACULA by BRAM STOKER

THE HOUND OF THE BASKERVILLES
    by SIR ARTHUR CONAN DOYLE

WUTHERING HEIGHTS by EMILY BRONTË

THE ODYSSEY by HOMER

A MIDSUMMER NIGHT'S DREAM by WILLIAM SHAKESPEARE

FRANKENSTEIN; DRACULA; DR. JEKYLL AND MR. HYDE
    by MARY SHELLEY, BRAM STOKER, AND ROBERT LOUIS STEVENSON

THE CLASSIC SLAVE NARRATIVES
    EDITED BY HENRY LOUIS GATES, JR.